MILTON'S MINOR POEMS

Milton's Minor Poems

J. B. LEISHMAN

EDITED, WITH A PREFACE, BY
GEOFFREY TILLOTSON

UNIVERSITY OF PITTSBURGH PRESS

First published in England 1969 by Hutchinson & Co (*Publishers*) Ltd.

© St. John's College, Oxford, 1969

Library of Congress Catalog Card Number 78-136095
ISBN 0-8229-1100-0

Manufactured in Great Britain by The Anchor Press Ltd.,
Tiptree, Essex

Contents

Preface

In his will James Blair Leishman, who died in 1963, appointed John Butt as his literary executor, and failing him myself. When Butt died two years later, the papers accordingly passed to me. Butt had already discovered that they included the lectures on Milton's minor poems, which along with Leishman's published essay on *L'Allegro* and *Il Penseroso* invited publication in book form.

Leishman's interest in these poems was of long standing, as the essay referred to attests, its date being 1951. There can be no doubt that he planned a book, and that the manuscript of his lectures represents a late stage in its preparation. An indication of the date of the text of the individual lectures survives in the titles of some of the scholars and critics quoted—'Dr' Tillyard, 'Professor' Lewis, and so on. I have let these titles stand as they stand in the manuscript. Nor have I tried to eliminate all traces of the lecturer's voice—the conversational 'very' and the salesman epithets and adverbs common in the lecture room have been retained, and the odd reference to the platinum blonde. It is one thing for an author to prepare his lectures for the press and another for an editor to presume to do it for him. Nor is a certain amount of the formal informality of lectures unpleasant when presented in print—witness that of Newman's *Idea of a University* and of several of Q's books.

A comment prompted by this book while it was still in manuscript is worth quoting: 'Lucky, lucky students to have such lectures!' And yet not many students, I believe, thought it worth their while to hear them. Now that books are so readily available, perhaps Carlyle was right, and the long reign of lectures has long

been over. In any event Leishman was rather the inky scholar than
the platform declaimer. Some of those who did go to hear him,
however, discovered something special. One of them, Mr Peter
Mudford, has kindly given me this account of his own experience:

> I remember him standing behind the high-table of St John's College,
> Oxford, one winter's morning when the blaze of a log-fire did little to
> warm the hall where his undergraduate audience were listening [to a
> general course on Shakespeare]. For a tall and broadly built man, the
> weight of his voice was thin and did not carry easily into the hall. He
> made no attempt at performance; and not many students had come
> through the winter to hear him. But he himself was impressive: not
> merely for the scope of his discriminating scholarship but because
> there penetrated through his secluded and difficult personality the sense
> of a man who had mined literature over a long period of time, and still
> found it gold.

The gold he found in Milton is now available more widely, for
defaulting students and others. Leishman's most satisfactory
medium was print.

'Over a long period of time.' Leishman had laboured to make
himself as nearly the ideal reader of Milton as he could manage.
He read what Milton had read, which meant in particular the
poetry written in Europe from its beginnings in Greece and Rome.
(Perhaps he was less familiar with English medieval poetry.)
At one point in the lectures he speaks of something being 'sufficient for any reader whom Milton cared to reach'. Chastening
phrase! Many of us nowadays have almost no equipment for
reading Milton as he should be read. For such he can be little
more than what Shakespeare was to L'Allegro, a warbler of native
wood-notes wild. He would not have much cared for reaching the
likes of many readers of today. And I can imagine the embarrassed
delight Leishman would have shown if anybody after reading this
book had said that he felt a little more ready to join the 'fit
audience . . . though few'.

These lectures are welcome also because, though we have
recently had plenty of books on *Paradise Lost*, we have had very
few on the minor poems—Rosemond Tuve's is the only one I
recall. And a book on those poems is welcome from Leishman in

particular. For the present volume may be seen as completing a tetralogy, by joining *Themes and Variations in Shakespeare's Sonnets*, the book on Donne's poetry (*The Monarch of Wit*) and *The Art of Marvell's Poetry*. There is, unfortunately, much poetry of the late sixteenth and the first half of the seventeenth century that Leishman did not write on, except incidentally, but now that the two posthumous volumes have been added to those that had the advantage of his completed attention, where else can we find, in all our literature, criticism of so long a stretch of English poetry in the briefer forms—criticism so close, so informed, and so expert in the weighing of evidence?

The labour of preparing this edition has been considerable. Leishman's handwriting is the sort that at first sight looks totally illegible—handwriting that is deciphered only after much poring over by all available well-wishers. Much the greater part of that labour has been done cheerfully and devotedly by Mr Anthony Burton.

I am grateful also to the following: to Professor Robert Browning for overseeing the Greek, to my wife, especially for help with knotty points in the deciphering, to Mr Brian Jenkins, who helped in the later stages, and to Miss Agnes M. C. Latham, who read the manuscript in typescript, adding footnotes bringing the scholarship up to date—her notes I have signed 'A. L.' (if a footnote is unsigned, it is Leishman's). Thanks are also due to the British Academy and Mr Geoffrey Carnall for kindly allowing us to reprint John Butt's obituary of Leishman (a document doubly sad) which first appeared in *Proceedings of the British Academy*, XLIX, 1963; while Chapter 6 first appeared in *Essays and Studies 1951*, published for the English Association by John Murray (Publishers) Ltd, reprinted by Wm. Dawson & Sons. For permission to quote liberally from Professor Bernard Wright's edition of Milton's *Shorter Poems* I am indebted to Messrs Macmillan & Co. Ltd.

Mr Burton has kindly supplied the following memorandum, explaining how the quotations from Milton have been dealt with:

For the poems Helen Darbishire's edition has been followed (2 volumes, 1952–5) and for prose the Columbia edition of the *Works* (20 volumes, New York, 1931–40).

The use of Darbishire's edition perhaps needs defence, as Leishman did not approve of her treatment of *Paradise Lost*. She does not, however, force her spellings on the minor poems, and her edition seems prefreable because (a) Leishman's book is in the nature of a commentary, and the reader will want to keep his copy of the poems handy, which meant the choice of one of the well-known, much-used editions; (b) he gives a fair amount of attention to textual matters, so that the reader needs an edition with an apparatus; (c) he takes 1645 as the definitive text, and Darbishire prints this (whereas Columbia, for example, follows 1673 to which Leishman does not refer). Darbishire in two volumes is therefore better than Wright (revised edition, 1966, which follows the 1673 text) or Bush (1966, which uses modern spelling) or Darbishire in one volume (1961, which has no apparatus) or Columbia (1931–40, in 20 volumes). The reader will not want to refer to the prose works, so it has been deemed reasonable to give references to the Columbia edition, which is the best so far. The Yale edition is nowhere near completion.

Birkbeck College, London   G.T.
10 May 1968

The young Milton

In these lectures on Milton's shorter poems I shall try to make a continual use of what Mr Eliot has called the critic's two chief tools, analysis and comparison. It is not really possible to use either of these tools successfully without also making an almost simultaneous use of the other. For if, as I believe, the chief purpose of serious literary study, above all, of the study of poetry, is to make ourselves more completely aware of the peculiar virtue, the essential *thisness*, of whatever works we are studying, it is very largely through our awareness of its numerous resemblances to and differences from other kinds of poetry that the essential *thisness* of a particular kind of poetry becomes really clear to us. In other words, in order to see what a thing is, we must also see what it is not. Milton's poetry is in some ways (but with great differences) like Spenser's, in some ways (but with great differences) like Jonson's, in almost no ways like Donne's, but in some ways (though with great differences) like Marvell's. Thus, if you want to see really clearly what Milton's earlier poetry both is and is not, you will also find it necessary to see clearly what a great deal of other poetry both is and is not, and in learning about Milton's poetry you will learn a great deal about other poetry as well. I often disagree (as others do) with that pugnacious and dogmatic critic Dr F. R. Leavis, but I agree most profoundly with his insistence that literary criticism should be based firmly upon the study of particular texts. Start from something precise and definite and you may hope to arrive at something precise and definite; start in the air and you are likely to remain in the air. I find more and more that the really valuable, the really illuminating generalisations about poetry (or rather, perhaps, about certain kinds of poetry) all arise out of the careful study of particular authors and particular poems. I may mention, as two very notable examples, Coleridge's discussion of Wordsworth's poems in *Biographia Literaria* and Matthew Arnold's lectures *On Translating Homer*.

In these lectures, then, one of my chief concerns will be to 'place' Milton's shorter poems in the landscape of seventeenth-century poetry, and, by comparing them with the poems of his predecessors and contemporaries, to try to see more clearly what kind of poet Milton was, what kind of poet he wanted to be.

It seems to me that in recent times Milton's shorter poems have not received the attention they deserve, that we have concentrated our attention too exclusively upon *Paradise Lost*, and that even in studying that great poem we have tended to devote too little time to the text and too much to the character, opinions, and beliefs of the man who wrote it. I do not wish to suggest that these matters are unimportant—far from it. More than with most poets there is a close relation between the work and the habitual life of its author: there is an intimate relation between the greatness of the poetry and the greatness of the man, as there is also, some would insist, between the occasional weaknesses and limitations of the poetry and the weaknesses and limitations of the man. Moreover, Milton, though one of our greatest artists in language—perhaps our very greatest—would have had no sympathy with the doctrine of art for art's sake, or with the conception of what has been called 'pure poetry'.

Like Wordsworth, he wished to be regarded as a teacher or nothing. Much of his poetry is the expression of large moral ideas and philosophical conceptions, and a consideration of the value of the expression cannot be wholly separated from a consideration of the value of these ideas themselves. And even in his least philosophical, even in what we might be tempted to call his most purely aesthetic poetry, there is a strong moral or religious element—a choosing of that which is truly better, a grateful acceptance and, as it were, sanctification of a beauty whose origin he recognises as divine. Nevertheless, although the relation between Milton's character, ideas, and opinions and Milton's poetry is close, interesting and important, the chief reason for reading *L'Allegro* and *Il Penseroso* is not in order to discover what sort of man Milton was in or about 1632, and the chief reason for reading *Paradise Lost* is not, in spite of Dr Tillyard, in order to discover the state of Milton's mind when he wrote it. Indeed, in recent years there has been so much speculation and controversy about the *ideas* behind *Paradise Lost* that many of us find it difficult to cut our way through and reach the poetry. It is therefore something of a relief, as well as a very useful exercise in criticism, to turn to the shorter poems and by means of analogies and comparison to attempt to reach a perception of their essential *thisness*. As a kind of prolegomenon to our study of the shorter poems, I will give a few facts about the environment, education and character of the young Milton, and offer a few reflections upon those facts.

The poet's father, also named John, was the son of Richard Milton of Stanton St John, a pleasant little village about two and a half miles north of Headington, near Oxford. Richard was a substantial yeoman and a staunch Catholic, who in 1601 was fined as a recusant. He sent his son to Christ Church, where, to the disgust of his father, who promptly disinherited him, he became a Protestant. Left without resources, he went to London to seek his fortune, and, after trying various means of gaining a livelihood, he finally adopted the profession of scrivener, in many respects akin to that of a modern solicitor. He progressed rapidly in this profession, and in the end had what Aubrey calls a plentiful estate. But besides being a successful man of business he was also a man of considerable culture, and, in particular, a musician and composer of some celebrity. It was into this household where both religion and the arts meant much that the musicianly poet and Christian humanist John Milton was born on the 9 December 1608. His only surviving brother, Christopher, who later became a judge, was not born until seven years later, and the father seems to have bestowed extraordinary care on the education of his first-born son. Indeed, Sir Arthur Quiller-Couch has made out an interesting parallel with the lonely and dedicated upbringing of the young Ruskin. In 1620, at the age of twelve, Milton was sent to St Paul's School, but for at least two years before that date he had received private tuition from Thomas

Young, a Scottish Presbyterian minister of considerable learning, who had settled in London and who seems to have supported himself partly by assisting Puritan ministers and partly by teaching. He was later to take part in the pamphleteering war against the bishops and to become a member of the Westminster Assembly of Divines. The fact that the elder Milton engaged such a man as his son's tutor suggests that he left the Church of Rome for an Anglicanism at least tinctured with Puritanism, and that he may even have held views about ecclesiastical organisation not very dissimilar from those which his son was later to champion with such passionate conviction. Milton's brother Christopher told Aubrey that 'When he went to Schoole, when he was very young he studied very hard and sate-up very late, comonly till 12 or one aclock at night, & his father ordered yᵉ mayde to sitt-up for him'[1]—a piece of information which is corroborated by Milton's own words in the *Second Defence*: 'My father directed me as a child to literature and learning, which I applied myself to so eagerly that from twelve years of age I hardly ever retired to bed from my studies before midnight.'[2] Milton remained at St Paul's School from 1620 to 1625, that is to say, from the age of twelve until the age of seventeen. The High-Master was Alexander Gill, 'old Dr Gill', as Aubrey calls him, a notable scholar and teacher and a notable flogger, about whom Aubrey has several amusing anecdotes. His son, also named Alexander, Aubrey's 'young Dr Gill', returned to his father's school in 1621 as under-usher. Although he was nine years older than Milton they became close friends, and corresponded and exchanged Latin verses after Milton had left for Cambridge. According to Wood, the younger Gill was 'accounted one of the best Latin poets in the nation', but it seems possible that he and Milton shared political as well as literary sympathies and that a disaster which befell Gill towards the end of 1628 made a considerable impression upon his young friend. While visiting his friends at Trinity College, Oxford, Gill drank a health to Felton, who had recently assassinated Buckingham the court favourite, and declared that the King 'was fitter to

---

[1] *The Early Lives of Milton*, ed. Helen Darbishire, 1932, p. 10.
[2] Columbia edn, viii. 118.

stand in a Cheapside shop, with an apron before him, and say *What lack you?* than to governe a kingdome.'[1] These impudent remarks seem to have been communicated to Laud by his nephew Chillingworth; Gill was examined in the Star-Chamber and sentenced to degradation from the Ministry, a fine of £2000, and the loss of both ears. As the result of his father's intercession the fine was reduced and the corporal punishment remitted, but Gill was dismissed from his ushership. Milton's most intimate friend at St Paul's, perhaps the only really intimate friend he ever had, was Charles Diodati, the son of a distinguished physician and native of Geneva, who had settled in England. The family was of Italian origin, and had left Italy for Geneva on account of religion. Diodati, who was an excellent classical scholar, went up to Trinity College, Oxford, became, like his father, a physician, and died of the plague in August 1638. Milton commemorated him in the *Epitaphium Damonis*.

Let me briefly recapitulate these facts and suggest to you why I have thought it worth while to mention them. Until he went up to Cambridge at the age of seventeen the only personal influences on Milton of which we have definite record were those of his father, of his tutor Thomas Young, of the younger Gill and of Charles Diodati. They were all passionately concerned with literature and they all held unorthodox views on either religion or politics or possibly on both. We have, it is true, no evidence about Diodati's religious opinions, but it seems reasonable to suppose that, like his family, he was some kind of Calvinist. The ridicule of Puritans by the Elizabethan and Jacobean dramatists, the behaviour of sectaries and saints during the Commonwealth period, and the satire upon them after the Restoration has no doubt led many people to assume that Puritanism and humanism, Puritanism and culture, were essentially incompatible. We should remember, though, that there were many kinds of Puritanism, and that some kinds could combine very well with admiration for the classics. On the close association between the bible and the classics, on the general intermingling of Pagan and Christian thought which was so characteristic of the Renaissance and which

---

[1] Joseph Mead, quoted by P. Bliss, *Athenae Oxonienses*, 1813–20, iii. 43.

is everywhere apparent in Spenser, you will find some excellent remarks in Professor Wright's Introduction to his edition of the Shorter Poems (1938). But there was something more than that. Presbyterianism and Calvinism were a kind of ecclesiastical republicanism, and they could easily lead to, or become associated with, political republicanism as well. Indeed, Hobbes complained that the study of the classics, especially of Plutarch's *Lives*, definitely encouraged republican and revolutionary opinions. Here it is worth recalling what John Aubrey, who had been personally acquainted both with Milton himself, with his brother, widow and nephews, and with many of his friends, wrote in his manuscript *Minutes of the Life of Mr John Milton*:

Whatever he wrote against Monarchie was out of no animosity to the King's person,\ or out of any faction, or Interest /but out of a pure zeall to the Liberty of Mankind, wch he thought would be greater under a free state than under a Monarchall goverñment. His being so conversant in Livy and the Rom: authors and the greatness he saw donne by the Rom: coñmonwealth & the virtue of their great Captaines induc't him to.[1]

I sometimes think that two of the most self-revealing lines Milton ever wrote occur in the second of the two Sonnets 'On the detraction which followed upon my writing certain treatises':

> I did but prompt the age to quit their cloggs
> By the known rules of antient libertie.

The ancients had left us 'known rules', not merely for the composition of epic and tragedy, but, in the examples of Harmodius and Aristogeiton, Brutus and Cassius and so many others, rules for ridding ourselves of tyrants. To Milton and many of his contemporaries the new 'liberty of conscience' which the Reformation had promised seemed more and more to demand as its corollary that political liberty, the idealised political liberty, which the ancient republics of Greece and Rome had practised.

In 1625, at the age of seventeen, Milton entered Christ's College, Cambridge, and remained in residence for the full period of seven years then required for the degree of M.A. He did not

---

[1] *The Early Lives of Milton*, ed. Helen Darbishire, 1932, pp. 13–14.

get on well with his first tutor, and during his first year was rusticated for a term. Milton's brother told Aubrey that his tutor whipped him, and a couplet in the front of Milton's Latin Elegies, addressed during his rustication to his friend Diodati, seems to confirm this tradition. It may well have been so, for it was an age of whippers. When Milton returned to his College he was transferred to another tutor, and in time seems to have become both respected and even popular, although in his prolusions, or public academic exercises, which he later printed, he lost no opportunity for expressing his contempt for the still largely medieval and scholastic curriculum, and for demanding a more humanistic learning. We have heard much of Jacobean and seventeenth-century melancholy and scepticism, and, although the fact has been considerably overemphasised, it is indeed possible to find in the tragedies of Webster, in Donne's *Anniversaries* and eleswhere, in Burton and in others, evidence of what might be called the disenchantment of the later Renaissance. There is no trace of this in the young Milton. In his seventh Prolusion he praises the blessings of learning with a Baconian confidence in the possibilities of man and of his future achievements, and in his verses on the theme *Naturam non pati senium*, That Nature does not suffer from old age, he opposes the fairly widely held view, memorably expressed in Donne's *Anniversaries*, that the world was decaying.

In respect of this forward-looking confidence in the possibilities of human achievement, Milton is nearer to Bacon and the exponents of 'new philosophy' and to the great rationalists and system-builders who followed than he is to many of his predecessors and contemporaries whose thinking and feeling was still to some considerable extent dominated by what may be called the Catholic or medieval world-picture. But before elaborating this important point, I will pause to remark that, in comparison with other seventeenth-century writers, both earlier and later, Milton appears sometimes as more old-fashioned and sometimes as more advanced or more modern. In respect of his allegiance to an older, or, perhaps one should say, to a more European tradition, his poetic style often seems to us, as no doubt it seemed to his contemporaries, more old-fashioned than that of Donne and that of other seventeenth-century poets, who rejected ornament and kept close to the rhythm and idiom of the spoken language. And his prose-writings, in respect both of their sentence-structure, their controversial and dogmatic tone, and their almost total lack of persuasiveness or of attempts at persuasion, seem old-fashioned, not merely in comparison with Dryden's, but even in comparison with those of several earlier seventeenth-century authors. On the other hand, in respect of his optimism, his rationalism, and what might almost be called his singleness of vision Milton is nearer to many thinkers of the later seventeenth and of the eighteenth century than, for example, to that greatest of all the Deans of St Paul's who died a year before he left Cambridge.

Here I will quote a passage from an interesting article by Sir Herbert Grierson on 'The Metaphysics of John Donne and Milton', which he reprinted in the volume *Criticism and Creation*: 'Donne's aim as a preacher,' he there declares,

is to define and illuminate by his learning and his imagination the great Catholic doctrines of God and Man, of sin and redemption, of death and the resurrection, not to cut out a path of his own; and he is happier and more eloquent when so employed than when denouncing Romish errors. The spirit in which he works, too, is neither mystical nor rationalist but the spirit of the great Catholic theologians who have always taken reason as the portal to faith, as not contradicted but transcended by revelation. The scepticism of Donne, on which modern criticism insists, was not the rationalist, dogmatic scepticism of the later deists and sceptics. It was that profounder, temperamental and spiritual, scepticism which torments the soul that realises too vividly the contradictions besetting all human speculation, the uncertainty of human values, the inextricable interweaving of good and evil—evil begetting good, good begetting evil:

There's nothing simply good nor ill alone:
Of every quality comparison
The only measure is, and judge opinion.

It was a mood, as Donne says, to be overcome, not reasoned with.

Milton had far more of the temper of the new rationalism, the dogmatism of the great individual system-builders from Descartes and Spinoza to Hegel. The Catholic tradition to which Donne always rallies is rejected by Milton without compunction.[1]

---

[1] *Criticism and Creation*, 1949, p. 38.

Closely connected with Milton's optimism and rationalism, or perhaps but another aspect of that in him of which they too are aspects, is what I have called his singleness of vision, which I would contrast with that doubleness of vision which is one of the distinguishing characteristics of so many of our earlier writers— of, to name but three, Chaucer, Shakespeare and Donne. Doubleness of vision: that vision for which the world is in a double sense a fair, a pilgrimage, a huge stage presenting shows on which the stars in secret influence comment; that vision for which man is now a little lower than the angels and now a quintessence of dust, now that *homunculus* whom Paracelsus, as Donne said 'would have undertaken to have made, in a Limbeck, in a Furnace,'[1] and now the heir of eternal glory; now drest in a little brief authority and playing fantastic tricks before high heaven, now unaccommodated and feeling what wretches feel. There was, it has often been remarked, nothing of the passionate reformer or crusader about Chaucer or Shakespeare, or, it might be added, about Donne. Habitually conscious as they were of man's ignorance, of his glassy essence and of the heart-ache and the thousand natural shocks that flesh is heir to, they could never have become more than very moderately interested in any particular political, ecclesiastical, social or material reform. Some good might come of it, but sooner or later there would be, as Donne once expressed it, another worm to devour that too. They would have whole-heartedly supported a war to keep the French or the Spaniards out of England, but they would have laughed at the notion of a war to end war or to establish the rule of the Saints. These poets' conception of man was essentially real, or realistic, and was based on a profound knowledge of their own natures and a wide experience of the natures of others; in comparison, the young Milton's conception of man was essentially ideal.

At this point I must resist various temptations to digress, and must remind myself and you that in this introductory lecture I am concerned only with those aspects of the younger Milton of which some knowledge and understanding are most relevant to the study of his poetry, and that I must not dwell too long upon

---

[1] *Sermons*, ed. G. R. Potter and Evelyn M. Simpson, Berkeley, U.S.A., 1953–62, ix. 136.

any one of them to the exclusion of the rest. I need not, for example, do more than hint at the way in which his bookish and idealised conception of humanity easily combined with that political and religious millennialism which possessed many of his Puritanical contemporaries at the outbreak of the Civil War; neither will I here do more than mention the probability that that singleness of vision which I have contrasted with the double vision of earlier poets is what Mr Eliot surely had in mind when he spoke of a dissociation of sensibility. I have already described Milton as a Christian humanist, and perhaps I can most profitably spend the time that remains to us by saying something of his humanism, and by suggesting some of the ways in which it modified, and was modified by, his Christianity.

In recent times the word 'humanist' has been appropriated by many different persons and has been made to mean many different things. It originally meant a student of the humaner letters, that is to say, of Latin, and later, after the study of Greek had been revived, of Greek as well. When we speak of Renaissance humanism or of Milton's humanism we ought to mean no more and no less than this—a passionate belief in the value of Greek and Latin literature and of the literary, political and human ideals there enshrined. On the same page of Milton's *Areopagitica* there occur two very revealing phrases; he speaks of the superiority of 'the old and elegant humanity of Greece' to 'the barbarick pride of a *Hunnish* and *Norwegian* statelines', and of 'those ages, to whose polite wisdom and letters we ow that we are not yet *Gothes* and *Jutlanders*'.[1] Behind such phrases, which are very plentiful, not only in Milton, but in the writings of Ascham and Bacon and other English humanists, there lies a quite definite and in many respects quite unhistorical conception not merely of European history but of ecclesiastical history. Such terms as 'gothic' and 'barbarous' are applied not merely to the barbaric destroyers of the Roman Empire but to the prelates and priesthood of the Roman Church, who were supposed somehow to have prolonged the age of darkness and ignorance in order to preserve their usurped authority, and who wrote their barbarous

---

[1] Columbia edn, iv. 295–6.

Latin and exercised their mummeries and superstitions during the whole of that long European night which was supposed to have extended almost without a break from the destruction of the Roman Empire until the Sack of Constantinople by the Turks. Greek scholars then poured over Europe with their manuscripts, light began to do battle with darkness, and in due course came the Reformation. This perhaps is a simplification, but scarcely a caricature, of what I may call the Protestant-humanist conception of ecclesiastical history, of the Middle Ages, of the Renaissance or Revival of Learning and of the Reformation. What was needed was first to go back and recover the right road in religion, in literature and in politics, and then to proceed confidently towards a glorious future. With the advent of Christianity, so Milton and many English humanists seem to have felt, there ought to have been a steady onward progress from the already achieved splendours of an idealised classical antiquity, and not, as there was, a relapse into Gothic barbarism, a relapse for which Milton and others often seem to regard the incurable gothicism of the Roman Church as having been even more responsible than the barbarian invaders themselves.

Among the Protestant humanists, especially in England, there was combined with admiration for classical literature, art, and institutions a deep ethical and religious strain which in other countries, especially in Italy, was far less pronounced, and often entirely absent. What exactly Milton believed that Christianity added, offered in addition, to the achievements of classical antiquity is very difficult to determine. Primarily, I think, he found in Christianity a positive and supernatural sanction for virtuous living, and a promise, as distinct from a mere hope, of immortality.

> Mortals that would follow me,
> Love vertue, she alone is free,
> She can teach ye how to clime
> Higher then the Spheary chime;
> Or if Vertue feeble were,
> Heav'n it self would stoop to her.

There is, as we shall see later, much Platonism in *Comus*, but the ringing confidence of those concluding lines is Christian rather than Platonic.

Some remarks on seventeenth-century poetry and Milton's place in it

When we generalise about seventeenth-century poetry we ought to distinguish more carefully than we commonly do, first, between the poetry which we remember and read now and that which was being written and read then, and, secondly, between the poetry which was then being read in print and that which was being read only in manuscript. It is often said, and with much truth, that the two great names, the two great influences, in the poetry of the first half of the seventeenth century are those of Ben Jonson and John Donne, that the so-called Cavalier poets (Herrick, Carew, Suckling, Lovelace and others) are in the main disciples of Ben Jonson, and that the so-called metaphysical poets are in one way or another disciples of Donne. That, I think you will agree, is the common view, and I have tried to state it in a single sentence; but the more I look at that sentence, the more it seems to me, as a statement of fact, to require modification and qualification. Jonson and Donne are certainly the two big names in that portion of earlier seventeenth-century poetry—and this is a most important qualification—which we still read and remember. Milton, the Milton of the poems from the Nativity Ode, 1629, to *Lycidas*, 1637, is as big a name as either of them, but he started to write much later and he exerted no influence, whereas Jonson and Donne are not only great names but great influences. Jonson, the author of tersely classical and sequacious lyrics, epigrams and epistles, where the emphasis is on phrasing and on substance, and where much of Elizabethan luxuriance and decoration has been pruned away; Donne, dramatic and para-

doxical Donne, who wrote as though Petrarch[1] and Spenser had
never existed, who chose the plainest and most colloquial
language, and who could sometimes make the purest poetry out
of almost bare argument—how different is the poetry of both of
them from the typical non-dramatic poetry of the Elizabethan age,
and how difficult it is for most of us to think of what we regard
as the typical non-dramatic poetry of the earlier seventeenth
century except in relation to the poetry of these two men. Let us
return to my sentence. Jonson, we say, begat the Cavalier poets.
Herrick is certainly a son of Ben, whom he several times ack-
nowledges as his master, but while Carew and Suckling would
also have been proud to be acknowledged as sons of Ben, they
were nevertheless, in several of their poems, by no means un-
affected by the example of Donne. But it is the concluding
assertion, that the so-called metaphysical poets were in one way or
another all disciples of Donne, which seems to me the most
questionable part of my brief re-statement of the common view.
There is indeed an affinity deeper than has been commonly
recognised between Donne's serious love-poetry and what one
might call Herbert's religious love-poetry; both can make the
purest poetry out of almost bare argument; both are masters of
what I am inclined to call the dialectical expression of personal
drama; nevertheless, with how much else in Donne's poetry—
his paradox, his outrageousness, his hyperbole, his sheer wit—
there is really no parallel in Herbert's. And how close is the
resemblance between Donne and Crashaw? And while Marvell's
Definition of Love might almost have been written by Donne, is not
his famous *Horatian Ode* far nearer to the ideal of poetry which
Ben Jonson was continuously striving to obtain? But I must
resist the temptation to discourse upon the true relationship
between the so-called metaphysical poets and upon the unsatisfactoriness of the term metaphysical. I merely want to suggest
to you that our familiar and handy generalisations about seven-

---

[1] In some respects Petrarch is a strong influence on Donne, who is often taking
Petrarchan arguments one stage further, twisting and sophisticating, but not ignor-
ing them. See A. J. Smith, 'Theory and Practice in Renaissance Poetry', *Bulletin
of the John Rylands Library*, vol. 47, 1964–5, pp. 212-43, and Donald L. Guss, *John
Donne, Petrarchist*, Wayne State University Press 1966. A.L.

teenth-century poetry, as about many other things, are not to be trusted too far.

Let me now take up another of the points I raised. From the tables at the end of Professor Douglas Bush's *English Literature in the Earlier Seventeenth Century* one may easily compile a fairly complete chronological list of books of non-dramatic poetry published between 1620 and 1650. How many poets are there in that list who may fairly be regarded as disciples of Jonson or disciples of Donne, and when do their books first appear? The question is not difficult to answer. George Herbert's *The Temple* was published in 1633, the year of his death, and a year after Milton had left Cambridge. The second edition of the precocious Cowley's *Poetical Blossoms*, to which was added a section entitled *Sylva*, in which some of the classical emulations, including the famous Ode 'A Vote', may perhaps be regarded as Jonsonian, was published in 1636. In 1638, three years after his death, were published the poems of the Son of Ben, Thomas Randolph. In 1640 appeared Thomas Carew's *Poems*, shortly after his death, the first printed volume, I think one may say with confidence, in which the influences both of Jonson and of Donne are equally apparent. Then for a time (remember always that we are only considering published poetry) Jonsonianism seems to be in the ascendant. In 1642 appeared (piratically) Denham's *Cooper's Hill*, and in 1645 (the same year as Milton) Waller published his poems. It was to become a critical commonplace, you will remember, among the Dick Minims of a later age that Waller and Denham were the first reformers of our numbers. During the remaining years of the half century sons of Ben, imitators of Donne, and poets who, rightly or wrongly, are commonly classified as metaphysical begin to crowd upon us thick and fast. In 1646 appeared Suckling's *Fragmenta Aurea*. Suckling, who had died in 1642, was, like many cavalier poets, an admirer and imitator both of Jonson and of Donne. In the same year appeared the poems of Shirley, whom I suppose one might call a minor Jonsonian; also Crashaw's *Steps to the Temple*, and Henry Vaughan's first volume, *Poems with the tenth Satire of Juvenal Englished*, full of sprightly imitations of various members of the tribe of Ben. In 1647 appeared the first edition of the poems of the metaphysical buffoon, as one might almost be justified in calling him, John Cleveland, who remained for nearly twenty years, if not the most popular, at any rate the most fashionable, of English poets; Cowley's *The Mistress*, that ingenious and for a time very popular imitation of the more superficial characteristics of Donne's love-poetry; the poems of John Hall, who wrote some agreeable lyrics sometimes in Jonson's manner, sometimes in Donne's, and the poems of Thomas Stanley, a notable classical scholar and an often very agreeable minor poet, who combines something of Donne's dialectical toughness with much use of the by now rather outworn conceits about fire and flame, ice and snow, and so forth. In 1648 appeared the *Hesperides* and *Noble Numbers* of the most notable of all the sons of Ben, Robert Herrick. In 1649 appeared the *Lucasta* of Lovelace, who at his best is in the main a disciple of Jonson, but who sometimes imitates Donne, and in the same year, *Lachrymae Musarum*, Elegies on the death of the Lord Hastings, where, among several others, Dryden, in the role of a disciple of Donne, or, one might almost say, of Cleveland, appears side by side with Herrick and Marvell. Finally, in 1650, appeared the first part of Henry Vaughan's *Silex Scintillans*.

It appears, then, from this brief examination that no collection of poems where either the manner of Jonson or the manner of Donne or the so-called metaphysical manner is really obvious and pervasive was published before 1633, the year in which Donne's poems were first printed and a year after Milton had left Cambridge: in other words, that most of what we usually have in mind when we speak or think of seventeenth-century poetry, or pre-Restoration seventeenth-century poetry, was, whether or no it had been written, not actually printed until in or after that year.

Let me now take up another of the points I raised. I said that in our generalisations about seventeenth-century poetry we ought to distinguish more carefully than we usually do between the poetry that was printed and the poetry that was merely circulating in manuscript. We always, and rightly, think of Donne as one of the great influences upon seventeenth-century poetry and yet with the exception of a contribution to the facetious commendations of Thomas Coryate and some Latin verses in commendation of Jonson's *Volpone*, Donne printed only two poems during his lifetime, the two *Anniversaries* upon the 'Religious Death of Mistris Elizabeth Drury', in 1611 and 1612. The first collected edition of his poems was not published until 1633, two years after his death, in which year George Herbert died and *The Temple* was published. Donne's great reputation as a poet during his lifetime, a reputation which he was beginning to establish during the last decade of the sixteenth century,[1] was gained entirely through the circulation of his poems in manuscript. Even with Ben Jonson the case was not entirely dissimilar. His plays, it is true, were both acted and published; and many of his lyrics appeared in his plays, and the folio edition of what, to the derision of some more humble playwrights, he called his *Works* and published in 1616, contained, besides the plays which he had so far written, his collection of somewhat more than 130 epigrams, and a small collection of fifteen songs, odes and epistles entitled *The Forrest*. Nevertheless, it was not until the posthumously published folio of 1640 that the great body of his non-dramatic poetry, with the general title *Under-woods*, first appeared in print. Moreover, Jonson, though a much more public poet than Donne, exerted, like Donne, a private rather than a public influence upon other poets. Though in a far less exclusive and intellectual sense than Donne, he too was the master, the *arbiter elegantiarum*, of a circle, of a coterie, of various young Templars and courtiers who gathered around him in taverns, hung upon his words, begged copies of his verses, and were proud to be known as his Sons. Now Jonson, as you may remember, told Drummond of Hawthornden that Donne was the first poet in the world for some things, and, since he was not a man to keep his opinions to himself, we may be pretty sure that he said much the same to his poetical sons: it is not strange, therefore, that in the work of many of these sons we should be able to detect now the manner of their master and now the manner of Donne. In general, these young disciples of Jonson and of Donne showed no inclination to rush into print. The

---

[1] On Donne's reputation as a poet during his lifetime, see Leishman, *The Monarch of Wit*, 6th edn, 1962, pp. 13–14, and *The Elegies and the Songs and Sonnets*, ed. Helen Gardner, Oxford 1965, General Introduction, pp. xlix-l. Ed.

collected poems (as distinct from complimentary verses and the like) of Randolph, Carew and Suckling were all published posthumously. Herrick did not publish his *Hesperides* until 1648, when he was fifty-seven years old. He had indeed entered it for publication in 1640, when he was nearly fifty, but he must have begun to write long before that since at least two of his poems can be dated as early as 1612. Like so many of these poets, he had evidently been content for his poems to circulate in manuscript among his friends. No doubt only a few of these friends were poets themselves, but they were all deeply interested in poetry, and many of them, one may assume, possessed manuscript collections and commonplace books into which they transcribed what most attracted them. The number of such manuscript collections of poetry which have survived from the seventeenth century is enormous, as you may easily convince yourselves by a brief visit to the Bodleian. Never, perhaps, has there been a time when poetry, even the practice of poetry, was so much part of the education and accomplishments of a gentleman. In the Preface to his reprint of the agreeable minor poet William Hammond, who was born in 1614, who published his poems in 1655, and who was the uncle of another agreeable minor poet, Thomas Stanley—in the Preface to his reprint of Hammond's poems Sir Egerton Brydges remarked that 'a laudable spirit of literature seems then to have prevailed among the gentilitial families' of Kent; and, after naming some of them, he continued:

The effects of example are so obvious, that it is easy to account for this honourable ambition having been so generally spread in a narrow neighbourhood when once excited. It seems to have expired with that generation; and I know not that it ever revived again.

But it was not only in Kent that such poetical circles were to be found; there were plenty of them in London and in many other places. It was, so far as we know, for a very small circle indeed, perhaps consisting only of the Lord General Fairfax and himself, that Marvell, sometime between 1651 and 1653, wrote some of the most charming and memorable of seventeenth-century poems, poems which were not printed until after his death and which remained almost unknown until their merits were discerned and proclaimed, first by Charles Lamb, and then by Tennyson and Palgrave.[1] Most of these poets, no doubt, were quite content with the admiration and occasional criticism of a small circle and simply did not bother about publication; others would probably have disdained it as much as they would have disdained to exhibit their musical skill by giving public performances upon the lute.

I have now perhaps said enough to persuade you that most of what we now chiefly remember of the secular, as distinct from the religious, poetry of the seventeenth century was written by brilliant amateurs, sometimes amateurs of genius, and written, not with any immediate view to publication, but partly for the writer's own pleasure and partly for circulation among certain literary circles, sets, coteries, or, if you will, cliques. (Today these terms have become terms of abuse; nevertheless, the answer to the question whether what is called coterie poetry is or is not a bad thing must, I suppose, depend on the qualities of those who compose the coterie, on those who set the tone and those who take it. Certainly, our poetry would be very much poorer but for those various circles and coteries which took their tone from Jonson and from Donne.) In fact, what we now regard as the main stream, or rather the two main streams of seventeenth-century poetry flowed underground during much of their course, and only began to emerge into public daylight in and after 1633. Very little of this poetry is what we today should call difficult. Indeed, I suppose that very little even of Donne's poetry is difficult according to modern standards of poetic difficulty. Nevertheless, many of the more unsophisticated seventeenth-century readers would have found the wit and compression, not merely of Donne's but of much other of this coterie poetry, difficult and obscure; and, in general, its terseness and elegance could only be fully appreciated by those who had some pretensions to connoisseurship. Only such readers, perhaps, would have felt that it was worth writing. To some of the old guard (if

---

[1] In J.B.L.'s *The Art of Marvell's Poetry* (2nd edn, 1968, p. 19). John Butt notes that Marvell's poetry was rather more widely known in the eighteenth century than Leishman's statements on the subject would suggest. Ed.

one may so call them without disrespect) this preoccupation of the young, the fashionable, and the advanced with short poems handed about in manuscript seemed contemptible and decadent—to (among others) that fine old Elizabethan survival Michael Drayton, who was born in 1563, a year earlier than Shakespeare, and, like Shakespeare, in Warwickshire, and who continued to live and write and publish until 1631, the year before Milton left Cambridge. Drayton was in the main a disciple of Spenser, with Spenser's high and serious conception of poetry. He sometimes did small things delightfully, but it was the writing of large-scale national and patriotic poems that lay nearest to his heart. In 1612 he published the first part of his immense *Poly-Olbion*, that 'Chorographicall Description of Tracts, Rivers, Mountaines, Forests, and other Parts of this renowned Isle of Great Britaine, With intermixture of the most Remarquable Stories, Antiquities, Wonders, Rarityes, Pleasures, and Commodities of the same', and in his preface to this poem we can hear the irritable and disappointed tones of one who, though he still retained his popularity with the world at large, had failed to win King James's patronage, and was perhaps regarded as a bit of a back-number by the young intellectuals of the Court and of the Inns of Court. 'In publishing this Essay of my Poeme', he declared,

there is this great disadvantage against me; that it commeth out at this time, when Verses are wholly deduc't to Chambers, and nothing esteem'd in this lunatique Age, but what is kept in Cabinets, and must only passe by Transcription; In such a season, when the Idle Humerous world must heare of nothing, that either savors of Antiquity, or may awake it to seeke after more, then dull and slothfull ignorance may easily reach unto: These, I say, make much against me.[1]

And later, in his epistle *To Henry Reynolds, Esquire, of Poets and Poesie*, the epistle that contains the famous lines about Marlowe and his brave translunary things, and which Drayton first published in the collection of poetry he put out in 1627, he again expressed himself contemptuously and rather bitterly about these private, these manuscript, these chamber poets, who wrote only

---

[1] *Works*, ed. J. W. Hebel, 1931–41, iv, p. v*.

for themselves and their friends. After reaching the end of his
description of English poets from Chaucer to the two Beaumonts
and William Browne, he added:

> but if you shall
> Say in your knowledge, that there be not all
> Have writ in numbers, be inform'd that I
> Only my selfe, to these few men doe tye,
> Whose workes oft printed, set on every post,
> To publique censure subject have bin most;
> For such whose poems, be they nere so rare,
> In private chambers, that incloistered are,
> And by transcription daintyly must goe;
> As though the world unworthy were to know,
> Their rich composures, let those men that keepe
> These wonderous reliques in their judgement deepe,
> And cry them up so, let such Peeces bee
> Spoke of by those that shall come after me,
> I passe not for them.[1]

Thus Drayton insists on that same distinction on which I have
myself been insisting between the manuscript and the printed
poetry of his time. What are the chief differences between the
printed and the manuscript poetry? Apart from those volumes,
chiefly posthumous, which I have already mentioned, and which
were appearing from 1633 onwards, apart from those, what
names, what volumes, would figure prominently in a list of non-
dramatic poetry published by still-living poets during the first
half of the seventeenth century? The manuscript poets, or coterie
poets, the chamber poets, as Drayton called them, were in the
main disciples of either Jonson or Donne or both; the publishing
poets were in the main disciples of Spenser. The manuscript
poets wrote mainly short poems; the publishing poets wrote
mainly long ones. The manuscript poets were mainly concerned
with what they called wit, with ingenuity, terseness, elegance,
compression, turns of phrase; the publishing poets wrote in a
much more popular style, and their matter was, in the main,
patriotic, heroic or religious. The manuscript poets, though far

---

[1] *Works*, iii. 230-1.

from being the mere triflers that Drayton suggests, were seldom didactic, and, although by no means unserious, their seriousness was nearly always mingled with a certain gaiety; whereas many, perhaps most, of the publishing poets were ambitious of writing something 'doctrinal to a nation'. Who then were the publishing, the selling poets? First, there was Drayton himself. Then—for I must mention one or two whose names do not actually appear after 1620—there was William Browne of Tavistock, author of *Britannia's Pastorals*. William Browne, by the way, is an example of the unsatisfactoriness of labels and of the tiresome way in which so many of these seventeenth-century poets won't stay put in their pigeon-holes. He is chiefly remembered for his pastorals and is generally classified as a Spenserian; but his best poem, his Epitaph on the Countess of Pembroke, was long attributed to Ben Jonson, who was anything but a Spenserian; and he wrote several ingenious epigrams and epitaphs which often appear in seventeenth-century commonplace books and miscellanies, and which were quite after that 'fancie of the tyme' which, as Ben Johnson told him in 1619, William Drummond's old-fashioned poetry no longer pleased. Nevertheless, he is in the main a Spenserian, and he may serve to remind you (if you need reminding) that not every seventeenth-century poet born later than Donne tried to write like Donne. Browne was probably born about 1590, the year in which the first three books of the *Faerie Queene* were published, and was about eighteen years younger than Donne. There was George Wither whose early pastoral poetry has much affinity with Browne's, and whose later religious and didactic verse has much affinity with Quarles's. There was Giles Fletcher, whose *Christ's Victorie and Triumph* (1610) is an heroic poem in four cantos, written in an eight-line stanza of his own invention and very Spenserian in style, on the birth, temptation, crucifixion and resurrection of Christ. There was his brother Phineas Fletcher whose most ambitious poem *The Purple Island*, published in 1633 though written much earlier, is an elaborate allegorical description, in twelve cantos of seven-line stanzas, of the human body and of human virtues and vices. Quarles hailed him as the 'Spenser of this age'. Quarles himself began by publishing numerous scriptural paraphrases, and then, in 1635, brought out his famous *Emblemes*, a collection of short meditations, in a great variety of metres, on various biblical texts, each illustrated by, and to some extent illustrating, a small allegorical engraving. This collection of, in the main, rather diffuse and never difficult poems, written in a style sometimes reminiscent of Spenser, sometimes of a very homespun George Herbert, became the most popular book of verse published during the seventeenth century.

What is the relation of Milton's shorter poems to the poets and poetry we have been considering? Where does he stand in relation to his predecessors and in relation to the publishing and to what I have called the coterie poets of his time? I don't wish to anticipate too much conclusions which should arise from our consideration of particular poems, but, to begin with, I will permit myself a few general observations. First, although in respect of that concentration of substance and distinction of expression which he always aimed at and which from the very beginning he often achieved, Milton resembles the coterie poets rather than the publishing poets of his time, he can only very doubtfully and occasionally be classified as a disciple of Donne and only with very considerable qualification as a disciple of Jonson. Secondly, while most (I might almost say, all) of the coterie poets were amateurs, with whom poetry was only an occasional occupation, Milton never seems to have considered seriously any other occupation or profession than that of being a poet, and from almost before he was out of his teens until the time when he set out on his Italian travels everything he did was guided by the single-minded purpose of making himself not merely a good poet but a great one. For although he wrote some of the most beautiful short poems of the seventeenth century, he regarded them as no more than preparations for his real task, his ultimate ambition, which was to write a lofty and elaborate poem, doctrinal to a nation. Moreover, even his shorter poems, with a few unimportant exceptions, are altogether more ambitious, more lofty, more uniformly serious than those of the coterie poets. He never wrote anything which might be called, as might many of their poems, an exquisite trifle, and only perhaps in *L'Allegro* and *Il Penseroso*, those two poems where it is both most possible and most profitable to compare Milton with his contemporaries, is there much of their light-heartedness and gaiety and wit.

I remarked that only with very considerable qualification could Milton be described as a disciple of Jonson. He does indeed resemble Jonson in his respect for craftsmanship, in his veneration of the classics, and even in some of his turns and phrases, but where he most resembles him is in his lofty conception of the poet and of poetry. While, though, Jonson, in his non-dramatic poetry, was content with the shorter forms, and while the tone and spirit of his best work is almost uniformly secular and, one might almost say, Horatian, Milton was from the first far more religious, idealistic and philosophical. If, indeed, we are to regard Milton as the disciple of anyone, it should be of another great professional poet, one who shared Jonson's high conception of the poet and of poetry, but to whom Plato and the Bible meant more than Horace, who was not content with the shorter forms, and who set out to recount in solemn cantos the deeds of knighthood. 'Milton', said Dryden, 'hath acknowledged to me that Spenser was his original.' We may be content to believe him. If Milton began as the disciple of anyone it was of the author of the *Faerie Queene*. Drayton, Browne, Wither, Giles and Phineas Fletcher, Quarles, to some extent—these publishing poets of the earlier seventeenth century were also, in one way or another, disciples of Spenser. The great public bought and admired them, although to many of the disciples of Jonson and Donne they seemed old-fashioned and out of date, as no doubt did Spenser too. Perhaps one can to some extent place Milton among his contemporaries by saying that he began as a poet to whom Spenser was not out of date, and to whom many of Spenser's preoccupations—Platonic idealism, classical mythology, medieval legend, militant Protestantism, British history and heroes—together with Spenser's large-scale poetic ambitions, were not out of date. In comparison with those superior persons to whom Drayton so contemptuously refers who were content to write short poems to be handed round in chambers, that is to say, in private, and to be preserved in cabinets, there was from the first something large

B

and public and patriotic about Milton's poetic ambitions. Pursuing his industrious and select reading, he might have seemed to be leading a cloistered life, but there was nothing fugitive or cloistered about either his conception of poetry or his poetic aims. With the exception of Drayton, the Spenserians I have mentioned were very minor poets indeed, even in comparison with the earlier Milton; and in design and craftsmanship and sheer poetic power not even Drayton at his best can be compared with him. Nevertheless, in many ways Milton was nearer to these survivors from an earlier age, these continuers of an earlier tradition, than to the disciples of Jonson and of Donne. There is more spiritual affinity between the disappointed and perhaps rather disappointing author of *Poly-Olbion* and the poet who for some time cherished the ambition of glorifying his native country by celebrating King Arthur than there is between Milton and Donne, or between Milton and Herrick, Milton and Carew, or Milton and almost any of the disciples of Jonson.

But although Milton's conception of poetry was larger and more public than that of the coterie poets, I do not for a moment want to suggest that it was popular or that there was any analogy between Milton and the ageing Wither, defending his 'lowly stile' and useful matter against the taste for what were called 'strong lines'. Milton always had in mind an audience fit though few and of considerable learning and sophistication. While, though, he disdained to court the approval of comparatively uneducated and simple-minded readers, he also disdained mere fashion and eccentricity; his ideal audience was one which, like himself, had been steeped in the classics and in Italian literature, which was habitually aware of what, in the Preface to *Samson Agonistes*, he called 'best example', and which judged according to European and international standards. Milton wished his poetry to be judged, not according to the measure of Donne, or even according to the measure of Jonson, but according to that of the greatest names in the history of European poetry. Fashion, the latest thing, being-up-to-date, and so forth, meant far less to him than to many of his contemporaries. Indeed, in a sense the great poets of antiquity whom he studied so assiduously were for him more contemporary than any poets then alive. In his shorter poems he is indeed a seventeenth-century poet, but nearly always a seventeenth-century poet with a difference, and what that difference is will, I hope, become clearer to us as we proceed.

I remarked that one might to some extent place Milton among his contemporaries by saying that he was a poet for whom Spenser was not out of date. His love of Spenser may well have dated from his schooldays, for the elder Gill, High-Master of St Paul's, had a great admiration for him. Gill wrote an English grammar, in Latin, but with numerous English quotations, and most of these quotations are from the *Faerie Queene*. Here let me quote some words of Dr Tillyard's which will help to unite what I have just been saying about Milton's European standards with his admiration for Spenser. 'Spenser', writes Dr Tillyard,

is assumed [by Gill] to be the English Virgil, the one undoubted English classic, international by his learning and his constant recourse to classical models, domestic by his having set the standard of English versification. During his school-days Milton would have come to believe in serious literature as belonging to one great humane tradition, whatever language it was written in. If it was modern, it should still be international: for it might be written in Latin, the common tongue of European culture; or if it was written in the vernacular, it should conform to a no less common tradition of literary imitation.[1]

On several different occasions Milton publicly expressed his admiration for Spenser. In *Comus*, as an introduction to his invocation of Sabrina, whom Spenser had celebrated in the second book of the *Faerie Queene*, Milton made his Attendant Spirit mention and praise Spenser under the name of Meliboeus:

> now I bethink me,
> Som other means I have that may be us'd,
> Which once of *Melibœus* old I learnt
> The soothest Shepherd that ere pip't on plains.

Then, in his *Animadversions upon the Remonstrant's Defence against Smectymnuus*, one of his many anti-episcopal pamphlets, Milton quoted a longish passage from the May Eclogue of Spenser's *Shepherd's Calendar*, the eclogue that consists of a controversial

---

[1] *Milton*, revised edn 1966, p. 9.

dialogue between the faithless and epicurean shepherd Palinode and the faithful and almost puritanical shepherd Piers who looks back regretfully to those primitive times when shepherds, that is to say, christian ministers, were content with such modest support as their own congregations could provide. Palinode, declared Milton, 'lively personates our Prelates. . . . Those our admired *Spencer* inveighs against, not without some presage of these reforming times.'[1] But the most famous of all Milton's allusions to Spenser is in the *Areopagitica*, where, after declaring that he cannot praise a fugitive and cloistered virtue, that what purifies us is trial, and that trial is by what is contrary, he continues:

Which was the reason why our sage and serious Poet *Spencer*, whom I dare be known to think a better teacher then *Scotus* or *Aquinas*, describing true temperance under the person of *Guion*, brings him in with his palmer through the cave of Mammon, and the bowr of earthly blisse that he might see and know, and yet abstain.[2]

Thus, whatever he may be for us, Spenser for Milton was above all soothest Spenser, reforming Spenser, sage and serious Spenser. At first sight, perhaps, contrasting the concentration and precision of Milton's mature style with the diffuseness and redundancy of Spenser's, one might be inclined to say that it was in respect rather of ends than of means that Spenser was Milton's original, and that what Milton inherited was Spenser's conception of the matter and purpose of poetry, not Spenser's conception of poetic style; that, in fact, his allegiance to Spenser was a moral and spiritual rather than an artistic allegiance. There would indeed be much truth in such a view, but it would not be the whole truth. One need not insist too much on the obviously Spenserian lines and phrases in the earliest of Milton's shorter poems and on the perhaps not quite so obvious Spenserian parallels, such as the list of flowers in *Lycidas*, in the later ones, but one ought to insist on the fact that the style of Milton's shorter poems, though more concentrated and precise than Spenser's, is still far nearer to Spenser's than to Donne's, or

---

[1] Columbia edn, iii. 165–6.   [2] Columbia edn, iv. 311.

even, on the whole, to Jonson's. The substance of Carew's praise of Donne as a poet in his famous elegy amounts to this, that Donne wrote his poetry, as children say, out of his own head, wrote almost as though no one had ever written poetry before: he purged the Muses' Garden of pedantic weeds, rooted out servile imitation and planted fresh invention; exiled the goodly train of gods and goddesses and silenced the tales of Ovid's *Metamorphoses*. For Milton, on the contrary, as for Spenser, classical allusions, classical mythology, a continual and recognisable deference to the whole classical and European tradition, an element of ritual and solemnity and deliberate assumption of the garland and singing robes, were not mere decorations, but inseparably connected with their whole conception of poetry as something lofty, elaborate and learned, something which demanded intense labour and study, industrious and select reading, the shunning of delights and the living of laborious days—something, moreover, that could only be fully appreciated by readers suitably prepared: one may compare Mark Pattison's assertion that a full appreciation of *Paradise Lost* is the last reward of consummated scholarship with Drayton's bitter and rather unjust remark (or implication), in the Preface to the first part of *Poly-Olbion*, that the manuscript poets (and I fear he was thinking mainly of Donne) wrote nothing but what 'dull and slothful ignorance may easily reach unto'. Milton, we may assume, had seen some of this manuscript poetry, and was perhaps occasionally influenced by its example. I said, indeed, at the beginning of my attempt to place him among his contemporaries, that in respect of that concentration of substance and distinction of expression which he always aimed at he resembles the coterie poets rather than the publishing poets of his time, although I might have added that in this respect he perhaps owed as much to his own industrious and select reading of the classics as to their example. Nevertheless, as I have tried to show, his real affinity was with Spenser, and like Drayton and many of the other publishing poets of his time he began as a poet for whom Spenser was not out of date.

In recent discussions of the various kinds of seventeenth-century poetry, including Milton's, there have been many attempts to relate them to what is called the main tradition or the main stream of English poetry. In most of these discussions it seems to me that certain important distinctions have not been sufficiently observed. If we think mainly of diction, and if we regard the dramatic poetry of Shakespeare and his contemporaries, with its closeness to the idiom and rhythm of the spoken language, as the chief glory of English poetry, then we may be inclined to say that Jonson's poetry and Donne's, and Donne's (in spite of the frequent eccentricity both of his subject-matter and of his treatment of it) even more than Jonson's, and the poetry of the continuers of this colloquial tradition, the poetry, that is to say, not merely of the later so-called metaphysicals, but the poetry of Dryden and, to a considerable extent, of Pope—that this essentially colloquial poetry is more English, more in the central tradition of English poetry, than that of either Spenser or Milton, especially Milton, who, as Dr Johnson said, 'had formed his style by a perverse and pedantick principle' and who was 'desirous to use English words with a foreign idiom'.[1] One of the final results of regarding English poetry and the English poetic tradition in this rather exclusive and one-sided way is that Milton comes more and more to appear (as he does in a recent book on English poetry) as one of the English Eccentrics, as a kind of lonely and provincial crank. If, though, we try to regard English poetry not merely from a Shakespearean (a rather narrowly Shakespearean) but from a European point of view, in relation to the main stream of European poetry, in relation to Homer and Virgil and Horace, to the Greek Dramatists, to Dante and Petrarch, to Ariosto and Tasso, if we try to look at English poetry in this way, then even Jonson, the great reverer and translator of the classics, seems in some respects a little narrow and provincial in comparison with Spenser, Donne seems eccentric and provincial in comparison with Jonson, and, while Milton is in the main stream, the successors of Jonson and Donne, even including Dryden and Pope, seem to be paddling in various kinds of backwater, seem, at any rate in comparison with the great European poets, to be essentially provincial. I admit, though, that to see Dryden and

---

[1] *Lives of the English Poets*, ed. G. B. Hill, 1905, i. 190.

Pope thus, or mainly thus, would be going too far to the other extreme. All I want to insist upon is that in many, and perhaps the most important respects Milton is a more central, a more classical, a more European poet than any of his English contemporaries.[1] And I will conclude what I have to say on this subject with two quotations from two distinguished scholars, one of them on the relation between Milton and Spenser and the other on the relation between Milton and Jonson. 'Spenser', wrote Sir Herbert Grierson, in the Introduction to his *Metaphysical Lyrics and Poems of the Seventeenth Century*,

was Milton's poetic father, and his poetic diction and elaborately varied harmony are a development of Spenser's art by one who has absorbed more completely the spirit, understood more perfectly the art, of Virgil and the Greeks, who has taken Virgil and Homer for his teachers rather than Ariosto and Tasso.[2]

'Among all Jonson's disciples', writes Professor Douglas Bush, in his *English Literature in the Earlier Seventeenth Century*,

the nearest heir of his Renaissance humanism, the ethical and scholarly solidity of his art, was the young Milton. The rest, in their various ways and degrees, and with varying responsiveness to the metaphysical fashion, cultivated such patches of the Jonsonian garden as amatory, complimentary, elegiac, and epigrammatic verse.[3]

---

[1] It must also be admitted that, while what may be called the Jonson-Donne tradition encouraged minor poets to attempt things within the scope of their talents and often, in so doing, to produce many small but beautiful or charming things, the 'European' tradition too often encouraged minor poets either to attempt things that were quite beyond them, such as epic and tragedy, or to borrow ancient conventions and ancient formulae which they had not the genius, such as Milton revealed in *Lycidas*, to re-animate.

[2] op cit., 1921, p. li.

[3] op. cit., 2nd edn 1962, p. 114.

≫ 3 ≪

The Latin poems

After having made some attempt to 'place' Milton's shorter poems in the landscape of seventeenth-century poetry, I must now proceed to a detailed examination of the poems themselves.

First, I will say a few, a very few, words about the Latin poems. Since these few words will be concerned almost exclusively with the matter of the poems, I will begin by reminding you that, as Sir Herbert Grierson has said, 'for a student of Milton's art it is not unimportant to realise how much Latin verse Milton had written before he composed any considerable poem in English'.[1] The composition of these Latin poems extended over the whole period of his shorter English ones: he wrote the first of his six elegies in 1626, a few months after the lines *On the death of a Fair Infant*, and he wrote the *Epitaphium Damonis* in 1640, a year after his return from Italy. Limiting myself to a consideration of the matter of these poems, as distinct from their style, I will say that some of them are of great interest for two reasons, first, for what they tell us about Milton's conception of poetry and of the poet, and, secondly, for what they tell us, or seem to tell us, about Milton as a man. The first elegy, written in 1626 when he was not quite eighteen, was addressed to his friend Charles Diodati from London, where Milton was living during the period of his rustication from Cambridge. He visits the theatres and sees both comedies, of which he speaks very sympathetically and without a trace of Puritanism, or of what we have come to regard as typical Puritanism, and tragedies, of which he speaks in language very similar to that later used in *Il Penseroso*, and—a matter which

---

[1] Preface to Florence Press edn of Milton's *Poems*, 1925, vol. i, p. v.

has seemed of quite exceptional significance to some modern commentators—he expresses fervent admiration for the beauty of the young women he sees walking in the parks. In the seventh elegy, written about two years later, he tells how he scorned love until Cupid punished him by making him fall passionately in love with a beautiful face which he saw for a few moments in a crowd and which then vanished from him for ever. In the 1645 edition of his poems Milton placed this seventh elegy, not in the chronological order, but at the end of the elegies, and added a kind of palinode, declaring that it was a memorial of his foolish youth. The fifth elegy, *In Adventum Veris*, on the coming of Spring, was written in April 1629, eight months before the Nativity Ode, and is a rapturous and one might almost say pagan celebration of the rebirth of love and of the fertility of the earth. The sixth elegy, written in December of the same year, just after he had completed the Nativity Ode, is addressed to Charles Diodati, who had excused the badness of his verses on the ground that he was in the midst of Christmas festivities. Milton replies that wine and festivity and the sight and sound of girls dancing and playing on the virginals are precisely the things most likely to inspire an elegiac (or, as we should say, lyric) poet to excel, although one who aspires to be an epic poet and to celebrate gods and heroes must live simply in the way Pythagoras prescribed. And he concludes by saying that he has just composed a poem on the nativity in English. The verses *Ad Patrem*, to his father, are full of Milton's characteristically lofty conception of poetry and of the poet. His father, the musician, seems to have suggested that it was time his son began to earn his living, in reply to which, with many expressions of gratitude for the care and generosity bestowed on his education, Milton gently but firmly put his father in his place, professed himself unable to believe that such a suggestion had been meant seriously, and declared that the musicianly father and the poetical son were, so to speak, the two halves of Phoebus. The poem *Mansus* was written at Naples during the winter of 1638–9 and presented to his magnificent host Giovanni Baptista Manso, Marquis of Villa, who had been the friend and patron of Tasso and Marino. It contains the earliest evidence that Milton had been meditating an heroic poem on the subject of King Arthur. He hopes that he himself may be able to find such a patron if ever he should be able to sing of Arthur and the Round Table and the victory of the Britons over the Saxons! Finally, in the *Epitaphium Damonis*, the pastoral elegy which he wrote in 1640[1] to commemorate his friend Diodati, who had died during his absence in Italy, he mentions many things which he would have loved to share with his friend: twelve days ago, he declares, he attempted a strain too lofty for his rural pipe, his theme being the Trojan settlement of Britain, the early kings, Arthur and Merlin. If life, he continues, is granted him, he will either put away his pipe or make it sound the harsh accents of his native tongue; for at the cost of losing eternal fame and of remaining unknown to the world at large, he will be content with the praises of his native land.

About what the Latin poems tell us of Milton's conception of poetry and of the poet there cannot, I think, be any dispute. Most notable, perhaps, is that clearly and sharply expressed distinction between elegiac poetry, by which Milton means not merely love-poetry such as Ovid and Propertius and others wrote in the elegiac couplet, but love poems and short poems in general —between this slighter kind of poetry, as he regarded it, which required no special dedication, and epic or heroic poetry, which, he believed, required not merely a technical but a moral preparation. Although it has not been generally recognised, I think Milton is making this same distinction in *Lycidas*, that by the strictly-meditated 'thankless Muse', who requires the shunning of delights and the living of laborious days, he means the muse of epic poetry, and that he is implicitly contrasting this muse with the elegiac muse which had inspired the celebrated Renaissance Latin poets Johannes Secundus and George Buchanan to sing the praises of Neæra and her hair. This clearly expressed distinction should remind us that Milton regarded his shorter English poems, even the best of them, as no more than *parerga*, by-products, preparations for something loftier and more elaborate. It is,

---

[1] In ll.9–11 of the *Epitaphium Damonis* Milton declares that two harvests and two springs have passed since Diodati's death in August 1638. He therefore must have written the poem in the late spring or early summer of 1640.

though, when we try to regard the Latin poems as evidence for
other things about Milton than his literary ideals and ambitions
that we may easily fall into misinterpretation and exaggeration.
Dr Tillyard and some other modern interpreters have seized upon
that celebration, at the end of the first elegy, of what Milton's
successors called the British Fair, that description, in the seventh,
of a beautiful face a moment seen then gone for ever, and that
celebration of the coming of spring in the fifth as pieces of what
they (rather self-revealingly, perhaps) call self-revelation—as a kind
of letting the cat out of the bag, as the spontaneous expression of
something which in his English poems Milton deliberately
suppressed. This is a subtle and difficult question, and to consider it fully would take far too much of the time which I want to
spend upon the English poems. I will therefore content myself
with saying that the most balanced and sensible discussion of it I
know is that by Professor Wright in his Introduction to the
Shorter Poems. Professor Wright's point, to put it very briefly,
is this: that while in Milton's life, as in his English poetry,
susceptibility to feminine charms was nearly always associated
with moral issues, with a kind of Platonic or idealistic way of
thinking, in his Latin poems it was separated from these moral
issues and from that idealistic strain by a literary convention, by
the fact that he was writing in the language and in the manner
of those whom he called the 'smooth elegiac poets', and that the
manner to a considerable extent dictated the matter, prescribed
what might and what might not be said. Moreover, that idealistic,
Platonic or Petrarchan strain which is absent from the Latin
poems is present enough in the contemporary Italian ones, which
Milton addressed to an accomplished Italian woman, or woman
of Italian descent, living in England.[1] For such details about her
—all we have—as may be gleaned from these Italian poems I
must refer you to Smart's edition of the Sonnets: her name was
Emilia, and she seems to have been Milton's first love. But
although in interpreting the Latin poems very much allowance
must be made for the tradition and convention in which they are

---

[1] On the Italian poems see Sergio Baldi, 'Poesie Italiane di Milton'. *Studi Secen-
teschi*, vol. vii, 1966. A.L.

written, the fact remains that they do, as Professor Wright admits, reveal a side of Milton's nature which we are apt to ignore or undervalue. George Herbert wrote in *The Pearl*:

> I know the wayes of Pleasure, the sweet strains,
> The lullings and the relishes of it;
> The propositions of hot bloud and brains;
> What mirth and musick mean; what love and wit
> Have done these twentie hundred yeares, and more:
> I know the projects of unbridled store:
> My stuffe is flesh, not brasse; my senses live,
> And grumble oft, that they have more in me
> Then he that curbs them, being but one to five:
>   Yet I love thee.

With Milton no less than with Herbert it was a river, not a rivulet, that was to be canalised.

4

English poems written at Cambridge

Let us now turn to the English poems, and begin by considering, briefly and in chronological order, those that Milton wrote during his residence at Cambridge. I do not propose to say all that might be said about each one of them, but shall try to keep continually in mind the question, what is the relation of these poems to those of Milton's publishing and unpublishing contemporaries?

The earliest of them is *On the Death of a Fair Infant*, written probably during the winter of 1625–6, when Milton was seventeen.[1] For some reason he did not include it in the 1645 volume, although he did include there two of his schoolboy paraphrases of the Psalms and the fragmentary and unsuccessful poem on the Passion. We cannot therefore assume too confidently, although it is not impossible, that he deliberately excluded it as being too immature and too imitative. It first appeared in the edition of 1673. It consists of eleven seven-line stanzas of a pattern only used, so far as I know, by Phineas Fletcher in some poems which were not published until 1633. It is Spenserian, perhaps, in its archaisms and in its easy flow, but it contains conceits which are less characteristic of Spenser than (to borrow

---

[1] In the 1673 edition it is said to have been composed 'Anno aetatis 17'. However, it is thought to refer to a child of Milton's sister Ann, wife of Edward Philips, and the first recorded death of a child of theirs is in January, 1628. See *Life Records of John Milton*, ed. J. Milton French, New Jersey, 1949, vol. i, p. 102. The two most recent editors of the poems, J. T. Shawcross (New York University Press, 1963) and Douglas Bush (Oxford University Press, 1966) accept that '17' is a printer's error, and that the correct date for the poem is 1628. A.L.

a phrase of Tillyard's) of such 'Ovidising' Elizabethan poems as *Venus and Adonis*, *The Rape of Lucrece* and *Hero and Leander*; for these conceits, or ingenious fancies, are not expressed in the witty, concentrated manner of the so-called metaphysicals, but developed in the ample and leisurely Elizabethan fashion. The poem, then, has almost nothing in common with those that were being written by the disciples of Jonson or of Donne, and is by their standards decidedly old-fashioned. What, though, has not, I think, been noticed is the very large number of compound adjectives it contains, and these are one of the most characteristic stylistic features of Milton's shorter poems. In this short poem there are no less than thirteen: long-uncoupled bed, ycie-pearled carr, Snow-soft chaire, cold-kind embrace, dearly-loved mate, low delved tombe, first-moving Spheare, sweet smiling Youth, white-robed Truth, golden-winged hoast, heav'n-lov'd innocence, Swift-rushing black perdition, false imagin'd loss. The compound adjective is not infrequent in Spenser ('sea-shouldering whales' is a famous example[1]) or in Shakespeare ('love-devouring death'[2]) or in Sidney's sonnets ('kiss-worthy face', 'long with love acquainted eyes'[3]) and also in his *Arcadia*, but it is, as I have said, a very noticeable feature of the style of Milton's earlier poems, especially, perhaps, of *Comus*. It may well be that Milton, like Sidney, was deliberately trying to transplant into English one of the beauties of Greek.

Even if one could not immediately adduce so-called 'parallel passages', the very first stanza of the poem is what anyone tolerably familiar with Elizabethan poetry would rightly call 'typically Elizabethan':

> O fairest flower no sooner blown but blasted,
> Soft silken Primrose fading timelesslie,
> Summers chief honour if thou hadst out-lasted
> Bleak winters force that made thy blossome drie;
> For he being amorous on that lovely die
>   That did thy cheek envermeil, thought to kiss
> But kill'd alas, and then bewayl'd his fatal bliss.

---

[1] *The Faerie Queene*, II. xii. 23.   [2] *Romeo and Juliet*, II. vi. 7.
[3] *Astrophel and Stella*, sonnets xxxi and lxxiii.

Consider (it was first cited in illustration by Todd) the beginning of the tenth poem in *The Passionate Pilgrim* (1599), which, whether or no it be by Shakespeare, may certainly be called typically Elizabethan:

> Sweet rose, fair flower, untimely pluck'd, soon vaded,
> Pluck'd in the bud, and vaded in the spring!
> Bright orient pearl, alack, too timely shaded!
> Fair creature, kill'd too soon by death's sharp sting.

Not only the movement of the verse, but the formal rhetorical pattern, a succession of what might be called apostrophical metaphors, is almost identical in both passages. Typically Elizabethan, too, 'Ovidisingly' Elizabethan, as distinct from being either in the manner of Spenser or of the so-called Metaphysicals, is that conceit about winter's killing where he meant to kiss. It is essentially the same conceit as that applied by Venus, in Shakespeare's poem, to the boar that killed Adonis:

> He thought to kiss him, and hath kill'd him so.[1]   (l.1110)

This kind of writing was still practised by some of the more old-fashioned of Milton's contemporaries, particularly by Giles and Phineas Fletcher, with whose poems the young Milton seems to have been well acquainted and by which he seems to have been, for a time, considerably influenced. Phineas Fletcher, in his *Purple Island*,

---

[1] I have called this conceit 'typically Elizabethan'; nevertheless, like many other conceits which may appropriately be so described, it is very much older than the earliest English poetry. It occurs in a short late Greek Anacreontic poem 'On the Death of Adonis', which was included in the collection of Greek pastoral poetry known as the *Bucolica*, apparently because of its affinity in subject with the Lament for Adonis. Aphrodite, says the poet, sent the Erotes to bring to her the boar which had killed Adonis. It swore that it had not meant to injure either him or her, but that, when it saw his naked thigh, it could not resist a burning desire to kiss it. It begged Aphrodite to cut off its too passionate tusks and even its lips. She forgave it, and from that day it followed her and, as penance and punishment, went to the fire and burnt away its tusks.

> γυμνὸν τὸν εἶχε μηρὸν
> ἐμαινόμαν φιλᾶσαι.   (ll.30-1)

('The thigh which he had naked I was mad to kiss.') The conceit may have reached Shakespeare either through Minturno's Latin epigram *De Adone ab Apro interempto*, or through an English version of the poem, which during the Renaissance was commonly ascribed to Theocritus, in a volume of translations from Theocritus entitled *Six Idillia*, which had been printed at Oxford in 1588.

had also, as Todd remarked, employed this kiss and kill conceit:

> Thus *Orpheus* wanne his lost *Eurydice*;
> Whom some deaf snake, that could no musick heare,
> Or some blinde neut, that could no beautie see,
> Thinking to kisse, kill'd with his forked spear.[1]

Such a conceit is scarcely conceivable except in some mythological or semi-allegorical context. Certainly, we should be more likely to find it in a poem of this formally and expansively rhetorical pattern, which I have called typically Elizabethan, than in the essentially colloquial and contemporary poems of Donne or in those of Donne's imitators. The double-epithets on which I have already commented also belong to a more formal and rhetorical kind of poetry than Donne's, and so too do many adjectival phrases which, though we might expect to find them, and often do find them, in Shakespeare's plays, we do not find in Donne's poems. There can be no doubt that at one time Milton delighted in Shakespeare, and his early poems contain not only many appropriations or variations of Shakespearean phrases but several Shakespearean observations of nature. It is perhaps unnecessary to insist upon the fact that by Milton and by many other poets for whom, unlike Donne, imitation was an essential part of the art of poetry, what we call plagiarism was not regarded as a crime. Consider the lines:

> Yet can I not perswade me thou art dead
> Or that thy coarse corrupts in earths dark wombe,
> Or that thy beauties lie in wormie bed.   (ll.29–31)

It is almost certain, I think, that Milton remembered the phrase 'wormie bed' from one of Puck's speeches in *A Midsummer Night's Dream*:

> damned spirits all,
> That in crossways and floods have burial,
> Already to their wormy beds are gone.[2]

Another phrase which one would never expect to find in Donne,

---

[1] Canto v, stanza 61. *The Poetical Works of Giles and Phineas Fletcher*, ed. F. S. Boas, 1908–9, ii. 66.
[2] III. ii. 384.

but which one might expect to find (although, as a matter of fact, one does not) in Shakespeare is 'nectar'd head'. It occurs in a stanza which is worth quoting as a whole, because it is a particularly striking example of the very Spenserian or Renaissance manner in which the young Milton blends classical mythology with the Christian consolation he is proffering:

> Wert thou some Starr which from the ruin'd roofe
> Of shak't Olympus by mischance didst fall;
> Which careful *Jove* in natures true behoofe
> Took up, and in fit place did reinstall?
> Or did of late earths Sonnes besiege the wall
>   Of sheenie Heav'n, and thou some goddess fled
> Amongst us here below to hide thy nectar'd head.
>
> (st. vii, ll. 43–9)

The word 'nectar'd' occurs twice in the poems of the early seventeenth-century satirist, John Davies of Hereford: 'Nectar'd *Streames of Helicon*'[1] and 'Hence flow all Nectard Sweets'[2]. Milton introduced the phrase 'nectar'd sweets' into a famous passage in *Comus*, where the Elder Brother declares that philosophy is a perpetual feast of nectar'd sweets where no crude surfeit reigns. This is most characteristic of Milton. He was always ready to appropriate, consciously or unconsciously, what seemed to him a good phrase, not merely from classical but from English poetry, and not merely from poets of the stature of Spenser and Shakespeare, but from poets whose works are to-day familiar only to a few scholars.

The English verses delivered as part of a vacation exercise in July 1628, when Milton was nineteen, are interesting, like some of the later elegies, for what they tell us about his poetic ideals. 'The Latin speeches ended, the English thus begun', is the subtitle, and Milton begins by hailing his native language:

> And from thy wardrope bring thy chiefest treasure;
> Not those new fangled toys, and trimming slight
> Which takes our late fantasticks with delight,
> But cull those richest Robes, and gay'st attire
> Which deepest Spirits, and choicest Wits desire. (ll. 18–22)

---

[1] *The Scourge of Folly*, [1611], p. 132.   [2] *Wittes Pilgrimage*, [1605], sig. C2v.

I confess I do not know whom Milton means by 'our late fantasticks', although everybody else seems to know that he means
those who wrote in the so-called metaphysical manner, Donne
and the imitators of Donne. If so, he must have been referring to
manuscript poetry, for, as we have seen, no distinctively metaphysical poetry was published before 1633. He cannot, I think,
have been referring to Donne himself, for 'our late fantasticks'
must mean either 'our recently arrived fantastics' or 'our recently
arrived and now departed fantastics', and Donne's poetic reputation had been established for some thirty years.[1] Moreover,
although Milton might well have been inclined to dismiss many
or most of Donne's Elegies and *Songs and Sonnets* as 'new fangled
toys', I doubt whether he would have spoken of 'trimming
slight', for the phrase suggests some rather trivial kind of
decoration, something sugary and tinselly, which is altogether
absent from Donne's poems. Indeed, however much Milton may
have disliked those poems, there is about nearly all of them an
intellectual toughness and an absence of 'trimming' which I
think he would have respected. I leave out of account the later
verses on the University Carrier, for although they exemplify
those elements in Donne's wit and poetry of which Cleveland
was the great exploiter, Milton was there very obviously con-
descending to write in a particular manner and very obviously
not being serious.[2] Who, then, 'our late fantasticks' were I do not
know; all I feel able to say is that Milton is here protesting against
some poetic fashion, probably in certain Cambridge circles, which
had either been recently established and was still flourishing, or
which had both been recently established and recently exploded.
Milton then proceeds to declare that he wishes he could employ
his native language on some graver subject than that now
entrusted to him:

---

[1] See above p. 26, n. 1.

[2] Several other poems, mostly anonymous, on the death of Hobson, the University
Carrier, have survived, and it is worth mentioning that, so far as I am aware,
Milton's two poems on the subject are the only poems of his that appeared in any
of the numerous miscellanies published during his life-time.

Such where the deep transported mind may soare
Above the wheeling poles, and at Heav'ns dore
Look in, and see each blissful Deitie
How he before the thunderous throne doth lie . . .
Then sing of secret things that came to pass
When Beldam Nature in her cradle was;
And last of Kings and Queens and *Hero's* old,

(ll. 33-6, 45-7)

such as Ulysses heard the minstrel Demodocus sing of when he feasted with King Alcinous.

Somewhat more than a year later, on Christmas Day, 1629, shortly after his twenty-first birthday, Milton wrote his first great poem. Professor Wright may well be correct in supposing that the Ode *On the Morning of Christ's Nativity* was the result of 'his first clear vision of the true power of poetry and of the kind of poet he should be', and that it was of this period that Milton was thinking when, in that famous Biographia Literaria which in 1642 he inserted into his *Apology for Smectymnuus* in order to defend his moral character against the aspersions of Bishop Hall, he wrote: 'And long it was not after, when I was confirm'd in this opinion, that he who would not be frustrate of his hope to write well hereafter in laudable things, ought him selfe to bee a true Poem';[1] for, as we have seen, it was in the sixth of his Latin elegies, at the end of which he mentioned the Nativity Ode, that Milton first expressed that sharp distinction between the preparation and regimen of an elegiac and an heroic poet.

Before examining some of the detail of this great and familiar poem, let us, as it were, stand back and look at it as a whole, and try to place it in relation to the poetry of Milton's contempories and predecessors. Obviously one cannot profitably compare it with any of the secular poetry of the seventeenth century. Can one profitably compare it with any of the religious poetry? When we think of the religious poetry of the seventeenth century, we probably think first of the poetry of Donne and Herbert, and perhaps nothing could be more unlike their religious poetry than Milton's Ode; for while their poetry is intensely personal

---

[1] Columbia edn, iii. 303.

and dramatic and undecorated and colloquial, what first strikes
us about Milton's poem is its loftiness, its elaborateness, and its
impersonality. Donne and Herbert did not write elaborate
celebrations of religious events: what they wrote of was the
intimate, the dramatic relation between God and their own souls.
The only seventeenth-century poet who in any memorable way
celebrated religious events was Crashaw, and perhaps the only
seventeenth-centurh religious poem that may at all profitably be
compared with the Nativity Ode is Crashaw's 'Sospetto d'Herode',
a free paraphrase from the Italian of Marino. Which reminds me
that Dr Tillyard, though without entering at all deeply into the
matter, has called Milton's Ode his first poem written in an
Italianate manner. Now although the celebration of Christ, in
something of an heroic manner, as a hero, is characteristic of
certain Italian poets, it is also, though perhaps only incidentally,
very characteristic of Milton's master Spenser, and of some of
Spenser's lesser disciples, among them Giles Fletcher who wrote
an heroic poem on *Christ's Victorie and Triumph*. Moreover, if, as
distinct from its substance, one attends mainly to the style and
tone of Milton's Ode, I think that for anything at all comparable
in English poetry one would have to go back to Spenser's
Epithalamion and the *Epithalamion* is an Italianate poem in so far
as its verse-pattern is modelled on that of the Italian canzone.
However, I am rather doubtful whether it is really necessary to
bring the Italians into a discussion of Milton's Ode. Let us stick
to Spenser, and let us content ourselves with saying that the
celebration of Christ as a hero is Spenserian, and that the lofty
and elaborate style of the poem, so different from that plain
colloquialism of, let us say, Herbert, is also Spenserian. Here let
me pause a moment to pay a tribute to the discrimination of that
excellent bookseller Humphrey Moseley who published Milton's
1645 volume and who said in his Preface to the Reader: 'Let the
event guide it self which way it will, I shall deserve of the age,
by bringing into the Light as true a Birth, as the Muses have
brought forth since our famous *Spencer* wrote; whose Poems in
these English ones are as rarely imitated, as sweetly excell'd.'
Moseley, I say, deserves credit for perceiving, long before Milton
himself admitted it to Dryden that Spenser had been Milton's

original, and that in point of style Milton had excelled what he began by imitating. In the Bodleian copy of the 1650 edition of the excellent anthology *The Academy of Complements* there is a list of Humphrey Moseley's publications, a list that includes, among other things, Beaumont and Fletcher's *Plays*, Suckling's, *Fragmenta Aurea*, Waller's *Poems*, Fanshaw's translation of the *Pastor Fido* and his Poems; Shirley's Poems, Crashaw's *Steps to the Temple*, Cowley's *Mistress*, Quarles's *Divine Poems*, three plays by Davenant, Denham's *Sophy* and *Cooper's Hill*, Heath's *Clarastella*, Carew's *Poems*, and 'Poems of Mr. *John Milton*'.

But before proceeding to examine particular passages in the Ode and trying to show that its diction and imagery are nearer to Spenser, to the Elizabethan and Jacobean pastoral poets, and to the more pastoral and folklorish portions of Shakespeare's plays than to the kind of poetry that was most fashionable among the young Milton's contemporaries—before proceeding to this, I will repeat and enlarge upon my remark that for anything comparable to the Nativity Ode in previous English poetry we must go back to Spenser's *Epithalamion*; for the *Epithalamion* is the only preceding poem of similar length that may be compared with the Nativity Ode, not merely in diction and imagery, but in design and organic unity and the presence of a continuously exciting and onward-carrying poetic energy. On this subject of the design and organisation of the Nativity Ode the best piece of writing I know is that by Miss Rosemond Tuve in her chapter on the Ode in *Images and Themes in Five Poems by Milton* (1957).[1] She rightly insists that the subject is the Incarnation rather than the Nativity, and that the poem is rather the celebration of a mystery and of the conquest of Darkness by Light than the description of an event, and that, as preparation for a full response to it, it is less important to have vividly in memory the Gospel narratives of the Nativity than certain sayings of St Paul about the significance of the Incarnation and about the hope, the peace, and the light that

---

[1] This seems to me by far the best chapter in Miss Tuve's book, although, like almost all her critical writing, it is very unequal. She often professes to discover what is not recognisably there, and she tends to worry at passages which we should prefer to be left alone, but the kernel of what she has to say, if you can break your way through to it, is excellent.

have come to men through Christ. After observing what Milton's
poem owes to the Pauline Epistles, to the Messianic interpretation of Virgil's Fourth Eclogue, that poem celebrating the
birth of a certain divine child who shall bring back the Golden
Age and universal peace, and to the two Proper Psalms for
Christmas, Psalm 85, which declares in verse 10 that 'Mercy
and truth are met together: righteousness (*iustitia*) and peace have
kissed each other', and Psalm 89, declaring in verse 15 that
'Righteousness and equity (*iustitia* et *iudicium*) are the habitation
of thy seat: mercy and truth shall go before thy face'—after
noticing these and other details, Miss Tuve declares:

Milton has thus formed our understanding of the full import of the
mystery he celebrates by a kind of orchestrated weaving of themes
carried by great symbols traditionally used to present such meanings.
It is highly original; no similar poem shows anything to match its
peculiar combination of dignity with light and happy charm. The
theme of how our peace is made, our darkness lightened, our harmony
new tuned to the celestial music, our nature transcended—is played in
key after key, repeated, varied, inverted, transposed.[1]

We may see here, as we shall see later in *At a Solemn Musick*, in
Arcades and in *Comus*, how strongly the originally Pythagorean
and Platonic but also, to some extent, traditionally Christian
notions of the just soul, of justice and of goodness as harmonies
and of the music of the spheres have possessed Milton's imagination and both modified and been modified by the way in which he
apprehended and experienced Christianity. The shepherds hear
the angels as a miraculously apprehensible echo of the celestial
harmony, of what Milton was later to describe as

> That undisturbed Song of pure concent,
> Ay sung before the saphire-colour'd throne,

and behold them as an effluence of the celestial light. As Miss
Tuve expresses it

Music, Harmonia, Concord (Love, Reconciliation, Peace, Order,
Unity in multiplicity) becomes the greatest and most conceptually

---

[1] op. cit., p. 62.

necessary symbol of the poem, except for that of Light, and the two interpenetrate each other. Without it Milton quite simply could not express his meanings, to say nothing of moving us by their depth of significance.[1]

What makes the Nativity Ode a great poem, and not merely a longish poem with fine passages, is the fusion in it of intense personal feeling with large traditional ideas and conceptions, all of which not only can be but are apprehended imaginatively and poetically as well as philosophically and religiously. A whole great chapter in the history of the human spirit is focussed and concentrated in a single imagination and made audible and visible in a single moment of time. There is something of this in Spenser's *Epithalamion*, which, as I have said, is the only preceding English poem with which, as a whole, the Nativity Ode is really comparable. Although he had behind him a long tradition of *epithalamia*, extending from Catullus and Claudian to the Renaissance, the form of Spenser's poem is highly original, for he has made of it a progressive and continuously energised celebration of the stages or stations of the wedding-day from dawn till dark, and into it he has brought, re-apprehending them all with full poetic imagination, all manner of traditional ideas, customs and images which had been or naturally could be associated with such celebration. As Professor Renwick has well said:

Its extraordinary quality arises from the complete fusion of personal feeling and literary tradition, strength made perfect by discipline, riches increased by the store of memories of which the tradition is made. The poetry of Europe was so much a part of Spenser's life, and his energy so habitually turned to poetry, that the happy day of worldly experience and the happy day of artistic power met and created this perfect poem. By the free use of the poetic tradition of mythology Spenser associates with his own joy the landscape round Kilcolman, the sea, the heavens and the moon. By the intermingling of Roman and English custom he controls and dignifies the action without freezing it.[2]

Besides these large and general resemblances, is it possible to

---

[1] op. cit., p. 57.
[2] Spenser, *Daphnaïda and other Poems*, ed. W. L. Renwick, 1929, p. 204.

find more particular examples of what may be called Spenserianism in the Nativity Ode? I think so. Consider the pastoralism of stanza 8:

> The Shepherds on the Lawn,
> Or e're the point of dawn,
>   Sate simply chatting in a rustick row;
> Full little thought they than,
> That the mighty *Pan*
>   Was kindly com to live with them below;
> Perhaps their loves, or els their sheep,
> Was all that did their silly thoughts so busie keep.

Consider also the fine use of a passage from Job—'when the morning stars sang together, and all the sons of God shouted for joy'—in stanza 12:

> Such Musick (as 'tis said)
> Before was never made,
>   But when of old the sons of morning sung,
> While the Creator great
> His constellations set,
>   And the well-ballanc't world on hinges hung,
> And cast the dark foundations deep,
> And bid the weltring waves their oozy channel keep.

Consider these passages, and compare them with some of Spenser's equally fine incorporations of Biblical phraseology into the *Epithalamion*:

> Open the temple gates vnto my loue,
> Open them wide that she may enter in,   (ll. 204–5)

or the description of the bride advancing 'Lyke Phœbe from her chamber of the East' (l. 149). Consider the perhaps slightly grotesque dragon in stanza 18, and compare it with Spenser's description of the dragon on which Duessa rode, 'scourging th' emptie ayre with his long traine.' Consider in stanza 25, a most characteristically Spenserian combination of pagan and Christian imagery, the suggested comparison of the divine babe to the infant Hercules who strangled the serpents which attacked him in his cradle.

It has often been said that various conceits, that is to say, ingenious and to our taste rather quaint comparisons in the poem are in the so-called metaphysical manner, and that Milton is here writing in a fashion which he later outgrew. I have not time to argue the matter fully, but I will ask you to believe, first, that the use of ingenious comparisons is only one, and by no means the most important characteristic, of Donne's poetry; secondly, that in Donne's poetry such comparisons are nearly always conceptual rather than pictorial, and nearly always used to illustrate some serious or unserious argument; thirdly, that comparisons both ingenious, picturesque, and often, as one might be inclined to say, decorated, are not infrequent even in Spenser and very frequent indeed in one of the most widely read books of the time, Sylvester's translation of Du Bartas' long poem on the Creation, *La Semaine*. Consider, in the seventh stanza, the conceit about the sun hiding his head for shame:

> And though the shady gloom
> Had given day her room,
> The Sun himself withheld his wonted speed,
> And hid his head for shame,
> As his inferiour flame,
> The new-enlightn'd world no more should need;
> He saw a greater Sun appear
> Then his bright Throne, or burning Axletree could bear.

Compare this with a stanza from the song in praise of fair Eliza, queen of shepherds all, in the April Eclogue of Spenser's *Shepherd's Calendar*, published in 1579, when Donne was about seven years old:

> I saw *Phœbus* thrust out his golden hedde,
> vpon her to gaze:
> But when he sawe, how broade her beames did spredde,
> it did him amaze.
> He blusht to see another Sunne belowe,
> Ne durst againe his fyrye face out showe:
> Let him, if he dare,
> His brightnesse compare
> With hers, to have the ouerthrowe.   (ll.73–81)

Consider also this stanza from Giles Fletcher's *Christs Victorie and Triumph*, which had been published at Cambridge in 1610:

> Who can forget, never to be forgot,
> The time, that all the world in slumber lies,
> When, like the starres, the singing Angels shot
> To earth, and heav'n awaked all his eyes,
> To see another Sunne, at midnight rise,
> On earth? was never sight of pareil fame,
> For God before Man like himselfe did frame,
> But God himselfe now like a mortall man became.[1]

This is stanza 78 of the first part of Fletcher's poem: I think it very possible that stanza 82 may have suggested to Milton the whole plan of his ode:

> The Angells caroll'd lowd their song of peace,
> The cursed Oracles wear strucken dumb,
> To see their Sheapheard, the poore Sheapheards press,
> To see their King, the Kingly Sophies come,
> And them to guide unto his Masters home,
> A Starre comes dauncing up the orient,
> That springs for joye over the strawy tent,
> Whear gold, to make their Prince a crowne, they all present.

I may add that in his Preface, where he mentions earlier religious poets, Fletcher speaks of 'thrice-honour'd *Bartas*, & our (I know no other name more glorious then his own) M\r. *Edmund Spencer*.'

As for the other conceits or quaintnesses in the poem, they are not really in Donne's manner: one could find much like them, or not very unlike them, in Sylvester's Du Bartas, or in Crashaw and the Italian pastoral poets with whom Crashaw, like Milton, was familiar, or sometimes in Cowley, especially the Cowley of the *Davideis*, or even graphically in the so popular emblems of the time. The description of the sun, in the first stanza of the Hymn, as the earth's 'lusty Paramour', and, in stanza 26, of how the sun

> in bed,
> Curtain'd with cloudy red,
> Pillows his chin upon an Orient wave

---

[1] *The Poetical Works of Giles and Phineas Fletcher*, ed. F. S. Boas, 1908–9, i. 37.

are quite in the manner of Sylvester's famous description of the periwigged woods, which Benlowes twice imitated in his *Theophilia*. And in fact the image of the sun in a red or crimson-curtained bed, though not of the sun pillowing his chin upon a wave, does actually occur in the second stanza of Crashaw's *An Himne for the Circumcision Day of Our Lord*, first published in his *Steps to the Temple*, 1646, but which I will quote in the revised version of 1652:

> All the purple pride that laces
>   The crimson curtains of thy bed,
> Guilds thee not with so sweet graces
>   Nor setts thee in so rich a red.[1]

Milton cannot have been imitating Crashaw, but I suppose it is just possible that Crashaw may have seen Milton's poem in manuscript, or even read it in the 1645 edition. The difference is that while Crashaw just fleetingly suggests the image of the sun as a noble or royal personage in a crimson-curtained bed, Milton dwells upon it and forces us to dwell upon it, until he has formed a more or less definite picture of his personified sun. Such over-pressed or over-elaborated comparisons are frequent in seven-teenth- and even in late sixteenth-century poetry, and, although they cannot properly be described as 'metaphysical', they may not unjustly be called 'quaint'. Crashaw is sometimes quaint in this way, but here, while Milton is, Crashaw is not. Such quaintness is comparatively infrequent even in Milton's earlier poetry, and he eventually discarded it. The more extended and pictorial conceit in stanza 2 is rather in the manner of Crashaw and the Italians:

> Onely with speeches fair
> She woo's the gentle Air
>   To hide her guilty front with innocent Snow,
> And on her naked shame,
> Pollute with sinful blame,
>   The Saintly Vail of Maiden white to throw,
> Confounded, that her Makers eyes
> Should look so neer upon her foul deformities.

---

[1] *Poems*, ed. L. C. Martin, 1927, p. 251.

Indeed, not merely the whole of this second stanza but the second part of the first stanza as well—

> Nature in aw to him
> Had doff't her gawdy trim,
>   With her great Master so to sympathize:
> It was no season then for her
> To wanton with the Sun her lusty Paramour.

—all this might be regarded as a development, an expansion, an elaborate working out of the image, or conceit, at the beginning of Petrarch's third sonnet, where he recalls that Good Friday on which he first saw Laura:

> Era il giorno ch' al sol si scoloraro
> per la pietà del suo fattore i rai;
> quando i' fui preso, e non me ne guardai,
> che i be' vostr' occhi, Donna, mi legaro.

('It was on that day when the sun's rays, for pity of their Creator, lost their colour that I was taken and did not perceive that your fair eyes, lady, had bound me.') The way in which, since the days of the Troubadours, the language and imagery of human and of divine adoration have borrowed from and lent to one another is one of the most interesting chapters in the history of European poetry.

The image in stanza 15 of Truth and Justice, with Mercy sitting between them, all dressed in the colours of the rainbow (or, as Milton later wrote, 'orb'd in a Rain-bow') and down-steering to men is reminiscent of some things in Cowley's *Davideis*. The quaint literalism, in the second stanza of the invocation, of the Son laying aside the glorious form

> Wherwith he wont at Heav'ns high Councel-Table,
> To sit the midst of Trinal Unity

and in the last stanza of the hymn of how

> Heav'ns youngest teemed Star,
> Hath fixt her polisht Car,
>   Her sleeping Lord with Handmaid Lamp attending

might well have been represented emblematically. Milton soon came to disdain these ingenious fancies and detailed personifications and to employ a much more suggestive and generalised kind of description, where most of the visual detail is left to the reader's imagination, although careful directions are given to it by well-chosen adjectives.

In the famous description of the silencing of the oracles, with its magnificent exploitation of the associations of proper names, Milton reveals his affinity not merely with Spenser, but also, as so often in his later poetry, with that most translunary and literary of poets, Marlowe. Milton has sometimes been called the last of the Elizabethans, and it is not merely in his admiration for Spenser and continuation of what one might call the Spenserian tradition that he is more Elizabethan than Donne or Jonson or their disciples. For, as I have already said, he admired Shakespeare, 'fancy's child' as he called him, and here in the penultimate stanza of the Ode, which contains that quaint image of the sun in bed, we find him exploiting the poetry of that world of folklore and popular superstition that Shakespeare had so notably exploited in the *Midsummer Night's Dream* and elsewhere. The pagan deities scatter before the heroic might of the new-born Saviour just as at sunrise,

> The flocking shadows pale,
> Troop to th' infernall jail,
>   Each fetter'd Ghost slips to his severall grave,
> And the yellow-skirted *Fayes*,
> Fly after the Night-steeds, leaving their Moon-lov'd maze.

'Fancy's child' had written:

> My fairy lord, this must be done with haste,
> For night's swift dragons cut the clouds full fast,
> And yonder shines Aurora's harbinger;
> At whose approach, ghosts, wandering here and there,
> Troop home to churchyards: damned spirits all,
> That in crossways and floods have burial,
> Already to their wormy beds are gone.[1]

And in another place:

---

[1] *A Midsummer-Night's Dream*, III. ii. 378 ff.

you demi-puppets that
By moonshine do the green sour ringlets make,
Whereof the ewe not bites.[1]

In both his earlier and later poetry Milton often worked this
mine that Shakespeare had opened, and it was one of the things
that led the Wartons and Hurd and other eighteenth-century
rediscoverers of the shorter poems to praise what they called the
romantic wildness of his fancy.

To come now to smaller units, we find several more of those
characteristic compound-epithets I mentioned in the lines *On
the Death of a Fair Infant*: far-beaming blaze of Majesty (l.9),
Star-led Wisards (l.23), Heav'n-born-childe (30), meek-eyd
Peace (46), new-enlightn'd world (82), shame-fac't night (111),
new-born Heir (116), well-ballanc't world (122), pale-ey'd
Priest (180), flowre-inwov'n tresses (187), twise batter'd god
(199), sable-stoled Sorcerers (220), yellow-skirted *Fayes* (235),
Moon-lov'd maze (236), youngest teemed Star (240), bright-
harnest Angels (244). The word 'inwov'n' (flowre-inwov'n
tresses) as an epithet, that is to say, as a word preceding, not
following, its noun was first used by Milton in this passage; and
the word *inweave* in the sense of 'to decorate with something
inserted or entwined' as distinct from the quite common sense of
'to weave one thread with another or one argument with
another', was first used by Spenser, that lover of flowers and
garlands, in *Muiopotmos*:

a faire border wrought of sundrie flowres,
Enwouen with an Yuie winding trayle.   (ll.298–9)

I may add that the word 'unexpressive', meaning 'inexpressible',
which occurs in stanza 11—

Harping in loud and solemn quire,
With unexpressive notes to Heaven's new-born
Heir—

was, so far as we know, only used three times in the whole history
of English literature: in this passage; in *Lycidas* (l.176),

---

[1] *The Tempest*, V. i. 36.

And hears the unexpressive nuptiall Song;

and by 'sweetest Shakespeare', its coiner, in *As You Like It*,

> Run, run, Orlando; carve on every tree
> The fair, the chaste and unexpressive she.[1]

In conclusion, without commenting upon them in any detail and without adducing, where that is possible, parallel passages, I will mention various phrases which one might expect to find in Spenser or Sylvester or Shakespeare, but which one would be very unlikely to find in the almost defiantly colloquial and un-literary poetry of Donne and of several other seventeenth-century poets. I will also mention one or two classical reminiscences, which again are quite alien to what we may call the Donne tradition, although not to that of Ben Jonson. Jonson, indeed, was much more of a phrase-maker than Donne, and a great appropriater of the phrases of classical poets. Although his diction is habitually far more plain and colloquial than Spenser's and far nearer to Donne's, he is at the same time a much more literary poet than Donne: he did not cultivate originality in the sense that Donne did, that out-of-one's-own-head kind of originality which, as I have shown, Carew praised in his famous elegy on Donne. Indeed, there are some passages in that elegy where Carew seems to be praising Donne at the expense of Jonson, although Jonson was a poet to whom in some ways Carew owed even more than he did to Donne:

> The subtle cheat
> Of slie Exchanges, and the jugling feat
> Of two-edg'd words, or whatsoever wrong
> By ours was done the Greeke, or Latine tongue,
> Thou hast redeem'd.[2]

By 'slie Exchanges' Carew meant, I suppose, appropriations and conversions into English of phrases from classical poets, a practice that Milton continued throughout his career. In this sense Milton was a Jonsonian: as Professor Douglas Bush remarks in the passage I have already quoted: 'Among all Jonson's

---

[1] III. ii. 10.   [2] *Poems*, ed. Rhodes Dunlap, 1949, p. 72.

disciples the nearest heir of his Renaissance humanism, the ethical and scholarly solidity of his art, was the young Milton.'[1]

Here, then, to begin with, are some characteristically un-Donnish phrases, as I may call them, in the Nativity Ode: 'the Suns team' (Invocation, st. iii, l.19); 'the spangled host' (loc. cit., l.21); *Cynthia's* seat' (Ode, st. x, l.103); 'stringed noise' (st. ix, l.97); 'speckl'd vanity' (st. xiv, l.136), possibly suggested by Horace's 'maculosum nefas' (*Odes*, IV. v. 22); 'leprous sin' (st. xiv, l.138). These phrases, by the way, together with many like them in earlier poets, are a complete refutation of Dr Johnson's remark, in his life of Dryden, that before the time of Dryden we had no poetical diction.[2]

Milton resembles Spenser in being a much more pictorial and descriptive kind of poet than either Donne or Jonson or their disciples. There is a certain amount of satirical or illustrative description in Jonson's non-dramatic poetry, but very little of what may be called scene-painting, and in Donne's poetry description is either satirical or sheerly witty. Milton, especially in *Paradise Lost*, owed even more to the remembered scenes and images of classical poets than to their phrases. In the famous allusion to the rape of Proserpine by Dis while gathering flowers in the Vale of Enna and of Ceres searching for her through the world he has borrowed nothing from the verbal detail of Ovid's description of the scene in the fourth book of the *Fasti* and in the fifth book of the *Metamorphoses*. It is the scene which had remained in his memory, the words with which he invokes it are his own. There are two good examples in the Nativity Ode of this kind of indebtedness to the classics.

> The Windes with wonder whist,
> Smoothly the waters kist,
> 　　Whispering new joyes to the milde Ocean,
> Who now hath quite forgot to rave,
> While Birds of Calm sit brooding on the charmed wave.
>
> 　　　　　　　　　　　　　(st. v, ll.64–8)

---

[1] *English Literature in the Earlier Seventeenth Century*, 2nd edn 1962, p. 114.
Lives of the English Poets, ed. G. B. Hill, 1905, i. 420.

There, as Warton observed, Milton had in mind a passage from his favourite Ovid's story of Ceyx and Alcyone in the *Metamorphoses*:

> perque dies placidos hiberno tempore septem
> incubat Alcyone pendentibus aequore nidis.
> tunc iacet unda maris: ventos custodit et arcet
> Aeolus egressu.[1]

('Through seven calm winter days Alcyone broods upon a nest suspended on the flood. At that time the wave of the sea reposes; Acolus guards the winds and prevents their outgoing.')

> And Hell it self will pass away,
> And leave her dolorous mansions to the peering day.
>
> (st. xiv, ll.139–40)

Here, as Warton also observed, Milton seems to have had in mind a simile that Virgil had used to decorate the den of Eacus:

> non secus ac si qua penitus vi terra dehiscens
> infernas reseret sedes et regna recludat
> pallida, dis invisa, superque immane barathrum
> cernatur, trepident immisso lumine Manes.[2]

('Not otherwise than as if the earth, gaping through some force deeply open, should unlock the infernal abodes and disclose those pale realms hateful to the Gods, and the vast abyss should be visible from above, and the shades tremble at the inrushing light.')

While Jonson's particular (as distinct from his general) indebtedness to the classical poets is mainly for phrases and moral ideas and precepts, Milton is as much (perhaps even more) indebted to them for scenes and images as for phrases.

I will conclude these remarks on the Nativity Ode by mentioning what is, I think, a hitherto unnoticed link between Milton, Jonson and Shakespeare in their use of the verb *take* in the sense of 'captivate, catch the fancy or affection'. Milton used it first of the music heard by the shepherds:

---

[1] xi. 745 ff.
[2] *Æneid*, viii. 243 ff.

C

> Divinely-warbl'd voice
> Answering the stringed noise,
>   As all their souls in blisfull rapture took.   (st. ix. ll.96–8)

At least three times more in his poetry Milton was to use this word memorably in describing the effect of music: Comus speaks of his mother Circe and the Sirens three,

> Who as they sung, would take the prison'd soul,
> And lap it in *Elysium*   (ll.256–7)

the Attendant Spirit of the Lady's singing,

>   that even Silence
> Was took ere she was ware, and wish't she might
> Deny her nature and be never more
> Still to be so displac't   (ll.557–60);

and in the Second Book of *Paradise Lost* comes:

> Thir Song was partial, but the harmony
> (What could it less than Spirits immortal sing?)
> Suspended Hell, and took with ravishment
> The thronging audience.   (ll.552–5)

Examples of the passive use, 'to be taken with', or simply 'to be taken', occur in Coverdale and in North's Plutarch, but the earliest examples of the active use of the verb in this sense cited by the *O.E.D.* are both by Ben Jonson: first, as a participle, in the first act of *Volpone* (1605):

>   that colour
> Shall make it much more taking;[1]

then in the famous song, 'Still to be neat, still to be drest', from *The Silent Woman* (1609):

> Such sweet neglect more taketh me,

a line which, together with the whole poem in which it occurs, Jonson's disciple Herrick had, I think, very much in mind when he concluded his scarcely less famous poem *Upon Julia's Clothes* with the line

---

[1] I. iv. 96 f.

O how that glittering taketh me.

Whether it was Jonson himself who first made the expression current, or whether it was already current in his circle when he, so to speak, ennobled it, is impossible to decide. Certainly, it was he who did ennoble it, and additional honours were conferred upon it by Shakespeare and Milton—the greatest of all, perhaps, by Shakespeare, who I think only once used the word in this sense, and who had no doubt been much 'taken' with his old friend's song and had treasured it in his memory for a year or two before he wrote:

> daffodils,
> That come before the swallow dares, and take
> The winds of March with beauty.[1]

Which should remind us, if we need reminding, that there are other kinds of originality besides that which Carew praised in Donne.

The Passion, an unsuccessful poem which Milton began in 1630 and left unfinished, 'as finding the subject to be above his years', is also written in that seven-line stanza which he had used in the lines *On the Death of a Fair Infant* and in the Introduction to the Nativity Ode, and which, as I have said, he may possibly have learnt from Phineas Fletcher. The opening lines:

> Ere-while of Musick, and Ethereal mirth,
> Wherwith the stage of Ayr and Earth did ring,
> And joyous news of heav'nly Infants birth,
> My muse with Angels did divide to sing

indicate that the poem was intended as a sequel to the Nativity Ode, and that it was probably begun at the following Easter. Its immeasurable inferiority to its predecessor may remind us that not even the greatest writers are always able to maintain a perpetual progress in achievement; that they sometimes, especially in their earlier years, slip back, and that, where other evidence is

---

[1] *The Winter's Tale*, IV. iv. 118. If J.B.L. had consulted the *Shakespeare-Lexicon* he would have found a few more examples, mostly from the late plays, but also from *Hamlet*: 'No fairy takes, nor witch hath power to charm' (I.i.163).

lacking, we should not be too confident in assuming that a poem or play which strikes us as being not merely inferior but immaturer must necessarily have been written earlier than a superior or maturer one.

For this poem, or rather, perhaps I should say, these lines, are the least Miltonic of all Milton's serious poems. In general the style might almost be described as an amalgam now of Sylvester, now of Giles Fletcher, now of Quarles, while in the last two stanzas Milton comes nearer than anywhere else in his poetry, except in his poem on Shakespeare, which is in a rather special category, and in his wholly unserious verses on Hobson the carrier, to the ingenious comparisons so often and often so inappropriately used in eulogy and funeral elegy by the contemporary imitators of Donne, or rather, of this particular element in Donne's poetry. If the authorship of the poem were unknown, one would be inclined to say that it had been written by some minor seventeenth-century Spenserian who tended at times (unable, old-fashioned though he was, to escape entirely from the fashion that surrounded him) to fall into the so-called metaphysical manner.

Perhaps the most fundamentally (as distinct from superficially) Spenserian thing about the poem is that conception of Christ as a hero which we have already noticed in the Nativity Ode:

> Most perfect *Heroe*, try'd in heaviest plight
> Of labours huge and hard, too hard for human wight.

Both in style and in conception I cannot but regard these two concluding lines of the second stanza as thoroughly Spenserian, true though it be that the conception of Christ as a hero, as the perfect pattern of the true wayfaring and warfaring Christian, was perhaps more immediately derived from the Spenserian Giles Fletcher, as well as from Vida's Latin poem the *Christiad*, which, in the fourth stanza, Milton alludes to in the line 'Loud o're the rest *Cremona's* Trump doth sound'. Ultimately, of course, it is derived from the Epistle to the Hebrews, ii, 10: 'For it became him, for whom are all things and by whom are all things, in bringing many sons unto glory, to make the captain of their salvation perfect through sufferings.' Nevertheless, I feel that here as elsewhere the Pauline presentation of Christ has combined with the tradition of Christianity and of the heroic poem. This, I think, always remained Milton's most fundamental and characteristic conception of Christ, and these two lines might almost be taken as a motto for *Paradise Regained*.

Now let us consider the two last stanzas, where, as I have said, Milton comes nearer than elsewhere in his serious poetry to the so-called metaphysical manner, to the kind of ingenuity practised, for example, by his contemporary at Christ's College, John Cleveland, and which at this time so many young men at both universities were cultivating and transcribing into their commonplace books.

> Mine eye hath found that sad Sepulchral rock
> That was the Casket of Heav'ns richest store,
> And here though grief my feeble hands up-lock,
> Yet on the softned Quarry would I score
> My plaining vers as lively as before;
>   For sure so well instructed were my tears,
> That they would fitly fall in order'd Characters.

Perhaps (as Warton suggests) from reading Sandys's *Travels*, Milton had formed a vivid image of the Holy Sepulchre; his tears, falling upon the rock ('quarry') will soften it, so that it will take their imprint 'as lively as before', as lively, that is to say, as in the Nativity Ode. This conceit of tears being so well instructed that they fall in ordered characters upon a rock which they soften so that it takes their imprint is so very much more ingenious and, as we should say, far-fetched that it differs almost in kind from the conceit in the seventh stanza of the Nativity Ode about the sun hiding his head for shame on seeing a greater sun appear, a conceit which Spenser had already used in his song of praise in Eliza Queen of Shepherds all, and which one would not be surprised to find in almost any characteristically Elizabethan poet. And I think it also differs almost in kind from that Anacreontic 'kiss and kill' conceit in the lines *On the Death of a Fair Infant*, which Shakespeare had used in *Venus and Adonis*. It is in fact the kind of conceit of which there are many examples in Donne's poem on Mrs Herbert entitled *The Autumnall* (to mention only one of

Donne's poems), and of which there are very many examples in the anthology of early seventeenth-century academic wit, *Parnassus Biceps*; it is the kind of conceit where the author seems (and often is) much more concerned with displaying his own ingenuity than with the professed subject of his poem. Indeed, in such poems the professed subject often seems to be entirely indifferent to the author, a mere occasion for intellectual gymnastics, for a display of sheer wit, for the production of something out of his own head. I will not go so far as to say that Milton's subject has here become indifferent to him, but here at any rate he is approaching the kind of poetry from which the ostensible subject seems to fade out, where the ingenious illustration completely smothers what it professes to be illustrating.

As a parallel with Milton's well-instructed tears falling in ordered characters Todd cites a passage about vocal eyes and rhetorical tears from Crashaw's poem *Upon the Death of a Gentleman*, written in 1633, three years later than Milton's. I think, though, you will agree that Crashaw's lines, unlike Milton's, are exquisitely poetical, and that, although they are indeed ingenious, there is a balance, a proportion, between ingenuity and propriety, in other words, a *decorum*, which Milton has not here achieved:

> Eyes are vocall, Teares have Tongues,
> And there be words not made with lungs;
> Sententious showers, ô let them fall,
> Their cadence is Rhetoricall.[1]

It is most important to perceive that all the sins and excesses of the so-called metaphysical manner are really sins against the great classical canon of *decorum*, of propriety,[2] and that a conceit which

---

[1] *Poems*, ed. L. C. Martin, 1927, p. 167.

[2] The offence of the metaphysical poets against the principle of decorum may be said to be the principal charge Dr Johnson brought up against them. In his Life of Cowley (*Lives of the Poets*, ed. G. B. Hill, 1905, i. 29) he notes that: 'As they sought only for novelty they did not much enquire whether their allusions were to things high or low, elegant or gross; whether they compared the little to the great or the great to the little'. cf. also p. 52. Johnson did not feel that these poets were properly in control of their theme, which was often emotional, when they departed as far as they did from the imagery traditionally associated with the expression of those emotions. Ed.

strikes one first and foremost as being merely ingenious, queer or odd is one where the poet's imagination has been insufficiently possessed by his professed subject. A much closer parallel with Milton's stanza and with his whole conceit of tears chiselling an inscription on stone, occurs in one of the elegies on the poet Richard Lovelace, who died about 1657. One Eldred Revett, a young Cambridge and Inns of Court man, who had himself published a volume of poems in 1657 and who was a friend of Lovelace's, contributed to the latter's *Posthume Poems* (1659), which he had helped the poet's youngest brother to edit, an elegy that concludes with some lines where Revett may well have been trying to improve upon that stanza from Milton's *Passion*:

> Why should some rude hand carve thy sacred stone,
> And there incise a cheap inscription;
> When we can shed the tribute of our tears
> So long, till the relenting marble wears?
> Which shall such order in their cadence keep,
> That they a native Epitaph shall weep;
> Untill each Letter spelt distinctly lyes,
> Cut by the mystick droppings of our eyes.[1]

Ingenuity of this kind was being very extensively cultivated by Milton's contemporaries, especially at the universities.[2]

The last stanza of this unfinished poem, in its hovering between different traditions, reveals a curious uncertainty, as though Milton did not quite know what kind of poetry he wanted to write. In the first line there is a characteristic borrowing from

---

[1] Lovelace, *Poems*, ed. C. H. Wilkinson, 1930, p. 229.
[2] Compare the concluding lines of Carew's poem *On the Duke of Buckingham* (Poems, ed. Dunlap, p. 57), which was perhaps originally intended for the monument which his widow erected over the tomb in Westminster Abbey where the murdered Duke had been buried in 1625:
> These are the pious Obsequies,
> Drop'd from his chast Wifes pregnant eyes
> In frequent showres and were alone
> By her congealing sighes made stone,
> On which the Carver did bestow
> These formes and characters of woe;
> So he the fashion onely lent,
> Whilst she wept all this Monument.

Shakespeare and in the second what one might call a characteristically Spenserian appropriation of a biblical phrase; the third and fourth lines, beautiful of their kind, might be called either Spenserian or Petrarchan, while the last three contain a conceit not unworthy of Cleveland:

> Or should I thence hurried on viewles wing,
> Take up a weeping on the Mountains wilde,
> The gentle neighbourhood of grove and spring
> Would soon unboosom all thir Echoes milde,
> And I (for grief is easily beguild)
>   Might think th' infection of my sorrows loud,
> Had got a race of mourners on som pregnant cloud.

The word 'viewless' in the first line was, so far as we know, first used by Shakespeare when in *Measure for Measure* he made Claudio mention, as one of the many possible horrors of death, that of being 'imprison'd in the viewless winds'.[1] Milton used it again, once in *Comus* (l.92) and once in *Paradise Lost* (iii. 518). The phrase 'viewless wing' is a good example of that poetic diction which Dr Johnson declared nonexistent before the time of Dryden, and which, as I have remarked before, belongs to a quite different poetical tradition from that which was being cultivated by so many of Milton's contemporaries. It was very probably in Keats's mind when he wrote:

> Not charioted by Bacchus and his pards,
> But on the viewless wings of Poesy.[2]

The beautiful second line,

> Take up a weeping on the Mountains wilde

is an obvious reminiscence of the tenth verse of the ninth chapter of Jeremiah: 'For the mountains will I take up a weeping and wailing.' The concluding conceit about his sorrows begetting a race of mourners on some pregnant cloud is an ingenious allusion to the legend of Ixion, who embraced a cloud which Zeus had caused to resemble Hera, and on it begot the Centaurs. Here

---

[1] III. i. 124.
[2] *Ode to a Nightingale*, st. iv, ll.32-3.

Milton is combining what one may call Donnish ingenuity with allusion to those Gods and Goddesses whom, as Carew said in his famous elegy, Donne had exiled.

Nowhere else, I repeat, does one find Milton so uncertainly hovering between different poetic traditions as in this poem; nowhere else in his serious poetry does he approximate so closely to contemporary academic taste. Some of his contemporaries, no doubt, might have lamented that he did not cultivate that very pretty wit which he had shown himself to possess. He left the poem unfinished, however, returned to an older and sounder tradition, and continued to write poetry which would have seemed to many of his academic contemporaries strangely old-fashioned and very deficient in wit.

The *Song. On May Morning*, also written in 1630 is, with its Spenserian and Shakespearian echoes, one of the most Elizabethan of Milton's shorter poems.

> Now the bright morning Star, Dayes harbinger,
> Comes dancing from the East, and leads with her
> The Flowry *May*, who from her green lap throws
> The yellow Cowslip, and the pale Primrose.

'And yonder shines Aurora's harbinger' wrote Shakespeare in, *A Midsummer Night's Dream*,[1] and I could produce numerous passages about dancing stars and the dancing sun, all of which seem ultimately to have been inspired by Spenser's *Astrophel*, st. vi:

> As Somers larke, that with her song doth greet
> The dawning day forth comming from the East;

and his *Faerie Queene*, I. v. 2 ff.

> At last the golden Orientall gate
> Of greatest heauen gan to open faire,
> And *Phœbus* fresh, as bridegrome to his mate,
> Came dauncing forth, shaking his deawie haire.

How frequent both in Spenser and in Shakespeare are such

---

[1] III. ii. 380.

poetical personifications—'the great eye of heaven', 'the eye of
Phoebus', and so forth—and how utterly alien they are to Donne's
poetry and to the whole Donne tradition: Donne who called the
sun 'Busie old foole' and 'Sawcy pedantique wretch'.

The personification of 'Flowry *May*' also seems to have been
suggested by Spenser. In his Masque of the Seasons and Months
in the seventh canto of the unfinished seventh book of the *Faerie
Queene* (st. 34) May is 'throwing flowres out of her lap around';
and at II. vi. 15 we have

<blockquote>
nature them forth throwes
Out of her fruitfull lap.
</blockquote>

But the adjectives—*green* lap and *pale* primrose—were, I think,
remembered from Shakespeare:

<blockquote>
The fresh green lap of fair King Richard's land;[1]
</blockquote>

Perdita's

<blockquote>
pale primroses,
That die unmarried;[2]
</blockquote>

and

<blockquote>
The flower that's like thy face, pale primrose[3]
</blockquote>

which Arviragus in *Cymbeline* declared that Fidele should not
lack. It is possible (as Todd observed) that Crashaw too, between
whose poems and Milton's we have already noticed several resemblances and affinities, may have had these Shakespearian
passages about the pale primrose in mind when he wrote in *The
Weeper* (first published in *Steps to the Temple*, 1646)

<blockquote>
The dew no more will weepe,
The Primroses pale cheeke to decke.
</blockquote>

Did Crashaw see some of Milton's poems in manuscript? He
came up to Pembroke in 1631, and Milton left Christ's in 1632,
so that they overlapped for a year. It is pleasant to suppose that
they became acquainted, and that the younger poet took copies of

---

[1] *Richard II*, III. iii. 47.
[2] *The Winter's Tale*, IV. iv. 122 f.
[3] *Cymbeline*, IV. ii. 221

some of Milton's poems and remembered some of their phrases. It would be well worth somebody's while to make a really careful examination of these borrowed Shakespearian phrases in Milton and other poets: many of them, I think, would be found to be tributes, not merely to Shakespeare's mastery of language, but also to his careful and loving observation of what Warton called 'real nature'. He taught other poets not merely to write but to see. And how fortunate it was that so many poets were still willing to learn, that they accepted the still potent tradition of imitation and did not insist on seeing (or not seeing) everything for themselves and doing everything out of their own heads!

Before leaving the *Song. On May Morning* I will mention an imitation, or it may be, merely a resemblance, of a more general kind, which not only unites Milton with his master Spenser but unites both Spenser and Milton with Spenser's master Ariosto. How much the allegory and incidents of the *Faerie Queene* owe to the example of the *Orlando Furioso* has often been insisted upon, especially by Mr C. S. Lewis. There are, though, rhetorical and stylistic as well as structural and narrative resemblances. Speaking of the opening lines of this *Song*, I said that it would be possible to produce numerous passages about dancing stars and the dancing sun, all of which seemed ultimately to have been inspired by Spenser, and that Milton's May throwing from her green lap the yellow cowslip and the pale primrose was, so to speak, a more Shakespearian presentation of the May of Spenser. Now it seems to me very likely that Spenser's descriptions both of dancing Phoebus and of May and Nature throwing flowers from their laps may all have been suggested to him by a single vivid stanza in the *Orlando Furioso*, although it is true that his description of dancing Phoebus also contains a reminiscence of the 19th Psalm, where the sun 'is as a bridegroom coming out of his chamber, and rejoiceth as a strong man to run a race'. Ariosto says of the net in which Vulcan caught Venus and Mars: 'Mercury then steals the net from the artificer, because he wishes to catch Chloris with it (Chloris is the Roman Flora), fair Chloris who flies through the air behind Aurora on the appearance of the sun, and from the ungathered hem of her robe scatters lilies, roses and violets' (canto xv, st. 57). It is indeed very likely that Milton himself may have had this stanza, as well as Spenser's descriptions, in mind, for his May led by Venus, the morning star, is nearer to Ariosto's Chloris flying behind Aurora than to any single image of Spenser's. Thus Milton has here derived what we may call the design of his picture from Spenser and Ariosto, and has added some characteristic Shakespearean particularisation, 'green lap', 'pale primrose', and a characteristic piece of Shakespearean poetic diction, 'Dayes harbinger', derived ultimately, as I have said, from Shakespeare's 'Aurora's harbinger', although immediately perhaps, as Warton suggested, from Richard Niccols's poem *The Cuckow*, published in 1607. Niccols in the poem calls the cock 'Daies harbinger', but Milton has almost certainly derived the phrase from Shakespeare, just as in his description of the day's bright king dancing from the east and of May throwing flowers from her fruitful lap he is certainly imitating Spenser.[1]

It may be suggested that many of the minor poets, even the very minor poets, of the early seventeenth century performed a useful function by giving a wider currency to the phrases, turns, and images of better poets, which they thus kept before the attention of better poets among their contemporaries, poets who had, so to speak, a better right to these phrases and who could introduce them into worthier contexts, where they appeared as both old and new. I will not say that Milton required a Niccols to remind him of Shakespeare's 'Aurora's harbinger' and to

---

[1] The Morning Star is the planet Venus (sometimes called Lucifer) when visible in the East before sunrise. Marlowe, towards the end of the Second Sestiad of *Hero and Leander*, which, though not published till 1598, must have been written before 1593 when he died, seems to have been the first to apply the word *harbinger* to the morning star, although he calls that star Hesperus, which, of course, is the name of the evening-star:

> By this *Apollos* golden harpe began
> To sound foorth musicke to the *Ocean*,
> Which watchfull *Hesperus* no sooner heard,
> But he the day(s) bright [? light]-bearing Car prepar'd,
> And ran before, as Harbenger of light,
> And with his flaring beams mockt ougly night.

Dyce conjectured 'bright Day-bearing'. However, the passage is full of corruption: the 'flaring beames' should be those of Apollo, not of 'Hesperus'.

suggest to him that it might, in this context, be advantageously altered into 'day's harbinger', but it is not at all improbable that Niccols actually did perform this service. You must have already observed that in these early poems of Milton there is a very large descriptive element, and it may perhaps have occurred to you that this is at least one of the reasons why there is so much more of what may be called poetic diction in Milton's poetry than in Donne's or even in Jonson's, and why Milton, though a greater poet than Donne, is so much more imitative and literary, and why his kind of originality, unlike Donne's, did not consist in doing things entirely out of his own head. Donne disdained to imitate anybody, or rather, perhaps I should say, to imitate anybody else's language; Jonson appropriated phrases from the classics rather than from English poets; and in Donne's poetry there is almost nothing and in Jonson's poetry very little of what, even in a wide sense, may be called poetic diction. Description, except when satirical or realistic, plays little part in their poetry; it was the poets who were largely concerned with description, the narrative and heroic poets, the cultivators of all the various kinds of pastoral (pastoral eclogue, pastoral ode, pastoral elegy) who used poetic diction and who pillaged Spenser and the translators and the descriptive passages in Shakespeare's plays. For the kind of poetry these poets were trying to write required again and again the descriptive adjective (the yellow cowslip and the pale primrose), the periphrasis (day's harbinger), the mythological or semi-mythological description of dawn or nightfall or the coming of spring. It required, that is to say, a poetic diction and a poetic tradition. Spenser did more than any other English poet to establish this tradition and diction, and although Donne and Ben Jonson did not think much of Spenser,[1] he had many successors, including Marlowe, who seems to have read the early part of the *Faerie Queene* while it was still in manuscript. Marlowe, several of his fellow-dramatists, including even Shakespeare (who did so many things) all continued in various ways the Spenserian

---

[1] During his later years, however—perhaps under the influence of that ardent Spenserian, his friend Sir Kenelm Digby—Jonson seems to have revised his opinion of Spenser: see *Ben Jonson*, ed. C. H. Herford and Percy and Evelyn Simpson, 1925–52, xi. 99–100.

tradition and cultivated and enriched the diction that Spenser had done so much to create. One is often tempted to be scornful about the great mass of Elizabethan pastoral poetry, with its nymphs and swains, crystal springs, fleecy flocks, and so forth; it seems so easy to write, so much a matter of properties and traditional phrases. And one might be inclined to say much the same about the narrative and pastoral poetry of William Browne and many other minor seventeenth-century Spenserians. There is indeed an affinity between this kind of poetry and the Latin verse which schoolboys, undergraduates and even graduates wrote on prescribed themes with the aid of a *Gradus* or Dictionary of Phrases. (One remembers Dr Johnson's scornful words about images, such as a college readily supplies.) It is a kind of poetry which seems too much to confirm that confident pronouncement of Scaliger's (hateful to modern ears) that poetry is an art which can be taught. Nevertheless, these many minor versifiers did at least help to give currency to phrases, images, and (if you like) properties which a great poet such as Milton could use greatly. And a study of them will help us to see more clearly the kind of poet Milton was and the kind of poetry he wanted to write. He, perhaps, is the final justification, as he is also the consummation, of the tradition they were continuing. He was from the beginning a scholar-poet, an industrious and select reader, continually appreciating, remembering, imitating, improving whatever seemed to him to exemplify 'best example'. One of the convictions behind the recent exaltation of Donne and his school at the expense of Milton seems to be this: that while Donne wrote poetry which he had not been taught but which, when he had written it, others could in certain respects very passably imitate, Milton wrote poetry which he had taught himself to write but which others could not attempt to imitate without disaster. Without entering further into this antithesis between Donne and Milton, I will admit that Milton's kind of poetry was the kind which only a very great poet could hope to write consistently and memorably well. With the minor Spenserians we find occasional good lines and good phrases embedded in masses of quite negligible verse, but Milton's vast poetic energy was able to infuse this highly artificial kind of poetry with life in every line.

He, at any rate, believed that poetry was an art which, given the 'strong propensity of nature', could be taught, and in these early poems we can watch him learning.

It was probably also in 1630 that Milton wrote his first English sonnet, 'O Nightingale . . .', at the same time as he was addressing Italian ones to the Emilia whose existence John Smart has done so much to elucidate. I need scarcely remind you, first, that the writing of sonnets was not a fashionable occupation in 1630, and secondly, that Milton was probably the first English poet to write sonnets precisely in what one might call the standard Italian form. It is not one of Milton's great sonnets, but it is an agreeable poem, and interesting because, for its time, it was so utterly un-fashionable, not only in form but in content and style; for while the Petrarchan lovelornness and invocation of the nightingale is quite alien to the manner of Donne and his school, the classical personifications—jolly hours (Homer's πολυγηθέες Ὧραι), propitious May, Jove's will, love and the Muse—are quite unlike the classicism which Ben Jonson cultivated in his non-dramatic poetry and much nearer to the elaborate and decorated classicism of Milton's Latin elegies. Indeed, the opening lines

> O Nightingale, that on yon bloomy Spray
> Warbl'st at eeve, when all the Woods are still,

are almost a translation of two lines in the fifth elegy, *In Adventum Veris*, which Milton had written a year before:

> Jam, Philomela, tuos foliis adoperta novellis
> Instituis modulos, dum silet omne nemus.

('Now it is that you, Philomela, hidden in new-appearing leaves, begin your measures when all the grove is still.')

The lines on Shakespeare, published in the second folio of 1632, are ascribed by Milton himself, in the 1645 volume, to the year 1630. They are interesting as an expression of Milton's admiration for Shakespeare, as indeed of the fact that he, like Jonson and so many later encomiasts, regarded Shakespeare as primarily the child of nature, and for the use of an elaborate conceit which has

been commonly regarded as a typical example of so-called
'metaphysical' wit.[1]

> For whilst to th' shame of slow-endeavouring art,
> Thy easie numbers flow

—here is that same distinction between nature and art which reappears in *L'Allegro*, in the distinction between Jonson's 'learned
Sock' and

> . . . sweetest *Shakespear* fancies childe
> Warbl[ing] his native Wood-notes wilde.   (ll. 132-4)

Here, though, the distinction is merely incidental, and is sand-
wiched into the middle of that ingenious simile or conceit, of
which I spoke:

> Thou in our wonder and astonishment
> Hast built thy self a live-long[2] Monument,

for, deduces Milton, while your artless and yet Delphic lines
impress themselves upon our hearts

> Then thou our fancy of it self bereaving,
> Dost make us Marble with too much conceaving;
> And so Sepulcher'd in such pomp dost lie,
> That Kings for such a Tomb would wish to die.

Shakespeare possesses in his readers an everlasting funeral
monument, or rather, series of monuments, cemetery of monuments, because their admiration of him transforms each one of
them into the likeness of a marble statue, within which, as in a
marble tomb, his lines are buried. The kernel of this conceit, the
idea, namely, that intense admiration transforms the beholder
into the likeness of a marble statue, is at least as old as Petrarch,
who in his Sonnet 131 declares that the pure ivory of Laura's
face

> fa di marmo chi da presso 'l guarda,

---

[1] There is an interesting article, by Mr H. W. Garrod, entitled 'Milton's Lines on
Shakespeare', in *Essays and Studies by Members of the English Association* for 1926.
Mr Garrod there considers (what I have not now time to do) the various small
textual differences between the printings of the poem in the second folio of 1632,
in the 1640 edition of Shakespeare's *Poems*, and in Milton's 1645 volume.
[2] The reading of 1632 is 'lasting monument'.

('turns to marble whoever gazes at it from anear'). This idea had been used at least twice by seventeenth-century poets before Milton took it up. In Thomas Tomkis's *Albumazar*, a comedy acted before the King at Trinity College, Cambridge, and published in 1615, a character exclaims:

> Wonder for me, admire and be astonisht,
> Maruaile thy selfe to Marble at these engines.[1]

But while Tomkis had used it to describe the effect of intense admiration, William Browne had used it, and Ben Jonson was to use it, in order to describe the effect of intense grief. In the second stanza of his famous epitaph on the Countess of Pembroke, 1621, Browne had written:

> Marble piles let no man raise
> To her name: for after days
> Some kind woman born as she
> Reading this, like Niobe
> Shall turn marble, and become
> Both her mourner and her tomb.[2]

This is a good deal more ingenious and elaborate than Petrarch. Petrarch was content to say that admiration for Laura transforms people into the likeness of marble statues; Browne declares that grief for the Countess of Pembroke will transform some future reader of his epitaph not only into a marble statue but into a marble tomb. A year after Milton's lines were written, Ben Jonson, in his Elegie On the Lady Jane Pawlet, the Marchioness of Winchester who died in 1631, and whom Milton also commemorated, got so far as declaring that grief had transformed him,

---

[1] *Albumazar*, 1615, sig. Blv (I. iv. 3 f.).
[2] If Giles Oldesworth, in his copy of Donne's poems, was right in identifying the subject of the 'Elegie on the L.C.' as 'L. Cary', i.e. Henry Carey, first Baron Hunsdon, who died in 1596, Browne was to some extent anticipated by Donne, whose elegy concludes:
> His children are his pictures, Oh they bee
> Pictures of him dead, senselesse, cold as he.
> Here needs no marble Tombe, since hee is gone,
> He, and about him, his, are turn'd to stone.
(See John Sampson, 'A Contemporary Light upon John Donne', *Essays and Studies by Members of the English Association*, 1921, pp. 95 ff.).

not indeed into a marble tomb, but at least into a marble tomb-
stone:

> I am almost a stone!
> And e're I can aske more of her, shee's gone!
> Alas, I am all Marble! write the rest
> Thou wouldst have written, Fame, upon my brest.

(ll. 11–14)

It seems just possible that Browne's ingenious fancy that grief
transforms the mourner into a marble tomb may have led Milton
to expand the familiar Petrarchan notion that admiration can
transform us to the likeness of marble statues into the still more
ingenious fancy that our admiration for Shakespeare transforms
us into marble statues that are both tombs and monuments. In
Il Penseroso he was to use this 'marble' conceit in a less ingenious,
more normal, more Petrarchan manner: Melancholy is to come
with her rapt soul sitting in her eyes, and

> There held in holy passion still,
> Forget thy self to Marble . . .

(ll. 41–2)

The interesting question is this: at what point does the development of a conceit become so ingenious that we call it metaphysical,
or say that it is in the metaphysical manner, or in the manner of
Donne? Or, to put the question in another and, perhaps, better
way, what characteristics must the development of a conceit
assume in order to make us call it (rightly or wrongly) metaphysical? For my part, I should be inclined to say that a conceit
is in the manner of Donne, is roughly in his manner, when its
working out is predominantly argumentative or dialectical, when
the intellectual or conceptual element is strong, and when the
pictorial element is only incidentally present, or perhaps scarcely
present at all. There is, then, I think, some resemblance between
the conceit in Milton's lines on Shakespeare and some of Donne's
conceits, although I think Donne would probably have rejected
the marble-making conceit as being too conventional, too much
common property. There is, nevertheless, some resemblance
between the conceit in Milton's poem and some of the conceits
in the quite unserious poem of Donne's about a flea on his

mistress's bosom—the poem in which Donne declares among
other things, that this flea, in which their bloods are mingled, is
both their marriage bed and the church in which they have been
married, and that if she kills it she will be committing first,
murder, through killing him in it; secondly, suicide, through
killing herself in it, and thirdly, sacrilege, through destroying in
it the church where they have been married. There is, though,
another respect in which this ingenious conceit of Milton's
resembles those sometimes used by Donne and often by his
successors, especially in funeral elegies and commendatory and
complimentary poems. For Milton would seem to have asked
himself, not, what can I say that is especially appropriate and
relevant about Shakespeare? but rather, what can I say that is
ingenious and original about the permanence of literary fame?
He does indeed bring in the contrast between Shakespeare's
'easie numbers' and the 'slow-endeavouring art' of others, but
almost incidentally and, as it were, parenthetically: his main
energy is concentrated upon the working out of his ingenious
fancy that our admiration for Shakespeare transforms us into
marble statues that are also marble tombs in which his verses lie
buried—a fancy which might have been applied with equal
propriety (or impropriety) to any other poet for whom the
eulogist had (or professed to have) great admiration.[1] This is
very characteristic of much seventeenth-century eulogy and
funeral elegy, where the authors are seldom concerned with saying something especially appropriate to the person commended
or lamented, but rather with saying something ingenious about
literary fame or about death or the manner of death: that, for
example, a mother who died in giving birth to a still-born child
was both a cradle and a grave, or that by the drowning of Edward
King Neptune obtained a university. Which brings me back to
my remarks suggested by the two last stanzas of Milton's poem
on the Passion: that in very much seventeenth-century poetry in
the so-called metaphysical manner the professed subject was merely
or mainly the occasion for a display of ingenuity, of wit. I said
that in the last stanzas of that poem Milton came nearer than

---

[1] This conceit recurs in its most acceptable form in Pope's *Epitaph on Gay*. Ed.

elsewhere in his serious poetry to that kind of verse where the professed subject seems to fade out and the ingenious comparison almost smothers what it professes to be illustrating. I there excepted this poem on Shakespeare, as being in a rather special category, by which I meant that it should be regarded, not so much as a temporary aberration, but rather as a temporary conformity with established usage. It is, after all, of a piece, and quite deliberate, while those two stanzas in *The Passion* are incompatibly and, as it were, unconsciously mingled with a different style and tradition.

The authors of these complimentary, commendatory and commemorative poems evidently felt that what was required of them was above all to say something memorably ingenious, striking, and astonishing, something which, because of its memorability, would perpetuate the memory of its professed subject. Where they were wrong was in assuming that posterity would continue to admire this kind of wit and ingenuity as much as they evidently did themselves.

The second, and by far the best, of the two poems *On the University Carrier*, 'who sickn'd in the time of his vacancy, being forbid to go to *London*, by reason of the Plague', written in 1631, is quite in the manner of some of Donne's many unserious elegies, especially the second entitled *The Anagram*, in which Donne undertakes to prove to an imaginary friend that it is far better to marry an old and ugly woman than a young and handsome one. Here, for the sake of comparison, are some lines from Donne's poem:

> If red and white and each good quality
> Be in thy wench, ne'r aske where it doth lye.
> In buying things perfum'd, we aske; if there
> Be muske and amber in it, but not where.
> Though all her parts be not in th'usuall place,
> She'hath yet an Anagram of a good face . . .
> She's faire as any, if all be like her,
> And if none bee, then she is singular.
> All love is wonder; if wee justly doe
> Account her wonderfull, why not lovely too?

Love built on beauty, soone as beauty, dies,
Chuse this face, chang'd by no deformities.
Women are all like Angels; the faire be
Like those which fell to worse; but such as shee,
Like to good Angels, nothing can impaire:
'Tis lesse griefe to be foule, than to' have beene faire.

(ll. 11–16, 23–32)

In the following lines Milton has produced a far more than averagely good specimen of this kind of wit, a specimen which I think Donne himself (the young Donne) would not have disdained.

Here lieth one who did most truly prove,
That he could never die while he could move,
So hung his destiny never to rot
While he might still jogg on, and keep his trot,
Made of sphear-metal, never to decay
Untill his revolution was at stay.
Time numbers motion, yet (without a crime
'Gainst old truth) motion number'd out his time;
And like an Engin mov'd with wheel and waight,
His principles being ceast, he ended strait.
Rest that gives all men life, gave him his death,
And too much breathing put him out of breath;
Nor were it contradiction to affirm
Too long vacation hastned on his term.

Several of Milton's contemporaries seem to have written poems on this subject. Six appeared in the first (1640) edition and are in later editions of that very popular miscellany *Wits Recreations*, three of them, it is true being only four lines, and one two lines, in length. Milton's second poem on the subject also appeared in 1640 in another Miscellany, *A Banquet of Jests*, and both his poems, together with one which had already appeared in *Wits Recreations*, were published in the Miscellany *Wit Restor'd* in 1658. There may well have been many other poems now lost, but I think any one who will take the trouble to read the seven which have survived will agree with me that Milton has beaten his contemporaries on their own ground. Only one of these poems seems to me to contain more than two lines that are worth quoting, and even this has a feeble concluding couplet, which I will omit.

> If constellations which in heaven are fixt,
> Give life by influence to bodies mixt,
> And every sign peculiar right doth claime
> Of that to which it propagates a name;
> Then I conjure,[1] *Charles* the great northern star
> Whistled up *Hobson* for to drive his car.
> He is not dead, but left his mansion here,
> Has left the Bull, and flitted to the Beare.[2]

Of the other poems, only the concluding lines of one and the opening lines of another seem to me anything like up to standard:

> He that with so much paper us'd to meet
> Is now, alas! content to take one sheet[3]

and

> Here *Hobson* lyes among his many betters,
> A man unlearned, yet a man of letters.[4]

In Milton's second poem there is much more of the fertile and exuberant ingenuity that Donne could bring to such subjects than there is in any of the poems I have mentioned. As I have said before, I very much doubt whether by our 'late fantasticks' Milton meant either Donne or his contemporary at Christ's John Cleveland, a great admirer of Donne, who may well have stimulated Milton to write these lines. But while Milton was content to show that he could write like this if he wanted to, it was and remained the height of Cleveland's ambition to write like this, and it was more or less in this style that, six years later, Cleveland and several of his contemporaries chose to commemorate, in a volume to which Milton also contributed, not another University Carrier, but Edward King. Milton knew who was who and what was what.

An Epitaph on the Marchioness of Winchester was also written in 1631. A certain amount of evidence suggests that there was a

---

[1] *Conjure*, surely meaningless in this context, would seem to be a corruption of either *conject* or *conceive*.
[2] *Facetiae. Musarum Deliciae, etc.*, reprint of 1817, ii. 249.
[3] ibid., p. 227.
[4] ibid., p. 250.

Cambridge collection of verses, in manuscript though not in print, on the death of this accomplished woman, whom Ben Jonson also commemorated, and that Milton was asked to contribute to it. His epitaph on the Marchioness is an unequal and, on the whole, not very good poem, but it is interesting for several reasons. Leaving aside such exceptions as the lines on Shakespeare and on the University Carrier, it is probably the most characteristically and typically seventeenth-century of Milton's Cambridge poems, at any rate in the sense in which most of us tend to think of seventeenth-century poetry. For one thing, it is written in that octosyllabic (or, as Milton here uses it, mainly heptasyllabic) couplet which was one of the great instruments of seventeenth-century poetry. Some of the most beautiful seventeenth-century epitaphs (and the earlier seventeenth century is the great age of the English epitaph) were written in this metre, and in choosing it Milton was conforming to a fashion, or to a recently established tradition. In many of these epitaphs there is a terse epigrammatic wit, but a wit blended with tenderness, and quite unlike the typical wit, serious or unserious, of Donne and his followers. It occurs in Browne's famous epitaph on the Countess of Pembroke:

> Death, ere thou hast slain another,
> Fair, and learn'd, and good as she,
> Time shall throw a dart at thee,

and in Jonson's *Epitaph on Salomon Pavy a child of Q. El Chappel* (I believe I have mentioned the paradox that some of the most characteristic seventeenth-century poetry was written before the end of Elizabeth's reign[1]):

> And did act (what now we mone)
>   Old men so duely,
> As, sooth, the *Parcæ* thought him one,
>   He plai'd so truely.
> So, by error, to his fate
>   They all consented;
> But viewing him since (alas, too late)
>   They haue repented.

---

[1] See J.B.L.'s *Monarch of Wit*, 6th edn 1962, p. 12.

And haue sought (to giue new birth)
  In bathes to steepe him;
But, being so much too good for earth,
  Heauen vowes to keepe him.   (ll.13–24)

There are several examples of his kind of wit in Milton's poem:

Once had the early Matrons run
To greet her of a lovely son,
And now with second hope she goes,
And calls *Lucina* to her throws;
But whether by mischance or blame
Atropos[1] for *Lucina* came;
And with remorsles cruelty,
Spoil'd at once both fruit and tree.   (ll.23–30)

What immediately follows might seem at first sight nearer to the
kind of wit displayed, as one might perhaps say, appropriately in
the various epitaphs on Hobson and inappropriately in, for
example, Cleveland's elegy on Edward King—nearer, in other
words, to that kind of writing where the ostensible subject seems
to fade out, or where from the first it has been no more than the
occasion for a display of ingenuity:

The haples Babe before his birth
Had burial, yet not laid in earth,
And the languisht Mothers Womb
Was not long a living Tomb.   (ll.31–4)

As a matter of fact, this same conceit had already been used by
William Browne, whom I have already mentioned as an example
of the difficulty of pigeon-holing seventeenth-century poets,
and who, although usually classified as a Spenserian and although
most of his poems are in what may be called the Spenserian
tradition, has several ingenious epigrams and elegies which
exactly hit what one may call the better academic taste in wit and
which regularly appear in seventeenth-century commonplace
books and in some miscellanies. Browne has a poem *On an
Infant Unborn, and the Mother dying in Travail*, which begins as
follows:

---

[1] 'Atrŏpos' is metrically a little clumsy: is it conceivable that Milton pronounced it
(incorrectly) 'Atrōpos'?

Within this grave there is a grave entomb'd:
There lies a mother and a child enwomb'd;
'Twas strange that Nature so much vigour gave
To one that ne'er was born to make a grave.
Yet, an injunction stranger, Nature will'd her,
Poor mother, to be tomb to that which kill'd her;
And not with so much cruelty content,
Buries the child, the grave, and monument.

But while in his poem on Shakespeare Milton seems to have expanded a conceit of Browne's and to have made it still more ingenious, and while that poem seems to exist almost entirely for the sake of the ingenious conceit, in this poem Milton has merely introduced lightly and, as it were, incidentally, and without expanding it or insisting upon it, a conceit which Browne had expanded into a whole poem. There is one passage which seems much more like Crashaw than like Jonson, that plucked-flower simile in ll.35–46.

But the fair blossom hangs the head
Side-ways as on a dying bed,
And those Pearls of dew she wears,
Prove to be presaging tears
Which the sad morn had let fall
On her hast'ning funerall.

It is interesting to discover that these lines are very close to what the seventeenth-century Italian poet Antonio Bruni, in the poem *Le Tre Gratie*, The Three Graces, says about the rose:

But scarcely born, O Phyllis,
Falls, languishes and dies:
The tender dew drops
Which impearl her breast
Are for her funeral
The grieving tears.

It was, perhaps, partly because Crashaw admired similar things in Italian pastoral poetry that he often wrote in a similar way. But today the beauty of this kind of poetry, its power to charm us, depends almost entirely on phrasing and cadence, and it is their phrasing and cadence which distinguish these lines of Milton:

> presaging tears
> Which the sad morn had let fall
> On her hast'ning funerall.   (ll.44–6)

That, many would be inclined to say, is seventeenth-century poetry at its best, and they would not be far wrong. Looked at in one way, the difference is merely one of degree, but looked at in another way it amounts almost to a difference of kind. The difference, in fact, is almost as great as that between Crashaw's vocal eyes and rhetorical tears in the poem *Upon the Death of a Gentleman* and Milton's conceit, in the penultimate stanza of *The Passion*, about well-instructed tears falling in ordered characters and softening and imprinting themselves upon a rock. I am not sure whether the octosyllabic couplet did not act as a kind of restraining influence and impel those who used it to a more epigrammatic, classic, and Jonsonian kind of wit. Certainly the most extreme examples of seventeenth-century ingenuity are all in the decasyllabic couplet, and nowhere, perhaps, is the difference between the controlled and the uncontrolled wit of the age so apparent as in the epitaphs in the octosyllabic couplet, which are among the most beautiful in English poetry, and those in the decasyllabic couplet, which are nearly all exercises in mere ingenuity.

As a further example of this more controlled, more classic, more Jonsonian kind of wit in Milton's poem, I may quote the lines:

> Sweet rest sease thee evermore,
> That to give the world encrease,
> Shortned hast thy own lives lease.   (ll.50–2)

And towards the end of his poem Milton declares that the Marchioness is like Rachel who, after the birth of her second child,

> Through pangs fled to felicity.   (l.68)

The last of Milton's Cambridge poems was the second of his English Sonnets, *On his being arrived to the age of twenty-three,* written on 9 December 1631, during his last winter in Cambridge.[1] It is the earliest of his poems to appear in the Trinity College Manuscript, that large folio commonplace book in the library of Trinity College, Cambridge, into which, probably very soon after he had left Cambridge for Horton in 1632 Milton began to transcribe fair copies of his poems, in which he also left copies of some of his letters, and in which he also noted possible subjects for a great dramatic or heroic poem. The manuscript opens with *Arcades* and *At a Solemn Musick*, both of them probably not written earlier than 1632, and this sonnet is not entered, like the other poems, as a fair copy at the time of its composition, but is quoted by Milton at the end of a letter to a friend; two drafts of this letter, both of which are full of corrections and alterations and seem to have been written in great haste, are addressed to an unknown correspondent who was evidently considerably his senior and who had remonstrated with him on what had seemed to be his neglect of Christ's commandment 'to labour while there is light'. Milton replies that if he seems to be neglecting this commandment it is not because of a mere love of learning and of studious retirement for their own sakes, since at his age such an inclination could not possibly be strong enough to withstand, on the one hand, the natural desire to obtain such a position as would enable him to found a family, or, on the other hand, that

---

[1] A title was first given to this sonnet in Tonson's edition of 1713. W. R. Parker has argued that Milton had a habit of counting years incorrectly, and that for Milton his 'three and twentith yeer' was that between his twenty-third and twenty-fourth birthdays. Parker concludes that the sonnet was written, not in December 1631 at Cambridge, but in December 1632 at Horton. See 'Some Problems in the Chronology of Milton's Earlier Poems', *Review of English Studies*, vol. xi, 1935. This new dating has now been accepted by most scholars. See, however, Ernest Sirluck, 'Some Recent Suggested Changes in the Chronology of Milton's Poems', *The Journal of English and Germanic Studies*, vol. lx, 1961. If December 1632 is the correct date for the sonnet, when the letter at the end of which it is entered in the Trinity Manuscript must have been composed some time in 1633, and *Arcades* and *At a Solemn Musick* might also have been written in that year, and not in 1632. These points should be borne in mind in the discussion which follows, and also in Chapter 7, pp. 162–3. On the difficult problem of the dating of this group of poems, see also A. S. P. Woodhouse, 'Notes on Milton's Early Development', *University of Toronto Quarterly*, vol. xiii, 1943, and J. T. Shawcross, 'Speculations on the Dating of the Trinity Manuscript of Milton's Poems', *Modern Languages Notes*, vol. lxx, 1960. A.L.

'desire of honour & repute & immortall fame seated in the brest of every true scholar wch all make hast to by the readiest ways of publishing & divulging conceived merits as well those that shall as those that never shall obtaine it'. No, declares Milton, it is not mere love of studious retirement that makes him seem disregard-ful of Christ's commandment, it is a reverent and scrupulous consideration of how he may best perform it, 'not taking thought of being late so it give advantage to be more fit, for those that were latest lost nothing when the maister of the vinyard came to give each one his hire'. 'Yet that you may see that I am something suspicious of my selfe, & doe take notice of a certaine belated-nesse in me I am the bolder to send you some of my nightward thoughts some while since (because they com in not altogether unfitly) made up in a Petrarchian stanza.'

> How soon hath Time the suttle theef of youth,
>   Stoln on his wing my three and twentith yeer!
>   My hasting dayes flie on with full career,
>   But my late spring no bud or blossom shew'th.
> Perhaps my semblance might deceive the truth,
>   That I to manhood am arriv'd so near,
>   And inward ripenes doth much less appear,
>   That som more timely-happy spirits indu'th.
> Yet be it less or more, or soon or slow,
>   It shall be still in strictest measure eev'n,
>   To that same lot, however mean, or high,
> Toward which Time leads me, and the will of Heav'n;
>   All is, if I have grace to use it so,
>   As ever in my great task-Masters eye.

Upon those last lines I will allow myself three remarks. First, there is a very interesting resemblance to a passage in Pindar's fourth Nemean Ode (ll.68–70)

> ἐμοὶ δ'ὁποίαν ἀρετὰν
> ἔδωκε πότμος, ἄναξ,
> εὖ οἶδ' ὅτι χρόνος ἕρπων πεπρωμέναν τελέσει:

('Whatever excellence Lord Fate has given me I know well that creeping time will bring to appointed perfection.') Secondly, how characteristically Miltonic is the conception of Christ as the great Task-Master, the Master of the Vineyard, almost, one might say, as a kind of King Arthur, sending out his knights on quests which they have sworn to achieve. Thirdly, how closely the Greek, especially the Platonic, conception of virtue and the chivalrous allegiance and romantic warfare of Spenser and medieval legend combine with Milton's conception of the true wayfaring Christian.

In the fourth line,

> But my late spring no bud or blossom shew'th

and in ll.7–8,

> And inward ripenes doth much less appear,
> That som more timely-happy spirits indu'th

it is very possible that Milton is alluding to the youthful Cowley's volume of poems entitled *Poetical Blossoms*. Although this book was not actually printed until 1633, two years later than Milton's sonnet, there is, I think, sufficient evidence to prove that it was circulating in manuscript and ready for the press as early as 1631, when Cowley was thirteen.[1]

Although many writers have repeated, as a strange paradox, the statement that the mature Milton placed Cowley with Spenser and Shakespeare as one of his favourite English poets, the earliest authority for it, so far as I am aware, is that of Newton in the *Life* prefaced to his edition of *Paradise Lost*.[2] Speaking of Milton's widow, he says:

... from the accounts of those who had seen her, I have learned, that she confirmed several things which have been related before. ... She was likewise asked whom he approved most of our English poets,

---

[1] See H. N. Nethercot, *Abraham Cowley*, 1931, pp. 22–3, and 'Milton, Jonson, and the Young Cowley' in *Modern Language Notes*, March 1934, pp. 158–62. J.B.L.

If the sonnet is dated 1632, there is no longer any need to assume that Milton had seen Cowley's work in manuscript. The date of the title-page of *Poetical Blossoms* is 1633, but the volume was entered in the Stationer's Register in October 1632, and it was a common practice to give books printed in the last month or two of one year the date of the next. A.L.

[2] 1749, vol. i, pp. lv–lvi.

and answered Spenser, Shakespear, and Cowley: and being asked what
he thought of Dryden, she said Dryden used sometimes to visit him,
but he thought him no poet, but a good rimist: but this was before
Dryden had composed his best poems.

Of those poems in the Trinity College Manuscript which also
appear in the 1645 volume, only *Comus*, 1634, and *Lycidas*, 1637,
together with the four Sonnets, can be dated precisely, or with
some approach to precision. Nevertheless, as I shall have occasion
to insist later, the letter containing the sonnet on his twenty-
third birthday cannot have been written later than 1632, and the
two poems which in the manuscript precede this letter must have
been written before the letter, which follows them, was composed. The second of them, *At a Solemn Musick*, was actually
composed in the book, although *Arcades*, which precedes it, was,
like most of the other poems, merely transcribed there. On the
whole, since the book contains none of the poems which we
definitely know to have been written before Milton left Cambridge, it seems to me probable that he began to keep it after he
had settled at Horton in July 1632, that *Arcades* and *At a Solemn
Musick* were both written in that year, and that the two short
poems which follow, *On Time* and *Upon the Circumcision*, were
written very shortly after them. *L'Allegro* and *Il Penseroso* do not
appear in the Trinity Manuscript, and since Milton transcribed
into the book almost everything he wrote after leaving Cambridge, Dr Tillyard and some others have regarded this fact as
evidence that the two poems had been written before Milton left
the university. I must confess that I find this argument from
negatives unconvincing and the fact which it is used to support
almost incredible. As Sir Herbert Grierson has insisted, it is
with the maturer art of the descriptive passages in *Comus* that
L'Allegro and *Il Penseroso* associate themselves, and I think there
may be something in his conjecture that Milton originally
intended to transcribe these two poems (of which the first drafts
may have been shorter) on the four blank leaves which he left
between p. 8, which contains *On Time* and *Upon the Circumcision*
and p. 13, on which *Comus* begins. 'If', Sir Herbert suggests,
' "Comus" absorbed Milton's time and the MS had to be lent to

Lawes for transcription,[1] and "L'Allegro" and "Il Penseroso" were expanded, we can understand that these poems never found their way into the volume.'[2]

I propose first to say a few words about the three short poems, and, incidentally, about *Arcades*, to which we shall have to return.

---

[1] See below, p. 175, n. 1.
[2] Preface to Florence Press edn. of Milton's *Poems*, 1925, vol. i, pp. xx–xxi.

5

Some poems written at Horton

Into the Trinity Manuscript Milton transcribed not merely fair copies of his poems, but sometimes what he may at first have regarded as fair copies, but with which he soon became so dissatisfied that he treated them as mere rough drafts. The result is that over and over again we catch him in the very act of composition, and when we compare his first drafts with his final versions, we may well say with the eighteenth-century editor Birch: 'Mr Waller's observation is a just one: poets lose half the praise they would get were it known how much they discreetly blot.' The most interesting and illuminating example of all is *At a Solemn Musick*, where we have a first and second draft of the complete poem, a third draft of a portion of the poem, and a fair copy. Here it seems quite possible that the heavily corrected first draft actually represents Milton's first attempt to write the poem. I wish it were possible for me to read you the whole of the first draft, omitting the corrections, and so to speak, replacing the erasures. Unfortunately, though, a large piece has been torn out of the top half of that page of the manuscript, leaving extensive gaps in the poem which I could only fill in partly from the second draft and partly from conjecture. But I will read you the whole of the second draft in its uncorrected form, and ask you, as I do so, to compare it with the final version which I presume you have in front of you.

> Blest paire of Sirens pledges of heavens joy
> Spheare-borne harmonious sisters Voice, & Verse
> Mixe yor choise chords, & happiest sounds employ
> dead things wth inbreath'd sense able to pierce

and whilst yor equall raptures temper'd sweet
in high misterious holie spousall meet
snatch us from earth a while
us of our selves & home bred woes beguile
and to our high rays'd Phantasie præsent
that undisturbed song of pure concent
ay sung before the saphire-colour'd Throne
to him that sits thereon
wth saintly shout, & solemne jubilie
where the bright Seraphim in tripled row
high lifted loud arch-angell trumpets blow
and the Cherubick hoast in thousand quires
touch thire immortall harps of golden wires
wth those just spirits that weare the blooming palmes
hymnes devout & sacred Psalmes
singing everlastingly
while all the starrie rounds & arches blue
resound and eccho Hallelu
that wee wth undiscording hart & voice
May rightly answere that melodious noise
by leaving out those harsh chromatick jarres
of clamourous sin that all our musick marres
& in our lives & in our song
may keepe in tune wth heaven, till God ere long
to his celestiall consort us unite
to live & sing wth him in endlesse morne of light.

This was Milton's second draft in its uncorrected form. Of the first draft, which it is impossible to reconstitute exactly, I will merely remark that it was only after many attempts and ponderings that Milton achieved the final phrase of the last line,

To live with him, and sing in endlesse morn of light.

Before he reached it he had tried no less than eight other possibilities: 'in ever-endlesse light', 'in ever-glorious light', 'in uneclipsed light', 'where day dwells w^{thout} night', 'in never parting light', 'in endlesse birth of light', 'in cloudlesse birth of light', 'in cloudlesse morne of light'.

If, disregarding all the intermediate revisions, one compares this second draft directly with the final version, one soon per-

D

ceives that, while even the second draft, like other people's poems, and like some of Milton's earlier poems, contains some very good lines, some which, though not very good, are perhaps adequate, and others which are either poor or definitely bad, the final version maintains a wonderful consistency of style from the first line to the last, almost every line being memorable, or containing some memorable phrase.

Notice first some slight alterations ('slight' is a comforting word, isn't it, and almost suggests that you or I could have made them), notice first some slight alterations, sometimes of a single word, which have sufficed to change rather commonplace lines into memorable ones:

> Mix yor choise chords, & happiest sounds employ
> Wed yor divine sounds, & mixt power employ (l.3)
>
> where the bright Seraphim in tripled row
> where the bright Seraphim in burning row (l.10)
>
> high lifted loud arch-angell trumpets blow
> thire loud up-lifted angell trumpetts blow (l.11)
>
> wth those just spirits that weare the blooming palmes
> wth those just spirits that weare victorious palmes (l.14)
>
> that wee wth undiscording hart & voice
> That wee on earth wth undiscording voice (l.17)

Notice next two quite pitiless excisions. Here is the first excised passage:

> and whilst yor equall raptures temper'd sweet
> in high misterious holie spousall meet
> snatch us from earth a while
> us of our selves & home bred woes beguile.

The idea of the 'holie spousall' had already been conveyed in the revised third line, 'Wed yor divine sounds', and Milton saw that the next two lines were also superfluous, since if Phantasy was once high-raised there would be no need for any subsidiary snatching or beguiling. Then, instead of the impressive pause and turn which now follows 'singing everlastingly', Milton retained even in the second draft:

> while all the starrie rounds & arches blue
> resound and eccho Hallelu.

I need not spend time in offering reasons for his exclusion of these lines from the final version.

Notice in conclusion the superb transformation and expansion of the three lines between 'may rightly answere . . .' and '. . . till God ere long', a transformation achieved, it is true, at the cost of bisecting the single sentence that the poem originally comprised.

> May rightly answere that melodious noise
> by leaving out those harsh chromatick jarres
> of clamorous sin that all our musick marres
> & in our lives & in our song
> may keepe in tune wth heaven . . .

Had Milton left it at that, I suppose we should still have felt it not to be beyond the reach of many far lesser seventeenth-century poets, of Giles Fletcher, for example, or even of Quarles. Milton seems to have been dissatisfied with it on two counts.

It is interesting to compare the extrusion of 'harsh chromatick jarres' from this poem with Milton's rejection of his original version of the last line of the Echo Song in *Comus* (l.243). In the version we all know the song concludes:

> So maist thou be translated to the skies,
> And give resounding grace to all Heav'ns Harmonies.

In the Bridgewater Manuscript, which was first printed by Todd in 1798, the last line reads:

> And hould a counterpointe to all heav'n's harmonies.

The Bridgewater Manuscript was a transcript, containing several cuts and adjustments, from Milton's original version. Warton, who had not, apparently, made any very careful collation of the Trinity and Bridgewater Manuscripts, assumed that the reading in the latter represented an attempt by Henry Lawes to improve on Milton 'by making a pleasant professional alteration'.[1] Todd, however, observed that although in the Trinity Manuscript the

---

[1] See below, p. 175, n. 1.

original version of the first half of the line had been almost illegibly deleted, it seemed to agree with the Bridgewater reading, and modern chemical treatment of the erasure has proved that Todd was correct. Mr C. S. Lewis, in the course of an article on *Comus* to which I shall refer later, remarks that it is 'almost the only rejected reading in Trinity which Milton took the trouble to scratch out illegibly—one might almost say vindictively'. Mr Lewis, however, has not observed that the probable reason for Milton's 'vindictiveness' was his perception, not that the conceit was too technical, but that it was musically inaccurate, and that, although Echo could 'hold a canon' to Heaven's harmonies, she could not 'hold a counterpoint'. In any case Milton preferred to drop the technical term, and he may have felt a similar distaste for the technical term 'chromatick' in *At a Solemn Musick*.

In the five lines from this poem which we have been considering, it seems to me that two—'by leaving out those harsh chromatick jarres' and '& in our lives & in our song'—are altogether more colloquial, nearer to prose and bread and butter, than 'Blest paire of Sirens pledges of heavens joy' or 'the bright Seraphim in burning row'. Milton evidently thought so too, for he set himself to revise the pitch and intensity of the passage to the level of such lines as I have quoted. Here is the result:

> May rightly answere that melodious noise
> as once we did till disproportion'd sin
> jarr'd against natures chime, & wth harsh din
> broke the fair musick that all creatures made
> to thire great Lord whose love thire motion sway'd
> in perfect diapason whilst they stood
> in first obedience, & thire state of good
> oh may wee soone againe renew that song
> & keepe in tune wth heav'n.

Thomas Warton said of this passage: 'Perhaps there are no finer lines in Milton, less obscured by conceit, less embarrassed by affected expressions, and less weakened by pompous epithets.'

I may remark parenthetically that the phrase 'nature's chime' is one which Milton seems to have remembered, consciously ro unconsciously, from Jonson's Weston Epithalamium, where (like even Donne in the Somerset Epithalamium) Jonson is writing more nearly than elsewhere to the manner of Spenser, the master, in some degree, of all later epithalamists:[1]

> It is the kindly Season of the time,
>   The Month of youth, which calls all Creatures forth
> To doe their Offices in Natures Chime.   (st. iv, ll.25–7)

It is also possible that he remembered a passage in Jonson's pastoral play *The Sad Shepherd*, where Aeglamour declares that the soul of Earine has seated herself

> Just in the midst with *Phœbus*; tempring all
> The jarring Spheeres, and giving to the World
> Againe, his first and tunefull planetting.[2]

But this topic of spheral and planetary music is one to which I must return. What I wish to insist upon now is that process of stylistic elevation or intensification which we can see at work between the first draft and the final version of *At a Solemn Musick*, that process which, as I have said, finally succeeded in revising every line to the pitch and intensity of 'Blest paire of Sirens pledges of heavens joy'.

Mr Eliot once declared that 'the great advantage of Dryden over Milton is that while the former is always in control of his ascent, and can rise or fall at will ... the latter has elected a perch from which he cannot afford to fall, and from which he is in danger of slipping'.[3] Well, that was a way of putting it, and although not a very good way, or even, perhaps, a very intelligent way, it will serve very well to illuminate the matter in hand. You may, if you happen to feel a bit unsympathetic towards Milton and if he compels you to admire him rather against your will, say that at the beginning of this poem he has elected a perch from which he cannot afford to fall and from which he is in danger of

---

[1] Except Tennyson at the close of *In Memoriam* and G. M. Hopkins in his fragment 'Epithalamion'. Ed.

[2] III. iii. 30–2.

[3] 'John Dryden', *Selected Essays 1917–1932*, 1932, p. 297.

slipping. The point is that Milton knew this a good deal better
than we do. We have seen him slip, or even fall, several times,
but each time he has picked himself up, and at last he has been
able to go through his performance without a single slip or a
single fall. Hopkins once wrote to Bridges of his conviction
that the language of poetry should be the common language
heightened. Now one of the great differences between Milton and
other seventeenth-century poets is that his language is more
heightened and more consistently heightened. I remarked that
Milton's transformation and expansion of the last lines was
achieved at the cost of breaking into two the single sentence
which the poem had at first consisted of. Even now, though,
the first sentence, perfectly articulated, continues for no less than
twenty-four lines. The main clause might be disentangled from
its numerous subordinate clauses and exhibited somewhat like
this: 'Voice and verse, make us imagine that we hear again that
celestial song to which human voices responded during the age of
innocence.'

There are two other, not indeed single-sentence, but what I
might call single-breath poems with which it is illuminating to
compare *At a Solemn Musick*: Donne's *Apparition* and Herbert's
The Collar. The most obvious difference between these two
poems and Milton's, the difference which, it seems to me, almost
involves and explains all the other differences, is that while these
poems are intensely dramatic, Milton's is not dramatic at all.
Milton's poem proceeds slowly, sweetly, solemnly, steadily,
swellingly, like some great melody played on an organ; in the
two poems by Donne and Herbert we hear voices excitedly
arguing and protesting, exclaiming and questioning. We might be
inclined to call the poems of Donne and Herbert more natural
or more spontaneous. Certainly, they communicate an impression of greater spontaneity—an impression that ideas and phrases
and exclamations are spontaneously occurring to the poet as he
writes, an impression of something almost like improvisation;
whereas with Milton's poem our impression is that everything
has been carefully foreseen and planned. The poems of Donne
and Herbert also seem to us far more personal: we are much more
aware than we are with Milton's of a particular person respond-

ing to experiences and circumstances in a particular way. In reading Milton's poem we are indeed continuously aware of Milton the artist, or of Milton's art, but we are not at all deeply or importantly aware of him as a particular kind of person, and we do not experience his poem as the expression of a particular kind of person, either of Milton himself, or of a person whom Milton, like Donne, in *The Apparition*, has imagined. What strikes us most in the poems of Donne and Herbert is not the diction or phrasing but the tremendous variety of inflection, or, to put the matter in another way, the fact that diction so plain, so colloquial, should somehow succeed in being so poetical. Clearly, in Herbert's poem such a phrase as 'wed your divine sounds' would be as out of place as (to take one of the most heightened phrases I can find in Herbert's poem)

> Recover all thy sigh-blown age
> On double pleasures

would be out of place in Milton's, would, in Mr Eliot's way of putting it, be a fall from the perch. It is perhaps dangerous to talk about the music of poety (all analogies are dangerous), but I think one may say that the rhythm of Milton's poetry, or of much of his poetry, including that of the poem we are considering, is a musical rhythm, while the rhythm of Donne and Herbert at their best is a speech rhythm. At any rate, I think one may say without fear of contradiction that Milton's voice is more often a chanting voice, a vaticinating voice, or even at times a pontificating voice than an arguing, expostulating, pleading, questioning, exclaiming voice. Sir Arthur Quiller-Couch, who in the course of his four lectures on Milton has continually insisted on Milton's love of music and of the musical element in his verse, thus takes leave of the author of *Paradise Lost*:

That is how I see Milton, and that is the portrait I would leave with you—of an old man, lonely and musical, seated at his chamber organ, sliding upon the keyboard a pair of hands pale as its ivory in the twilight of a shabby lodging of which the shabbiness and the gloom molest not him; for he is blind—and yet he sees.[1]

---

[1] *Studies in Literature. Second Series*, 1922, p. 168.

That, perhaps, is how many of us see him; but here we encounter
a paradox, or apparent paradox, which should perhaps make us
beware of our musical analogy: it is the musical poet (as we call
him) who has to attend so carefully, and who forces us to attend
so carefully, to his diction and phrasing; it is the (comparatively
speaking) unmusical poets, the colloquial, dramatic, speech-
rhythm poets, who can use successfully almost whatever words
and phrases first come to hand. If we are not very good at
remembering whole poems, when we try to remember *At a
Solemn Musick* we remember, of course, the swelling, organ-like
progression of the whole poem, but the lines or passages that we
remember we remember for the sake of their exquisite diction,
their *curiosa felicitas*:

> the bright Seraphim in burning row . . .
> To live with him, and sing in endles morn of light.

On the other hand, the lines or passages that we remember from
The Apparition or *The Collar* we remember not so much for the
sake of their phrases as for the sake of the rhythm, inflection and
tone of voice in which those phrases are uttered.

> I'had rather thou shouldst painfully repent . . .

> Call in thy deaths head there: tie up thy fears,
>   He that forbears
> To suit and serve his need,
>   Deserves his load.

The diction of these lines is perfectly adequate, but neither
astonishing nor inevitable: the power of the passage resides in
the dramatic rhythms and inflections, which might have found
expression equally well in and through quite different words and
phrases, if the sense of those different words and phrases had been
approximately the same, and if they had still been plain and
colloquial and had not drawn too much attention to themselves
and away from the tone of voice in which they were uttered. If,
then, we call Milton a musical poet, if we call *At a Solemn Musick*
a musical poem, we should ask ourselves what that means. It
does not mean (as it has sometimes in recent years been suggested) that he is an empty poet, an author of poems where

sound is more important than sense. It might be maintained that sound, not as mere magniloquence, but as variety of inflection, rhythm and cadence, as sound of the voice, is a more important element in Donne's poetry and in Herbert's than it is in Milton's, and that Coleridge's definition of poetry as 'the best words in the best order', laying, as it does, more emphasis on the element of diction than on the element of rhythm, is more applicable to Milton's poetry than to theirs. I return to my paradox: if *At a Solemn Musick* is a musical poem, its music is of a kind that not only comports with but demands a quite exceptional choiceness of diction. The slow, stately, swelling rhythm throws (if I may suddenly change my metaphor) as searching a light upon every word and phrase as do those Greek lyric measures which Horace introduced into Latin poetry. Matthew Arnold declared that Milton was the only English poet who possessed 'sureness of perfect style': this perhaps was the first poem in which he achieved it, and we have seen what pains the achievement cost him.

Commenting upon the phrase 'nature's chime', I said that the topic of spheral and planetary music was one to which I would return. I will begin by insisting that the correct reading of the last word in the sixth line is 'concent':

> That undisturbed Song of pure concent,

and that the word is from the Latin *concentus*, from *concinere* (*com* and *cano*), 'sing together', and, like Italian *concento*, means harmony, or, as the Elizabethans often said, *consort*. It is indeed very possible that Milton may have been remembering a passage in Tasso's *Gerusalemme Liberata* (canto ix, st. 58), describing the celestial consort or concent:

> Al gran concento de' beati carmi
> lieta risuona la celese reggia

('To the great concent of blessed songs happily resounds the celestial kingdom.') There is another line of Tasso's (canto xviii, st. 19)

> d'aure, d'acque, d' augei dolce concento

which Fairfax has rendered

Birdes, windes, and waters sing, with sweete con[c]ent.

'Concent', with a *c*, is the reading of the Trinity Manuscript, but the compositor of the 1645 edition printed 'content', and many modern editors have followed him, although Milton himself, in the 1673 edition, corrected it back to 'concent'. A fresh error, 'consent' with an *s*, was introduced by Tonson in 1695. The matter is important for a proper understanding of the poem, because the 'song of pure concent' in l.6 corresponds with the 'perfect diapason' in l.23:

> the fair musick that all creatures made
> To their great Lord, whose love their motion sway'd
> In perfet Diapason.

And Milton is here using the word *diapason* not merely, I think, in the figurative sense of concord or harmony, but in the original and technical sense, ἡ διὰ πασῶν χορδῶν συμφωνία, the symphony through all the strings, that is to say, the concord through all the notes of the scale, and, more particularly, the concord of the octave made by the eight notes of the eight revolving spheres. For, as Dr Tillyard has elaborately demonstrated in an appendix to his book on Milton, Milton has characteristically introduced into this poem not merely the sapphire-coloured throne of Ezekiel's vision and the song sung before the throne in the Book of Revelation, but also the Platonic doctrine of the music of the spheres. In the vision of Er at the close of Plato's *Republic* Socrates describes in a myth the judgement of souls in the other world.

The souls come to a place where they see the Spindle of Necessity, made of adamant, which holds the universe together and by which its revolutions are produced and maintained; it is driven as an axis through the centre of the earth and the eight spheres, and rests in the lap of Necessity. On each of the spheres sits a siren who utters one note at one pitch, the eight notes making together the harmony of the octave. Seated at equal distances about Necessity are the Fates, Lachesis and Clotho and Atropos, the daughters of Necessity; Lachesis sings of the past, Clotho of the present, and Atropos of the future, and it is they who turn the Spindle of Necessity.[1]

---

[1] Milton, *The Shorter Poems*, ed. B. A. Wright, 1938, p. 144.

It is of these Platonic sirens that Milton is thinking when he hails
voice and verse as 'Blest pair of Sirens', and I rather think that
'Spheare-borne' (spelt with an 'e' in the Trinity MS) means, not
born of the spheres, daughters of the spheres, but 'borne round,
carried round, by the revolving spheres'. And the song sung
before the throne in the Book of Revelation is associated in
Milton's imagination with the perfect harmony sung by Plato's
sphere-borne sirens, and the Fall of Man is, partly at least, interpreted Platonically: before it occurred all creatures responded in
perfect diapason to this celestial music which Milton imagines
both apocalyptically and Platonically. And this leads me to a
passage in *Arcades*, the short entertainment or brief masque
which in the Trinity MS precedes *At a Solemn Musick* and which
I think was composed very shortly before it. Milton there makes
the Genius of the Wood declare:

> in deep of night when drowsines
> Hath lockt up mortal sense, then listen I
> To the celestial *Sirens* harmony,
> That sit upon the nine enfolded Sphears,
> And sing to those that hold the vital shears,
> And turn the Adamantine spindle round,
> On which the fate of gods and men is wound.
> Such sweet compulsion doth in musick ly,
> To lull the daughters of *Necessity*,
> And keep unsteddy Nature to her law,
> And the low world in measur'd motion draw
> After the heavenly tune, which none can hear
> Of human mould with grosse unpurged ear.   (ll.61-73)

Warton, I think, was the first editor to observe that this notion
that only purged ears can hear the spheral music seems to have
been grafted on to the Platonic myth by Milton himself, and he
referred to one of Milton's Cambridge prolusions *De Sphærarum
Concentu*, on the harmony, the 'concent', of the spheres, where
Milton had declared:

The reason why we are quite unable to hear this harmony is the fool-
hardy theft of Prometheus, which, among so many ills that it brought
to mankind, robbed us of this faculty of hearing. Nor shall we be

allowed to enjoy the faculty again, so long as we are overwhelmed by sin and grow brutish with beastly desires. . . . But if our hearts should grow to a snowy purity, . . . then our ears would be filled and ring with the most sweet music of the revolving stars.[1]

It is possible, as Dr Tillyard seems to suggest, that this addition into the Platonic myth was suggested to Milton by a passage in the Book of Revelation:

And they sung as it were a new song before the throne, and before the four beasts, and the elders: and no man could learn that song but the hundred and forty and four thousand, which were redeemed from the earth. These are they which were not defiled with women; for they are virgins. These are they which follow the Lamb whithersoever he goeth.[2]

It is indeed true that in the *Apology for Smectymnuus*, defending himself against charges of scandalous living, Milton declared that he did not slumber 'over that place [in the Bible] expressing such high rewards of ever accompanying the Lambe, with those celestiall songs to others inapprehensible, but not to those who were not defil'd with women',[3] which, he characteristically added, 'doubtlesse meanes fornication: For mariage must not be call'd a defilement.' Warton too noticed this passage, but he thought that what he called 'this part of the system' might have been more immediately suggested by a more secular writer:

> There's not the smallest orb which thou behold'st
> But in his motion like an angel sings,
> Still quiring to the young-eyed cherubins;
> Such harmony is in immortal souls;
> But whilst this muddy vesture of decay
> Doth grossly close it in, we cannot hear it.[4]

And there is yet another passage suggesting that Milton's 'with gross unpurged ear' may have been a recollection of the language of 'Fancy's Child'—that where Titania says to Bottom:

---

[1] Columbia edn, xii. 156.   [2] xiv. 3–4.
[3] Columbia edn, iii. 306.   [4] *The Merchant of Venice*, V. i. 60–5.

And I will purge thy mortal grossness so
That thou shalt like an airy spirit go.[1]

Thus by this most eclectic of poets Greek philosophy and
Christian doctrine, the Platonic myth and the Apocalyptic vision,
together with some of Shakespeare's midsummer night fancies,
are all associated and ensphered.

Before leaving 'Blest Pair of Sirens' for the lines *On Time*
I will remark that, as Professor F. T. Prince, in his excellent
book on *The Italian Element in Milton's Verse*, has recently
reminded us, the metrical pattern—one might almost say, the
form—of each of those poems was inspired by the Italian madrigal, a kind of poetry that had been much used by Tasso, Marino
and others as an equivalent for the Greek epigram. [Here J. B. L.
interposed a reading of Professor Prince's book, pp. 64-5, to
demonstrate this point.]

The only one of Milton's English predecessors who had
closely imitated the Italian madrigal was Drummond of Hawthornden. Most of his madrigals are paraphrases or imitations of
Italian originals, and few of them have much distinction. Here,
though, is one for which, so far as I am aware, no original has
been discovered, and which Palgrave found good enough for
the *Golden Treasury*:

My Thoughts hold mortall Strife,
I doe detest my Life,
And with lamenting Cries
(Peace to my Soule to bring)
Oft calles that Prince which here doth Monarchise,
But Hee grimme-grinning King,
Who Catiues scornes, and doth the Blest surprise,
    Late hauing deckt with *Beauties* Rose his Tombe,
    Disdaines to croppe a Weede, and will not come.[2]

I will conclude these remarks on *At a Solemn Musick* with two
notes.

That we on Earth with undiscording voice
May rightly answer that melodious noise.

---

[1] *A Midsummer Night's Dream*, III. i. 162-3.
[2] *The Poetical Works*, ed. L. E. Kastner, 1913, i. 64.

'Noise' here is a good example of the fact that some knowledge
of the history of the language is often necessary in order to
enable us to recover the original colour of a word. Sixteenth-
and seventeenth-century writers very often used the word *noise*
as equivalent to *music*: a good example is the fifth verse of the
47th Psalm: 'God is gone up with a merry noise, and the Lord
with the sound of the trump'; and, in a less exalted context, the
words of the First Drawer to the Second Drawer in the Second
Part of *Henry IV*: 'See if thou canst find out Sneak's noise;
Mistress Tearsheet would fain hear some music.'[1]

> till disproportion'd sin
> Jarr'd against natures chime, and with harsh din
> Broke the fair musick that all creatures made;

or, as Milton originally wrote:

> by leaving out those harsh chromatick jarres
> of clamourous sin that all our musick marres.

This metaphor, with its extensions ('perfet Diapason', 'keep in
tune with Heav'n') is quite different from the ingenious conceits
in the poem on Shakespeare and in the last two stanzas of *The
Passion*. There is indeed an element of surprise in it, but it arises
naturally out of what has gone before, it illuminates and is
itself illuminated by the whole subject of the poem, and it takes
up and concludingly unites both the spheral and Platonic music
of the opening lines and the celestial song which follows. It
is also the kind of metaphor which, less elaborately and perfectly
expressed, might have been used by any European poet from the
time of Petrarch, or even of Dante. Todd quotes a comparatively
simple example of it from Sylvester's *Du Bartas*:

> The World's *transform'd* from what it was at first:
> For *Adams* sin, all creatures else accurst:
> Their Harmony distuned by His iar:
> Yet all again concent, to make him war.[2]

The lines *On Time*, which follow a few pages after *At a Solemn*

---

[1] II. iv. 12–4.   [2] *Du Bartas His Divine Weekes And Workes*, [1621], p. 201.

Musick in the Trinity MS, where they bear the sub-title, '[to be] set on a clock case', constitute another almost single-breath poem, with long and short lines intermingled in the manner of the Italian canzone or madrigal and of Spenser's *Epithalamion* and *Prothalamion*. The rhythm and progression is as slow and stately and solemn as in *At a Solemn Musick* and, as in that poem, positively compels us to linger over and admire the exceptionally choice diction which it requires and which here too Milton has achieved: whether at equal cost we cannot tell, for the manuscript contains only the fair copy. Observe the emphasis which in l.12 falls upon the word 'individual' and in l.14 upon the word 'sincerely'.

> Then long Eternity shall greet our bliss
> With an individual kiss ...
> When every thing that is sincerely good
> And perfetly divine ...

'Individual' here means undividable, inseparable,[1] and 'sincerely' is used, not in the restricted modern sense of honestly, with no disproportion between profession and belief, but in the larger Latin sense of purely, entirely, uncorruptedly, of a piece through and through. Milton may perhaps have been remembering a passage in his favorite Ovid, in the *Metamorphoses*, where Aegeus, rejoicing at his son Theseus's escape from Medea's attempt to murder him, learns that Minos is preparing to make war upon himself:

> Nec tamen (usque adeo nulla est sincera voluptas,
> sollicitumque aliquid laetis intervenit) Aegeus
> gaudia percepit nato secura recepto:[2]

('Yet (for no pleasure's perfect here below, And even with our joy is mixed some woe) Aegeus, with son restored, was none the less Not to enjoy untroubled happiness'). Milton is not here liable

---

[1] G. B. Hardison Jnr sees Aristotelian influence in this poem, and interprets 'greet ... with an individual kiss' as 'greet individually with a kiss'. A Christian is an individual who may be either saved or damned. His soul does not necessarily return to its source. See Hardison, 'Milton's "On Time" and its Scholastic Background', *Texan Studies in Literature and Language*, 1961. A.L.

[2] op. cit., vii. 453 ff.

to Dr Johnson's accusation of using English words with a Latin idiom, since these two words were frequently used in this sense by Milton's contemporaries: nevertheless, as we often find him doing in his later poetry, Milton places such an emphasis upon them by means of rhythm and context that they seem suddenly to release all the meaning they had acquired and carried since Roman times.

This kind of writing is far removed from the manner of Donne and his imitators. In comparison it might almost be called 'literary'. And yet, because of the demands it makes upon the reader's attention, it has some affinity with the kind of verse which some seventeenth-century readers and writers called 'strong-lined', a term which they used to describe a close-packed and strenuous way of writing, less immediately and easily appreciable than 'the soft, melting and diffuse style of the Spenserians'.[1] For them both Donne and Jonson were, in comparison with Spenser, strong-lined poets, and perhaps Milton, had his poetry been more generally known, would have seemed so too. Indeed, if Professor Wright's interpretation of the fourth line of this poem were correct, I should be inclined to say of it what Hopkins said of two of Patmore's lines: 'If I understand this at all, it seems to me a thought condensed beyond what literature will bear.'[2]

> Fly envious *Time*, till thou run out thy race,
> Call on the lazy leaden-stepping hours,
> Whose speed is but the heavy Plummets pace;
> And glut thy self with what thy womb devours,
> Which is no more then what is false and vain,
> And meerly mortal dross.

Professor Wright holds that 'womb' is in the accusative and is the object of 'devours'—'Glut thyself on that which devours thine own womb'—and that the meaning is: Time devours the Hours which themselves devour those mortal things which Time brings forth.[3] I doubt, though, whether this explanation is either

---

[1] See an article by G. Williamson, 'Strong Lines', in *English Studies*, xviii (1936), 152 ff
[2] *Further Letters*, ed. C. C. Abbott, 2nd edn 1956, p. 318.
[3] Milton, *The Shorter Poems*, 1938, p. 121.

possible or necessary: I think rather that 'womb' is nominative, that Milton is using it in the then quite common sense of belly or maw, and that the meaning is no more than 'glut yourself with your favorite food', that is to say, with mortal dross. Time is not, I think, represented as devouring the Hours, but as calling upon them to help him track down and devour mortal things. In fact, I don't think that Milton is being so 'strong-lined' as Professor Wright thinks he is.[1]

There are in this poem three of Milton's characteristic compound epithets: 'leaden-stepping hours', 'happy-making sight', 'heav'nly-guided soul'. Bowle remarked that the line 'Call on the lazy leaden-stepping hours' was 'much in the manner' of a phrase in the chorus to the fourth act of Shakespeare's *Henry V*:

> the cripple tardy-gaited night
> Who, like a foul and ugly witch, doth limp
> So tediously away.

I have already remarked that Milton's fondness for double-epithets may have owed something to the example of Sidney, and that Milton, like Sidney, was trying to introduce into English one of the beauties of Greek. Nevertheless, some of Milton's double-epithets, like 'leaden-stepping' here, are rather in what one might call the Shakespearean than the classical idiom. Indeed, it is interesting to contrast 'the lazy leaden-stepping hours', that quite Shakespearean phrase, with the completely classical and un-Shakespearean:

> The Graces, and the rosie-boosom'd Howres

in *Comus* (l.986). 'Rosie-boosom'd' is a translation of the Greek

---

[1] My interpretation seems to be supported by a passage in the Chorus to the third act of Fulke Greville's *Mustapha* (ll.133–6), where Eternity says to Time:

> Ruine this Masse; worke Change in all Estates,
> Which, when they serue not me, are in your power:
> Giue vnto their corruption doomes of Fate;
> Let your vast wombe your *Cadmus*-men deuoure.

(*Poems and Dramas*, ed. G. Bullough, [1939], ii. 109.) Milton may well have read this chorus (it did not appear in the 1609 quarto of *Mustapha*) in Greville's *Workes*, 1633; I doubt, though, whether the resemblance between the passage I have quoted and his poem *On Time* is more than casual.

ῥοδόκολπος, a word which, I think, occurs only once in what
has survived to us of Greek literature, in a lyric of the classical
period included in his anthology by Stobaeus, a scholar of the
fifth century A.D. This lyric, a prayer addressed on behalf of a city
to the Fates, contains these lines:

> πέμπετ᾽ ἄμμιν
> ῥοδόκολπον Εὐνομίαν, λιπαροθρόνους τ᾽ἀδελφάς, Δίκαν
> καὶ στεφανηφόρον Εἰράναν

('Send to us rosy-bosomed Concord and her gleaming-throned
sisters, Justice and garland-bearing Peace.') It is certain, I think,
that Milton, in the course of his industrious and select reading,
had met with and remembered this passage; it is also probable
that he remembered various epithets applied in late Greek poetry
to the personified Hours: for example, Nonnus, the epic poet
who flourished around A.D. 400 has ῥοδοπήχεες Ὧραι 'rosy-
armed Hours', and ῥοδωπίδες Ὧραι,[1] 'rosy-faced Hours' and
that, following such precedents, he applied to the Hours the
epithet 'rosy-boosom'd', which the anonymous lyrist had applied
to Concord. Both Thomson and Gray paid Milton the compliment of imitation: Thomson spoke of 'the rosy-bosomed Spring'
(*Spring*, l.1010), and Gray, in the first line of his *Ode on the Spring*,
appropriated the whole phrase:

> Lo! Where the rosy-bosom'd Hours,
> Fair Venus' train appear.

I hope you will agree with me that it is worth spending some
time in trying to perceive, or, at any rate, in trying to feel how
'the lazy leaden-stepping hours' of this poem is more Shakespearean, nearer to 'the cripple tardy-gaited night' than to 'the
rosy-boosom'd Hours' of *Comus*. It is true that behind Shakespeare's compound epithet and his personification of Night there
is ultimately classical precedent and example, but there is nothing
to suggest that Shakespeare was aware of this. The whole phrase,
especially, perhaps, as the result of the preliminary epithet
'cripple', is as natively English as the word *street*, although that
word is ultimately derived from Latin. And there is something of

---

[1] *Dionysiaca*, xlvii. 90 and xi. 487.

this same native Englishness about Milton's phrase, although his
personification of the Hours is more sophisticated, more consciously classical, than Shakespeare's personification of Night.
It would be interesting to compile a list of memorable personifications in Milton's early poetry, including *Comus*, and to distinguish between the more classical and what one might call the
more Shakespearean—between those where we are immediately
aware of, or suspect, classical example or precedent, and those
where we are not. In spite of some modern denigrators of Milton,
I do not think that any one disinterestedly interested in literature
would care to maintain that those where Milton's industrious
and select reading was most apparent were inferior to the
seemingly more unsophisticated and Shakespearean.

I will conclude what I have to say about this poem by remarking
that in it there is the same mingling of Platonic and Christian
idealism as in *At a Solemn Musick*; for if the vision of eternity,
where

> Truth, and Peace, and Love shall ever shine
> About the supreme Throne

is manifestly Christian, the contrast and opposition between Time
and Eternity, appearance and reality, earthly grossness and
spiritual purity, is no less manifestly Platonic. There is, in fact,
as in the other poem, what may be called a strong Platonic
undertone.

Upon the Circumcision follows the lines *On Time* on the same page
of the Trinity manuscript. It is less powerful and less perfect
than its two predecessors, but it has been rather unjustly neglected. It consists of two fourteen-line stanzas, with admixture
of long and short lines, stanzas which, as Professor F. T. Prince
has noticed,[1] are an exact reproduction of the stanza used by
Petrarch in his *Canzone* to the Blessed Virgin. This is the only
occasion where Milton has imitated a complete stanza that must
be repeated throughout the poem, a fact which, together with the
fact that this poem contains only two stanzas, suggests that he
found such a procedure too constricting. As Professor Prince

---

[1] *The Italian Element in Milton's Verse*, 1954, p. 61.

observes, 'the only stanza-form he continued to use was that of the sonnet, and then only in a manner which very considerably modified its stanzaic character'.[1] The last twelve lines of the second stanza compose a single sentence, and each stanza composes a so closely-woven and logically articulated verse-paragraph that no line or phrase could be transposed without injuring either the sense or the rhythm. It is more typically seventeenth-century than its two predecessors in the Trinity manuscript; that is to say, it might more easily be regarded as a kind of sublimation of the art of various seventeenth-century Spenserians, such as Giles Fletcher.

In the first stanza there is a typical piece of seventeenth-century ingenuity (or, as some would say—inappropriately, I think—metaphysicality) which is the last and latest thing of its kind in Milton's poetry. He begins by exhorting the 'flaming Powers' who had rejoiced at the Nativity to mourn: then, recollecting that spirits whose essence is fire cannot produce water, he suggests that they should imitate the Sun and with their burning sighs draw up vapour from the seas of tears we have wept:

> Now mourn, and if sad share with us to bear
> Your fiery essence can distill no tear,
> Burn in your sighs, and borrow
> Seas wept from our deep sorrow.

This is very similar to one of Donne's ingenious conceits in that fiendishly ingenious poem, *A Valediction: of weeping*, a poem which, if he knew it, Milton could only have seen in manuscript —unless we assume, which is difficult indeed, that he wrote his poem after the posthumous publication of Donne's poems in 1633. Do not, says Donne in that poem, do not, like a moon, draw up my sea-like tears in order to shed them again and drown me in your embrace:

> O more then Moone,
> Draw not up seas to drowne me in thy spheare.

Later, as Dr Tillyard has observed, Milton was content to write of 'Tears such as angels weep'. If the ingenious conceit about sunlike sighs drawing up sea-like tears is rather in Donne's manner

---

[1] op. cit., p. 63.

and a good example of what many of Milton's academic contemporaries understood by wit, the general style of the poem is
Spenserian, and that partly Spenserian, partly Italian, and very
characteristically Miltonic conception of Christ as a hero, which
first appears in the Nativity Ode and on which I have so often
commented, reappears in the lines

> He who with all Heav'ns heraldry whileare
> Enter'd the world, now bleeds to give us ease.

I have also (not, I hope, altogether improperly) several times
described as Spenserian Milton's various appropriations of
Biblical phrases. There is a very notable one in the second stanza
of this poem:

> till he that dwelt above
> High thron'd in secret bliss, for us frail dust
> Emptied his glory, ev'n to nakedness.

It was clearly the Greek text, not the Authorised translation of
the sixth, seventh and eighth verses of the second chapter of St
Paul's Epistle to the Philippians which Milton had in mind. The
Authorised version, with various necessary changes, would read
as follows: 'Let that mind be in you which was also in Christ
Jesus: Who, being from the beginning in the form of God,
thought it not a thing to be grasped to be equal with God: But
emptied himself, and took upon him the form of a servant, and
was made in the likeness of men.' ἑαυτὸν ἐκένωσεν: the Authorised Version paraphrases it as 'made himself of no reputation',
but 'emptied himself' is the literal meaning of the Greek, which
suggested to Milton the phrase 'emptied his glory'. This passage
is immediately followed by one in which Milton reveals himself
to hold what may be called the substitution theory of the Atonement. This was the theory generally held by the Reformers, and
there is about it something of the atmosphere of a criminal
law-court. The Atonement is regarded merely as a legal trans-
action: Adam's transgression compelled the Divine Justice, as a
punishment, to deprive him and his posterity of the gift of
Eternal Life, a gift which could be restored only through the
substitution for Adam of God's own son and the payment by him

of that satisfaction which Adam could not make. This is what Milton, in *Paradise Lost*, calls

> The rigid satisfaction, death for death.

It is too often supposed that the legalism which pervades so much of the celestial speeches in *Paradise Lost* is something characteristically Miltonic, whereas it is actually something that appears in all seventeenth-century discussions of the Atonement, by the great Anglican divines no less than by the Presbyterians and other dissenters. This passage in the second stanza of the Circumcision poem is, I think, the first expression of the doctrine in Milton's poetry, and it is entirely characteristic of his time:[1]

> And that great Cov'nant which we still transgress
> Intirely satisfi'd,
> And the full wrath beside
> of vengeful Justice bore for our excess.

While the first stanza begins, or almost begins, with a piece of ingenuity, a conceit (that about sun-like sighs drawing up sea-like tears), quite in the manner of Milton's academic contemporaries, the second stanza begins with these lines:

> O more exceeding love or law more just?
> Just law indeed, but more exceeding love!

—lines of which Dr Tillyard (the only critic, I think, who has done some justice to this neglected poem) rightly declares that they 'have the accent of the more dialectical speeches of *Paradise Lost* as none of the other early poems have'.[2] They are also a good example of what Dryden, in a curious passage towards the end of his *Discourse concerning the Original and Progress of Satire*, calls 'beautiful turns of words and thoughts' and to which, though this is the first time he has mentioned them, he declares that his attention had been directed by 'that noble wit of Scotland, Sir George Mackenzie' about twenty years ago.[3] These 'turns',

---

[1] Milton's legalistic view of the Atonement is treated very fully by A. C. Patrides in *Milton and the Christian Tradition*, Clarendon Press 1966. A.L.

[2] *Milton*, revised edn 1966, p. 54.

[3] *Essays*, ed. W. P. Ker, 1900, ii. 108.

Dryden declares, are frequent in Virgil and Ovid, and in the
Italian poets and in Spenser, who translated them from Virgil
and Ovid, in Waller and Denham and in contemporary French
poets, but he complains that he has been unable to find any
examples of them in Milton, who he here chooses to consider as
a predominantly Homeric, and, as it were, rough-diamond sort
of poet, in contrast to his master, the Virgilian Spenser. There are
nevertheless plenty of such 'turns' in *Paradise Lost*, and if
Dryden had been really familiar with Milton's shorter poems
he could not have found a better example of what he had in mind
than the two lines I have quoted. Richardson cited as a kind of
parallel a passage from Virgil's eighth Eclogue in which Medea's
murder of her children is mentioned as an example of the cruelty
to which human beings are driven by love:

> saevus Amor docuit natorum sanguine matrem
> commaculare manus; crudelis tu quoque, mater:
> crudelis mater magis, an puer improbus ille?
> improbus ille puer; crudelis tu quoque mater. (ll.47–50)

('Savage love taught a mother to stain her hands with the blood
of her own offspring; cruel yourself, O mother. More cruel the
mother, or that relentless boy? Relentless that boy: cruel you
yourself, O mother.')

> O more exceeding love or law more just?
> Just law indeed, but more exceeding love!

Nowhere perhaps is the likeness and the unlikeness of the
younger Milton to his contemporaries more apparent than in the
co-existence in this short poem of an extreme example of academic
ingenuity and an insurpassable example of Virgilian elegance.

6

L'Allegro and Il Penseroso in their relation to seventeenth-century poetry

My only reason for not describing *L'Allegro* and *Il Penseroso* as the most typically seventeenth-century of Milton's shorter poems is that I cannot conceive how any other seventeenth-century poet could possibly have written them. What, though, may be safely asserted is that many of the most delightful characteristics of seventeenth-century poetry in general are there more perfectly exhibited than elsewhere.

It is not an accident that they are written in that octosyllabic couplet which various poets of the earlier seventeenth century brought to perfection: it was precisely the right form both for Milton's subject-matter and for his attitude towards it; and both subject-matter and attitude (or tone) are here further from Spenser (who never used this metre) and nearer to some of the best seventeenth-century poets than anywhere else in what may be called Milton's major minor poems. There is more wit here than elsewhere in his serious poetry—wit, not in the narrower sense of ingeniousness and the devising of ingenious analogies and comparisons (although there are some traces of this), but wit in the wider sense, as denoting a certain flexibility of mind and mood, a certain balance between seriousness and light-heartedness.

There is also some trace in them of that dialectical, argumentative, and debating strain which is so strong in Donne and in some of his successors.

How strong is this debating strain, and what exactly is the debate about? Most of us, I suppose, have always assumed that it

was about Mirth and Melancholy, but Dr Tillyard, partly perhaps
because he was looking for evidence to support his belief that the
two poems, because they do not appear in the Trinity College
Manuscript, must have been written before Milton left Cambridge,
has declared that they grew out of Milton's *First Prolusion,* a
semi-serious academic exercise, delivered not later than July
1628, on the subject 'Whether Day or Night is the more excellent'.
Noticing, in his lecture[1] on the two poems, Dr Johnson's

---

[1] Published by the English Association, July 1932, and reprinted in *The Miltonic
Setting*, 1938. Dr Tillyard believed that the two poems had been written in the
summer of 1631, during Milton's last Long Vacation. More recently Mr F. W.
Bateson (*English Poetry*, 1950, pp. 155–6) has argued (unconvincingly, as it seems to
me) in favour of a still earlier date, and would persuade us that the two poems
preceded the Nativity Ode and were written during the late summer or autumn of
1629. Mr Bateson's view stands or falls with his own interpretation of the concluding
lines of *Elegia Sexta*, where, after having described his composition of the Nativity
Ode, Milton says to Diodati:

> Dona quidem dedimus Christi natalibus illa,
>   Illa sub auroram lux mihi prima tulit.
> Te quoque pressa manent patriis meditata cicutis,
>   Tu mihi, cui recitem, judicis instar eris.

All things considered, the natural translation and interpretation of these lines
seems to me to be as follows: 'These strains I offered as some sort of gift to Christ's
nativity, these were brought to me by the first fore-dawning light. You too they
await, these strains, withheld as yet from publication (*pressa*: cf. Horace, *Ars
Poetica*, 1.388, "nonumque *prematur* in annum"), composed upon my native pipes;
you shall be as a judge to whom I may deliver them in speech (though not in
writing).' Mr Bateson, however, would, in the first place, accept the Columbia
edition's translation of the third line, which takes *quoque* with *meditata* and mis-
translates *pressa*: 'For you other strains too are waiting, strains oft practised, strains
struck out from my native country's reeds'. Secondly, on the ground that the word
cicuta is 'invariably used in Latin poetry, in a literary context, to describe pastoral
poetry', he assumes that these 'other strains' must be pastorals; and, thirdly, he
assumes that the only surviving poems of Milton which could be so described are
L'Allegro and *Il Penseroso*. Of the three stages in this argument I do not know which
is the more precarious. (1) As a whole, the Columbia translation of the third line is
impossible. At the best, Mr Bateson would have to content himself with something
like: 'For you too some print-shy verses are waiting, composed upon my native
pipes'. This interpretation, however although grammatically possible, is neither
necessary nor self-evident, and, except for one bent on proving an early date for
L'Allegro and *Il Penseroso*, it solves no old problems and raises many new ones.
If the traditional and (semantically) more natural interpretation convicts Milton's
Latinity of a certain harshness and inelegance, the new one is open to the objection
that *meditata* can be much more naturally referred back to the *dona* and *illa* of the
preceding lines than taken as a kind of substantive: if this was really what Milton
wanted to say, he should somehow have contrived to introduce a new noun, such

objection that the cheerful man and the meditative man are too much alike, Dr Tillyard declares:

Nevertheless, the poems *are* sharply contrasted, and the contrast is that between day and night. *L'Allegro* written in praise of day corresponds to the *First Prolusion*; *Il Penseroso* written in praise of night corresponds to what Milton would have said had he been called on to take the other side.

To this it may be shortly replied that *L'Allegro* cannot be described either as a poem about day or as a poem in praise of day, and that *Il Penseroso* cannot be described either as a poem about night or as a poem in praise of night. In each poem, as Warton observed long ago, there is a day piece and a night piece; both the cheerful man and the pensive man have their characteristic day-time and their characteristic evening pleasures, although, as might be expected, in *L'Allegro* it is the day-time and in *Il Penseroso* the evening pleasures that preponderate; and while the list of pleasures in *L'Allegro* begins at dawn, with the lark, that in *Il Penseroso* begins at night, with the nightingale. L'Allegro's evening pleasures begin after the rustic company have heard tales of Robin Goodfellow and gone to bed: he then goes to town ('Towred Cities please us then, And the busie humm of men'), sees tournaments, masques and comedies and hears soft Lydian airs. And just as L'Allegro has his evening pleasures, Il Penseroso has his day-time ones: his dawn is ushered in by a shower; he goes for a solitary walk in the woods; meditates, sleeps and dreams beside a stream, paces the studious cloister, hears organ and choir

---

as *carmina*. And as for the *patriis cicutis*, their position here may be satisfactorily explained by the fact that Milton has not hitherto mentioned that he has written the Nativity Ode in English. (2) In *classical* Latin poetry *cicuta* (hemlock pipe) is indeed, generally used to describe pastoral poetry; but what of Renaissance Latin poetry, and what, above all, of Milton's? No classical Latin poet ever found it necessary to apologise for writing with that humble and rustic instrument the Latin tongue; Milton, though, the Milton of the shorter poems, was continually making a distinction between his English and his Latin poetry and by his native pipes or his native reeds he meant, primarily, not any particular kind of poetry, but any kind of poetry composed in his native tongue. (3) If, however, it be insisted that Milton *must* mean pastoral poetry, and if it be assumed that he preserved every poem he ever wrote, it may be replied that the Nativity Ode, with its shepherds, might be more (though still not very) appropriately described as a pastoral than either *L'Allegro* or *Il Penseroso*.

in a cathedral or in a college chapel. If, then, there is a contrast
between the two poems, it is not that between day and night, and
if there is a debate, it is not on the respective merits of day and
night. In spite of Dr Tillyard, we may be content to believe that
when Milton exorcised Melancholy and invoked Mirth he supposed himself to be writing a poem about Mirth; that when he
exorcised Mirth and invoked Melancholy he supposed himself
to be writing a poem about Melancholy; and that mirth and
melancholy did not mean precisely the same to him, in spite of
Dr Johnson's complaint that the two characters were not kept
sufficiently apart.

The question, what exactly did Milton mean by melancholy? is
complex and interesting and will detain us for some time. First,
though, it is worth observing that for the idea of two contrasted
poems, one praising the pleasures of mirth and the other praising
the pleasures of melancholy, there existed far better and more
obvious precedent than his own early prolusion on the superiority
of day to night. It was, I think, Sympson, one of the co-editors
of the edition of Beaumont and Fletcher's plays published in
1750, who was the first to point out certain obvious resemblances
between *Il Penseroso* and Fletcher's song in *The Nice Valour*
beginning 'Hence, all you vaine Delights'. Both play and song
were first printed in the folio of 1647, but long before that date
the song had become very popular, and it appears in several
manuscript collections from about 1620 onwards. In one of these,
MS Malone 21 in the Bodleian, it is followed by a reply entitled
Against Melancholy and ascribed to 'Dr Strode', that is, to William
Strode (1602–1645), Canon of Christ Church, Chaplain to Bishop
Corbet, and Public Orator at Oxford. Both Fletcher's poem and
Strode's reply to it were printed in the Miscellanies *Wits Interpre-
ter* (1655) and *Wit Restor'd* (1658).

After having dismissed, rather summarily perhaps, Dr Tillyard's
hypothesis, I rather hesitate to advance one of my own. I will,
though, venture to suggest that someone may have shown Milton a
manuscript of Fletcher's poem and Strode's reply and that this may
have started him off. This hypothesis has four great merits: it is
simple; it conflicts with no existing facts; it involves no new interpretation of Milton's poems; no one can prove that it is untrue.

Let us, before proceeding, have the two poems before us. Here is Fletcher's:

> Hence, all you vaine Delights,
> As short as are the nights,
>   Wherein you spend your folly.
> Ther's nought in this life sweet,
> If man were wise to see 't,
>   But onely Melancholy,
>   O sweetest melancholy.
> Welcome, folded Armes and fixed eyes,
> A sigh that piercing mortifies,
> A look that's fastned to the ground,
> A tongue chain'd up without a sound.
>
> Fountaine heads, and pathlesse Groves,
> Places which pale passion loves;
> Moon-light walkes, when all the fowles
> Are warmly hous'd, save Bats and Owles;
> A mid-night Bell, a parting groane,
> These are the sounds we feed upon;
> Then stretch our bones in a still gloomy valley,
> Nothing's so daintie sweet as lovely melancholy.

Strode's reply, though not without merit, is far less memorable and distinguished. It is also less romantic and less pictorial than Fletcher's poem, and nearer to some of Jonson's more epigrammatic lyrics.

> Returne my joyes and hither bring
> A heart not taught to speak but sing,
> A jolly spleen, an inward feast,
> A causelesse laugh without a jest;
> A face which gladnesse doth anoint,
> An arme for joy flung out of joynt;
> A sprightfull gate that leaves no print,
> And makes a feather of a flint;
> A heart that's lighter then the aire,
> An eye still daunceing in its spheare;
> Strong mirth which nothing can controule,
> A body nimbler than a Soule;
> Free wandring thoughts not ty'de to muse,
> Which thinke on all things, nothing choose,

Which ere wee see them come are gone:
These life itselfe doth live upon.
    Then take no care, but only to be jolly:
    To be more wretched then we must is folly.

I may, perhaps, be too confident in my hypothesis, but it seems
to me almost self-evident that it was Fletcher's

Hence, all you vaine Delights

which suggested

Hence vain deluding joyes

and the rest of the elaborate abjuration at the beginning of *Il
Penseroso*, and that it was Strode's catalogue of the qualities which
his returning joys were to bring with them which suggested the
various personified qualities and moods which Mirth and
Melancholy are exhorted to bring with them in Milton's poems.
It also seems to me that the luxurious, or, as a seventeenth-
century writer might have called it, the humorous and self-
pleasing, the on the whole very agreeable, melancholy of
Fletcher's poem is much like the kind of melancholy which
Milton invokes and describes in *Il Penseroso*, as distinct from the
kind which he abjures at the beginning of *L'Allegro*.

There is a further and rather important resemblance between
Milton's poems and the pair which I think may have suggested
them. Fletcher and Strode do not *argue* as Donne would have
done had he chosen to exert himself upon this topic; they merely
describe. Fletcher says in effect: 'Melancholy's a delicious thing:
feel, look, listen'; Strode says in effect: 'Mirth's the thing I want
—makes you feel like this'. This is very different from Donne's
method, when, in *The Anagram*, he sets himself to persuade an
imaginary friend that it is in all respects better and wiser to marry
an old and ugly woman than a young and handsome one, or when
he argues with an imaginary mistress that she is refusing to him
what she has permitted to a flea. There is *something* of argument,
of debate, of paradox, of hyperbole in these poems of Fletcher
and Strode and Milton, but not that mock-serious application of
close and ingenious argument to the maintenance of mon-
strously absurd paradox which we often find in Donne. Their

poems are also, though far from solemn, more serious than those two of Donne's which I have mentioned. They take their subject more seriously and they treat it more seriously; their subject, one may say, *means* more to them. Milton's poems, as I need scarcely insist, are more serious and elaborate and important than those of Fletcher and Strode, which, in comparison, are almost trifles; nevertheless, Milton's poems too are, partly at least, in the same tradition, the same fashion, the fashion of serious, and yet at the same time light-hearted, poetical debate.

There is indeed a relation between Milton's First Prolusion and his *L'Allegro* and *Il Penseroso*, but it is very much slighter and more distant than Dr Tillyard seems to suppose. For the fact is that the relation between these two poems and Milton's First Prolusion is no more and no less intimate than that between these poems and several of Milton's other prolusions, or, for that matter, between these poems and the whole tradition of academic paradox and debate. Something of the same kind of wit, something of the same kind of intention, namely, to show your wit, to show what you could do, is present both in the poems and in the prolusions. Something, but only something. For, after the abjurations with which each poem begins, the purely paradoxical or hyperbolic element in Milton's poems ceases, if it is present at all, to be felt as paradox or hyperbole. In this respect *L'Allegro* and *Il Penseroso* differ greatly, not only from some of the outrageously and quite unseriously paradoxical poems of Donne, but even from such a poem as Marvell's *The Garden*.

> No white nor red was ever seen
> So am'rous as this lovely green.

Throughout Marvell's praise of the garden we are delightfully aware of the element of hyperbole and paradox, whereas Milton's praise of the pleasures of mirth and of melancholy is, in comparison, as unhyperbolical as, let us say, Ben Jonson's Virgilian and Horatian praise of a country life in his epistle To Sir Robert Wroth.

Each of Milton's poems might almost be described as a Catalogue of Delights, a formula which relates them, not merely to the two poems of Fletcher and Strode, but also to Marlowe's *Passionate Shepherd*, Ralegh's reply thereto (both printed in

England's Helicon) and to the many imitations (including Donne's *The Baite*) which those two poems provoked. Todd, indeed, in his introductory remarks to *L'Allegro*, says that it has been observed (he does not say by whom) that the concluding lines of Marlowe's and Ralegh's poems,

> If these delights thy mind may move,
> Then live with me, and be my love,

'seem to have furnished Milton with the hint for the last lines both of his *Allegro* and *Penseroso*'[1].

The subject of the two poems, then, is the contrast between the pleasures of mirth and the pleasures of melancholy, and they have some relation, though not, perhaps, a very close one, to a well-established academic and poetic tradition of witty and paradoxical debate. Let us now return to Dr Johnson's complaint that the contrast between the two poems and the two kinds of pleasure is not great enough, and to the question of what exactly Milton meant by melancholy. 'I know not' Johnson remarked,

whether the characters are kept sufficiently apart. No mirth can, indeed, be found in his melancholy; but I am afraid that I always meet some melancholy in his mirth.[2]

In a sense Johnson was right. He was aware of some apparent inconsistency, and it lies, I think, in a certain disparity between programme and performance, between what we are led to expect and what we actually get: that is to say, the melancholy abjured in the introductory stanza of *L'Allegro* as

> loathed Melancholy
> Of *Cerberus*, and blackest midnight born,

is not the kind of melancholy which is invoked and of which the pleasures are described in *Il Penseroso*; and the heart-easing mirth invoked at the beginning of *L'Allegro*, together with

> Jest and youthful Jollity,
> Quips and Cranks, and wanton Wiles,

---

[1] *Poetical Works of John Milton*, 2nd edn 1809, vi. 69.
[2] *Lives of the Poets*, ed. G. B. Hill, 1905, i. 167.

and so forth, has only the very slightest connexion with the mood or moods whose pleasures are actually described in the course of the poem. The mood of *L'Allegro* is not really the mood of Strode's lines against melancholy, although, as I have suggested, it was probably Fletcher's praise of melancholy and Strode's reply to it which suggested to Milton the idea of his two companion poems. Milton's two poems are less antithetical than Fletcher's and Strode's. The mood of Strode's poem,

> Returne my joyes and hither bring
> A heart not taught to speake but sing,
> A jolly spleen, an inward feast,
> A causelesse laugh without a jest,

and so forth, is indeed the mood of the opening lies of *L'Allegro*, of the invocation of 'heart-easing Mirth' and of 'Laughter holding both his sides'; but although Milton can abstractly approve of such a mood and abstractly personify it, he is, of course, quite incapable of evoking, with pleasure to himself and to his readers, a succession of scenes in all of which he shall appear laughing and holding both his sides, tripping on light fantastic toe, and otherwise joyfully-jollificating. Therefore, as soon as the invocation is finished, as soon as personification gives place to exemplification, as soon as L'Allegro himself appears and proceeds to go through his round of day-time and evening pleasures, there is a very considerable sobering down. As Warton observed:

There is specifically no mirth in contemplating a fine landschape. And even his landschape, although it has flowery meadows and flocks, wears a shade of pensiveness; and contains *russet* lawns, fallows *gray*, and *barren* mountains, overhung with *labouring* clouds. Its old turreted mansion peeping from the trees, awakens only a train of solemn and romantic, perhaps melancholy, reflection. Many a pensive man listens with delight to the milk-maid *singing blith*, to the mower *whetting his scythe*, and to a distant peal of village-bells. He chose such illustrations as minister matter for true poetry, and genuine description. Even his most brilliant imagery is mellowed with the sober hues of philosophic meditation.[1]

---

[1] *Poems upon Several Occasions by John Milton*, 1785, p. 95.

And just as the exemplifications of cheerfulness in *L'Allegro* are very different from the personifications of it, so too both the personifications and exemplifications of melancholy in *Il Penseroso* have nothing in common with the 'loathed Melancholy' abjured at the beginning of *L'Allegro*, and much in common with the rather attractive, romantic, and luxurious melancholy exemplified in Fletcher's poem. Indeed, one may say that Strode, whose poem does not get beyond personifying various aspects of cheerfulness, suggested to Milton the idea of personification, while Fletcher, who exemplifies what he means by melancholy,

> Fountaine heads, and pathlesse Groves,
> Places which pale passion loves,

suggested to him the idea of exemplifying, as distinct from merely personifying, the two moods; although, when he actually got to work, Milton found that he could follow Fletcher more closely than he could follow Strode. He could, that is to say, amplify and diversify and sublimate Fletcher's exemplifications of melancholy, but he could not exemplify, as distinct from merely personifying, the boisterousness of Strode's reply. And exemplification rather than personification was to provide the main substance of his poems, if only because they were to be very much longer than the pair which suggested them.

Nevertheless, although the moods of *L'Allegro* and *Il Penseroso* are less sharply contrasted than in the poems of Fletcher and Strode, although it is only in the rhetorical introductory abjurations and in the personification of Mirth and her companions that anything of the originally crude antithesis appears, and although even Warton, a great admirer of these poems, agrees with Johnson in finding some mixture of melancholy in Milton's mirth, there still remains a contrast between the moods of the two poems which is both greater and subtler than has commonly been noticed, if not by readers, at any rate by critics. Perhaps I can best indicate the nature of this contrast by remarking that while L'Allegro's pleasures, though far from boisterous, nearly all have some admixture or suggestion of human society and are of the kind which, in some degree, take one, as the saying is, out of oneself, the pleasures described in *Il Penseroso* are more

E

solitary, more introspective, more purely the pleasures of reverie and of solitary contemplation and imagination. L'Allegro, although he scarcely, perhaps, takes any very active share in them, is still fairly continuously aware of the doings of his fellow-men, and reflections of their activities and pleasures largely determine and largely colour his moods. What would his morning walk be without the sound of the huntsman's horn, the whistling ploughman, the singing milkmaid, the scythe-whetting mower, and the counting shepherds? Later he approaches the smoking cottage chimney of Thyrsis and Corydon and closes his round of day-time pleasures among country-dancers and story-tellers. His evening pleasures are essentially sociable: tournaments, masques, and comedies. And even when he is alone he looks around him with delighted attention and is taken out of himself by what he sees: nibbling sheep, labouring clouds, daisy-pied meadows, brooks and rivers, romantically embowered towers. The pleasures of Il Penseroso are much more brooding and solitary. Indeed, only once is there any suggestion of human society, when, at the very end of the poem, he hears organ and choir in some cathedral or college chapel. He begins his night (for apparently he does a good part of his sleeping by day), with a stroll in some lonely wood, listening to the nightingale, gazing at the wandering moon, hearing the distant curfew—sights and sounds more likely to prolong than to interrupt his reverie. He then sits alone by the glowing embers of his hearth and ascends to his lonely tower, where he reads Plato, Greek tragedies (L'Allegro did not read, but visited, comedies) and various romantic poems. When day comes he again repairs to his wood to rest and dream by a brookside, and then, after pacing the studious cloister, first encounters his fellow-beings at divine service.

During the seventeenth century the word melancholy had many different senses and shades of meaning. The noun, in what may be called its strict or proper sense, denoted that dark and dangerous mental disease of melancholia, produced partly by physical causes, such as lack of exercise or ill-regulated diet, and partly by indulgence in certain mental habits, which Burton describes and for which he suggests remedies in his famous book.

Loathed Melancholy
Of *Cerberus*, and blackest midnight born.

In Shakespeare the word nearly always denotes a disposition which is regarded as unpleasant, unfortunate, or deplorable: Viola's imaginary sister fell into a green and yellow melancholy, and Hamlet feared that the ghost might be a devil which, out of his weakness and his melancholy, was abusing him to damn him. And in Elizabethan usage generally the word denoted, if not the actual disease of melancholia, at any rate a mood of habitual sadness and depression, true though it be that the mood was often affected by persons with pretensions to superior refinement. It was, characteristically, during the more analytic and introspective seventeenth century that the word came to be used to denote a certain tender and pensive sadness which, at times perhaps not without some sense of guiltiness and of playing with fire, was regarded as positively agreeable. William Drummond, for example, declared in one of his madrigals that when his mistress wept

A sweet Melancholie my Senses keepes;[1]

Fletcher declared that

Nothing's so daintie sweet as lovely melancholy;

while Milton in *Il Penseroso* invokes 'divinest Melancholy', and in *Comus* (l.546) makes the Attendant Spirit describe himself as having been

Wrapt in a pleasing fit of melancholy.

The history of the adjective is similar. Shakespeare's 'melancholy Jaques' is saturnine rather than sweetly pensive; when Capulet, after the discovery of the supposed death of Juliet, declares

All things that we ordained festival,
Turn from their office to black funeral.

and speaks of 'melancholy bells'[2] he means sad, gloomy, dismal

---

[1] *Poems*, ed. L. E. Kastner, 1913, i. 35.
[2] *Romeo and Juliet*, IV. v. 84–6.

bells, and when Orlando in *As You Like It* exclaims to the banished
Duke and his company

> But whate'er you are
> That in this desert inaccessible,
> Under the shade of melancholy boughs,
> Lose and neglect the creeping hours of time,[1]

he means that he finds their situation gloomy and depressing,
rather frightening, perhaps a little pathetic: certainly not that he
finds it agreeably romantic. Nevertheless, some forty years later
(8 October 1641) Evelyn thus described the royal park at Brussels:

From this wee walked into the Parke, which for being intirely within
the Walles of the Citty is particularly remarkable; nor lesse divertissant,
then if in the most solitary recesses; So naturally it is furnish'd with
whatever may render it agreable, melancholy & Country-like.

In the early part of 1659 Anthony à Wood was taken by a friend
to visit one Hannibal Baskervyle who inhabited 'a private and
lone house in or neare to Bagley wood', 'an old house situated in a
romancey place'. This Mr Baskervyle was very civil, 'but A. W.
found him to be a melancholy and retir'd man'; nevertheless

A. Wood afterwards frequented the house, especially in the time of
his son Thomas Baskervyle, to refresh his mind with a melancholy
walke, and with the retiredness of the place.[2]

Thus, while Wood found the melancholy and retiredness of the
elder Baskervyle rather depressing, he found the melancholy
and retiredness of his grounds, with their 'romancey' situation,
rather refreshing. And the fact that Wood calls the situation of
the place where he took these refreshingly melancholy walks
'romancey' suggests that 'melancholy' might well have been added
to those *Four Words* of which Logan Pearsall Smith so delightfully
and illuminatingly investigated the sense-history, and that,
accordingly, the origin of romanticism, the romantic mood, and
even of the romantic movement might have been taken yet a
little further back. For it has often been remarked that something

---

[1] II. vii. 109–12.
[2] *The Life and Times of Anthony à Wood*, ed. Llewelyn Powys, 1932, pp. 64–5.

like a new taste had been formed when, shortly after 1650, the words 'romancy' and 'romantic' began to be commonly applied to scenes which recalled those in old romances, 'old castles, mountains and forests, pastoral plains, waste and solitary places.'[1] It is true that it is not until the eighteenth century that we hear, from Thomson, of a 'fine romantic kind of melancholy'[2], but, already in 1659 we find Wood enjoying a refreshing melancholy in a romancy place, and more than forty years before that Fletcher had discovered the sweetness of melancholy and of scenes where that sweetness could be most luxuriously savoured. It is appropriate that the romantic discovery of the sweetness of melancholy should have been made during the seventeenth century, when so many other important discoveries were made, and when so many characteristically modern movements, including, for all I know, the Romantic Movement, began. Fletcher, perhaps, was the first romantic. Donne was not of the movement, nor, I think, was Jonson, but Milton, the Milton of *Il Penseroso*, certainly was, and, as I shall insist in a moment, it is significant that the Wartons and Hurd and other unimpeachable eighteenth-century romantics, revolting, as school-children say, against the Age of Prose and Reason, should have continually praised his 'romantic' scenes and descriptions.

Before leaving this topic of the kind of melancholy exemplified in *Il Penseroso*, I will notice a conjecture advanced by Thomas Warton in his edition of Milton's Shorter Poems. Neglecting Fletcher and Strode, Warton believed that Milton's two poems had been suggested by a poem of Burton's:

He seems to have borrowed the subject of L'ALLEGRO and IL PENSEROSO, together with some particular thoughts, expressions and rhymes, more especially the idea of a contrast between these two dispositions, from a forgotten poem prefixed to the first edition of Burton's ANATOMNE OF MELANCHOLY entitled 'The author's ABSTRACT of Melancholy, or a Dialogue between Pleasure and Pain.' Here Pain is Melancholy.[3]

Now although it seems to me more than likely that Milton knew

---

[1] L. Pearsall Smith, 'Four Romantic Words', in *Words and Idioms*, 1925, p. 79.
[2] op. cit., p. 76.
[3] *Poems upon Several Occasions by John Milton*, p. 93.

both Burton's poem and Burton's book, and that he took some
suggestions from both, I must insist that Burton's poem is not
what Warton says it is. It is not really a dialogue between Pleasure
and Pain, and certainly not a debate between Mirth and Melancholy, but a series of alternate representations of the pleasures
and pains of melancholy in the serious Burtonian sense: of those
oscillations between exaltation and dejection which attend the
unrestrained indulgence of solitary imagination, and which, if
not checked, may finally unhinge the mind. Here is a repre-
sentative passage:

> When to my selfe I act and smile,
> With pleasing thoughts the time beguile;
> By a brooke side or wood so greene,
> Vnheard, vnsought for, or vnseene,
> A thousand pleasures doe me blesse,
> And crowne my soule with happinesse.
>> All my ioyes besides are folly,
>> None so sweete as Melancholy.
> When I lie, sit, or walke alone,
> I sigh, I grieue, making great moane,
> In a dark groue, or irkesome denne,
> With discontentes and Furies then,
> A thousand miseries at once,
> Mine heauy heart and soule ensconce.
>> All my griefes to this are iolly,
>> None so soure as Melancholy.[1]

Burton's poem might, in fact, be regarded as a series of alternate
representations of Fletcher's 'sweetest Melancholy' and Milton's
'loathed Melancholy', that melancholy into which, as Burton
insists, sweetest melancholy, if excessively indulged in, may easily
turn. For Burton sweetest melancholy is a dangerous thing, and
it is against such 'pleasing melancholy and vaine conceits' that, in
his chapter 'Exercise rectified of Body and Minde', he recom-
mends sight-seeing, recreation and study. I will quote some
scattered sentences from the chapter, for it contains, as Warton
observed, many parallels with Milton's poems.

---

[1] I quote from the poem as it was first printed, in the third edition, 1628. Warton
wrongly supposed that it had appeared in the first edition, 1621.

To walke amongst Orchards, Gardens, Bowers, & Arbors, arteficiall
Wildernesses, and greene thickets, Arches, Groues, Pooles, Fishponds,
betwixt wood and water in a faire Meddowe, by a riuer side, to dis-
port in some pleasant plaine, or runne vp a steepe hill, or sit in a shady
seat, must needs bee a delectable recreation. . . . To see some Pageant,
or sight go by, as at Coronations, Weddings, and such like solemnities, to see an Embassadour or a Prince met, receaued, entertained
with Masks, shews, fire-works, &c. . . . The Country hath it's
recreations, the Citty it's severall Gymnicks and exercises, Maygames,
Feasts, Wakes, & merry meetings to solace themselues . . . *Dancing,
Singing, Masking, Mumming, Stage-playes*, howsoeuer they be heauily cen-
sured by some seuere *Catoes*, yet if opportunely and soberly vsed, may
iustly be approued . . . To read, walke and see Mappes, Pictures, Stat-
ures, old Coynes of severall sorts in a fayre Gallery, arteficiall workes,
perspectiue glasses, old reliques, Roman antiquities, variety of colors.[1]

Burton is here recommending to the man carried away with 'a
pleasing melancholy and vaine conceits' various things that will
'take him out of himself', make him less introspective and more
extravert. And if anyone positively insists on somehow bringing
Burton into *L'Allegro* and *Il Penseroso*, I think we might at least
allow him to maintain that in *L'Allegro* Milton has exemplified
various pleasures and activities (many of them mentioned by
Burton) which will correct the pleasing, the sweetest, the divinest
melancholy of *Il Penseroso*, and prevent it from turning into
Melancholia. Not that Il Penseroso lives entirely in his own
solitary imagination; he does, after all, spend considerable time
reading in his lonely tower and he regularly attends divine service.
Even when Milton is most characteristically seventeenth-century
he nearly always is so with a difference. His divinest melancholy
is less paradoxical than Fletcher's sweetest melancholy, less illicit,
less a kind of secret indulgence. Milton, after all, identifies himself, at least to a considerable extent, with the two characters, and,
he just cannot imagine himself as indulging in any mood or
pleasure that is at all reprehensible.

Having now seen more clearly what is the real nature of the
contrast between the two poems and what Milton meant by

---

[1] Part 2, sec. 2, memb. 4, edn 1621, pp. 342–51.

melancholy, let us proceed to consider *L'Allegro* and *Il Penseroso* as descriptive poems.

It will be well to apply first the method of comparison and to decide in what sense they are not descriptive, and then to apply the method of analysis, and, proceeding from the more general to the more particular, to decide precisely in what sense they are. Let us begin with Warton's statement that they may be called 'the two first descriptive poems in the English language'. What Warton and his contemporaries meant by a descriptive poem was one where description was not merely incidental or illustrative but essential, a poem which existed purely for the sake of its descriptions, and whose descriptions were mainly of natural sights and sounds, not of individual human beings, though sometimes, perhaps, of typical human activities. Milton's poems, it is true, are not purely descriptive in this sense, since they are controlled by an idea, that of the exemplification of the pleasures appropriate to two contrasted but complementary moods; nevertheless we may be content without quibbling to regard them as examples of what is ordinarily meant by descriptive poetry.

Have they any predecessors? They are obviously different from, on the one hand, the purely topographical or guide-book description of Drayton's *Poly-Olbion* and, on the other hand, from the almost purely witty description of Donne's two verse-letters entitled *The Storme* and *The Calme*. The Donne who wrote these two poems may perhaps be regarded as the originator of a kind of descriptive, or professedly descriptive, poetry which became very popular during the seventeenth century, and of which the formula would seem to be: to how many other things, ideas, experiences can this particular experience, or this particular object in front of me, be related? Clearly, *L'Allegro* and *Il Penseroso*, although they do contain one or two ingenious similes, are quite outside this tradition. The only predecessor or proto-types of Milton's two poems are certain 'Catalogues of Delights' (if I may repeat my own phrase) and certain descriptive exemplifi-cations of more or less romantic moods—Fletcher's lines on melancholy, Burton's poem prefixed to the *Anatomy*, some of the descriptions in Beaumont and Fletcher's plays, notably, perhaps, those of and by the wronged Aspasia in *The Maid's Tragedy*.

What, then, of their successors? How do they stand in relation
to later poems which may be classified as descriptive? An interesting piece for comparison is that long and rather rambling poem
on Appleton House which Marvell wrote sometime in 1651 or
1652, after, I cannot but think, he had bought and read Milton's
1645 volume. For *Appleton House* stands somewhere between the
purely witty manner of Donne and Milton's manner in *L'Allegro*
and *Il Penseroso*: Marvell is as witty and ingenious as Donne, but,
like Milton, he is also in love with what he is describing:

> And now to the Abbyss I pass
> Of that unfathomable Grass,
> Where Men like Grashoppers appear,
> But Grashoppers are Gyants there:
> They, in there squeking Laugh, contemn
> Us as we walk more low then them:
> And, from the Precipies tall
> Of the green spir's, to us do call.
>
> To see Men through this Meadow Dive,
> We wonder how they rise alive
> As, under Water, none does know
> Whether he fall through it or go.
> But, as the Marriners that sound,
> And show upon their Lead the Ground,
> They bring up Flow'rs so to be seen,
> And prove they've at the Bottom been.   (st. xlvii, xlviii)

Milton is obviously far less witty than Marvell, but, on the other
hand, he is far wittier in the seventeenth-century sense than the
almost professional nature poets of the eighteenth and nineteenth
centuries. *L'Allegro* and *Il Penseroso* are not descriptive poetry in
the sense in which Thomson's *Seasons*, or Wordsworth's *Poems
on the Naming of Places*, or many famous things by Tennyson
are descriptive poetry. Milton does not set out to give minute
descriptions of natural scenes and natural objects, but to give
precise descriptions, precise exemplifications, precise evocations
of the pleasures appropriate to two contrasted moods. His out-
lines, the directions he gives to our imagination, are as precise
and concise as possible, but he generally leaves us to fill in the
visual detail for ourselves.

> Or let my Lamp at midnight hour,
> Be seen in som high lonely Towr—
>
> (Il Penseroso, ll.85–6)

that example will do as well as any: a *seen* lamp in a tower that is
high and lonely. Whether the tower be old and grey, round or
square, ruinous, ivy-mantled, moss-grown or lichenous, we may
decide for ourselves. This very important distinction between
precision of outline, or of imaginative direction, achieved mainly
by the use of most carefully chosen adjectives, and minuteness of
visual detail, is one that has been completely overlooked by Mr
Eliot in perhaps the most unfortunate of all his writings on
Milton[1]: after declaring that, for his purposes, the most important fact about Milton is his blindness, he there complains that
'the imagery in *L'Allegro* and *Il Penseroso* is all general', and that,
among other things, the whistling ploughman is not individual-
ised. Was Mr Eliot, I wonder, like Irving Babbitt, recoiling from
what seemed to him a symptom of romanticism? For there can,
I think, be little doubt that it was the essentially evocative nature
of Milton's descriptions which led many of his eighteenth-century
admirers to call them romantic. Thomas Warton, for example,
in the Preface to his edition, sees in Milton's shorter poems 'fiction
and fancy ... picturesque description, and romantic imagery'.
Consider, as a description that would probably have seemed to
Warton and his contemporaries especially romantic, this from
Il Penseroso:

> And missing thee, I walk unseen
> On the dry smooth-shaven Green,
> To behold the wandring Moon,
> Riding neer her highest noon,
> Like one that had bin led astray
> Through the Heav'ns wide pathles way;
> And oft, as if her head she bow'd,
> Stooping through a fleecy cloud.
>
> (ll.65–6)

What, especially the third of those couplets, could be more
'romantic'? Shelley might almost have written it, the Shelley of

---

[1] 'A Note on the Verse of John Milton' in *Essays and Studies by Members of the
English Association*, xxi. (1935).

'Art thou pale for weariness . . . ?' It is true that Shelley dwells on the imagined loneliness of the moon more lingeringly and emphatically than Milton, but the two descriptions, the two ways of seeing it, even the two ways of saying it, still remain strikingly similar. Critics have often complained of a lack of mystery in *Paradise Lost*, but both there and in Milton's shorter poems there is no lack of suggestiveness that may not inappropriately be called romantic. Milton is commonly regarded, and perhaps rightly, as the most classical of our poets, and yet, as I have observed, we find many eighteenth-century precursors of the so-called Romantic Revival continually praising what seem to them his romantic descriptions, his romantic wildness, his romantic fancy. One could quite plausibly maintain that the classical Milton is the most romantic of seventeenth-century poets. One could also maintain that the official romantics (if I may so describe them) tended to exploit and overemphasise what in Milton remain elements in a balanced whole. The wandering moon and the sound of the far-off curfew,

> Over som wide-water'd shoar,
> Swinging slow with sullen roar;   (ll. 75-6)

occupy only a few lines of *Il Penseroso*, whereas with a full-blown romantic each might well occupy a whole poem. We have already noticed some interesting differences and resemblances between *L'Allegro* and *Il Penseroso*, as descriptive poems, and Marvell's *Appleton House*: compare them with those two indisputably beautiful and indisputably romantic poems, Collins's 'Ode to Evening' and Keats's 'Ode to Autumn'. In comparison with Milton, Collins and Keats (I do not say it in any pejorative sense) are much more monotonous, much more willing to linger and luxuriate in single images and single moods. I will leave the subject with a pregnant observation of W. P. Ker's: 'Romance is often near its best with authors who are not thinking about it, or who think other things more important.'[1]

The precisely evocative descriptions in these two poems sometimes have a touch (it is no more) of that wit which is still

---

[1] *Collected Essays*, 1925, ii. 318.

popularly and, as it seems to me, inappropriately, termed 'metaphysical'.

> Towers, and Battlements it sees
> Boosom'd high in tufted Trees,
> Where perhaps som beauty lies,
> The Cynosure of neighbouring eyes.   (*L'Allegro*, ll.77–8)

Here there is a truly remarkable combination of romantic suggestiveness (what precision and concentration in that second line, where every word counts!), of characteristically seventeenth-century wit, and of characteristically Miltonic scholarship. The Cynosure is the Dog's Tail or Lesser Bear, the star by which the Phoenician sailors steered, and the wit, the conceit, is reminiscent of Marvell, although the word itself, like the epithet Hippotades for Aeolus in *Lycidas*, is Miltonically recondite. There are a few other examples of such conceits in these poems. The description of sunrise in *L'Allegro*:

> Right against the Eastern gate,
> Where the great Sun begins his state,
> Rob'd in flames, and Amber light,
> The clouds in thousand Liveries dight.   (ll.59–62)

The sun, that is to say, begins his royal progress or 'state' from the eastern gates, attended by courtier-like clouds in robes of a thousand different colours. This, though far more appropriate and decorous, has perhaps some affinity with the description of

> the Sun in bed,
> Curtain'd with cloudy red,
> Pillow[ing] his chin upon an Orient wave

in the Nativity Ode, a conceit in the manner of Sylvester or of Crashaw rather than of Donne or Marvell. For what distinguishes Crashaw's conceits from Donne's and from those of many of Donne's imitators is their picturesqueness, their bright visual images. Indeed, the picturesqueness is often more striking than the ingenuity, although the ingenuity, the wit, prevents the images from being just conventionally pretty. Todd compares with Milton's image of the sun beginning his state some lines from a poem in Drummond's *Flowres of Sion* (1623). Drummond is freely translating from a poem of Sannazaro's, and in his passage he greatly elaborates his original. Sannazaro merely says:

> E se vedendo il Sol dall' Oriente
>   Venir di' rai vestito,

('and if, seeing the sun from the East come clad with rays')—a passage which Drummond expands and elaborates as follows:

> If, when farre in the East yee doe behold
> Foorth from his Christall Bed the Sunne to rise,
> With rosie Robes and Crowne of flaming Gold.[1]

From Petrarch onwards, Italian poetry, of which Drummond was a devoted admirer and imitator, abounds with such images, and so too does Spenser's. It is such essentially picturesque, Italianate, or Spenserian imagery that Crashaw's wit generally combines and permeates. And when such imagery (quite unlike Donne's) is presented in some strikingly ingenious or epigrammatic or antithetical way we call it a conceit, or even (inappropriately, as I think) metaphysical. What exactly is the difference between a characteristically Italianate or Spenserian personification and a characteristic early seventeenth-century conceit? Is it a difference of kind, or merely one of degree? Perhaps it is like the point where day passes into night, of which Burke said that, although no one could define it exactly, everyone knew when it had taken place. The chief difference between Milton's personification of the sun and Drummond's is that in Milton's the implied comparison of the sun to an earthly monarch is several degrees more particularised. Drummond's sun only resembles an earthly monarch in having robes and a crown. Earthly monarchs do not rise from crystal beds. In other words, in Drummond's personification the resemblance is not more insisted upon than the difference. But Milton's sun resembles an earthly monarch in setting out on a progress and in being attended by courtier-like clouds, although it is true that these detailed resemblances are rather fleetingly suggested than insisted upon and, as it were, underlined, as they might have been by

---

[1] *Poetical Works*, ed. L. E. Kastner, 1913, ii. 14.

Cowley in the *Davideis*. Nevertheless, there is in Milton's personification an ingenuity, a wit, a quaintness (as we might be inclined to call it) which there is not in Drummond's, or in the nineteenth Psalm, where the sun 'is as a bridegroom coming out of his chamber, and rejoiceth as a strong man to run a race', or in Spenser's famous personification which that passage in the nineteenth Psalm partly suggested.[1]

What needs to be insisted upon is that the ingenious comparison, which, although it is only one element, and by no means the most important one, in Donne's poetry, has so often been regarded as *the* characteristic of so-called metaphysical poetry in general, can, and often does, take as its substance or subject-matter precisely that picturesque, Italianate, Spenserian, or, as one might be inclined to say, typically Elizabethan imagery which Donne seems to have deliberately rejected. Such witty or ingenious combinations of traditional and picturesque imagery are very frequent in certain sixteenth- and seventeenth-century Italian poets, Guarini, Marino, and the rest, poets whom Crashaw seems to have admired; and in Milton's early poems the kind of ingenuity so assiduously cultivated by most of his academic contemporaries is sometimes applied, not always successfully, to his predominantly Spenserian or Italianate imagery. Wit, though, except in the wide sense, was never more than a very occasional intruder into Milton's poetry. It is above all in Marvell, a poet in some respects even more eclectic than Milton, that we may observe how wit and ingenuity can be combined in all manner of ways with traditional imagery, traditional forms, and traditional themes. Too much tidy-mindedness and love of classification have prevented readers from seeing in what a variety of ways the manners of Spenser, of Jonson, and of Donne, poets commonly regarded as the founders of distinct schools, could be combined.

While, then, 'The Cynosure of neighbouring eyes' is the kind of conceit one might almost expect to find in Marvell, that about the sun beginning his state is more like what one might expect to find in Sylvester or Crashaw. Much more like Marvell is the astrological metaphor in

---

[1] *The Faerie Queene*, I. v. 2. See above, p. 73.

> store of Ladies, whose bright eies
> Rain influence, and judge the prise
> Of Wit, or Arms.
>
> (*L'Allegro*, ll.121–3)

Here too, though, the wit is no more than the lightest of flashes,
and how much more appropriately might this passage, like so
many others in these poems, be called an evocation rather than a
description! There are a few other flashes or gleams of this ingenious and surprising kind of wit that was so popular with
many of Milton's contemporaries, but in every case the ingenious or surprising comparison is merely implied, never
elaborated or insisted upon. There is the Platonic conceit, as one
might call it, in

> Untwisting all the chains that ty
> The hidden soul of harmony,
>
> (*L'Allegro*, ll.143–4)

where the soul of harmony is conceived of as a kind of sleeping
beauty, a mere potentiality, first actualised, awakened into life,
by the singer and the instruments. There is some likeness between
this conceit and a very famous one at the beginning of Michael-
angelo's sixteenth sonnet:

> Si come nella penna e nell' inchiostro
>   É l'alto e basso e l'mediocre stile,
>   E ne' marmi l'imagin ricca e vile,
>   Secondo che 'l sa trar l'ingenio nostro—

('As in pen and ink is the high and the low and the middle style,
and as in marble the image rich or mean according as our genius
is able to extract it.') There is the almost Shakespearean conceit in

> While the Cock with lively din,
> Scatters the rear of darknes thin
>
> (*L'Allegro*, ll.49–50)

—scatters, that is, like a routed army the last thin wreaths of
dark mist that linger after sunrise. The praise of Melancholy's
blackness in *Il Penseroso* has something, if only a little, in common
with many paradoxical praises of dark or 'black' beauty by
seventeenth-century poets,[1] and even with Donnes's praise

---

[1] e.g. Walton Poole's *On Black Hayre and Eyes* (Grierson's *Donne*, I. 460), *On his Black Mistress* in *Wits Interpreter*, 1655, 76.

(greatly wanting in propriety and *decorum* though, for the most part, it is) of the 'autumnal' beauty of Mrs Herbert:

> Hail divinest Melancholy,
> Whose Saintly visage is too bright
> To hit the Sense of human sight;
> And therfore to our weaker view,
> Ore laid with black staid Wisdoms hue,
> Black, but such as in esteem,
> Prince *Memnons* sister might beseem,
> Or that Starr'd *Ethiope* Queen that strove
> To set her beauties praise above
> The Sea Nymphs, and their powers offended.

One may also, perhaps, recall one of the items in Sir Thomas Browne's 'Musaeum Clausum', that imaginary and characteristic descriptive catalogue of 'some remarkable Books, Antiquities, Pictures and Rarities of several kinds, scarce or never seen by any man now living':

a fair English Lady drawn *Al Negro*, or in the Aethiopian hue excelling the original White and Red Beauty, with this Subscription,

> *Sed quandam volo nocte Nigriorem.*[1]

In his later exhortation to Melancholy,

> There held in holy passion still,
> Forget thy self to Marble,

Milton is using a conceit the development of which we have already studied.[2] In his lines on Shakespeare, Milton had exercised elaborate ingenuity upon it, but by the time he came to write *L'Allegro* and *Il Penseroso* he had left this kind of extravagance behind him. In comparison with that of many of his contemporaries, his wit is now as unextravagant, as decorous, as Pope's, when (no doubt with this passage in *Il Penseroso* in mind) he makes Eloisa exclaim

> Tho' cold like you, unmov'd, and silent grown,
> I have not yet forgot my self to stone.   (ll. 23–4)

---

[1] *Works*, ed. Sayle, III. 359.   [2] See above, pp. 80–2.

In every one of these passages the wit, the ingenuity, is strictly subordinated to the purpose of illuminating or sharpening the particular delight Milton is evoking, just as each delight is dwelt upon not a line longer than his conception of his subject and the plan of his poem require. We never feel that any of these not very extreme examples of ingenuity is there merely *because* it is ingenious. Indeed, the strict *decorum* which in these two poems Milton observes even in his wit seems to me one of the strongest arguments for assuming that they were written during the Horton period, for several times in his Cambridge poems we find him elaborating conceits in the inappropriate and indecorous manner of his academic contemporaries.

In the introduction to *Il Penseroso*, which is largely an appropriation and transformation of phrases in the description of the Cave of Sleep in Sylvester's *Du Bartas*, one might regard 'The fickle Pensioners of *Morpheus* train' as a conceit. Elizabeth, like Henry VIII, had a bodyguard of tall, handsome young men called pensioners, to whom Mrs Quickly alludes in *The Merry Wives of Windsor*: 'And yet there has been earls, nay, which is more, pensioners'.[1] The only figurative use of the word before Milton recorded by the Oxford Dictionary is in *A Midsummer Night's Dream*: 'The cowslips tall her pensioners be'.[2] This is by no means the only place in these two poems where Milton is indebted to 'sweetest *Shakespear* fancies childe'. The 'fresh-blown Roses washt in dew' at the beginning of *L'Allegro* were almost certainly suggested by Petruchio's

> Say that she frown; I'll say she looks as clear
> As morning roses newly wash'd with dew

in *The Taming of the Shrew*.[3] The 'dappled dawn' in l.44 was probably suggested by

> And look, the gentle day . . .
> Dapples the drowsy east with spots of gray

in *Much Ado About Nothing*,[4] and the 'nibling flocks' in l.72 by

---

[1] II. ii. 77–9.   [2] II. i. 10.   [3] II. i. 173–4.   [4] V. iii. 25.

'Thy turfy mountains, where live nibbling sheep' in *The Tempest*.[1]
The 'Chequer'd shade' in 'Dancing in the Chequer'd shade'
almost certainly owes something to the lines which so incongruously appear in Queen Tamora's seductive speech to Aaron
the Moor in *Titus Andronicus*:

> The green leaves quiver with the cooling wind
> And make a chequer'd shadow on the ground.[2]

Only twice more did Shakespeare use the verb *chequer*, and then
still only in its participial forms: the present participle in *Romeo
and Juliet*, 'Chequering the eastern clouds with streaks of light',[3]
and the past participle once again, this time in a context with
which numerous contemporary parallels could be produced, in
Venus and Adonis (l.1168), 'A purple flower sprung up, chequer'd
with white'. He was, I think, the first to describe, and perhaps
also, in what might be called the Wordsworthian sense, to notice,
the pattern made by sunlight and shadow on the grass beneath
trees. Of the many writers who have described it since, most, I
believe, consciously or unconsciously, have used the word which
he used, which Milton used after him, and which Pope used in
Windsor Forest:

> Here waving Groves a checquer'd Scene display,
> And part admit and part exclude the Day.   (ll.17–18)

How many later poets Shakespeare taught not merely to write but
to see! Of the following lines in *Il Penseroso*,

> Far from all resort of mirth,
> Save the Cricket on the hearth,   (ll.81–2)

Warton remarked that

Shakespeare, the universal and accurate observer of real nature, was
the first who introduced the crying of the cricket, and with the finest
effect, into our poetry.

He was thinking of a famous scene in *Macbeth*:

> 'I have done the deed. Didst thou not hear a noise?'
> 'I heard the owl scream and the crickets cry.'

---

[1] IV. i. 62.   [2] II. iii. 14–15.   [3] II. iii. 2.

Dr Johnson said of Milton:

He saw Nature, as Dryden expresses it, 'through the spectacles of books'; and on most occasions calls learning to his assistance.[1]

However that may be, it is certainly true that when in these poems there appears in Milton's precise evocations (evocations rather than descriptions) some more than usually arresting detail, it will often be found that he is looking at nature through the eyes and through the language of Shakespeare.

There is, though, at least one example of what Wordsworth would have called a new image from external nature for which Milton does not seem to have been indebted either to Shakespeare or to anyone else—in that passage where he declares that, after one of his studious vigils, he would have dawn ushered in with a shower,

> Ending on the russling Leaves,
> With minute drops from off the Eaves.   (ll.129–30)

'Minute drops', drops, that is to say, falling at intervals of a minute, a phrase formed on the analogy of minute-gun, minute-bell, and so forth, is a precise expression of a hitherto unrecorded phenomenon which is not unworthy of the wild woodnote warbler himself. (That famous phrase, by the way, seems, as Todd observed, to be a free translation of one in Tasso's *Gerusalemme Liberata*—vii. 6—where Erminia hears a sound

> di pastorali accenti
> Misto, e di boscareccie inculte avene

> commingled
> Of shepherd accents and rude woodland reeds.)

'Minute drops', both as a phrase and as an observation, is original, although it is possible that in admitting into his catalogue of delights that of listening to the sound of rain upon one's roof Milton may, as Todd suggested, have been remembering a fragment of Sophocles quoted by Cicero in one of his letters to Atticus (II. vii):

---

[1] *Lives of the Poets*, ed. G. B. Hill, 1905, i. 178.

I had grown weary of piloting the state even while I was allowed to do so. Now, though, that I have been turned out of the boat, and have not abandoned the tiller but had it snatched out of my hands, my desire is to watch their shipwreck from the shore; my desire, as your friend Sophocles says, is

> beneath my roof
> To hear with drowsing mind the frequent drop.[1]

But to return to Shakespeare: Milton, like so many of his predecessors and contemporaries, was indebted to him not merely for new images from external nature but for his fairy-lore. In his notes on the passage in *L'Allegro* about Mab and Robin Goodfellow, Warton prefaces his numerous illustrations with the remark that 'All this is a part of the pastoral imagery which now prevailed in our poetry.' He might have added that it was a part which came to prevail through the example of Shakespeare, for Shakespeare in *A Midsummer Night's Dream* seems to have been the first to exploit the poetic possibilities of popular superstition, seems, in fact, to have started a new fashion, in which he was soon followed by Ben Jonson (*The Satyr*, 1603), William Browne, Drayton (*Nimphidia*), Herrick ('Oberon's Chapel', 'Oberon's Feast', 'Oberon's Palace', etc.), and many others.

This, though, is by no means the end of Milton's indebtedness to Shakespeare, both here and elsewhere. Shakespeare taught him not merely to see but to say, and even in passages of a much more general and figurative kind we often find him appropriating Shakespeare's diction—almost, I might say, his 'poetic diction'.

Milton's indebtedness to Shakespeare's diction is sometimes direct and sometimes indirect: sometimes, that is, he appropriates Shakespearean phrases without, or with only slight, modification; sometimes, especially in personifications, he uses phrases and images which, although one cannot positively assert that they *must* have been suggested by particular passages in Shakespeare, are yet thoroughly Shakespearean and without Shakespeare's example would almost certainly have been different. 'Weeds of Peace' in *L'Allegro*,

---

[1] πυκνῆς ἀκούειν ψακάδος εὐδούσῃ φρενί.

Where throngs of Knights and Barons bold,
In weeds of Peace high triumphs hold,   (ll. 119–20)

is from *Troilus and Cressida*: 'To see great Hector in his weeds of peace.'[1] 'Hit the Sense' in *Il Penseroso*,

Whose Saintly visage is too bright
To hit the Sense of human sight,   (ll. 13–14)

is from *Antony and Cleopatra*:

From the barge
A strange invisible perfume hits the sense.[2]

'Civil-suited Morn' in *Il Penseroso* is almost certainly a re-combination of epithets which Shakespeare in *Romeo and Juliet* had applied to night:

Come, civil night,
Thou sober-suited matron, all in black.[3]

But Milton was also, I think, though less directly, indebted to that same speech of Juliet's, as well as to the general imagery of the play, when in *Il Penseroso* he wrote of Philomel

Smoothing the rugged brow of night.   (l. 58)

He was also very probably, and, at first sight, more deeply indebted, as Todd suggested, to some lines in Spenser's sonnet to Sir Christopher Hatton, prefixed to *The Faerie Queene*:

So you great Lord, that with your counsell sway
The burdeine of this kingdom mightily,
With like delightes sometimes may eke delay,
The rugged brow of carefull Policy,

where the obsolete verb *delay* (derived, unlike the verb meaning 'retard', 'defer', from *dis-ligare*, unbind) means to smooth. Nevertheless, although the diction here is partly Spenserian, it is also partly Shakespearean, and the image itself is as characteristically Shakespearean as that in Comus's description of the Lady's singing:

---

[1] III. iii. 239.   [2] II. ii. 216–17.   [3] IV. ii. 10–11.

How sweetly did they float upon the wings
Of Silence . . .[1]   (ll.249–50)

There are at least three other places in these poems where
Milton seems to have combined the diction of Shakespeare with
that of other Elizabethans. In these lines from *L'Allegro*:

Com, and trip it as ye go
On the light fantastick toe   (ll.33–4)

it is hard not to suppose that the phrase 'Come, and trip it' and
the rhyme 'go—toe' are recollections, or even deliberate imitations, of Ariel's

Before you can say 'I come' and 'go'
And breathe twice and cry 'so, so',
Each one, tripping on his toe,
Will be here with mop and mow,[2]

just as it is also hard not to suppose that the combination of
'light fantastick', both here and in *Comus*,

Com, knit hands, and beat the ground,
In a light fantastick round   (ll.143–4)

was not remembered, or imitated, from Drayton's *Nimphidia*,
'My pretty light fantastick mayde.' Similarly, in the 'Meadows
trim with Daisies pide' of *L'Allegro*, it would surely have been
impossible for Milton or any other poet to write of 'Daisies
pide' without reminding his readers of Shakespeare's famous
song, even if the phrase had occurred to him quite spontaneously;
nevertheless, it is interesting to learn from Todd that the phrase
'trim meadow' actually occurs in Bartholomew Young's translation of Boccaccio's *Amorous Fiametta* (1587): 'I went singing vp
and downe in this pleasant and trym meadowe', and it is difficult
to suppose that *both* phrases could have come to Milton, as
children say, 'out of his own head'. In 'Hide me from Day's
garish eie' Milton seems to have been recollecting both Juliet's
exclamation that the 'starred' Romeo

---

[1] See below, p. 241.   [2] *The Tempest*, IV. i. 44–7.

> will make the face of heaven so fine
> That all the world will be in love with night,
> And pay no worship to the garish sun[1]

and, as Todd suggested, the phrase 'a woman's garish eye' from Barnaby Riche's *Adventures of Simonides* (1584).

For both here and elsewhere Milton reveals a very considerable indebtedness, not merely to the diction of Shakespeare, but to that of many other sixteenth- and seventeenth-century poets, some very minor ones. Some of his most memorable phrases are often appropriations, with certain additions and modifications of his own, of what were almost *clichés*. Examples are so numerous that it is hard to suppose that it can have been a matter of mere memory, conscious or unconscious. Milton's 'industrious and select reading' embraced, one must assume, English as well as classical and Italian poets, and almost certainly demanded the companionship of a notebook (would it had been preserved!) into which he copied any passage or phrase, any 'elegances or flowers of speech', which happened to take his fancy and of which he felt that he might at some time be able to make good use himself. He had been taught to write Latin verse with the aid of a *Gradus* and a *Flores Poetarum*, and even after he had become able to dispense with such aids he remained continuously careful of Virgilian and Ovidian precedent. When he turned to English poetry he wrote it on, so to speak, the same principles as those on which he had written his Latin poetry. He sometimes complied with the contemporary academic taste for the ingenious comparison, but it would no more have occurred to him to cultivate in his English poetry that out-of-one's-own-head kind of originality which Carew praised in Donne than it would have occurred to him to try to write Latin poetry as though no one had ever written it before. The only difference was that, while in Latin poetry, 'best example' was not a matter of dispute, in English poetry it was a matter upon which Milton had to decide.

As an example of what I mean by the appropriation and transformation (whether by addition, modification, or context) of

---

[1] *Romeo and Juliet*, III. ii. 23-5.

phrases that were almost *clichés*, I will mention *L'Allegro*'s
'bucksom, blith, and debonair'. That *buxom* and *blithe* had been
keeping company for some considerable time is suggested by their
appearance in the slightly ludicrous context of Gower's Prologue to the first act of *Pericles*:

> This king unto him took a fere,
> Who died and left a female heir,
> So buxom, blithe, and full of face,
> As heaven had lent her all his grace.

It also seems possible that *buxom* and *debonair* may long have been
accustomed to hunt in couples, for in James Bell's *Answer
Apologetical to Hierome Osorius*, 1581 (quoted by *O.E.D.*) we
find: 'The Consuls should ... sweare faythfully to become
bonnaire and buxome to the Pope', although it is true that *buxom*
is here used in the more restricted sense of 'obedient'. At any
rate, when Milton's Cambridge contemporary, Thomas Randolph
of Trinity, writes in his comedy of *Aristippus* (1630)

> A Bowle of wine is wondrous boone, cheere,
> To make one blyth, buxome, and deboneere,[1]

it does not seem absolutely necessary to assume that either he
must have been borrowing from Milton or Milton from him. If
one of them was borrowing, it is rather more likely to have been
Milton, who, as his manner was, had entered the phrase in his
notebook; but it seems possible that each of them, quite inde-
pendently, was, as it were, telescoping two time-hallowed and
traditional phrases. The point is, though, that but for Milton the
phrase (or combination of two phrases), however often it had
been used by earlier poets, would have died a natural death. The
mere words themselves might well have appeared together in a
line in one of those painfully undistinguished poems in Poulter's
Measure which make up the greater part of *Tottel's Miscellany*,
and there they would have been as unlikely to arrest the attention
of any but philologists or lexicographers as in the line from Randolph's *Aristippus*. Milton, by means of context and rhythm,
has conferred upon them a modest immortality: in their place in

---

[1] p. 18.

his poem they have struck, and will continue to strike, most readers as being exquisitely original and right.

One might say almost the same of *Il Penseroso's*:

> Com pensive Nun, devout and pure,
> Sober, stedfast, and demure.   (ll.31–2)

The combination 'sober and demure' seems to have been almost as much of a fixed phrase as were 'fair and free' and the like in those metrical romances parodied by Chaucer in 'Sir Thopas': in Skelton's 'Philip Sparrow' we have

> Goodly Mistress Jane,
> Sober, demure Diane[1],

in the old *Chronicle History of King Leir* Ragan says of Cordella:

> Besides, she is so nice and so demure;
> So sober, courteous, modest, and precise;[2]

and in the Catholic devotional manual *Partheneia Sacra* (1633, p. 209) occurs the invocation 'most sober and demure Virgin'. Here again by means of rhythm and context Milton has transmuted copper currency into gold. And when I say 'by means of context', I mean very largely that, because of the extreme economy and *decorum* which Milton observes in these two poems, every detail receives the maximum emphasis and produces the maximum effect: everything stands out clearly, nothing gets lost in the crowd.

The line 'Nods, and Becks, and Wreathed Smiles,' which has probably struck most readers as delightfully original (as indeed, in the most valuable sense, it is), seems to have been compounded from a ballad-like translation of a passage from Musaeus's *Hero and Leander* in Burton's *Anatomy of Melancholy*:

> With becks and nods he first beganne,
>   To try the wenches minde,
> With becks and nods and smiles againe,
>   An answere he did finde.[3]

---

[1] *Poems*, ed. Philip Henderson, 1931, p. 95.
[2] ed. Sidney Lee, 1909, I. ii, 9–10.
[3] Part 3, sect. 2, memb. 2. subs. 4 (Allurements of Loue), edn 1621, p. 583.

The exquisite use of the verb *ride* in

> To behold the wandring Moon,
> Riding neer her highest noon,   (*Il Penseroso*, ll.67–8)

may well have been inspired, as Todd suggested, by a passage in Archbishop Parker's translation of *The Whole Psalter* (?1567, p. 199):

> Sweet peace shalbe on euery side,
> As long as moone her sphere doth ryde.[1]

Poets who had used such phrases before him did not, one might say, know what to do with them; they fumbled, they dropped their catches. Milton picked them up, and phrases which might otherwise have quietly disappeared from the language are now among the most memorable in these two poems—or rather, perhaps I should say, as memorable as any, since the distinction of *L'Allegro* and *Il Penseroso* is that nearly all their phrases are memorable. Nowhere do we find such striking confirmation of that hard saying:

Unto every one that hath shall be given, and he shall have abundance: but from him that hath not shall be taken away even that which he hath.

At least twice in these poems not just a phrase or a metaphor but an extended passage seems to have been suggested to Milton by something he had remembered (or transcribed into his notebook) from earlier poets. In *Britannia's Pastorals* (1616) William Browne, with a touch of epigrammatic wit, had written of Spenser:

> He sung th' heroic knights of fairyland
> In lines so elegant, of such command,
> that had the Thracian play'd but half so well,
> He had not left Eurydice in hell.[2]

It was perhaps the possibility he saw of exquisitely refining and

---

[1] cf. also *P.L.*, i. 769: 'In spring time, when the Sun with *Taurus* rides'. *O.E.D.* quotes no earlier examples of the application of the verb to the heavenly bodies: its later examples all seem to have been imitated from Milton.

[2] II. i. 991–4.

pointing this touch of epigrammatic wit which led Milton to
bring Orpheus and Eurydice into the last lines of *L'Allegro*, and
to express the wish that from the marriage of Lydian airs and
immortal verse he might hear such strains as would move even
Orpheus in Elysium to listen

> and hear
> Such streins as would have won the ear
> Of *Pluto*, to have quite set free
> His half regain'd *Eurydice*.

Nowhere else in these poems is Milton's power of compressed
statement so brilliantly and astonishingly revealed as in the last
two lines of this passage. 'Quite set free'—that is, without any
conditions, since, as it was, Orpheus only 'half-regained' her,
regained her subject to the condition of not looking back until
they had reached the upper world.[1] The monosyllables 'quite'
and 'half' are not only unimprovably and magisterially right, but
each is so placed in its line that it receives the maximum emphasis
and performs the maximum amount of work. One might almost
say that the 'wit' which so many of his contemporaries expended
upon the devising of ingenious similes, Milton came more and
more to spend upon the rightness and economy of his choice of
words. Most of the poets he borrowed from habitually used far
too many words, and when they did hit upon a good phrase or a
good idea its potential energy was nearly always damped or
dissipated by an undistinguished context.

The other example of such extended imitation (or transmutation) is less remarkable. Drayton had written in *The Owle*
(1604 and 1619, ll.117–21),

> See the small brookes as though these Groves they travell ...
> With the smooth cadence of their murmuring.
> Each *Bee* with Honey on her laden thye.[2]

It was almost certainly with these lines in his memory (or in
his notebook) that Milton begged Melancholy to hide him

---

[1] Milton then reintroduced Orpheus and Eurydice into what may be called the
corresponding place in *Il Penseroso*, ll.105–8.
[2] *Works*, ed. J. W. Hebel, 1931–41, ii. 483.

from day's garish eye by some shady brook,

> While the Bee with Honied thie,
> That at her flowry work doth sing,
> And the Waters murmuring
> With such consort as they keep,
> Entice the dewy-feather'd Sleep.   (ll. 142–6)

'Flowry work' is the translation of a phrase (*laboris floriferi*) from Lucan's *Pharsalia*, in a description of how bees, at the sound of beaten brass,

> Attonitae posuere fugam, studiumque laboris
> Floriferi repetunt et sparsi mellis amorem.[1]

('in alarm they stop their flight and go back to their task of bearing pollen, and renew their love of scattered honey.') In his translation (1627) Thomas May rendered it as 'flow'ry taskes', a phrase which Milton may possibly have remembered and improved upon. Such periphrases—'watery plain', 'heavenly round', 'finny tribe', 'feathered choir', etc.—which are still popularly supposed to constitute almost the sum total of 'poetic diction' and to have been introduced by Pope, are very numerous in the work of the seventeenth-century translators, from Sylvester's *Du Bartas* onwards. They are generally translations of more or less equivalent Latin phrases, but where he speaks in *L'Allegro* of the lubber fiend's 'hairy strength', Milton seems to have coined one of his own.

But just as such periphrases constitute only a small and rather specialised portion of what may properly be called poetic diction, they also constitute only a small portion of Milton's Latinisms, of those phrases which he has either adapted directly from Latin authors or into which, although they had been used by his English predecessors, he has re-injected some of their original virtue. There are two very notable examples in four consecutive lines of *L'Allegro*:

> And ever against eating Cares,
> Lap me in soft *Lydian* Aires,

---

[1] ix. 289–90.

Married to immortal verse
Such as the meeting soul may pierce.   (ll.135-8)

'Eating cares' is a translation of the phrase *edaces curae*, which
occurs several times in Horace's Odes, e.g., 'Dissipat Euhius
curas edaces'.[1] 'Meeting', in the phrase 'meeting soul', is an
anglicisation of Latin *obvius*, in the sense of 'coming forward in
response or welcome', as in Virgil: 'cui mater media sese tulit
obvia silva,' ('to whom in the midst of the forest rose meetingly
his mother').[2] The only pre-Miltonic example cited by *O.E.D.* is
from Udall's translation of Erasmus's *Paraphrase upon the First
Epistle to Timothy*, 1548, where the phrase *obviis, ut aiunt, ulnis
amplectendum* is rendered 'to be embraced (as they saye) with
meting armes'. Nevertheless, it would seem that by Milton's
time the word had become, and for some time remained, quite
current English: Saltmarshe, 1639, has 'Bee not too meeting, and
seeme not too hasty in accepting graces and favours', and South
in a sermon speaks of 'all the meeting readiness of appetite and
desire'. Dr Johnson declared that both in prose and verse Milton
had 'formed his style by a perverse and pedantick principle', and
that he was 'desirous to use English words with a foreign idiom';
very often, though, investigation will reveal that what seems
Latin or 'foreign' idiom now was good English idiom at the time
when Milton wrote, although it is true that, by means of context
and emphasis, he not infrequently injected into such Latinate
phrases a new dose of their original virtue. 'Decent' in *Il
Penseroso* is an excellent example:

And sable stole of *Cipres* Lawn,
Over thy decent shoulders drawn.   (ll.35-6)

Latin *decens* means either 'seemly' or 'becoming', sometimes both,
and the word 'decent' was similarly used by Milton's predecessors
and contemporaries. Here, though, by means of context and
emphasis, he has contrived to give it a depth of meaning such as
Horace often achieves. Here are some instances from Horace's
Odes. Europa is speaking:

---

[1] II. xi.   [2] *Aeneid*, i. 314.

antequam turpis macies decentis
occupet malas[1]—

('before hideous wasting seizes upon my comely cheeks'). Or
again we read of 'iunctaeque Nymphis Gratiae decentes'.[2] Or of
a noble and comely youth: 'et nobilis et decens'.[3] Or this taunt:

quo fugit Venus, heu, quove color? decens
quo motus?[4]

(Whither, alas, has fled thy grace, whither thy bloom?
Whither thy decent carriage?)

Collins, undoubtedly imitating Milton, used the same word to
achieve precisely the same effect in the second stanza of his
'Ode to Simplicity' (where he has also borrowed the phrase
'meeting soul'):

Thou, who with Hermit Heart
Disdain'st the Wealth of Art,
And Gauds, and pageant Weeds, and trailing Pall:
But com'st a decent Maid
In *Attic* Robe array'd,
O chase unboastful Nymph, to Thee I call!

Neither here nor elsewhere in these two poems is there anything perverse or pedantic, odd or eccentric, startling or stunning
about Milton's 'originality', which in almost every one of its
manifestations consists simply in doing better, more economically,
more tellingly, things which other poets had done, or had
tried to do, before. All his materials, one might almost say, lay
ready to his hand, and his whole art and power consists in his
judicious selection and combination of them. The observance of
decorum, the subordination of the parts to the whole, the placing
of words in a line, of lines in a passage, of passages in a poem—
nowhere, perhaps, is that sheer craftsmanship which is the founda-
tion of all great poetry so apparent as in *L'Allegro* and *Il Penseroso*.
Almost everything that is commonly understood by 'originality',

---

[1] III. xxvii. 53-4.   [2] I. iv. 6.   [3] IV. i. 13.   [4] IV. xiii. 17-18.

almost everything that Carew meant when he praised the
originality of Donne, is missing: Milton's originality in these
two poems consists almost entirely in his manipulation and
craftsmanship—in his style, which, 'by certain vital signs it had,
was likely to live'.

≫ 7 ≪

Arcades

On 9 February 1646 (new style) Milton addressed to his friend Henry Lawes a sonnet beginning

> *Harry* whose tuneful and well measur'd Song
> First taught our English Musick how to span
> Words with just note and accent, not to scan
> With *Midas* Ears, committing short and long . . .

The exact meaning of these lines has long baffled, and will probably long continue to baffle, if not all Milton's editors, at any rate all musicologists whose attention may be directed to them. Is Milton really declaring that all Lawes's predecessors, including Dowland and Campion, habitually 'committed', that is to say, put together, misjoined strong musical accents and unaccented syllables in a manner that might be expected of a composer imperfectly acquainted with our language? For if that is really what Milton meant, it would almost seem necessary to assume that he was permitting himself to indulge in that hyperbolical compliment characteristic of a poetic style he had long outgrown.[1] Be that as it may, this puzzling sonnet was by no means the only fruit of Milton's friendship with Lawes, for it was almost certainly through him that Milton became acquainted with the Bridgewater family and was commissioned (or, if that word

---

[1] On Lawes and the new style of setting words to music, see E. A. J. Honigmann, *Milton's Sonnets. The Texts with an Introduction and Commentary*, London 1966, p. 127 et seq. Milton's draft acknowledged that Lawes was not the only composer who knew how to 'scan'. It reads 'that didst reform thy art, the chief among. . . .' A.L.

seems too commercial, was requested) to write, first an entertainment, and then a masque. Without Lawes we should have
had neither *Arcades* nor *Comus*, just as without Wordsworth we
should never have had *The Ancient Mariner*. For although *Paradise
Lost*, *Paradise Regained*, and *Samson Agonistes* are not, any more
than the *Aeneid* or the *Divine Comedy*, the work of a poet who
required, as it were, to be nudged into activity, and although
a combination of literary ambition and moral, religious and
patriotic fervour was for Milton a sufficient motive for composition, we must remember that the Milton of the Horton period
was still completing to his mind the full circle of his private
studies and preparing himself to write at some future time a
great poem of what Aristotle called 'a certain magnitude'. We
must remember that the Milton of this period seems to have
regarded the writing of any but very short poems as a deflection
and distraction, and that both in the Latin motto he placed on
the title-page of the Masque which he allowed Lawes to publish
anonymously in 1637 and in the opening lines of *Lycidas* (a
poem requested—one might perhaps say, exacted— by the editor
or editors of the Cambridge volume of elegies on Milton's fellow-
collegian Edward King) he apologised for writing and publishing before his genius was ripe.

Henry Lawes, a Gentleman of the King's Chapel, a member of
the King's Music, and, like Mr Alfred Deller, a counter-tenor,
was one of the most considerable musicians of his time, and for
the beginning of Milton's friendship with him it is perhaps not
necessary to look further than that not inconsiderable musician
Milton's father, who was probably acquainted with most of the
musicians of his time. It is even possible that, for a while at any
rate, Lawes and the Miltons had been near neighbours, for we
know that Lawes had been employed by the Earl of Bridgewater
to instruct his daughters in music, and Harefield, the seat of
the Bridgewater family, was only twelve miles from Horton.
When in 1653 he dedicated his *Ayres and Dialogues* to the Earl's
daughters, Alice, now Countess of Carbery, who had taken the
part of the younger brother in *Comus*, and her sister, Mary, now
Lady Herbert of Cherbury, he declared that most of the songs had
been composed 'when I was employed by Your ever Honour'd

F

Parents to attend your *Ladishipp's* Education in Musick'; and in
dedicating the anonymous, 1637, edition of *Comus* to the Earl's
son, the young Viscount Brackley, he begged him to receive it
'from the hands of him, who hath by many favours been long
oblig'd to your most honour'd Parents', and reminded him that
he had taken the part of 'your attendant *Thyrsis*'.

We know that *Comus* was performed on Michaelmas Night,
that is, on 29 September 1634, and we may assume that Milton
was fairly continuously at work upon it during the earlier part of
that year. The exact date of the writing and presentation of
Arcades is uncertain, although I think we can say almost with
certainty that it must have been not earlier than 1630 and not
later than 1632.[1] The *terminus ante quem* depends on an answer to
the question, when did Milton first begin to transcribe poems
into the manuscript book now preserved in the library of Trinity
College, Cambridge, the book which opens with a transcript of
Arcades? On pages 6–7, after *Arcades* and after *At a Solemn
Musick*, there are two drafts of a letter to an elderly friend,
presumably a friend of Milton's father, who had apparently
remonstrated with Milton for idling and drifting. Milton defends
himself against these charges, and in the course of his defence
quotes the sonnet on his twenty-third birthday, which must have
been written in December 1631, and which Milton refers to as
having been written 'some while since'. It seems clear to me that
Milton's 'some while since' cannot mean more than 'a few
months since', 'a few months ago', and that, accordingly, Milton,
after having already transcribed *Arcades* and composed *At a
Solemn Musick*, had reached that page of his manuscript book not
later than about the autumn of 1632. It is true that Masson,
because he thought *Arcades* must have been written very shortly
before *Comus*, and that, accordingly, Milton could not have
started his transcription book before 1633, took Milton's 'some
while since' to mean 'about two years ago'; but, as Sir Herbert
Grierson acutely remarked, 'it would surely be impertinent to say
to an elderly friend who rebuked me for apparently idling and
drifting that I should show him a sonnet I had written on that

---

[1] See above, p. 91.

two years before'.[1] This, then, gives us a *terminus ante quem*: we can say quite definitely that *Arcades* must have been written before the autumn of 1632. But since, unlike *At a Solemn Musick*, Milton did not compose it in his manuscript book, but merely transcribed it there, we can only guess how long he may have had it by him before he transcribed it. Since, though, Milton has not transcribed into this book any of the poems which we know to have been written during his Cambridge period, I think we may assume that he used it only for poems written after he had begun to keep it, that *Arcades* was the first of these poems, and that it was written shortly after he had left Cambridge and settled with his father at Horton in July 1632. And since the entertainment of which *Arcades* formed a part was presumably an open-air one, it seems reasonable to suppose that it took place before the end of the summer.

In the 1645 volume, where it was first published, Milton described *Arcades* as 'Part of an entertainment presented to the Countess Dowager of *Darby* at *Harefield*, by som Noble persons of her Family'. The dowager Countess of Derby was the widow and third wife of Donne's patron Sir Thomas Egerton, later Baron Ellesmere, and both step-mother and mother-in-law of his only surviving son, the first Earl of Bridgewater. She had been born about 1560, one of the daughters of Sir John Spencer of Althorpe, and before her marriage to Sir Thomas Egerton she had been the wife of Ferdinando Stanley, Lord Strange and later Earl of Derby, patron of Shakespeare's company the Chamberlain's men. 'The span of a human life', wrote Sir Walter Greg, in his book on *Pastoral Poetry and Pastoral Drama*,

The span of a human life appears strange when measured by the rapidly moving events of the English renaissance. The wife of Shakespeare's patron, who may have witnessed the early ventures of the Stratford lad at the time of his first appearance on the London stage—the 'Amarillis' of *Colin Clout*, with whom, and with her sisters 'Phillis' and 'Charillis,' Spenser claimed kinship, and to whom he dedicated his *Tears of the Muses* in 1591—lived to see her grandchildren perform for her amusement in the reign of the first Charles an enter-

---

[1] Introduction to Florence Press edn of Milton's *Poems*, 1925, i. p. xiv.

tainment for which their music-master Lawes had requisitioned the pen of the future author of *Paradise Lost*.[1]

The whole family continued to reside at Harefield, only twelve miles from Horton, and it is probable that this was Milton's first introduction to them, and that both the introduction and the request for a contribution to the entertainment came from Henry Lawes, who may already have been residing at Harefield as the children's tutor in music. It is also possible, or even probable, that the three children who were later to take the principal parts in *Comus*, the Lady Alice Egerton, the Lord Viscount Brackley, and little Master Thomas Egerton, also took part in this compliment to their grandmother.

Arcades, which contains a little more than a hundred lines and is only about a tenth of the length of *Comus*, was only a part of this entertainment presented to the Countess of Derby. When Milton began to transcribe it on the first page of the Trinity College manuscript he at first headed it 'Part of a maske'; then deleted this title and wrote

'Arcades

Part of an Entertainment at'

—*cetera desunt*, for this first leaf of the manuscript book has been badly damaged. Milton's original title may serve to remind us of the relationship between a masque and an entertainment, an entertainment being a simplified form of the masque suitable for performance out of doors. Indeed, the relationship between the entertainment and the Court Masque proper, as it was developed by Ben Jonson and others, is so slight that I think it is perhaps better to regard the entertainment not as a simplified kind of masque, but rather as just one rather specialised example of those various outdoor pageants that were so fashionable during the sixteenth and seventeenth centuries. The core of the masque, as I shall insist later on, is what might be called the pulling of the cracker, the opening of the Easter egg: that is to say, the ingenious and surprising discovery or revelation of the concealed masquers who first dance among themselves and then with the

---

[1] *Pastoral Poetry and Pastoral Drama*, 1906, p. 389.

spectators. The core of the entertainment, on the other hand, is the address of welcome or the complimentary speech. *Arcades* contains better poetry than any other surviving example of the entertainment, but Milton has not there attempted to transform the entertainment in the way that in *Comus* he has transformed the masque. Neither could he have attempted to do so, for while in *Comus* he was, as it were, constituted Master of the Revels and given a completely free hand, in *Arcades* he was simply requested to provide a small poetical contribution to a piece of pageantry which had already been designed. *Arcades*, therefore, is a much more conventional piece of work than *Comus*, and in at least one place we can almost see Milton vainly attempting to soar above the restrictions imposed upon him. In considering *Comus* it will be necessary to examine several examples of the masque, but it will be sufficient to compare *Arcades* with a single typical example of the entertainment. In June 1603, when the Queen and Prince Henry first came into England, they were received at Althorpe by Sir Robert Spencer, who had requested Ben Jonson to compose an entertainment to welcome them. This entertainment, which Jonson, when he published it, entitled *The Satyr*, is pleasant enough to read, although, like so many of Jonson's entertainments and masques, as pure literature it is rather slight and scarcely able to survive the occasion for which it was written. We commonly think of Jonson, who insisted on 'language such as men do use', who disliked Spenser, admired Donne, wrote so much satirical and realistic poetry and drama, and who tried in so many poems to reproduce what he admired in the Roman poets—we commonly think of Jonson as a kind of neo-classic poet, or, at any rate, as one resolutely opposed to the pastoralism and the rather easy prettiness of so much Elizabethan poetry. Nevertheless, in his masques and entertainments Jonson is often very typically Elizabethan. Here, for example, he continues that exploitation—one might almost say, that transformation— of popular fairy lore which Shakespeare began in *A Midsummer Night's Dream* and which soon found so many imitators; and his heptasyllabic couplets contain a fair amount of typically pastoral or Spenserian diction. Jonson's initial stage-direction, or description (a great part of his printed masques and entertainments consists of descriptions of scenes and actions) is as follows:

The inuention was, to have a Satyre lodged in a little Spinet [i.e., a spinney or copse, not a musical instrument], by which her Maiestie, and the Prince were to come, who (at the report of certayne Cornets that were diuided in seuerall places of the Parke, to signifie her approch) aduanced his head aboue the top of the wood, wondring, and (with his pipe in his hand) began as followeth.

After expressing his ecstatic admiration, the satyr runs back into the wood

whilst to the sound of excellent soft Musique, that was there conceald in the thicket; there came tripping up the lawne, a beuy of *Faeries*, attending on MAB their Queene, who falling into an artificiall ring, that was there cut in the path, began to dance a round, whilst their Mistris spake as followeth.

FAERIE

Haile, and welcome worthiest Queene,
Ioy had neuer perfect beene,
To the Nymphs that haunt this greene,
Had they not this euening seene.
Now they print it on the ground
With their feete in figures round,
Markes that will be euer found,
To remember this glad stound.[1]

Mab presents a jewel to the Queen, and then the Satyr leads out of the wood Lord Spencer's eldest son dressed as a huntsman, and presents him to the Prince. The first night's show concluded, as Jonson tells us, with the starting and killing of a brace of deer in the sight of Her Majesty.

In structure, in substance, and in style *Arcades* is far nearer to this entertainment of Ben Jonson's than *Comus* is to any of Jonson's masques. Although, as I have said, it contains better poetry than any other surviving example of the entertainment, it remains nevertheless an occasional poem in a sense in which *Comus* does not; it does not, that is to say, really transcend the

[1] *Ben Jonson*, ed. C. H. Herford, Percy and Evelyn Simpson, Oxford, 1925–52 vol. vii, pp. 121–2.

occasion for which it was written. Most of it is very close to what might be called the average manner of Elizabethan pastoral, and I think there is only one passage that really soars beyond the scope of several of Milton's English predecessors and contemporaries. For this reason, some critics, among them Sir Herbert Grierson, would like to suppose that it may have been written as early as 1630, rather than, as I have suggested, in 1632. Perhaps, though, a sufficient explanation of the fact that the style of *Arcades* is so much less characteristically Miltonic than that of *Comus* is that in *Arcades* Milton was so much more limited by his commission and by the nature of the occasion: he was, in fact, limited to the devising of courtly and hyperbolical compliments, and even Milton, when so limited, was unable to produce much more than an agreeable trifle. As in *L'Allegro* and *Il Penseroso* and in *Comus*, we can see him availing himself here of the stock of poetic diction, which had been accumulated by Spenser and his successors, by the Elizabethan dramatists, and by the translators, but he does not here carry the process of modification and transformation nearly so far as he does in these poems.

At the beginning of Milton's contribution to the entertainment certain members of the Countess's family 'appear on the Scene in pastoral habit, moving toward the seat of State, with this Song.' The song, though perhaps a shade more distinguished, more dexterous, more craftsmanly, is not fundamentally different from many similar hyperbolic compliments in Jonson's masques: consider the last two stanzas:

> Mark what radiant state she spreds,
> In circle round her shining throne,
> Shooting her beams like silver threds,
> This this is she alone,
>   Sitting like a Goddes bright,
>   In the center of her light.
>
> Might she the wise *Latona* be,
> Or the towred *Cybele*,
> Mother of a hundred gods;
> *Juno* dare's not give her odds;
>   Who had thought this chime had held
>   A deity so unparalel'd?

Between this and the two concluding songs come some sixty lines of decasyllabic couplets addressed to the advancing nymphs and shepherds by the Genius of the Wood. Except for one passage, they are very much in the average manner of Elizabethan and Jacobean pastoral, and contain many echoes and parallels. I will content myself with offering two comments on the following lines:

> For know by lot from *Jove* I am the powr
> Of this fair Wood, and live in Oak'n bowr,
> To nurse the Saplings tall, and curl the grove
> With Ringlets quaint, and wanton windings wove.
> And all my Plants I save from nightly ill,
> Of noisom winds, and blasting vapours chill.
> And from the Bough brush off the evil dew ...   (ll. 44–50)

Notice first lines 46–7. Four times in his *Poly-Olbion* Drayton speaks of 'curled groves' or the 'curled heads' of groves; Jonson, in his Epistle *To Sir Robert Wroth* speaks of 'curled woods and painted meades', and William Browne speaks of the 'curl'd tops', of oaks and makes trees 'nod their curled heads'. It is clear, I think, that this favourite metaphor came into early seventeenth-century poetry through Sylvester's translation of Du Bartas, which had begun to appear in 1592 and which first appeared in complete form in 1605;

> When through their green boughs, whiffing Winds do whirl
> With wanton pufs their wauing locks to curl.[1]
>   une aure gentille
> S'esbatant à travers les rameaux verdoyans,
> Se plaît é frisoter leurs cheveux ondoyans.

This passage was first printed in French in 1578, but it is an interesting fact that Du Bartas' contemporary Jean Passerat in his *L'Hymne de la Paix*, printed in 1562, had written

> Zephire seul souffloit de qui la doulce haleine
> Frisoit mignardement les cheveus de la plaine,

a passage which Drummond of Hawthornden transcribed into

---

[1] *Du Bartas His Divine Weekes and Workes*, [1621], p. 30.

his commonplace book as one of Passerat's striking lines and which he inserted in a sonnet on the Spring:

The *Zephyres* curle the greene Lockes of the Plaine.[1]

This interesting piece of information I owe to the editor of the standard edition of Drummond's poems, for I must admit that I have only a very slight acquaintance with Du Bartas' French contemporaries and do not know to what extent what seem to be his own peculiar stylistic devices may also have been practised by them.[2]

One thing, however, is clear: that Du Bartas had a special fondness for describing nature in terms of art and that through Sylvester's translation the practice was introduced into English poetry, where it at once found many imitators. For example, the second song in *Arcades* begins:

O're the smooth enameld green.

It is, I suppose, just possible that Milton himself borrowed this phrase directly from the fourth canto of the *Inferno* (ll.118–19), where Dante says:

Colà diritto, sopra 'l verde smalto,
mi fuor mostrati li spiriti magni,

('There directly, upon the green enamel, were shown to me the great spirits'). Ruskin, in the third volume of *Modern Painters*[3] has a lengthy attack on what he regards as the abuse and misuse by later poets of the word 'enamelled' as applied to grass. He does not insist (as he perhaps might have done) that they had all ultimately derived the phrase from Dante, but he insists that

---

[1] *Poetical Works*, ed. L. E. Kastner, 1913, I, 61 and 212.

[2] I have noticed at least one example of the same metaphor in Ronsard, 'Le Narssis', ll.22–3 (*Bocage*, 1554; *Oeuvres*, ed. Laumonier, vol. vi, Paris 1930, p. 74):

    & ja la forest veufve
    Herisse sa perruque.

It seems likely that Du Bartas, Passerat, Ronsard and the rest believed that they had classical precedent for these extravagances in the almost habitual use by Roman poets of the word *comae*, tresses, to describe the leaves of trees. If, the French poets may well have thought, it is comely and classical to say that trees have tresses, why should not we go one better, and speak of the wind as curling or frizzing their tresses; or why should we not even occasionally speak of their periwigs?

[3] Part IV, ch. xiv, § 47–50.

Dante alone is using the phrase correctly, and that he is comparing, not grass in general, but, quite specifically, the grass of
the Inferno, 'laid as a tempering and cooling substance over the
dark, metallic, gloomy ground', to enamel. If, then, Milton took
the phrase directly from Dante he is using it in what Ruskin
would regard as the inappropriate manner of Du Bartas, for in
such contexts the word *enamelled* occurs repeatedly in Sylvester's
translation and in many Elizabethan and Jacobean poets. Sylvester has, for example, 'th' inammeld meads' (edn. 1621, p. 208),
'this enammeld vale' (p. 262), and—a passage where nature is
very much 'trickt and frounc't' by art—

> Th' inammell'd Vallies, where the liquid glass
> Of silver Brooks in curled streams doth pass. (p. 282)[1]

In the last line of the passage I quoted, 'And from the Boughs
brush off the evil dew,' there is one of those Shakespearean
reminiscences or rather, perhaps, one of those conscious adaptations of Shakespearean phrases, of which we have already
noticed several examples in *L'Allegro* and *Il Penseroso* and of
which we shall notice many more in *Comus*. Milton is remembering Caliban's words in *The Tempest*, although he is

---

[1] Ronsard was a great enameller: *I. Livre des Amours*, no. clxiii, 'Voicy le bois,
que ma sainte Angelette', l.8:

> Le bel émail de l'herbe nouvellete;

cxcix, ll.1–2;

> Pille, Garçon, d'une main larronnesse
> Le bel esmail de la verte saison;

II. Livre des amours, 'Quand ce beau Printemps je voy', ll.43–5:

> Quand je voy tant de couleurs
>   Et de fleurs
> Qui esmaillent un rivage;

Elegie 'Voicy le temps, Candé, qui joyeux nous convie', ll.23–4:

>   les Nymphes dans ces prez
> Esmaillez, peintunez, verdurez, diaprez.

(Text of 1578: *Oeuvres*, ed. Vaganay, Paris 1923–30, i. 179, 212; ii. 137; iv. 276.)
The word does not occur in Chaucer, but it occurs in Dunbar, *The Twa Mariit
Wemen and the Wedo*, ll.30–1:

> Arrayit ryallie about with mony rich vardour,
> That nature full nobillie annamalit with flouris.

applying them in a quite different sense, and transforming the
maleficent magic of Sycorax into the beneficent magic of the
Genius of the Wood:

> As wicked dew as e'er my mother brush'd
> With raven's feather from unwholesome fen
> Drop on you both![1]

The greater part of this speech of the Genius of the Wood,
charming and elegant though it is, is what might be called
gradus work, a skilful combination and adaptation of the properties
and diction of the Elizabethan and Jacobean pastoral poets and
sometimes of Shakespeare. There is one passage, however, which
I have already mentioned in connection with *At a Solemn Musick*,
which is far more characteristically Miltonic, and which seems to
soar considerably beyond the context and the occasion—the
passage where Milton remembers the Platonic myth about
Necessity, the Fates, the spheres and the sirens.[2]

> But els in deep of night when drowsines
> Hath lockt up mortal sense, then listen I
> To the celestial *Sirens* harmony,
> That sit upon the nine enfolded Sphears,
> And sing to those that hold the vital shears,
> And turn the Adamantine spindle round,
> On which the fate of gods and men is wound.
> Such sweet compulsion doth in musick ly,
> To lull the daughters of *Necessity*,
> And keep unsteddy Nature to her law,
> And the low world in measur'd motion draw
> After the heavenly tune, which none can hear
> Of human mould with grosse unpurged ear.   (ll.61–73)

This passage reads to me like a first expression of what was to
find such memorable expression in *At a Solemn Musick*; and
suggests that *Arcades* was written only a very little earlier than
At a Solemn Musick and that Milton resumed his Platonic
meditation almost immediately after he had been compelled to
pretend—no doubt rather against the grain—that his first

---

[1] *The Tempest*, I. ii. 321–3.   [2] See above, pp. 105–9.

expression of it had been no more than the artful climax of an elaborate and courtly compliment to the old Countess of Derby. 'And yet', continues the Genius of the Wood,

> And yet such musick worthiest were to blaze
> The peerles height of her immortal praise,
> Whose lustre leads us, and for her most fit,
> If my inferior hand or voice could hit
> Inimitable sounds . . .   (ll.74–78)

If the general style of *Arcades* seems immature and conventional in comparison with that of *Comus*, the explanation lies only partly in the fact that *Comus* was written two years later; it lies mainly, I think, in the fact that in *Comus* Milton was so much less circumscribed. He would, one cannot but think, have been very unwilling to write any more short entertainments, or contributions to entertainments: if, when he had condescended to steal some hours from his private studies in order to compose a few lines of elegant *gradus* work, the muse suddenly visited him and inspired him to write something worthy not merely of the occasion but of himself, he would be most unwilling that it should be lost in a trivial or unworthy context. That, perhaps, is why he almost immediately set about transforming the Platonic passage on the spheral music, the most Miltonic thing in *Arcades*, into 'Blest pair of *Sirens*' for, as I have tried to show in my examination of *L'Allegro* and *Il Penseroso*, Milton's chief poetic gift was his wonderful sense of design, his architectonic power, his ability to write, not merely good lines and good passages, but poems which were organic wholes, poems in which the beauty of the parts depended very largely on their subordination to the whole and on our continued awareness of the whole in the parts, poems where

> totam . . . infusa per artus
> Mens agitat molem.

And closely connected with this sense of design (indeed, only another aspect of it) was Milton's sense of *decorum*, of the importance of preserving unity of tone and a style and diction appropriate to the subject. When he was merely asked for a graceful poetic compliment, his very sense of *decorum* prevented him, so to speak, from ever getting into top gear. In Ben Jonson's masques, in spite of Jonson's attempts to persuade himself and others of the importance of what he was doing, we are continually aware of the way in which the exercise of his poetic gift is being cramped and circumscribed by the essential ephemerality, or even, from a strictly literary point of view, the essential triviality, of the occasion. When at last Milton was persuaded to write what he called a masque, he wrote it, so to speaak, on his own terms. He did indeed accept certain restrictions, but only in so far as he was able to transform them into conditions of fruitful activity. The spectacular, the occasional, the complimentary elements are all there, but they are there in what Milton regarded as their proper places, that is to say, in very subordinate ones. Such restrictions as he has accepted are no more fettering to him than are the verse-forms he has employed.

≫ 8 ≪

Comus

As early as July 1631, the Earl of Bridgewater had been made Lord President of the Council of Wales and of the Marches, that, is, of the counties on the Welsh border, a position comparable in nature, if not in importance, with that of Lord Lieutenant of Ireland. For some reason he did not formally enter upon his duties until the autumn of 1634, and it was on Michaelmas Night, the 29th of September, on the occasion of his inauguration at his official residence of Ludlow Castle, that *Comus* was performed. Since Lawes composed the music for the singing parts, himself took the part of Thyrsis, and in 1637 published the poem, without mentioning Milton's name, but obviously with Milton's consent, we may assume that it was through him that Milton received this second request to provide poetic entertainment for the Bridgewater family.

'When', I said, 'Milton was at last persuaded to write what he called a masque': that, and that alone, is what he called it; in the two surviving manuscripts and in the three printed texts the only title of the poem is 'A Mask'. The first editor of Milton who entitled the poem 'Comus' was Thomas Warton, in his first edition of the shorter poems (1785):[1] 'I have ventured', he there wrote (p. 126), 'to insert this title, which has had the full sanction of use.' In his second edition (1791) Warton omitted this explanation, apparently because it seemed to him no longer necessary.

---

[1] It seems that the first person so to entitle the poem in print was John Toland, who in his *Life of Milton*, 1698, wrote of Milton's '*Comus* or Mask presented at *Ludlow* Castle'. See *The Early Lives of Milton*, ed. Helen Darbishire, 1932, p. 114. A.L.

Warton, as his words imply, was not the inventor of the title. It was first used by John Dalton for his adaptation of Milton's masque as what was then called a 'mixed opera'. This adaptation, in which Dalton inserted passages from several other of Milton's poems, together with several songs of his own, and for which Arne composed the music, was first performed in 1738. It was several times revived, in 1750, with a prologue by Dr Johnson, for the benefit of Milton's granddaughter, and it became one of the most popular mixed operas of the eighteenth and early nineteenth centuries. It was thus only after it had reached the public stage, where every piece must have a title, that Milton's masque acquired the title *Comus*.

Before beginning my investigation of *Comus*, I will mention one very interesting and important matter which, although it could well repay careful investigation, I shall only be able to treat occasionally and incidentally, that, namely, of the relation between the two manuscripts and the three printed texts.[1]

The original, or uncorrected, version in the Trinity College manuscript was obviously made before the performance of the masque on the Michaelmas Night 1634, for the Egerton or Bridgewater manuscript, which is assumed to be in the handwriting of Henry Lawes, does not contain the alterations which Milton subsequently made in the Trinity manuscript, and which were incorporated in the edition which Lawes published in 1637. The only textual value of the Bridgewater manuscript which, together with some errors in transcription, contains several cuts and alterations evidently made by Lawes for the performance, is that it sometimes enables us to recover original readings which in the Trinity manuscript have been illegibly erased. Milton made two further alterations in the Trinity manuscript after the edition of 1637 had been published; he also made various alterations in the editions which he himself published in 1645 and 1673. Our examination of the drafts and the fair copy of *At a Solemn Musick*

---

[1] J. T. Shawcross in his detailed study, 'Certain Relationships of the Manuscripts of *Comus*', comes to very different conclusions concerning the Bridgewater manuscript. He finds that it was not transcribed until autumn–winter 1637–8, and that the handwriting is not that of Henry Lawes. See *The Papers of the Bibliographical Society of America*, vol. 54, 1960. A.L.

has already shown us how much a study of Milton's revisions can teach us about the nature of his art. That poem, however, is a rather exceptional case, since it was one of the two which Milton did not merely transcribe but actually composed in the Trinity manuscript. Moreover, it is a short poem, and to attempt to deal in the same detached manner with all the revised passages in *Comus* and then to draw some general conclusions would take far more time that we can now afford. I shall therefore only occasionally and incidentally attend to the revisions in *Comus*, and I will refer any who may care to pursue the matter further to an important study by Professor C. S. Lewis entitled, '*A Note on Comus*', in the *Review of English Studies* for 1932. Professor Lewis, after numerous comparisons, reaches the interesting conclusion that in all, or nearly all, of his revisions Milton was guided by his sense of *decorum*, his sense of the style and diction appropriate to the particular kind of poem he was writing, his desire to preserve unity of tone. In order to preserve this unity of tone Milton was willing to sacrifice many things which, in themselves, might well seem to us more striking or more beautiful than what he substituted for them, and we might often be tempted to call these substitutions conventional. But, insists Professor Lewis, they are conventional only in the sense that Milton, 'having determined on what plane of convention (at what distance from real life and violent emotion) he is to work, brings everything on to that plane; how many individual beauties he must thereby lose is to him a matter of indifference'. If, in the light of the evidence he produces, you regard Professor Lewis's conclusion as correct, you will also, I think, regard it as an important confirmation of something on which I have been continually insisting, namely, that Milton's greatness as a poet consists very largely in his architectonic power. He was not, like so many of his contemporaries and predecessors, a poet of fine passages, but a poet of fine poems.

Even if I leave almost entirely aside this important matter of the revisions, it will still be difficult briefly to do anything like justice to *Comus*. There are so many ways in which it can and should be considered. Milton himself called it simply 'A Mask', and although it differs greatly from the many typical examples of the masque which have been preserved, it is important to see *how* it differs, and this will require an examination of at least some other examples of the masque. Many critics have insisted that it should be regarded rather as an example of the Pastoral Drama than of the masque, and there is much justice in this contention, but here again we can reach no conclusion until we have made some comparisons. Professor Wright has suggested that *Comus* should be regarded as a kind of Platonic dialogue in verse, and he has himself done more than any other commentator to reveal the nature and extent of Milton's indebtedness to Plato. This question of the young Milton's Platonism and, more generally, of his intense preoccupation with moral, philosophical, and religious ideas, is a most important one. How far is his sense of design—as distinct from his sheer power of handling words, a power which many lesser poets have perhaps equalled—how far is that ever-present sense of design, in which he excels most poets, connected with, dependent upon, the spiritual ardour, the moral and intellectual fire within him? Or, if that question is too difficult and too speculative, consider this: although *Comus* is far more than a collection of fine passages, it does in fact contain numerous passages of far greater poetry than are to be found in all Jonson's or any other masques; and the fineness of many of these fine passages is closely connected with the weight and substantiality of what they express and with the fact that Milton is only really incidentally concerned with the celebration of a particular occasion and with the devising of elegant compliments to the Earl of Bridgewater and his family. Then, having considered *Comus* in relation to the masque, in relation to pastoral drama, and in relation to Milton's Platonism, idealism, and religious faith, we must proceed from the more general to the more particular and consider it as a poem by John Milton, revealing, as do *L'Allegro* and *Il Penseroso*, but on a much larger scale, his characteristic sense of design, and of *decorum*, his industrious and select reading, and his eclectic use or adaptation of the diction of earlier poets.

ITS RELATION TO THE COURT MASQUE

I will begin by saying something of the Court masque.[1] I cannot
here enter into the question of its possible origin in folklore and
ancient superstition, nor does it seem necessary to insist at
any length upon its many affinities with the allegorical shows,
spectacles, pageants, devices and entertainments which were so
popular during the sixteenth and seventeenth centuries and which
find so many reflections in Spenser's *Faerie Queene*. Ronald Bayne,
in his excellent chapter on 'Masque and Pastoral' in the *Cambridge
History of English Literature*, remarks that

Such famous descriptions as the cave of Mammon and the bower of
Bliss are like the set pieces which Inigo Jones tried to make real to
the eye when the masque became a fixture at the end of the great hall;[2]

to which I may add that, in spite of his professed dislike for his
poetry, Jonson in his masques is often very close to Spenser and
to the disciples of Spenser, for he there cultivates, with the
appropriate style and diction, an allegorical, mythological, sometimes pastoral vein which is only very occasionally apparent in
his other work. First, though, let us concentrate our attention,
not on those features which the masque shares with other
forms of entertainment and other forms of literature, but on that
which is peculiar to itself.

   As a definition of the courtly or complimentary masque in its
simplest form I will offer the following slightly modified version
of a description by Sir E. K. Chambers:

The mask is not primarily a drama; it is an episode in an indoor revel
of dancing. Masked and otherwise disguised persons [bringing with
them torch-bearers and musicians] come, by convention unexpectedly,
into the hall, as a compliment to the hosts or the principal guests.
Often they bring them gifts; always they dance before them, and then
invite them to join the dance.[3]

Such a complimentary 'mumming', as the records call it, was

---

[1] Recent studies of the masque form include Stephen Orgel, *The Jonsonian Masque*,
Harvard 1965, and J. G. Demaray, *Milton and the Masque Tradition*, Harvard 1968.
A.L.

[2] vi. 335.   [3] *The Elizabethan Stage*, 1923, i. 149.

performed by a company of London citizens before Prince Richard at Candlemas 1377, but whether, before they departed, the mummers actually danced with the Prince and his courtiers, or whether the two parties danced separately, is a fact which the records do not make absolutely clear. At any rate, this very important, this distinguishing, characteristic of the masque, namely, the concluding invitation of the masquers to their hosts to dance with them, seems, if it ever existed in England, to have dropped out during the fifteenth century, or to have been forgotten; and when it was first introduced (or revived) at the court of Henry VIII, it was noticed by the chronicler Halle as an Italian innovation.

On the Twelfth Night of 1522, the Kyng with xi other wer disguised, after the maner of Italie, called a maske, a thynge not seen afore in Englande, thei were appareled in garmentes long and brode, wrought all with gold, with visers and cappes of gold, and after the banket doen, these maskers came in, with six gentlemen disguised in silke bearyng staffe torches, and desired the ladies to daunce, some were content, and some that knew the fashion of it refused, because it was not a thyng commonly seen. And after thei daunced and commoned together, as the fashion of the maskes is, thei toke their leave and departed, and so did the Quene, and all the ladies.[1]

Henceforth, this 'commoning together' (to keep Halle's phrase), implying as it did a community of status between them, remained a characteristic (one might say, *the* characteristic) feature of the masque, and by the end of Henry VIII's reign 'Mask' had become the official name for such entertainments and the old name of 'disguising' had become obsolete.

The masque was and remained essentially an amateur, not a professional performance, although it might be either very simple or very elaborate, and although not merely professional musicians and scene-painters, but even professional actors, might be called in, to serve as presenters, to sing, or to speak passages of dramatic or semi-dramatic dialogue. But in spite of all this professional paraphernalia, the whole performance revolved around the masquers, who neither spoke nor sang, but only

---

[1] E. K. Chambers, *Eliz. Stage*, i, 153.

danced. As Sir Edmund Chambers remarks:

The spectacular and literary elaboration of the Jacobean mask must not be allowed to blind our eyes to the fact that after all it was not a dramatic illusion but a choregraphic compliment which remained the central purpose of the entertainment. Scenery and speech and song occupy perhaps a disproportionate share of the attention of the poets who, to their own glorification and that of the architects, wrote the descriptions; but the greater part of the considerable number of hours during which the mask lasted was devoted to the actual dancing. And the dancing involved an intimacy, and not a detachment, in the relation between performers and spectators.[1]

The most notable and most ample provider of Court masques was Ben Jonson, who during the twenty years between 1605 and 1625 supplied nearly thirty. Let us consider some of their characteristics. First, though, I must remark that the printed texts of them often bear about the same relation to the performance as does a programme note to the performance of a ballet. A great part, often a very great part of the text consists of elaborate prose descriptions of scene, change of scene, costumes, and so forth, and, apart from this, the text contains only a few songs and a few lines of dialogue, whose intrinsic literary value is very slight. Perhaps only from a small minority of these texts can we derive much specifically literary pleasure; often the chief, or even the only, pleasure consists in attempting to reconstruct in our imaginations the occasion and the scene.

I will begin with the element of spectacle. In *The Masque of Blackness*, Jonson's first Court masque the long-voyaging twelve daughters of Niger, who, discontented with their blackness, have been commanded in a vision to seek a land whose name ends in -tania, at last reach Britannia, which, they are assured, is ruled by a sun able to 'blanch an ÆTHIOPE', and are told that if they return to their native land, perform certain rites, and then come back to Britannia a year hence their skins will be made white. Here are some details from Jonson's elaborate prose description which precedes the dialogue and the songs: a landscape of small woods; an artificial sea; six tritons, a pair of

---

[1] *Eliz. Stage*, i. 195.

sea-naiads; Oceanus and Niger on sea-horses. 'These induced the
Masquers, which were twelve *Nymphs, Negro's*; and the daughters
of NIGER; attended by so many of the OCEANIAE, which were
their *light-bearers.*' These masquers were placed in a great concave
shell, which moved up and down on the artificial sea; around it
swam six sea-monsters bearing the twelve torch-bearers. In the
sequel, *The Masque of Beauty*, performed three years later, where
the twelve daughters of Niger, together with four of their sisters,
return to Britannia and are transformed, the spectacular element
is still more elaborate—so elaborate that I must ask you to read
Jonson's description for yourselves. *Hymenaei*, celebrating the
wedding of the Earl of Essex and Frances Howard, opens with a
bridal procession, ushered by Hymen, to Juno's altar, of which
Jonson has given a most elaborate prose description and in which
he has tried to incorporate every detail of the Roman ritual. At
the beginning of *The Hue and Cry after Cupid*, celebrating the
marriage of the Earl of Haddington and Lady Elizabeth Radcliffe,
daughter of the Earl of Sussex, Venus, in a triumphal car drawn
by doves and swans, and attended by the three Graces, appears on
the top of a red cliff which emblematises and honours the family
of Radcliffe.

I have begun by describing a few examples of the spectacular
elements, because it is what first strikes a reader of Jonson's
masques, and because even the few examples and details I have
mentioned should at once suggest how far the mere printed
texts are from possessing anything like the literary self-sufficiency
and substantiality of Milton's *Comus*. Nevertheless, pageantry and
spectacle, although an indispensable concomitant, is not in itself
the specific characteristic of Jonson's masques; the specific and
peculiar characteristic of Jonson's and of all other masques, the
centre around which everything else revolves, is what I have
called the pulling of the cracker, the opening of the Easter egg,
the cutting of the pie: that is to say, the ingenious discovery or
revelation of the concealed masquers and their dancing, first with
one another and then with members of the audience. Let us now
examine a few of Jonson's masques and try, so far as we can, to concentrate our attention exclusively upon the cracker and its pulling.

In *The Hue and Cry after Cupid*, after the anti-masque of Joci and Risus and the entry of Hymen, Vulcan appears, strikes the red cliff which has formed the back of the scene and reveals a vast sphere in which the masquers, representing the signs of the Zodiac, are placed. In due course they descend and dance. In the *Masque of Queens*, after an anti-masque of witches, representing various kinds of ill-fame, has suddenly vanished at the sound of a loud music, the House of Fame is discovered, with the twelve masquers (the Queen herself and eleven noble ladies) representing various kinds of female heroic virtue, enthroned above it. While Fame is speaking they descend and re-appear in triumphal chariots, to which the hags, who have formed the anti-masque, are bound. After riding about the stage while a triumphal song is sung

they alighted from they^r *Chariots*, and daunc'd forth they^r first *Daunce*; then a second, immediately following it: both right curious, and full of subtile, and excellent Changes ... The first was to the *Cornets*, the second to the *Violins*. After wch they tooke out the Men, and dauncd the *Measures*; entertayning the time, almost to the space of an hower, wth singular variety.

After pausing for some rest while another song was sung, the masquers apparently danced a third formal dance among themselves, and then galliards and corantos with members of the audience.

And then they^r last *Daunce*, no lesse elegant (in the place) then the rest. wth wch they tooke they^r *chariots* agayne, and triumphing about the stage, had they^r returne to the *House of Fame* celebrated wth this last *song*, whose *Notes* (as to the former) were the worke, & Honor of my excellent Freind, *Alfonso Ferrabosco*.[1]

I have quoted at some length from Jonson's description here because it illustrates particularly well how the dancing with which it concluded was the crown and consummation, the *raison d'être*, of the whole performance. Whatever poet, musician and architect, professional actors and singers, had done before was only a prelude to the real business of the evening, only a splendid

---

[1] *Ben Jonson*, ed. C. H. Herford, Percy and Evelyn Simpson, Oxford, 1925–52, vol. vii, pp. 315–16.

introduction to a kind of fancy dress ball. In *Oberon*, after some agreeable but rather inconsequential anti-masquing of Satyrs before Oberon's palace, the cock crows, and the palace opens, revealing the fairies, the Knights Masquers in their seats, and Oberon in a triumphal car drawn by two white bears. In *Pleasure reconciled to Virtue*, after unvirtuous pleasures have been represented by anti-masques of Comus and his revellers and of pigmies, Mercy announces that Pleasure and Virtue are going to be reconciled in the sight of 'Hesperus, ye glory of ye West', and the twelve masquers, one of them Prince Charles, emerge from the top of Mount Atlas, which throughout has composed the scene. In *Time Vindicated* Fame declares that she has been sent by Time to summon all sorts of worthy persons to view a great spectacle he means to exhibit. After a dramatic blank-verse induction, in which false fame is satirised, and after two anti-masques, the scene opens and reveals Saturn (Time) sitting with Venus and certain votaries who form the chorus. Fame declares that Venus has discovered that Hecate keeps certain glories of the time obscured, and has persuaded Saturn to set them free,

> As being fitter to adorne the age,
> By you restor'd on earth, most like his owne:
> And fill this world of beautie here, your Court.[1]

Whereupon the masquers are discovered. Here the discovery of the masquers is retarded until the very end, and there is, as it were, a cracker within a cracker; on the other hand, in *Pan's Anniversarie*, after some introductory pastoral song, the masquers are revealed almost immediately, sitting around the fountain of light, with the musicians, attired like the priests of Pan, standing beneath them, and they remain seated above until the Boeotian visitors have danced their anti-masque, when they are called upon, as the true Arcadians, to descend. In *The Fortunate Isles*, after an induction which has little connection with the masque proper, the Intelligence of Jupiter's sphere informs that great Neptune, King James, that the floating island of Macaria, the island of the blest, has been commanded to adhere to his Britannia,

---

[1] ibid, p. 664.

That where the happie spirits liue, hereafter
Might be no question made, by the most curious.[1]

The island is then 'discovered', with the masquers 'sitting in their
seuerall seiges'.

In reviewing these examples of the discovery of the masquers
I have sometimes had to refer incidentally to the anti-masque.
This device is not present in Jonson's earliest masques, and he
seems to have hit upon it almost by chance. Since it pleased
both himself and his patrons, he made it a regular feature of his
masques for several years, and then, not always very successfully,
replaced it by more or less realistic inductions which preceded
the masque proper, and, even when enjoyable in themselves, did
not really blend with it. The anti-masque first appears in his
Hue and Cry after Cupid, where Cupid is attended by twelve boys,
'most antickly attyr'd', representing Joci and Risus. Jonson
describes his conception of it at the beginning of the printed
text of his *Masque of Queens*.

And because her Ma.tie (best knowing, that a principall part of life
in these *Spectacles* lay in theyr variety) had commaunded mee to think
on some *Daunce*, or shew, that might præcede hers, and haue the
place of a foyle, or false-*Masque*; I was carefull to decline not only
from others, but mine owne stepps in that kind, since the last yeare
I had an *Anti-Masque* of Boyes.

Since, therefore, his argument was the celebration of honourable
and true fame, he devised an anti-masque of twelve women
representing the opposites of good fame,

not as a *Masque*, but a spectacle of strangenesse, producing multiplicity of Gesture, and not vnaptly sorting wth the current, and whole
fall of the Deuise.[2]

In *Oberon* the anti-masque is formed by eleven satyrs and a
Silenus. In *Pleasure reconciled to Virtue*, there are two anti-masques
representing unvirtuous pleasure, one by Comus and his attend-
ants, who vanish on the appearance of Hercules, and one by some
pygmies, who prepare to murder Hercules while he is asleep.

---

[1] ibid, p. 722.   [2] ibid, p. 282.

In *Pan's Anniversarie* there is an anti-masque of Boeotians who have come to challenge the true Arcadians, represented by the masquers proper, at fencing and other sports. In all these anti-masques the parts are taken by professionals, who, unlike the masquers proper, speak and sing as well as dance. For this reason, the anti-masque, unlike the masque proper, could be developed dramatically, and in his later masques Jonson developed it into, or rather, I should say, replaced it by, a kind of induction, which was really an almost independent dramatic scene, not artistically *in pari materia* with the masque that followed. In these inductions one may observe the immeasurable inferiority of Jonson's satirico-comical prose to his satirico-comical blank verse. For example, *News from the New World discovered in the Moon* opens with some intolerably tedious prose dialogue between a printer, a chronicler, a news-factor, and two heralds, who bring them news of a country in the moon. The satirical blank verse induction to *Time Vindicated* is incomparably superior. Since persons really worthy of the time's admiration are ultimately going to be presented, there is first an anti-masque composed of the ignorant and absurd admirers of a vainglorious verse-satirist, followed—rather inconsequentially—by a second anti-masque of tumblers and jugglers brought in by the Cat and Fiddle. In *The Fortunate Isles* Mere-Foole, a gullible student of magic, is fooled by Jophiel, the Intelligence of Jupiter's sphere, who persuades him that all his prayers have been answered and that he may now call up whatever spirits he pleases; those of his choice form an incongruous anti-masque, which Jophiel dismisses, with an apology to the King. The blank verse, in some ways reminiscent of *The Alchemist*, is greatly superior to the prose dialogue in other masques, although, just as in *Time Vindicated*, there is no real artistic unity between this induction and the masque proper.

Just as what may be called the architecture of the masque culminates in the ingenious discovery of the concealed masquers, even so, as you must already have observed from my brief descriptions, the poetic lines, or poetic flight, culminates in an elaborate compliment to the King, the Queen, or the Prince. In *The Masque of Blackness* the daughters of Niger are told that Britannia is ruled by a sun able to 'blanch an Æthiope'; in *The Masque of Queens* Perseus declares how far Bel-anna surpasses all the other eleven representatives of female heroic virtue; Pleasure and Virtue are reconciled in the sight of 'Hesperus, ye glory of ye west'; the conclusion of *Time Vindicated* is an elaborate compliment to King James on his love of hunting, and in *The Fortunate Isles* the royal Neptune is informed that Macaria, the floating island of the blest, has been commanded to adhere to his Britannia.

Without labouring the contrast between these hyperbolical eulogies and the concluding lines of *Comus*, what can we say about the positive literary value of Jonson's masques? As pure literature, several are quite negligible, and the only pleasure to be derived from them consists, as I have said, in trying to reconstruct imaginatively the spectacle and the occasion. Some are faintly charming; some contain a few memorable lines, or, occasionally, a really remarkable song; one or two can be read with pleasure almost throughout, but not one, regarded purely as literature, forms a really satisfying artistic whole. Apart from a few memorable songs, I am inclinded to say that the best pieces of continuous writing in Jonson's masques are the anti-masque of witches in *The Masque of Queens* and portions of *Oberon*, where Jonson is working the vein which Shakespeare had opened in *A Midsummer Night's Dream*, and, in doing so, adding a certain slightly grotesque and earthy beauty that was peculiarly his own—these together with the blank-verse inductions to *Time Vindicated* and *The Fortunate Isles*, where Jonson is really forsaking the masque-form and returning to something like the comic style of *Volpone* and *The Alchemist*. The grotesquely fantastic beauty, the grotesquely fantastic satire, in these four pieces of writing is peculiarly and characteristically Jonsonian; but in the pastoral, mythological and complimentary verse which predominates in his masques he seldom achieves anything at all noticeably different from the many other Elizabethan and Jacobean poets in whose manner he was writing. His hand was too much subdued to that it worked in; he was unable to transform the traditional properties, traditional imagery and traditional diction and to confer upon them that ineffable distinction which Milton has done in *Comus* and elsewhere. He was too

circumscribed by the machinery and the occasion: except in anti-
masques and inductions, his dialogue had, generally speaking, to
be confined to mere presenters, and by the time he has explained
why something is going to appear, interpreted it when it has
appeared, and delivered his compliment, the masquers are ready
to dance, and he is hustled off the stage. In the introductions to
the printed texts of his masques it is pathetic to observe him trying
to persuade himself and his readers that what he has been doing
has a permanent literary value and has not merely served to
grace an occasion. In his long introduction to *Hymenaei*, a
masque celebrating the marriage of the Earl of Essex and Frances
Howard, he declares:

It is a noble and iust aduantage, that the things subiected to *understanding* haue of those which are obiected to *sense*, that the one sort are
but momentarie, and meerely taking; the other impressing, and lasting:
Else the glorie of all these *solemnities* had perish'd like a blaze, and gone
out, in the *beholders* eyes. So short-liu'd are the *bodies* of all things, in
comparison of their *soules*.

Therefore, he declares, the greatest princes have not merely
insisted that their spectacles should be magnificent, but have been

curious after the most high, and heartie *inuentions*, to furnish the inward
parts: (and those grounded vpon *antiquitie*, and solide *learnings*).[1]

Such language suggests that Jonson really believed, or had
persuaded himself to believe, that he had achieved something
comparable with what Milton was to achieve in *Comus*—a claim
which cannot survive the briefest inspection. The spectacle, no
doubt, was magnificent; the procession which Hymen ushers to
Juno's altar is indeed grounded, almost to the point of pedantry,
'vpon *antiquities* and solide *learnings*'; but how sadly undistinguished is the verse, limited as for the most part it is to
commenting upon and interpreting the spectacle. After a first
masque of eight men, representing the four humours and the
four affections, have threatened to disturb the procession to
Juno's altar and have been restrained by Reason, Heaven is
discovered above, with Juno enthroned, Jupiter above her,

[1] ibid, p. 209.

brandishing his thunderbolt, Iris below her, and on either side
eight ladies, representing her powers as goddess of marriage,
who form the second masque. Reason then begins:

> ANd see, where IVNO, whose great name
> Is VNIO, in the *anagram*,
> Displays her glistering state, and chaire,
> As she enlightened all the *ayre*!
> Harke how the charming tunes doe beate
> In sacred concords 'bout her seat!
> And loe! to grace what these intend,
> Eight of her noblest *powers* descend,
> Which are enstil'd her *faculties*,
> That gouerne nuptiall mysteries.[1]

This is a not unfair specimen of the kind of verse to be found in
this and in many other of Jonson's masques. Any number of
his minor contemporaries could have done as well, but could
even Milton, or Shakespeare either, for that matter, have produced anything very much more memorable if they had been so
confined?

Milton did not allow himself to be so confined. He called his
poem 'A Mask', but, as some commentators have observed, it
really has more affinity with the pastoral drama, a form which we
shall have to consider later, than with the court masque as
practised by Ben Jonson and others. The specific and central
characteristic of the masque, that which differentiates it from
other forms of entertainment, is absent, and such other
characteristics of the masque as are present are present only in a
very attenuated and subordinate fashion.

There are, in the first place, no masquers and no cracker. In all
Jonson's masques everything, as we have seen, revolves around
the masquers, who neither speak nor sing, who are usually revealed by some ingenious device after curiosity has been excited,
and whose dancing, first with one another and then with
members of the audience, is the *raison d'être* of the whole performance. There are no such masquers in *Comus*. Milton's central
figures are the two brothers and their sister, who are not masquers

---

[1] ibid, p. 217.

at all; they all speak, and the sister even sings, and, if they dance at all, it is apparently only in some general revel at the very end of the performance and before the Spirit's epilogue. The entry of Comus and his crew and their dancing may indeed be regarded as a kind of anti-masque, although there is no masque proper, only the general revels, the 'victorious dance', at the very end of the performance, to which it can be regarded as the foil. And how simple and attenuated is that spectacular element on which Ben Jonson and Inigo Jones lavished such ingenuity and such vast expense, and how unobtrusive and incidental, among all the philosophic debate and pastoral description, are the occasional compliments to the Earl of Bridgewater and his office and to Henry Lawes in comparison with those elaborate and hyperbolical compliments to King James and his Britannia in which the text of so many of Jonson's masques used to culminate!

Let us examine in detail (it will not take very long) such masque-like characteristics as we can discover in this masque without masquers. And let us begin with the dancing. At lines 92–3 in the 1645 edition comes the stage-direction:

Comus enters with a Charming Rod in one hand, his Glass in the other, with him a rout of Monsters headed like sundry sorts of wilde Beasts, but otherwise like Men and Women, their Apparel glistring, they com in making a riotous and unruly noise, with Torches in their hands.

The direction in the Trinity College manuscript is substantially the same, except that it is supplemented by the words 'intrant κωμάζοντες', enter conversing, which reminds us that Milton was thinking of the κῶμος, that processional revel of Attic villagers at the winter festival of Dionysus, out of which comedy κωμῳδία, the song of the Comos, ultimately developed. At line 143 Comus exclaims:

Com, knit hands, and beat the ground,
In a light fantastick round.

Here the 1643 edition simply prints '*The Measure*', but in the Trinity manuscript this direction is supplemented by the bracketed words, 'in a wild rude & wanton antick'. There is no more dancing until the very end of the performance, and the

stage-directions in the 1645 edition do not make quite clear what
actually took place. After Sabrina has risen and released the Lady
from her enchantment, the Attendant Spirit proposes to conduct
the children to their father's residence, where many friends have
met this night to congratulate him, and where they shall catch
the rural swains at their sport. That they leave the stage at line
957, before the change of scene to Ludlow town and castle, is
made clear by the direction 'Exeunt' in the Trinity manuscript.
The 1645 edition then reads:

The Scene changes, presenting *Ludlow* Town and the Presidents
Castle, then com in Countrey-Dancers, after them the attendant
Spirit, with the two Brothers and the Lady.

This does not mean that there is a kind of procession, headed by
the country dancers and followed by the Spirit and the children,
but that the Spirit and the children enter while the country
dancing is in progress: this is made clear by the direction in the
Trinity manuscript: 'At those sports the Dæmon wth ye 2 bro.
& th Ladie enter.' Milton originally wrote 'After those sports',
but replaced 'After' by 'at' in order to make it clear that the
children and the Spirit (or, as he originally called it, the Dæmon)
enter while the sports are still in progress. The Bridgewater
manuscript, a transcript made by Lawes for the actual performance,[1] makes this still clearer: 'towards the end of these sports
the demon with the 2 brothers and the ladye come in'. The
country dances, then, may have lasted for a considerable time. At
line 958 the Spirit sings:

> Back Shepherds, back, anough your play,
> Till next Sun-shine holiday,
> Here be without duck or nod
> Other trippings to be trod
> Of lighter toes, and such Court guise
> As *Mercury* did first devise
> With the mincing *Dryades*
> On the Lawns, and on the Leas.

Then the Spirit sings a second song, which in the 1645 edition is

---

[1] See above, p. 175, n. 1.

headed 'This second Song presents them to their father and mother'. It begins 'Noble Lord, and Lady bright', and declares that Heaven has sent their children

> With crown of deathless Praise,
>   To triumph in victorious dance
> O're sensual Folly, and Intemperance.

This is followed by the only other stage-direction in *Comus*: 'The dances ended, the Spirit Epiloguizes', or, in the Bridgewater manuscript: 'They daunce, the daunces al ended, the Daemon singes or sayes.' From these directions we can only conjecture how the presentation was effected and who were the dancers. It is, I suppose, just conceivable that the Spirit merely led the children to the front of the stage, and that, after they had bowed and curtsied to the prominently seated Earl and Countess, the four of them proceeded to execute a series of triumphant and victorious dances on the stage, while the audience remained in their seats, and that the Spirit then spoke his epilogue and everyone went off to supper. It is just conceivable that this is what happened but I must admit that the more I try to imagine the spectacle of Lawes and the three children alone on the stage and triumphing in victorious dance for perhaps half an hour, while the audience sat and watched, the more ludicrous and even bathetic it appears. Either, I think, they must have danced a single short dance on the stage and then have joined a general revel in the hall, or else, at the conclusion of, or during, this second song the Spirit stepped down with them from the stage, led them to where their parents were seated, and that it was at this point that the dancing began. When, in the preceding song, the Spirit orders the country dancers to make way for 'other trippings', 'lighter toes' and 'Court guise', he can scarcely, I think, be referring merely to dances which he and three children are going to perform: both these phrases and the direction in the Bridgewater manuscript, 'the daunces *al* ended', suggest that there was a lot of dancing, and that at the conclusion of this most un-masque-like masque, as at the conclusion of other masques, a good time was had by all. Indeed, Milton and Lawes may well have regarded the rather hobbledehoyish country

dancing of the 'rural swains', with their 'ducks and nods', as a
kind of second anti-masque and as a foil to the more courtly
'trippings' of the Lord and Lady and their guests. It is even possible to regard all that has gone before as one vast Induction,
to regard the appearance of the children when the scene has
changed to Ludlow as the pulling of the cracker, and henceforth
to regard the children, who do not speak during this last scene,
as the masquers. We might then say that Milton, characteristically,
only allowed the masque proper to begin after he had first secured
an uninterrupted recital of his poem. The complimentary and
strictly occasional element is, as I have remarked, very unobtrusive, and almost incidental. It might even be said that the
selection of the Earl's children as the principal actors and the
weaving of the plot around an incident which, so tradition has
it, actually befell the children, namely, a benightedness in
Hogwood Forest while they were returning from a visit—it
might be said that this, from Milton's point of view, was a
brilliant idea; for throughout the Earl's children, in spite of
their supernatural adventures and the 'divine philosophy' they
utter, remain the Earl's children, on their way to congratulate
their father on his 'new-entrusted Scepter'. Since, therefore, the
whole plot was a kind of family affair and might in itself be
regarded as an elaborate compliment, Milton was able to devote
all his energies to the kind of poetry he really enjoyed writing,
and to dispense almost entirely with the kind of compliment that
Jonson and others had to be continually devising. Since the
illusion he was trying to create was rather a musical than a
dramatic one (one remembers Socrates's words about philosophy
as the greatest music), since the children appeared throughout
as the glorified but recognisable children of glorified but recognisable parents, and since they were continuously journeying,
albeit 'through hard assays', to their parents, it was unnecessary
to introduce continual reminders that it was their parents and the
festivities at Ludlow towards which they were journeying. And,
in any case, would not the Earl have been better pleased to hear
his own children talking, almost *in propria persona*, like three
little Miltons than to hear himself continually alluded to as a
kind of Western divinity? In fact, the brilliant choice (conscious

or unconscious) of this complimentary plot relieved Milton from the necessity of devising what he 'would have regarded as trivial compliments. All he had to do was to write at the top of his bent in the conviction that every piece of 'divine philosophy', every exquisite phrase the children uttered could not be but regarded as a compliment both to the parents of such children and to the children themselves.

The few complimentary, occasional and local allusions, which no doubt sufficiently gratified those who first heard them, are completely worked into the texture of the poem and do not remain as, so to speak, historical excrescences. At line 27 of his opening speech, after declaring how Neptune has assigned the various islands to various tributary gods, the Spirit continues:

> but this Ile
> The greatest, and the best of all the main
> He quarters to his blu-hair'd deities,
> And all this tract that fronts the falling Sun
> A noble Peer of mickle trust, and power
> Has in his charge, with temper'd awe to guide
> An old, and haughty Nation proud in Arms:
> Where his fair off-spring nurs't in Princely love,
> Are coming to attend their Fathers state,
> And new-entrusted Scepter, but their way
> Lies through the perplex't paths of this drear Wood.

Throughout Milton continually finds occasion to exploit the poetic and descriptive possibilities of this sylvan setting, but his next definitely local allusion does not, I think, come until the long description and invocation of Sabrina, the river-goddess of the Severn, which begins at line 820; and his next allusion to the Earl, the new honour conferred upon him, and the evening's festivities does not come until line 946, where the Spirit promises to conduct the children to

> your Fathers residence,
> Where this night are met in state
> Many a friend to gratulate
> His wish't presence, and beside
> All the Swains that there abide,

G

> With Jiggs, and rural dance resort,
> We shall catch them at their sport,
> And our sudden coming there
> Will double all their mirth and chere

—a speech which immediately precedes the change of scene to Ludlow, the country-dancing, and the presentation of the children to their parents. Between these two allusions to the Earl and to the occasion Milton has for more than nine hundred lines been circumscribed only by his own conception of his own poem. Even the introduction of the local river-goddess is sufficiently motivated and enables him to indulge in a kind of description which he thoroughly enjoyed and in which he excelled. He has also found occasion to introduce quite naturally two graceful compliments to Henry Lawes, compliments which also contain graceful allusions to the fact that Lawes was then a member of the Earl's household in his capacity as the children's music-master. At line 84 the Spirit declares that he must

> take the Weeds and likenes of a Swain,
> That to the service of this house belongs,
> Who with his soft Pipe, and smooth-dittied Song,
> Well knows to still the wilde winds when they roar,
> And hush the waving Woods;

and at line 494, when the disguised Spirit enters, the Elder brother exclaims:

> *Thyrsis*? Whose artful strains have oft delaid
> The huddling brook to hear his madrigal,
> And sweeten'd every muskrose of the dale.

And Thyrsis, with his

> O my lov'd masters heir, and his next joy

helps to preserve that intimate, family atmosphere, that gracious idealisation of real relationships and that dream-like self-enacting of idealised selves, which the original spectators must have found so intriguing and which we can still to some extent recapture.

As for the element of spectacle, its simplicity is far removed, not only from the elaborate architectural machinery of Jonson's masques, but even from such complexity of stage-effect and stage-device as Shakespeare permitted himself in *The Tempest* and elsewhere. The only machine required would be a trapdoor to enable Sabrina and her attendant water-nymphs to rise and descend. The only prearranged set, the one interior scene, simple enough even by Elizabethan playhouse standards, is that of Comus's palace, where the drawing of the 'wild wood' backcloth would reveal some sort of inner stage (ll.658–9):

The Scene changes to a stately Palace, set out with all manner of deliciousness: soft Musick, Tables spred with all dainties. *Comus* appears with his rabble, and the Lady set in an inchanted Chair, to whom he offers his Glass, which she puts by, and goes about to rise.

At line 957, after Comus and his rout have been 'driven in' and Sabrina has released the Lady from her enchantment, the Spirit and the three children leave the stage: all that was then required was to draw across the inner stage or recess, which had represented the interior of Comus's palace, a painted backcloth or canvas 'presenting *Ludlow* Town and the Presidents Castle'. But while the stage-devices were few and of the simplest kind, there is no reason why the costumes, just as on the Elizabethan public stage, should not have been magnificent. Every now and then there is a piece of brilliant and spectacular action—the entry of Comus and his crew, headed like animals and bearing torches, the brothers rushing in with drawn swords, the rising of Sabrina and her nymphs; but there is not, as in Jonson's masques, a continually changing spectacular background to inaction. Jonson, one might say, except in his Inductions and sometimes in his anti-masques, is poetically limited to commenting upon elaborate dumb-shows. With all the spectacle and the machinery, the poet can only get in edgeways, whereas in *Comus* one might almost say that it is the masquers who can only get in edgeways. In Jonson's masques the appeal to the eye was overwhelming, in *Comus* it is only occasional and incidental. Milton is in this respect as unfettered as Shakespeare; he can appeal throughout to the intellect and the imagination, and he can mingle with his philosophic argument an amount of sylvan and pastoral description that would have failed to produce its proper effect had the inner eyes of his audience been reduced to inactivity by the fact that their outer eyes were continually preoccupied with elaborate stage-effects.

In the total impression which *Comus* leaves upon us this descriptive element plays a most important part. It is not, as is sometimes suggested, an exclusively philosophic poem. Since I shall have to consider some of these descriptions in detail when I come to examine the style of *Comus* and its relation to the work of earlier poets, and since I am at present concerned rather with form and outline, I will mention a few of them with no more detail than may be necessary to enable you to recall them: the Spirit's opening description of the ancestry of Comus, of his orgies, and of the spells he casts on travellers (ll.46–77); the amount of incidental sylvan, pastoral and fairy description in the Lady's first speech, where she tells how at the approach of 'gray-hooded Eev'n' her brothers left her while they went in search of berries and how a thousand fantasies begin to throng into her memory of airy tongues that syllable men's names (ll.190 ff.); Comus's description of her singing, which surpasses that of his mother Circe with the sirens three (ll.244 ff.); his description of how he met her brothers

> What time the labour'd Oxe
> In his loose traces from the furrow came,
> And the swink't hedger at his Supper sate;   (ll.291 ff.)

the large amount of sylvan and pastoral description in the first dialogue of the Brothers, their longing for some beam of light from a cottage, some sound from wattled cotes or pastoral reed, and their imagination of their sister leaning her unpillowed head against the rugged bark of some broad elm (ll.331 ff.); the Spirit's second description of Comus and his crew when, disguised as Thyrsis, he meets the brothers, and his own description of their sister's singing, rising like a stream of rich distilled perfumes in such strains as might create a soul under the ribs of death (ll.520–64), followed by his description of the magic-conquering herb given him by a certain shepherd lad, more medicinal than the moly Hermes once gave to wise Ulysses (ll.619–43); Comus's description of his 'cordial julep', more joy-inspiring than

that *Nepenthes* which the wife of *Thone*,
In *Egypt* gave to *Jove*-born *Helena*   (ll.672–8)

the Spirit's description (ll.824–58) of the transformation of
Sabrina and of her beneficient magic,

> For which the Shepherds at their festivals
> Carrol her goodnes lowd in rustick layes,
> And throw sweet garland wreaths into her stream
> Of pancies, pinks, and gaudy Daffadils

Professor Wright has declared that

'Comus' should be read as a dramatised debate on a moral or philosophical theme, a sort of Platonic dialogue in verse; and although
there are moments of ordinary drama, the main dramatic interest, as in
a Platonic dialogue, consists in following the developments and turns
in a skilfully conducted debate.[1]

This is admirable as a reply to that charge of inactivity which
Dr Johnson brought against the poem when he judged it according
to ordinary dramatic standards, but it does not insist, as I think
it should, upon that pervasive element of controlled and subordinated *description* which I have been trying to recall, and which, as
a source of pleasure, is scarcely less important than the element
of debate. Thomas Warton, who also defended the poem against
Dr Johnson's strictures, got the emphasis, as it seems to me,
approximately right when he wrote:

Comus is a suite of Speeches, not interesting by discrimination of
character; not conveying a variety of incidents, nor gradually exciting
curiosity: but perpetually attracting attention by sublime sentiment, by
fanciful imagery of the richest vein, by an exuberance of picturesque
description, poetical allusion, and ornamental expression.[2]

And, because of his choice of scene, Milton can indulge in these
numerous and memorable descriptions without ever seeming to
be irrelevant. In a note on line 185, where the Lady recalls that
her brothers said they would step to the next thicket side

---

[1] John Milton, *The Shorter Poems*, ed. B. A. Wright, p. 142.
[2] *Poems upon several Occasions, by John Milton*, 1785, pp. 264–5.

> To bring me Berries, or such cooling fruit
> As the kind hospitable Woods provide,

in a note on this passage Thomas Warton remarked:

By laying the scene of his Mask in a wild forest, Milton secured to himself a perpetual fund of picturesque description, which, resulting from situation, was always at hand. He was not obliged to go out of his way for this striking embellishment: it was suggested of necessity by present circumstances. The same happy choice of scene supplied Sophocles in PHILOCTETES, Shakespeare in As YOU LIKE IT, and Fletcher in the FAITHFUL SHERHERDESS, with frequent and even unavoidable opportunities of rural delineation, and that of the most romantic kind. But Milton has additional advantages: his forest is not only the residence of a magician, but is exhibited under the gloom of midnight.[1]

Fletcher's forest also, as Warton immediately remembers, has this additional advantage of being 'exhibited under the gloom of midnight', and so too, he might have added, has Shakespeare's in *A Midsummer Night's Dream*, together with the second advantage of being likewise exhibited by a magician, though a less sinister one than Comus.

I will conclude this discussion of the relation of *Comus* to the Court masque by saying that, while the mere printed texts of Jonson's masques are, with few exceptions, of very minor literary interest and sometimes little more than programme notes, the printed text of *Comus* is a self-sufficient work of literature, which, while it might perhaps receive some super-added charm from a perfect performance, loses almost nothing by being merely read.

Milton, in fact, contrived to have it both ways: he produced something that was entirely suitable to the occasion and yet immeasurably transcended it; he adopted certain features of the masque, yet without allowing them in any way to cramp his style; he contrived to please those for whom he wrote without at any point displeasing himself. The Bridgewater manuscript does indeed reveal that Lawes found it necessary to cut three speeches for the actual performance: he omitted (evidently because he found it too long) about thirty lines (195–225) from

---

[1] ibid, p. 154.

the Lady's first speech, including the beautiful passage about the
airy tongues that syllable men's names; and, evidently because
he found in them some want of propriety with the very tender
years of the person by whom they were to be uttered and to whom
they were to be addressed, he omitted four lines (697–700)
from one of the Lady's speeches to Comus and about twenty
lines (737–55) from Comus's argument against virginity. Milton
replaced all these passages when he printed the poem, and he
even added some twenty-five lines to the Lady's last speech (779–
806) making her declaim the 'sage and serious doctrine of
virginity' in such a way that he himself might almost be speaking
in propria persona.

ITS RELATION TO PASTORAL DRAMA

At line 496 of *Comus*,

> And sweeten'd every muskrose of the dale,

Thomas Warton quotes an observation of his brother Joseph:

> In poetical and picturesque circumstances, in wildness of fancy and
> imagery, and in weight of sentiment and moral, how greatly does
> COMUS excell the AMINTA of Tasso, and the PASTOR FIDO of Guarini;
> which Milton, from his love of Italian poetry, must have frequently
> read! COMUS, like these two, is a Pastoral Drama, and I have often
> wondered it is not mentioned as such.[1]

There is much in this apparently original observation of Joseph
Warton's, and indeed in some respects *Comus* has more affinity
with the pastoral drama than with the masque. Pastoral drama was
a peculiar and characteristic Renaissance development of what
may be called the Arcadian Pastoral, and the Arcadian Pastoral
was invented, as Mr Highet has reminded us, by Virgil. In most
of his Eclogues (or Bucolics) Virgil imitated Theocritus, whose
pastoral Idylls (for only a minority of Theocritus's Idylls are
Pastorals) may be regarded as idealisations of real life, but in
two of them, the seventh and tenth, Virgil pláced the scene in
Arcadia. 'Vergil', says Mr Highet,

---

[1] ibid, p. 195.

was the discoverer of Arcadia, the idealized land of country life, where youth is eternal, love is sweetest of all things even though cruel, music comes to the lips of every herdsman, and the kind spirits of the country-side bless even the unhappiest lover with their sympathy. In reality, Arcadia was a harsh hill-country in the centre of the Peloponnese: it was known to the rest of Greece chiefly for the very ancient and often very barbarous customs that survived in it long after they had died elsewhere. ... But Vergil chose it because (unlike Sicily) it was distant and unknown and 'unspoilt'; and because Pan— with his love of flocks, and nymphs, and music (the untutored music of pan-pipes, not the complex lyre-music of Apollo and his choir, the Nine)—was specifically the god of Arcadia. It was in this unreal land of escape that Vergil placed his friend Gallus, a poet and an unhappy lover, to receive consolation from the wild scenery of woodland and caves, from music, and from the divinities of art and nature.[1]

The immense vogue of Arcadianism, which found expression in so many literary forms—eclogue, lyric, drama, prose romance— may perhaps be said to have begun with the publication in 1504 of Sannazaro's prose and verse romance *Arcadia*. Pastoral drama, then, was a variety of what may be called Arcadian Pastoral, and on its origin and development I will again quote Mr Highet:

In several of Vergil's *Bucolics* two characters speak, and dispute, and compete, so much so that the poems were actually staged in the theatre of Augustan Rome. The rediscovery of classical drama suggested to modern playwrights that they might create complete plays on the romantic love-themes appropriate for pastoral characters, with the charming costumes, music, and scenery of Arcadia.[2]

The two most famous (though not the first) of these Italian pastoral dramas were Tasso's *Aminta*, acted before the Duke of Ferrara and his court in 1573, when Tasso was twenty-nine, and printed in 1580, and the much longer and more elaborate *Pastor Fido* of Guarini, presented to, but not, it would seem, as was perhaps intended, represented before,[3] Charles Emanuel, Duke of Savoy, on the occasion of his marriage to Catherine of Austria at Turin in 1585, and printed in 1590. Tasso's *Aminta* is a most beautiful poem. In spite of its exquisite artificiality and patterned

---

[1] *The Classical Tradition*, 1949, p. 163.   [2] op. cit., p. 139.
[3] See W. W. Greg, *Pastoral Poetry & Pastoral Drama*, 1906, p. 206.

rhetoric, it has a certain Greek simplicity and clarity of outline, and, one might almost say, a certain Greek freshness. It is in blank verse, with admixture of shorter (heptasyllabic) lines in some of the more impassioned and tender passages, and there are rhymed choruses at the end of each act, including the famous 'O bella età de l'oro', 'O beautiful age of gold'—beautiful, not because of its unlaborious earth and eternal spring, but because 'onor', in the sense in which Donne had in mind when he spoke of 'the Giant Honour', was unknown and 'S'ei piace, ei lice', 'if it pleases, it is permitted', was the universal law. Aminta (or, as we should call him, Amyntas) Pan's nephew, loves Silvia, Diana's niece, but Silvia rejects love and cares only for hunting. Even when Aminta, in the nick of time, saves her from a satyr who has stripped her naked and bound her to a tree with her own hair, she is ungrateful: as soon as her hands are free she tells him not to touch her, and that she can do the rest of the untying herself. She relents only when it is apparently too late— when she hears that Aminta, maddened by a false report that she had been killed by a wolf, has committed suicide by throwing himself from a cliff. The last act concludes with a description of how, when she went to seek what she supposed would be his dead body, she found that his fall had been broken by a bush, and how he regained consciousness in her arms.

One reason why I have given this brief description of the *Aminta* is that I may ask you to consider for a moment what seems to me a surprising and over-confident assertion by Professor Mario Praz:

One has heard much about the Spenserian character of *Comus*, but nobody seems to have been aware that Tasso's *Aminta* is the real model. Comus's arguments to persuade the Lady to forsake her virginity are a development of those Dafne uses with Silvia at the beginning of Tasso's pastoral drama; Comus himself acts the part of Tasso's Satyr. *Comus* is a spiritualized *Aminta*; the Satyr binds Silvia naked to a tree and tries to violate her, but Comus's fetters are the invisible work of a spell. Thus sensuality has been carried away from the senses.[1]

---

[1] 'Milton and Poussin', in *Seventeenth-Century Studies presented to Sir Herbert Grierson*, 1938, p. 202.

This surprising statement occurs in the course of a very interesting and, on the whole, well-supported parallel between Milton and Poussin, and may be regarded as an example of the way in which, while pursuing some general identity, one too often tends to obliterate important differences and distinctions. Is not the attempt to make out a parallel between the Satyr who binds Silvia with her hair to a tree and Comus who binds the Lady with his spells to a chair so forced as to be ludicrous? One cannot, in fact, point to any particular work and say confidently, this was Milton's source. Thomas Warton, following Isaac Reed, extracted from the mass of fantastic detail that surrounds it the main plot of Peele's *Old Wives' Tale*, in which two brothers rescue their sister from an enchanter, and by retaining details that were similar and omitting many that were not, was able to suggest quite plausibly that Milton might have been indebted to Peele for the outline of his plot. This suggestion seems to have been accepted as a certainty by most modern editors, but I am not convinced that any of the resemblances are more than accidental. Warton also greatly exaggerated Milton's supposed indebtedness to Fletcher's *Faithful Shepherdess*, of which I shall speak in a moment. Meanwhile, to return to the *Aminta*: although I cannot agree with Professor Praz that Comus's arguments against virginity are a development of those which Dafne uses with Silvia in Tasso's play, since both in narrative, in dialogue, and in short poems arguments for and against fruition were very popular with sixteenth- and seventeenth-century English poets and might almost be regarded as one of the commonplaces of the time, I will agree that in respect of this dialectical and debating strain there is some affinity between *Comus* and the *Aminta*. Silvia listens and replies to arguments in favour of love, Aminta listens and replies to arguments against despair, and at the beginning of the last act the philosophical Elpino expatiates on the strange arts and unknown paths by which love leads men to felicity, and when they have reached (as they suppose) the depths of misery, suddenly places them in paradise. Moreover, although the poetry of the *Aminta* has not the power and splendour of Milton's, it has a certain elegance and solidity, a certain exquisite artifice, which is nearer to *Comus* than to the *Faithful Shepherdess*.

I need not insist that the emotions and ideals expressed in the two poems are utterly different, and that while Tasso's is Arcadian and, I suppose one might say, neo-pagan, Milton's is Platonic and Christian. Neither perhaps need I insist that the *Aminta* is dramatic in a sense in which *Comus* is not. It does indeed contain arguments and debates, but these are only incidental, and its mainspring is the conflict between persons and passions, between Aminta's love and Silvia's contempt for love; and new situations and new reactions to those situations, with much alternation of fear and hope, are produced by various turns of fortune: by the Satyr's attempt to ravish Silvia, by the false report of her death which leads Aminta to attempt suicide, and then by the false report of Aminta's death which leads Silvia to accept the love she has so long rejected. In comparison with this *Comus* is static and, as Professor Wright has said, may be regarded as a kind of Platonic dialogue in verse. Nevertheless, although there is more action in the *Aminta* than in *Comus*, much of it is not represented, but narrated by messengers or eyewitnesses, and it is in these descriptive passages that some of Tasso's most beautiful poetry occurs. Indeed, some would maintain that in our total impression of the *Aminta* the purely descriptive element plays a part no less important than it does in our total impression of *Comus*.

Guarini's *Pastor Fido* is much longer than the *Aminta* and much more complex. Indeed, in the complexity of its plot or situation it follows a pattern set by the earliest of all full-scale pastoral dramas, Beccari's *Sacrifizio*, where, as Mr Highet neatly says: 'A loves B, B loves C, C loves D, and D is vowed to chastity; E loves F and his love is returned, but they are forbidden by a cruel kinsman to marry.'

Although in almost every other poetic form what may be called Arcadian pastoralism flourished exceedingly in England during the sixteenth and seventeenth centuries and even persisted until the days when it so disgusted Dr Johnson, pastoral drama never took root as it did in Italy. The only really notable pastoral drama of the Italian kind in English is Fletcher's *Faithful Shepherdess*. Peele's *Arraignment of Paris*, that rather over-praised hotch-potch, is nearer both to the masque and to Lyly's mythological and courtly comedies than to pastoral drama as practised by the Italians, and Ben Jonson's unfinished *Sad Shepherd* is too un-Arcadian and too natively English. There were, it is true, some rather pale and insipid imitations of the Italian form by Daniel and others, and there was the intolerably tedious and feeble *Amyntas* by Thomas Randolph, but these exceptions only prove the rule. Fletcher was the only dramatist who in this form achieved a poetic level at all comparable with that of the best Italian examples, and even Fletcher's play was, as he himself admitted when he printed it, a complete failure on the public stage, where the audience neither understood nor appreciated Arcadianism, and missed the Whitsun ales and other lively touches which they associated with shepherds.

It has often been said that *The Faithful Shepherdess* is an imitation of Guarini's *Pastor Fido*, but this is only very limitedly true. Fletcher imitates scarcely any of the detail in either the *Pastor Fido* or the *Aminta*: what he reproduces is the Arcadianism of the Italians and that pattern of ill-assorted lovers which appears both in the *Pastor Fido* and in many other Italian pastoral plays. The action takes place in a forest during the noon, night and early morning following a Festival of Pan. Perigot loves Amoret; Amaryllis loves Perigot; the Sullen Shepherd loves Amaryllis, who promises to reward him if he will use magic to part Perigot and Amoret. The wanton Chloe loves Thenot, who is in love with Clorin, the Faithful Shepherdess, who is vowed to chastity and good works and the tending of her dead lover's grave. Chloe then proffers her love to the modest Daphnis, whom, finding too squeamish, she forsakes for the lascivious Alexis. After a night of assignations, mistakes, enchantments, pursuits, assaults, and flights, the unfortunate and the guilty are all rounded up by the Priest of Pan and the guardian Satyr and brought to Clorin's bower for judgement and advice. Clorin has already cured Thenot of his passion for herself by pretending to yield to it, thereby destroying his belief in the superhuman fidelity which had been the cause of his love. Clorin now banishes the Sullen Shepherd, pardons the jealous but now penitent Amaryllis, and cures with her magic and fortifies with good advice the wanton Chloe and the lascivious Alexis.

Throughout his commentary on *Comus* Thomas Warton has greatly exaggerated what he calls (in a note on line 891) 'Milton's

perpetual and palpable imitations of the FAITHFUL SHEPHERDESS',
and most of his imaginary parallels are, I am convinced, purely
accidental resemblances, where an occasional similarity in detail
is the result of an accidental similarity of incident and situation.
There is, for example, a river-god in *The Faithful Shepherdess*
and there is a river-goddess in *Comus*, but there is no more
significance in this than in the fact that in both poems there is a
wood. Sabrina appears in *Comus* because she is the divinity of the
local river, the Severn, and it did not require Fletcher to remind
Milton that the banks of an English river are often fringed with
osiers. Milton had undoubtedly read Fletcher's play and it may
well have suggested to him how much pleasure and variety might
be introduced by exploiting the descriptive possibilities and the
romantic and mythological associations of the woodland scene.

We can often point to particular phrases which Milton has
either appropriated or adapted from earlier poets and we can
often say, 'This is the kind of thing which many earlier poets
did and which Milton has done better', but we cannot say confidently that either the plot or any particular incident in *Comus* was
suggested by any one particular source. I have already expressed
scepticism about Milton's supposed indebtedness to the main
plot of Peele's *Old Wives' Tale*, and I have not been convinced
that Comus himself was suggested to Milton by the bouncing
belly-god of that name in the first anti-masque of Jonson's
Pleasure reconciled to Virtue. I have noticed only one really striking
detailed resemblance between a passage in *Comus* and a passage
in *The Faithful Shepherdess*, and these are both descriptions of the
almost magically defensive power of chastity. At the beginning
of Fletcher's play Clorin, the Faithful Shepherdess, who has
resolved to devote her life to tending her lover's grave and to
curing witchcraft and diseases, is astonished by the respectful
adoration of a Satyr who brings her a present of fruit, and recalls
how her mother told her that no enchantment or other power
could harm a maiden who remained chaste:

> Yet I have heard (my Mother told it me)
> And now I do believe it, if I keep
> My Virgin Flower uncropt, pure, chaste, and fair,
> No Goblin, Wood-god, Fairy, Elfe, or Fiend,

Satyr or other power that haunts the Groves,
Shall hurt my body, or by vain illusion
Draw me to wander after idle fires;
Or voyces calling me in dead of night,
To make me follow, and so tole me on
Through mire and standing pools, to find my ruine:
Else why should this rough thing, who never knew
Manners, nor smooth humanity, whose heats
Are rougher than himself, and more mishapen,
Thus mildly kneel to me? sure there is a power
In that great name of Virgin, that binds fast
All rude uncivil bloods, all appetites
That break their confines: then strong Chastity
Be thou my strongest guard, for here I'le dwell
In opposition against Fate and Hell.[1]

It is almost certain, I think, that Milton had these lines, consciously or unconsciously, in his memory when he introduced into the Elder Brother's long speech about that 'hidden strength' which would defend their sister, and which the anxious Younger Brother seemed to have forgotten, the following passage:

'Tis chastity, my brother, chastity:
She that has that, is clad in compleat steel,
And like a quiver'd Nymph with Arrows keen
May trace huge Forests, and unharbour'd Heaths,
Infamous Hills, and sandy perilous wildes,
Where through the sacred rayes of Chastity,
No savage fierce, Bandite, or mountaneer
Will dare to soyl her Virgin purity,
Yea there, where very desolation dwels
By grots, and caverns shag'd with horrid shades,
She may pass on with unblench't majesty,
Be it not don in pride, or in presumption.
Som say no evil thing that walks by night
In fog, or fire, by lake, or moorish fen,
Blew meager Hag, or stubborn unlaid ghost,
That breaks his magick chains at *curfeu* time,
No goblin, or swart Faëry of the mine,
Hath hurtfull power o're true virginity.   (ll.420–37)

---

[1] *Works*, ed. A. Glover and A. R. Waller, 1905–12, ii. 375.

There can, I think, be no doubt that this conception of chastity as a kind of magical power or charm was suggested to Milton by Fletcher, and that what one might call the Shakespearean exploitation of popular superstition and fairy lore in Clorin's speech was thoroughly congenial to Milton's imagination. It was something he liked doing and knew he could do well, and he has here improved upon Fletcher with an almost Shakespearean profusion of intensely evocative detail, and has produced one of those passages which seemed to Collins and Hurd and the Wartons so wildly and thrillingly romantic. Milton, though, unlike Fletcher, is not content with the conception of chastity as a kind of magical charm. He immediately proceeds to associate it with his Platonic and Christian idealism and to describe it in terms reminiscent of Plato's description of that supreme good which can subdue all the lower passions. This is one of the great differences between *Comus* and *The Faithful Shepherdess*, a difference which, when we perceive it, enables us to see each poem more clearly for what it is. Fletcher's ostensible, or professed, theme is chastity, the miseries caused by unchaste love and the punishment, cure and repentance of unchaste lovers. But Fletcher is only able to make poetry out of this theme when, as in Clorin's speech, he exploits it magically and romantically; as a moral quality, an active virtue, he can make nothing of chastity, and his few lines on the subject are conventional, trivial, and thin. In the last scene, in reply to Clorin's question

> Is your Love yet true and chaste,
> And for ever so to last?

Alexis declares

> I have forgot all vain desires,
> All looser thoughts, ill tempred fires,
> True Love I find a pleasant fume,
> Whose moderate heat can ne'r consume.

And Chloe follows with

> And I a new fire feel in me,
> Whose chaste flame is not quencht to be.[1]

---

[1] *Works*, ii. 437–8.

Fletcher, in fact, is able to make nothing of his professed theme, and his play is only memorable because of its many incidental beauties. It is held together by the mechanism of its plot, but not by any intensely felt idea, ideal, or emotion. Milton, on the other hand, is able to make even finer poety out of chastity as a virtue than out of chastity as a kind of magic. The purely descriptive poetry in *Comus*, although a great source of pleasure, is only incidental: the central thing is the philosophic debate. Milton reveals himself not merely as a descriptive, but as a moral and philosophic poet and his poem has both a unity and a range which Fletcher's lacks.

It is, then, only in respect of its descriptive element, its exploitation of the romantic and picturesque associations of a nocturnal woodland, that *Comus* has affinity with *The Faithful Shepherdess*, and here, if Milton was really indebted to Fletcher for anything more than the most general suggestions, he has greatly surpassed them. Fletcher's verse is always agreeable, often charming, but almost never really distinguished in the way that Milton's and Shakespeare's is. Take, for example, a passage that was a great favourite with Hazlitt, Chloe's exhortation to rustic delights:

> Shepherd, I pray thee stay, where hast thou been?
> Or whither go'st thou? here be Woods as green
> As any, air likewise as fresh and sweet,
> As where smooth *Zephyrus* plays on the fleet
> Face of the curled Streams, with Flowers as many
> As the young Spring gives, and as choise as any;
> Here be all new Delights, cool Streams and Wells,
> Arbors o'rgrown with Woodbinds, Caves, and Dells,
> Chuse where thou wilt, whilst I sit by, and sing,
> Or gather Rushes to make many a Ring
> For thy long fingers; tell thee tales of Love,
> How the pale *Phœbe* hunting in a Grove,
> First saw the Boy *Endymion*, from whose Eyes
> She took eternal fire that never dyes;
> How she convey'd him softly in a sleep,
> His temples bound with poppy to the steep
> Head of old *Latmus*, where she stoops each night,
> Gilding the Mountain with her Brothers light,

To kiss her sweetest.[1]

This is delightful in its way, and, incidentally, both in matter, in diction, and in versification, as near to the kind of poetry Keats was trying to write in *Endymion* as anything in our earlier literature, but it is an altogether easier and slighter kind of poetry than that of the best descriptive passages in *Comus*. Or take this speech of Amaryllis, pursued by the Sullen Shepherd:

> If there be
> Ever a Neighbour Brook, or hollow tree,
> Receive my Body, close me up from lust
> That follows at my heels; be ever just,
> Thou god of Shepherds, *Pan*, for her dear sake
> That loves the Rivers brinks, and still doth shake
> In cold remembrance of thy quick pursuit:
> Let me be made a reed, and ever mute,
> Nod to the waters fall, whilst every blast
> Sings through my slender leaves that I was chast.

In *The Faithful Shepherdess* the heroic couplet predominates over blank verse, while in *Comus* Milton only uses it in one short passage of eighteen lines (ll.495–512); but Fletcher also has numerous octo-syllabic passages, and these perhaps were Milton's chief example. If so, he has again greatly surpassed his original.

DOCTRINE

Comus, then, has only incidental affinities with the pastoral drama, just as it has only incidental affinities with the court masque. It is really *sui generis*. It might be described as a semi-dramatic poetical debate on a moral theme, with a pastoral and mythological setting affording much opportunity for beautiful description; self-sufficient as a piece of literature, but with just enough action, incident, spectacle, song and dance to make it enjoyable as a performance. In most of Jonson's masques there is a mythological element, and in some of them there is a moral theme, the contrast, for example between virtuous and un-virtuous pleasure, or between true and false fame, but this moral theme is generally so smothered by the spectacular, choreographic

---

[1] *Works*, ii. 383.

and complimentary elements that Jonson is only able to treat it poetically in the most superficial and conventional way. Milton, though, has made this incidental, and, strictly speaking, accidental element in some of Jonson's masques the central and constituent element of *Comus*. It is, indeed, profitable to compare *Comus* with various examples of the masque and of the pastoral drama in order to see more clearly both what it is not and what it is, but I know of only one other poem with which it has a real and deep affinity, another poem that is also *sui generis*, *Paradise Regained*. For *Paradise Regained*, in spite of obvious differences which I need not insist upon, may also be described as a semi-dramatic, philosophic, moral and religious debate, diversified with passages of description. In *Comus* Lawes found it necessary to cut some of the Lady's speeches, and in writing them Milton scarcely seems to have considered for a moment what would and what would not be appropriate in the mouth of the child who was to deliver them. In fact, he seems to have thought of the Lady, not as a person, but simply as an incorporation of the kind of virtue or excellence he wished to expound, and there are moments when we might almost be listening to the Christ of *Paradise Regained* demolishing the arguments of Satan.

The argumentative and philosophic passages in *Comus* are the completest poetical expression of the young Milton's moral and religious idealism, of those ardours and aspirations which he was later to describe so eloquently in the various autobiographical passages in his prose pamphlets. Hints and glimpses of this *Weltanschauung* we have caught from time to time in our study of the preceding poems: the conception, derived partly from St Paul, partly from Spenser and from Vida and other Italian poets, of Christ as a hero, a captain of salvation, a kind of King Arthur sending out his knights on quests, a great taskmaster, a master of the vineyard; the conception, derived partly from the Book of Revelation, partly from Plato, and partly, it would seem (strangely enough) from Shakespeare, of a spheral music, a divine harmony, audible only to purified ears; above all, though we have noticed it only in the sixth Latin Elegy, in the sonnet on his twenty-third birthday, and in the letter accompanying that sonnet, the conception of dedication, of vocation, of preparation for a great and noble task. As Dr Tillyard has observed,[1] the whole body of Milton's Prolusions, those Latin academic exercises delivered at various times during his Cambridge years, provides conclusive proof of his early and deep devotion to Plato; nevertheless that passage in *Arcades* about the spheral music and the poem 'Blest pair of *Sirens*' suggest that round about 1632 Platonism was becoming more and more important as a binding and unifying element in Milton's whole conception of life, and that it enabled him more and more both to apprehend his religion and his morality imaginatively and to express them poetically. For Milton had long regarded himself as a dedicated spirit, and the philosophic life as described by Plato in those great central dialogues, the *Symposium*, the *Phaedrus*, the *Phaedo* and the *Republic*, is essentially a life of dedication, an *askesis*, a sublimation of matter into spirit, an ascent from physical to intellectual beauty, from the visible and temporal to the invisible and eternal; a progress, as Plato sometimes expressed it, in remembering—a gradual remembering of those eternal forms or patterns of all excellence which our souls had known in their pre-natal state. About these Platonic conceptions there is a grandeur, a spaciousness, and (in spite of the frequent subtlety of Plato's thought) a simplicity of outline which has always powerfully appealed to many poetic minds, above all when they have been somewhat lonely idealists like Milton. And Plato's philosophy combined so well with all that he had learnt from our sage and serious Spenser about the purification of virtue through trial and with his own conception of Christianity as a kind of personal pilgrimage through the world and a kind of personal loyalty to the great quest-giver and taskmaster. Indeed, I sometimes think that at this time Milton had come to apprehend Christianity very largely in and through Platonism, had come to regard it primarily as a confirmation and consummation of Platonism, confirming by divine revelation the truths which Plato had reached after by reason, and proclaiming as an absolute certainty that immortality which Plato could regard as no more than probable and often adumbrated in myth.

---

[1] *Milton*, revised edn 1966, p. 47.

Just as *Comus* immeasurably transcends the occasion for which it was written, so too the virtue which Milton there celebrates under the name of chastity is really far more than chastity as ordinarily understood. This too, perhaps, is essentially Platonic, for with Plato himself the virtues are continually sliding into one another, and, when any particular virtue is being discussed at length, it soon seems to have swallowed up all the rest. For, since wisdom is the highest good, every virtue, in so far as it is a virtue, turns out to be some form of *philosophia* or love of wisdom. Moreover, Plato is less often concerned with promulgating truths, or, as some might say, with dogmatising, than with describing the method, the temper, the regimen by which truth may be reached. He appears, one might say, more often as a moralist than as a metaphysician. The chastity, then, which Milton celebrates may be regarded as the Platonic love of wisdom considered more especially in relation to that purity and dedicatedness which wisdom demands of her lovers.

I propose to examine in some detail the Platonic passages in *Comus*, and in doing so I shall often refer to Professor Wright, by whom the extent of Plato's influence on the poem has been for the first time fully revealed.[1] I will begin at the beginning, with the first eleven lines of the Attendant Spirit's prologue:

> Before the starry threshold of *Joves* Court
> My mansion is, where those immortal shapes
> Of bright aëreal Spirits live insphear'd
> In Regions milde of calm and serene Ayr,
> Above the smoak and stir of this dim spot,
> Which men call Earth, and with low-thoughted care
> Confin'd, and pester'd in this pin-fold here,
> Strive to keep up a frail, and Feaverish being
> Unmindfull of the crown that Vertue gives
> After this mortal change, to her true Servants
> Amongst the enthron'd gods on Sainted seats.

Commentators from the eighteenth century onwards have

---

[1] Sears Jayne, 'The Subject of Milton's Ludlow *Mask*', *Publications of the Modern Language Association of America*, 1959, claims Ficino as the chief influence on the poem. M. Lloyd, 'Comus and Plutarch's Dæmons', *Notes and Queries*, vol. 205, 1960, has an interesting comparison of the Attendant Spirit with Platonic dæmons. A.L.

noticed how pagan and Christian, classical and Biblical reminiscences have been combined in the description of this heaven
where virtue is rewarded. We may recall Homer's description of
Olympus in the sixth book of the *Odyssey* (42 ff.) as it is magnifi-
cently imitated by Lucretius:

> apparet divum numen sedesque quietae
> quas neque concutiunt venti nec nubila nimbis
> aspergunt neque nix acri concreta pruina
> cana cadens violat semper*que* innubilus aether
> integit, et large lumine ridet.[1]

('The majesty of the gods appears and their quiet seats, which
neither winds shake nor clouds drench with showers, nor does
snow congealed of sharp frost violate them whitely falling, but
ever-cloudless aether encompasses and laughs with large-spread
light.') Milton may also have had in mind the vision of St John:

And immediately I was in the spirit: and, behold, a throne was set in
heaven, and one sat on the throne. . . . And around about the throne
were four and twenty seats: and upon the seats I saw four and twenty
elders sitting, clothed in white raiment; and they had on their heads
crowns of gold.[2]

Similar collocations of pagan and Christian imagery also occur in
Lycidas, where they so offended Dr Johnson, and in the
Epitaphium Damonis, and they are frequent in Milton's master
Spenser, who in his elegy on Dido in the November eclogue of
The Shepherd's Calendar declares

> She raignes a goddesse now emong the saintes. (l.175)

They are indeed frequent in very much Renaissance poetry, and
they cannot, I think, be explained entirely in terms of the doctrine
of imitation, by the assumption that a poet who was trying to
imitate one of the classical forms would think it necessary to
imitate classical imagery and allusions as well. Something of the
old medieval practice of allegorical interpretation was also, I
think, at work, together with some now more, now less conscious attempt to appropriate and Christianise the classics, and to
regard all that had ever deeply moved the human spirit as portions

---

[1] *De Rerum Natura*, iii. 18 ff.   [2] *Revelation*, iv, 2–4.

of one great progressive revelation. To many humanists, especially, I think, to Milton in his younger years, Christianity was not the irreconcilable opposite of what seemed to them most admirable in the life and literature of the ancient world, but rather its completion ('with this over and above, of being a Christian'[1]). But to return to the passage we were considering, although eighteenth-century commentators had noticed the combination of Homeric and Apocalyptic imagery in the Spirit's description of his abode, it was Professor Wright who first revealed the presence in these lines of something more, something of Platonic doctrine and Platonic myth. The Platonic dialogue which seems to have been most in Milton's mind at this time, the one, at any rate, of which *Comus* contains by far the greatest number of demonstrable reminiscences, is the *Phaedo*, in which Socrates, awaiting death in prison, discusses with some of his friends the evidence and arguments in favour of the immortality of the soul. (It is, by the way, interesting to remember that it was this portion of Plato's philosophy in which Il Penseroso was chiefly interested:

> . . . or unsphear
> The spirit of *Plato* to unfold
> What Worlds, or what vast Regions hold
> The immortal mind that hath forsook
> Her mansion in this fleshly nook.)

Partly because it seems to be supported by his doctrine of reminiscence—reminiscence, that is, of those absolute ideas and perfections of which in this world we experience only approximations and shadows—Socrates accepts as probable the Orphic doctrine that the soul undergoes a succession of incarnations in the forms of men and animals before it is finally purified and released from the cycle of birth. The body, in fact, is the tomb of the soul, which even in this life the soul learns to dispense with in so far as it attains to the contemplation of reality and truth. Those souls which by the practice of such contemplation have completely liberated themselves from dependence on the body and the senses are the truly virtuous, and at death they are

---

[1] Columbia edn, iii. 236.

released into perfect freedom and dwell for ever with the gods. Socrates concludes his argument with a typical Platonic myth, of which I will quote Professor Wright's summary:

I believe, says Socrates, that the earth is a globe in the centre of the universe, and within its surface are many hollows where we and other races of men dwell. But the true surface of the earth is above in the pure air of heaven, which we call the ether and of which the air and mist and water collecting in our hollows are the sediment. We who dwell in these hollows ignorantly suppose that we are living on the true surface of the earth; but if a man could arrive at the surface he could see the true earth, and the true heaven beyond. On the true earth all things are fairer than here; and men are living there, some inland, some on the coasts of the air as we on the coasts of the sea, and some on islands in the air: for air is to them what the sea is to us, and the ether what air is to us. Also they have temples where the gods really dwell, and they see and talk with them face to face. Now those who are judged to have been holy in their lives on earth come to those pure mansions above and dwell on the true earth; whilst those who have purified themselves by philosophy go to the heaven beyond and live for ever without bodies in mansions fairer still. Wherefore, concludes Socrates, having regard to these things, it behoves us to leave nothing undone to obtain virtue and wisdom in this life: fair is the prize, and the hope great.[1]

καλὸν γὰρ τὸ ἆθλον καὶ ἡ ἐλπὶς μεγάλη is perhaps the most memorable phrase in all Plato's writings.

Let us now return to the passage we were considering, and see whether certain phrases in it have not now acquired a deeper and preciser meaning. Consider these lines:

> . . . where those immortal shapes
> Of bright aëreal Spirits live insphear'd
> In Regions milde of calm and serene Ayr,
> Above the smoak and stirr of this dim spot,
> Which men call Earth.

The spirit dwells, that is to say, on Plato's true earth, at the threshold of that heaven inhabited by gods and philosophers, up in the pure ether, far above this dim spot, these hollows, this

---

[1] Milton, *The Shorter Poems*, ed. B. A. Wright, 1938, p. 147.

pinfold, which men *call* earth. On this earth men remain:

> Unmindfull of the crown that Vertue gives
> After this mortal change, to her true Servants:

'this mortal change', this change from immortality to mortality, this imprisonment in the entombing and fettering body, which the soul must continually undergo until by the practice of virtue and the pursuit of wisdom it has finally liberated itself from the cycle of birth and comes to dwell for ever on the true earth, or even, if it has been a truly philosophic soul, among the 'enthron'd gods'. It is also possible, as Professor Wright has suggested, that Milton may have had another Platonic passage in mind, one in the tenth Book of the *Republic* (611c–d), where Socrates declares that the soul on earth is so fettered and contaminated by the body and the senses that its original form is no more recognisable than that of the sea-god Glaucus, all encrusted with seaweed and shells. And 'the crown that Vertue gives' may well have been suggested both by Platonic and by New Testament metaphors from the games: by Plato's comparison in the tenth book of the *Republic* (613) of just men to runners who complete the course, receive the prizes, and are crowned; by the exhortation in the Epistle to the Hebrews to 'run with patience the race that is set before us' (xii, 1); by St Paul's words to the Corinthians,

> Know ye not that they which run in a race run all, but one receiveth the prize? So run, that ye may obtain. And every man that striveth for the mastery is temperate in all things. Now they do it to obtain a corruptible crown; but we an incorruptible;[1]

and by the Apocalytic promise to the church in Smyrna, 'Be thou faithful unto death, and I will give thee a crown of life'.[2]

Milton's Platonism, as expressed in this poem, is sometimes more and sometimes less modified by his Christianity. The present passage, I am inclined to say, is essentially Platonic, and perhaps only in the Apocalytic allusion to 'Sainted seats' at all distinctively Christian. This is particularly true of its continuation, which concludes the Spirit's account of himself and his abode:

---

[1] *I Corinthians*, ix. 24–5.   [2] *Revelation*, ii. 10.

Yet som there be that by due steps aspire
To lay their just hands on that Golden Key
That ope's the Palace of Eternity:
To such my errand is, and but for such,
I would not soil these pure Ambrosial weeds,
With the rank vapours of this Sin-worn mould.

The 'golden key' that opens this, that or the other was a common
poetic metaphor and does not in itself contain any necessary
allusion to St Peter's keys. What is significant is the Platonic and
absolute contrast between 'these pure Ambrosial weeds' and 'the
rank vapours of this Sin-worn mould': that absolute contrast,
which we so often find in Plato, and above all in the *Phaedo*,
between the impure, enfettering and entombing body and the
soul which can only escape from it when, through the contemplation of absolute purity, it has become absolutely pure—a
condition which only 'some' souls can ever hope to achieve. It
is a contrast not really consistent with the characteristically
Miltonic conception, which we shall encounter later, of the possible sublimation of body or matter into spirit. For the body
that can be sublimated into spirit is not a Platonic and irredeem-
able body but a Christian and redeemed body, not a body that is
the tomb of the soul but a body that is the Temple of the Holy
Ghost:

What? know ye not that your body is the temple of the Holy Ghost
which is in you, which ye have of God, and ye are not your own?
For ye are bought with a price: therefore glorify God in your body,
and in your spirit, which are God's.[1]

Although in this examination of what I may call the doctrine
of *Comus* my emphasis is necessarily more on substance than on
form, I must insist that Milton has both apprehended and
expressed these partly Platonic and partly Christian conceptions
in a manner that is essentially poetic. From the beginning until
the end of his poetic career he loved to contemplate vast expanses
of time and space, and to imagine his own most vivid experiences
of visual, aural, moral, and intellectual beauty prolonged and

---

[1] *I Corinthians*, vi. 19–20.

expanded into a celestial order, harmony and illumination. The spacious architectural, musical quality of Plato's thought, ever gyring, ever expanding, and progressing as it so often does by means of metaphors and analogies, was especially congenial to him, and it is fascinating to observe how natively, as it were, his own imagination clothes itself in Plato's metaphors and Plato's myths. The only English predecessors who can at all compare with him in this essentially poetic expression of large philosophic and moral ideas are Marlowe, Shakespeare, and, occasionally, Spenser.

Dr Johnson, who once insisted to Boswell on the importance of little things, wrote of the author of *Paradise Lost* that his natural port was gigantic loftiness. To some extent this is true also of the young Milton. That he was intensely responsive to the beauty around him *L'Allegro* and *Il Penseroso* and the descriptive passages in *Comus* sufficiently reveal; nevertheless, he did not, I think, in the Johnsonian sense, love little things—not, at any rate, for their own sakes: they were always suggesting to him the idea of some more absolute beauty, some more exact goodness, some vaster order, some celestial harmony, just as that 'Solemn Musick' he so finely commemorated raised his phantasy from itself to the celestial consort and the endless morn of light. This irrepressible tendency to pass immediately from things as they were to things as they might be is the sufficient explanation of the fact that when he turned from poetry to politics Milton began with such vast expectations, suffered so many bitter disappointments, and ended in such deep disenchantment.

When the Lady first appears and has delivered that Fletcherian passage about the magically defensive powers of chastity, she continues:

> O welcom pure-ey'd Faith, white-handed Hope,
> Thou hovering Angel girt with golden wings,
> And thou unblemish't form of Chastity,
> I see ye visibly, and now beleeve
> That he, the Supreme good, t' whom all things ill
> Are but as slavish officers of vengeance,
> Would send a glistring Guardian if need were
> To keep my life and honour unassail'd.   (ll.213–20)

This substitution of Chastity for love in the triad of Christian virtues is partly imposed on Milton by dramatic necessity, and by the fact that the Lady, at any rate professedly, ostensibly and *prima facie*, represents, not virtue in general but one particular virtue, although, as I have insisted, Chastity as Milton conceives it comes, quite Platonically, to include and swallow up all the other virtues. Nevertheless, I think Milton could quite naturally come to identify the Christian virtue of love with the φιλία in Plato's φιλοσοφία, the love, as Professor Wright expresses it, of that Supreme Good 'which subdues the lower passions and produces "those happy twins of her divine generation, knowledge and virtue" '.[1] For the love that is centred upon an ideal of perfection involves at the same time a fastidious shrinking from imperfection and defilement, and one might even be content to suggest the positive by insisting on the negative, and speak of 'that chastity of perfectionism that shrinks from impurity', just as Burke spoke of 'that chastity of honour, which felt a stain like a wound'.

Later, in the dialogue between the Brothers, the elder declares that he does not find in the mere fact that their sister is alone any cause for anxiety:

> Vertue could see to do what vertue would
> By her own radiant light, though Sun and Moon
> Were in the flat Sea sunk. And Wisdoms self
> Oft seeks to sweet retired Solitude,
> Where with her best nurse Contemplation
> She plumes her feathers, and lets grow her wings
> That in the various bussle of resort
> Were all to ruffl'd, and sometimes impair'd. (ll.373–80)

This is a superb example of the way in which Milton not only adopts Plato's thought but expresses it in Plato's own metaphors. 'This central passage', declares Professor Wright,

once more reveals the influence of Plato. Note first the transition from virtue to wisdom: 'Wisdom's self' (which we might translate by the

---

[1] Milton, *Shorter Poems*, p. 156.

platonic 'Philosopher') is introduced as the ideal of virtue. Secondly, the imagery derives from Plato's 'Phaedrus' ... love is desire for that heavenly beauty the soul once knew and of which earthly beauty arouses the remembrance. In a typical Platonic myth Socrates likens the soul to a winged chariot, the wings representing the desire and power of the soul to mount to the heaven from which it is an exile; the wings of the virtuous soul are quickened and nourished by the desire and search for the truth, but the wings of the soul intent on worldly affairs and carnal desires are maimed and drooping.[1]

Later in this long dialogue between the two Brothers there is a most interesting passage (ll.453–63) where that insistence on purity which may be regarded both as Platonic and Christian ('Blessed are the pure in heart, for they shall see God') is combined, first with the expression of an unshakeable confidence in divine assistance, divine grace, which may be regarded as specifically Christian; then with that notion that only purged ears can hear the celestial harmony, which we have already met with in *Arcades* and *At a Solemn Musick*, a notion derived partly from Plato, partly from the *Apocalypse*, and partly, it would seem, from Shakespeare; and finally with that characteristically Miltonic, and, one might almost say, characteristically un-Platonic conception of the possible sublimation of matter into spirit, to which I have already alluded in my remarks on the Spirit's Prologue.

> So dear to Heav'n is Saintly chastity,
> That when a soul is found sincerely so,
> A thousand liveried Angels lacky her,
> Driving far off each thing of sin and guilt,
> And in cleer dream, and solemn vision
> Tell her of things that no gross ear can hear,
> Till oft convers with heav'nly habitants
> Begin to cast a beam on th'outward shape,
> The unpolluted temple of the mind,
> And turns it by degrees to the souls essence,
> Till all be made immortal.

From Thyer onwards, all the commentators have noticed that the

---

[1] Milton, *Shorter Poems*, pp. 158–9.

last few lines of this passage contain the germ of that speculation so fully developed in Raphael's speech to Adam in the fifth book of *Paradise Lost*, and occasioned, so incongruously, as it has seemed to many readers, by a description of the processes of Angelic digestion:

> O *Adam*, one Almightie is, from whom
> All things proceed, and up to him return,
> If not deprav'd from good, created all
> Such to perfection, one first matter all,
> Indu'd with various forms, various degrees
> Of substance, and in things that live, of life;
> But more refin'd, more spiritous, and pure,
> As neerer to him plac't or neerer tending
> Each in thir several active Sphears assignd,
> Till body up to spirit work, in bounds
> Proportiond to each kind. So from the root
> Springs lighter the green stalk, from thence the leaves
> More aerie, last the bright consummat floure
> Spirits odorous breathes . . .
>   time may come when men
> With Angels may participate, and find
> No inconvenient Diet, nor too light Fare;
> And from these corporal nutriments perhaps
> Your bodies may at last turn all to spirit,
> Improv'd by tract of time, and wing'd ascend
> Ethereal, as wee, or may at choice
> Here or in Heav'nly Paradises dwell.   (ll.469–500)

This is one of Milton's fundamental ideas. Matter and spirit, he insists, do not differ in kind, but are simply lower and higher manifestations of that single divine substance, or divine effluence, out of which God created all things and arranged them in a graduated scale of being, ascending from the inorganic to the angelic. I must admit that I do not know enough of the various neo-Platonic and Hermetic doctrines that were so much studied and discussed in Milton's day to be able to declare whether this characteristically Miltonic conception is or is not entirely original. Few ideas are entirely original, and Milton may possibly have taken hints from various sources. Two things, however, are certain: first, it was a conception which he made peculiarly his own and to which he attached great importance, for he has expressed it at length not only in that passage in *Paradise Lost* from which I quoted but also in the *De Doctrina Christiana*; secondly, it is definitely not Platonic. For Plato the distinction between matter and spirit, sense and intellect, is ultimately absolute and ultimately inexplicable: by which I mean that there seems to be an unresolved dualism or contradiction in Plato's thought. He never really explains why matter should have been created, or why the pure soul should ever have been condemned to this imprisonment in the contaminating body. This absolute opposition between the world of ideas and the world of phenomena, between spirit and matter, soul and body, the pure λόγος and the corrupting flesh, was a problem and a difficulty for many later Greek thinkers, and no doubt it was with them and their problem very much in mind that the author of the prologue to St John's Gospel announced the triumphant, the miraculous, solution: καὶ ὁ λόγος σὰρξ ἐγένετο ('And the word became flesh'). Milton's world, unlike Plato's, is a Christian world, a redeemed world, in which the word made flesh can raise even matter to the ethereality of spirit. For Milton matter is not evil in itself. Evil came into the world through man's abuse of his free-will, and although, as the result of Christ's victory and triumph, man, with the aid of divine grace, has the possibility of re-entering regained paradise, he also has the possibility of sinking in the scale of being, sinking further from God, and, instead of making himself more spiritual, of making himself more material, less divine, less human, more brutish. Evil, as Milton conceives it, is degraded spirituality. Here, then, Milton (in his own way, as always) is specifically Christian, although even here some Christians might still find his Christianity strongly, perhaps too strongly, tinged with Platonism. Is there not, they might ask, something exclusive and esoteric, something emphatically for the few, some indifference to ordinary humanity, about this refined and solitary progress in a kind of poetic spirituality? And is there not, so to speak, too little weight of conquered negation behind the sublime confidence? Certainly this was also the man who really seems to have believed that, with the abolition of bishops, the Kingdom of God was at hand. He was to suffer many disenchantments and to learn much about

humanity and much about evil before he came to write his last
and greatest poems, and the entering regained Paradise was then to
seem a harder and longer task than it did to the author of *Comus*.

At the conclusion of this Christian passage Milton again turns
to Plato for his imagery, and associates what Plato had said about
the clogged and contaminated soul with his own conception of
the scale of being and the relativity of matter and spirit:

> but when lust
> By unchaste looks, loose gestures, and foul talk,
> But most by leud and lavish act of sin,
> Lets in defilement to the inward parts,
> The soul grows clotted by contagion,
> Imbodies, and imbrutes, till she quite loose
> The divine property of her first being.
> Such are those thick and gloomy shadows damp
> Oft seen in Charnell vaults, and Sepulchers
> Lingering, and sitting by a new made grave,
> As loath to leave the body that it lov'd,
> And link't it self by carnal sensualty
> To a degenerate and degraded state.   (ll.463–75)

From Warton onwards all the commentators have noticed this
is almost a paraphrase of a passage in Plato's *Phaedo* (81b–d), of
which the most relevant portions are thus given by Professor
Wright:

If the soul departs from the body [at death] polluted and impure, as
having constantly held communion with the body, and having served
and loved it, bewitched by sensual desires and pleasures, thinking
that there is nothing real except the corporeal, which one can touch and
see, eat and drink, and employ for sensual purposes ... such a soul
after death is weighed down and drawn again into the visible world ...
wandering, as it is said, amongst monuments and tombs, about which
indeed certain shadowy phantoms of souls have been seen.[1]

It is in these philosophical passages in *Comus* that one first becomes really aware of the oneness of Milton's life and art and of
the fact that his moral ardour and idealism must almost be regarded as portions of his distinctively poetic equipment and as

---

[1] Milton, *Shorter Poems*, p. 160.

scarcely less important than his sheer command over language. His vision of life was in many ways distinctively poetic, one, at any rate, that was peculiary adapted to his own powers of poetic expression.

'How charming is divine Philosophy!' exclaims the Younger Brother at the conclusion of the speech we have been examining,

> How charming is divine Philosophy!
> Not harsh, and crabbed as dull fools suppose,
> But musical as is *Apollo's* lute,
> And a perpetual feast of nectar'd sweets,
> Where no crude surfet raigns.   (ll.476–80)

Milton's Christian Platonism or Platonic Christianity certainly was so: it consisted of a few grandly general and simple conceptions, such as that of the scale of being, which could be both visually and, as it were, musically, apprehended, and endlessly amplified and illustrated with metaphors and analogies. In his poetry, at any rate, he generally starts from and develops assumptions rather than painfully searches for conclusions, and is thus for the most part able to dispense with that analysis and logic-chopping which is apt to impede the progress of poetry. What might be called the poetic passages in Plato are those where he is amplifying, unfolding and illustrating, or mythologically pro-longing beyond the reach of argument, conclusions reached by methods far more prosaic and far more severe. It is, though, not Plato's arguments but Plato's conclusions, metaphors, and myths that Milton appropriates and Christianises. He can see and hear all that he thinks: his imagination is full of ethereal spirits, liveried angels, celestial harmonies and shining spaces. He is the great master of what might be called spiritual architecture. His thought is never vague, but it is almost never what is com-monly called abstract: it is always imaginative, and always poetic. Here, in the philosophical parts of *Comus*, is already revealed much of the poetic equipment of the author of *Paradise Lost* and *Paradise Regained*.

But of all these philosophic speeches in *Comus* I am inclined to think that the poetically greatest is that in which the Elder Brother utters the final expression of his confidence in the inviolability of virtue. It is also, as regards metaphor and imagery, one of the plainest. It is the sound, the music of it, that is so impressive; and that means, if we examine the matter, that it communicates the profound inner vibration with which Milton responded to the moral, philosophical and religious convictions he is expressing:

> against the threats
> Of malice or of sorcery, or that power
> Which erring men call Chance, this I hold firm,
> Vertue may be assail'd, but never hurt,
> Surpriz'd by unjust force, but not enthrall'd,
> Yea even that which mischief meant most harm,
> Shall in the happy trial prove most glory.
> But evil on it self shall back recoyl,
> And mix no more with goodness, when at last
> Gather'd like scum, and setl'd to it self
> It shall be in eternal restless change
> Self-fed, and self-consum'd; if this fail,
> The pillar'd firmament is rott'nness,
> And earths base built on stubble.   (ll. 586–99)

Some of what may be called the philosophic speeches in *Tamburlaine* and *Faustus* have this quality—what distinguishes them is the impressiveness and memorability with which they communicate the vibration set up in the poet by contemplation of the ideas expressed:

> And, to be short, when all the world dissolves,
> And every creature shall be purified,
> All places shall be hell that is not heaven.[1]

> Our souls, whose faculties can comprehend
> The wondrous architecture of the world,
> And measure every wandering planet's course,
> Still climbing after knowledge infinite,
> And always moving as the restless spheres,
> Wills us to wear ourselves and never rest.[2]

There are indeed images in this speech of Tamburlaine's— 'wondrous architecture of the world', 'wandering planets',

---

[1] *Dr Faustus*, II. i. 125 ff.   [2] *Tamburlaine*, Part I, II. vii. 21 ff.

H

'restless spheres'—but we do not see them, we only feel them; or, if you like, we see them vaguely but feel them intensely. It is their emotive, not their visual, connotations that Marlowe is exploiting. In this sense the speech, like that of Milton's I have just quoted, may be called musical. In *Paradise Lost* and *Paradise Regained* there are numerous passages which are also musical in this sense, passages where Milton is above all concerned to communicate the inner vibration excited in him by the moral idea or the scene he is contemplating. It was, I think, some failure to make these necessary distinctions that led Mr Eliot to complain of what he called the predominance of the aural over the visual and tactile in Milton's poetic style.[1] Sometimes Milton says in effect: 'I both feel and see it like this.' To write great moral and philosophical, as distinct from merely didactic, poetry, the poet must be able to apprehend ideas, as it were, musically, and to communicate the rhythms and vibrations which they excite in him. He may only occasionally be able to make us see them, but he must always be able to make us feel them and vibrate with them. I may add that the style of some of the most impressive moral and philosophic passages in Shakespeare is not nearly so unlike that of the philosophic parts of *Comus* as might be supposed by readers who had not made the comparison, and who had been persuaded by modern critics that Shakespeare and Milton were unlike in everything they did. And certainly it is only in Marlowe and Shakespeare before him that we shall find anything at all like the *height* of style which Milton has achieved in *Comus*.

The ringing confidence of that splendid passage we have been considering is more Christian than Platonic; so too, I think, in spite of Professor Wright, are the concluding lines of the Spirit's Epilogue:

> Mortals that would follow me,
> Love vertue, she alone is free,
> She can teach ye how to clime
> Higher then the Spheary chime;
> Or if Vertue feeble were,
> Heav'n it self would stoop to her.

---

[1] 'A Note on the Verse of John Milton', in *Essays and Studies by Members of the English Association*, xxi (1935).

Professor Wright, concentrating his attention too exclusively, as I think, upon 'the Spheary chime', declares that Milton is thinking of Plato's myth in the *Phaedrus*, where souls who have loved the highest beauty, that of truth and goodness, are represented as following Zeus and the gods in their journeys beyond the outermost sphere of this universe and beholding all things as they really are, and that Milton is closing on the Platonic theme with which he opened, 'the free immortal life awaiting the virtuous soul, the lover of wisdom'. It is indeed very probable that the 'Spheary chime' contains a reminiscence of the *Phaedrus*, but Milton does not end there, and Professor Wright does not comment upon the last two lines,

> Or if Vertue feeble were,
> Heav'n it self would stoop to her,

which Milton transcribed into the album of a Neapolitan refugee at Geneva in June 1639, adding

> Caelum non animum muto dum trans mare curro.

A descendant of Milton's Earl of Bridgewater, Mr Egerton as he then was, communicated to Todd, while he was preparing his edition of Milton's poems, some severe animadversions upon Thyer's interpretation of these last two lines by reference to *The Table of Cebes*, a school-book by a Greek philosopher, which consists of a dialogue upon an allegorical picture. There, Thyer had remarked,

Patience and Perseverance are represented stooping and stretching out their hands to help up those, who are endeavouring to climb the craggy hill of Virtue, and yet are too feeble to ascend of themselves.

Egerton insisted to Todd that Milton was concluding his poem

in rapt contemplation of that stupendous Mystery, whereby *He*, the lofty theme of *Paradise Regained*, stooping from above all height, 'bowed the Heavens, and came down' on Earth, to atone as Man for the Sins of Men, to strengthen feeble Virtue by the influence of his Grace, and to teach Her to ascend his throne.

I think the descendant of Milton's Lord President was right, and that, in spite of his admiration for Plato and his deep indebtedness to him, Milton's last word is not the Platonic but the Christian λόγος, the Word made flesh.

Before leaving this topic of the Doctrine of *Comus* for a closer examination of some of the verbal detail of the poem, I will permit myself a general observation about the argument between Comus and the Lady. Although *Comus* is not to be judged by ordinary dramatic standards, and although, as I have already observed, Milton scarcely seems to have considered for a moment whether the speeches he wrote for the Lady would or would not seem appropriate in the mouth of a child, there is nevertheless in the dialogue between her and Comus a power which may not unfitly be called dramatic, and which, both here and elsewhere in Milton's poetry, has too often been overlooked. There is nothing of deliberate caricature about the presentation of Comus and his case; he is allowed to be as eloquent and as plausible as it is possible to make him, and in his arguments in favour of fruition and enjoyment of the present hour Milton is, as it were, recapitulating the best that had been written on that subject by many sixteenth- and seventeenth-century poets, including Shakespeare in his earlier sonnets. This dramatic power, as I can only call it, this power of fully comprehending and fully presenting arguments and attitudes with which he disagrees, Milton has revealed still more strikingly in his later poems: in the arguments of Satan and the rebel angels and in Adam's failure to subordinate love of Eve to love of God; in the arguments used by Satan to tempt Christ in *Paradise Regained*, those superbly presented and superbly illustrated arguments which seem unanswerable until they are answered by the Son of God; in the speeches of Dalila in *Samson Agonistes*, of which Goethe exclaimed when Crabb Robinson was reading the poem to him: 'See the great poet! he *putt* her in right!'[1] It is only in his poetry, not in his prose, that Milton reveals and exercises this power. Of Milton as a controversialist Saintsbury very justly remarked that

His capital fault is that he never succeeds in bringing, or, apparently, attempts to bring, the matter under any consideration, or upon any

---

[1] W. P. Ker, *The Art of Poetry*, 1923, p. 65. This remark, which Crabb Robinson did not record in his *Diary*, was communicated by him to Masson and by Masson to Ker.

ground, which his opponents can be imagined as sharing, or reasonably invited to share.[1]

Partly, perhaps, because not sufficient distinction has been made between the pamphleteer and the poet, and because it has been too readily assumed that this dogmatic and egotistical controversialist would never even try to penetrate a mind and attitude different from his own, it has often been suggested in recent times that in the speeches of Comus and of Satan and of the Eve-dominated Adam, Milton, that most conscious of artists, is behaving unconsciously, and that something he has imperfectly suppressed in his own nature is here finding expression. From which it is clear that failure to appreciate this dialectically dramatic, or dramatically dialectical, power of Milton's may lead to serious misunderstanding and misinterpretation. I have not time to say more on this important subject; fortunately, though, it has been said for me, and with admirable lucidity, by Mr A. E. Dyson in an article on 'The Interpretation of *Comus*' in *Essays and Studies by Members of the English Association* for 1955. I would particularly recommend to you the passage where Mr Dyson expresses what he calls a 'few assumptions which I am making' about some of Milton's beliefs, a passage from which I will quote a few sentences:

Milton believed ... that the arguments of devils were particularly likely to appeal to fallen man, whose understanding is clouded by the effect of sin, so that he cannot clearly distinguish truth from error, and his will infected, so that he is more than half in love with sin. The notion of 'truth' as a discovery made by the intellect alone would no doubt have shocked Milton deeply. 'Truth' on the spiritual level was reserved for the pure in heart to know. Those who relied upon their intellects alone would fall ready victims, he would have supposed, to the rationalizations and sophistries of devils. (pp. 93f.)

STYLE AND DICTION

(1) *Classicism*

In this examination of the style and diction of *Comus* I propose

---

[1] *The Cambridge History of English Literature*, vii. 124.

to proceed from the more general to the more particular, and I will begin with a brief review of the evidence it affords for Milton's 'industrious and select reading' of the classics. In comparison with the rather unscholarly and haphazard classicism of his master Spenser, Milton's is of that much more learned and accurate kind that was practised, óften to the point of pedantry, by certain other writers and poets of the later Renaissance, and with which Professor Mario Praz has found a most interesting and instructive parallel (which, it is true, he often presses too far) in the paintings of Nicholas Poussin. Matthew Arnold has a famous phrase about the function of criticism being the attempt to see the object as in itself it really is. From the earliest dawn of the Renaissance in Italy we may observe European poets gradually coming to see the classics more and more as they really are. For the authors of the medieval romances and even, to a considerable extent, for Chaucer, Virgil and Ovid, Statius and Lucan are simply story-tellers who treat of the matter of Greece or the matter of Rome the Great, and they reveal little or no awareness of the distinctively poetic art of these poets, or that it differs in any remarkable way from that of Dares and Dictys. Dante was the first European poet to reveal any deep sense of the art and power of Latin poetry, and it may well be that it was he who enabled Petrarch and Boccaccio to perceive it too, just it was Boccaccio, it would seem, who suggested to Chaucer a conception of narrative poetry which he had been unable to derive from his own reading of the Latin poets, for Chaucer seems to have read them much as his medieval predecessors had done. Even Spenser still sees the classics through a kind of medieval glass, but Milton, at any rate as regards art and style, seems to have seen them almost face to face.

Let us begin with a very famous passage, Comus's description of the Lady's singing:

> I have oft heard
> My Mother *Circe* with the Sirens three,
> Amidst the flowry-kirtl'd *Naiades*
> Culling their potent hearbs, and balefull drugs,
> Who as they sung, would take the prison'd soul,
> And lap it in *Elysium*, *Scylla* wept,

And chid her barking waves into attention,
And fell *Charybdis* murmur'd soft applause.   (ll.252–9)

About the splendid clarity and concentration of this there is
absolutely nothing medieval; it is saturated in reminiscence of
Milton's own loving and careful reading of the classical poets.
And yet at the same time it is profoundly original, for by a
wonderful process of invention, selection and combination
Milton has produced something that is both new and yet entirely
in the manner and tradition of his favourite poets. The making
Circe Comus's mother was a brilliant invention of his own. How,
though, did he bring Circe and the Sirens, Scylla and Charybdis
together? In Homer they are quite separate. Homer, in the
tenth book of the *Odyssey*, describes how Odysseus and his
companions came to Circe's island of Aeaea. After consulting
Teiresias in Hades they return to Aeaea to bring Elpenor, and
Circe, giving instructions to Odysseus about the voyage which he
hopes will at last bring him home to Ithaca, warns him against
the island of the Sirens (xii. 39–54) and against Scylla and
Charybdis, the monsters who dwell on either side of the Straits
of Messina (xii. 73–110). Homer mentions the sweet singing of
Circe (x. 221), and says that she had four handmaidens
ἀμφίπολοι, x. 348), who were 'children of the springs and groves,
and of the sacred rivers that flow forth to the sea' (350–1), that
is, they were Naiades, although Homer does not employ the
word here. Ovid, though, in the fourteenth book of the
Metamorphoses (ll.264 ff.) describes how Nereids and nymphs
arrange the flowers and herbs of which Circe alone knows the
use, and it was undoubtedly his recollection of these two passages
in Homer and Ovid that suggested to Milton the beautiful phrase,
'Amidst the flowry-kirtl'd *Naiades*'. It was through Ovid, too,
that Milton came to establish a relation between Circe and
Scylla, for Ovid in the thirteenth and fourteenth books of the
Metamorphoses describes how Circe, jealous because she was loved
by the sea-god Glaucus, transformed Scylla into a sea-monster;
and, having thus brought in Scylla, it was natural to bring in the
Homeric Charybdis as well. How, though, did Milton come to
bring Circe and the Sirens together, a relationship for which,

so far as I know, there is no classical precedent whatever? And, again so far as I know, the only modern predecessor of Milton's who brought Circe and the Sirens together was William Browne in his Inner Temple Masque, which, although it was presented in January 1614–15, remained in manuscript until the eighteenth century. Browne, whose masquers are the enchanted companions of Ulysses, places Circe and the Sirens on the same island, and makes them as much servants of Circe as her nymphs and Nereids. Unless Milton had seen either a manuscript of Browne's masque or a revived performance of which we have no record, we must assume either that his conflation of the legends of Circe and of the Sirens was original or that it had already been made by some other writer or writers now forgotten. Warton suggested that it might at first have been made as the result either of misunderstanding or of quotation out of its context of a single line in one of Horace's Epistles (I. ii. 23), where Horace, who has been re-reading Homer, reminds Lollius that in Ulysses Homer has given us a pattern of wisdom and temperance: You remember, he says, the Siren's songs and Circe's cups,

> Sirenum voces et Circae pocula nosti.

I may add that Milton has departed from Homer and followed later writers in making the number of the Sirens not two, but three. Finally, Milton's 'potent herbs' was suggested to him by his recollection of a brief allusion in the seventh book of the *Aeneid* (ll.19–20), where Aeneas and his companions, skirting Circe's isle, hear the raging of beasts,

> quos hominum ex facie dea saeva potentibus herbis
> induerat Circe in voltus ac terga ferarum,

('whom from the likeness of men Circe, cruel goddess, with her potent herbs had clothed in the features and forms of beasts.') Behind the lines:

> Amidst the flowry-kirtl'd *Naiades*
> Culling their potent hearbs, and balefull drugs—

even behind those two lines alone what loving recollection there is and what skilful combination of passages in Homer, Ovid and Virgil!

Sometimes, too, Milton combines classic and romantic tradition, in, as it were, a seamless fashion that is quite unlike Spenser's. The Spirit tells the Brothers that, armed with the herb Hæmony, they may

> Boldly assault the necromancers hall;
> Where if he be, with dauntless hardihood,
> And brandish't blade rush on him, break his glass,
> And shed the lushious liquor on the ground,
> But sease his wand ...   (ll.649–53)

Here, it seems probable, there are recollections, not only of Ulysses assaulting Circe and her proffered cup (as described by Ovid in the *Metamorphoses*[1] rather than by Homer in the *Odyssey*[2]), but also of Guyon in the *Faerie Queene* spilling the bowl proffered by Acrasia's Porter[3] and breaking Acrasia's golden cup.[4] On 'necromancers hall' Warton comments: 'Milton here thought of a magician's castle which has an inchanted Hall invaded by christian knights.' And there may also be some reminiscence of Caliban's plotting against Prospero:

> Remember,
> First to possess his books.[5]

Similarly, in the Spirit's account of the restoration of Sabrina Milton has almost completely classicised the romantic legend. When, fleeing from her stepmother Gwendolen, Sabrina had flung herself into the Severn, the water-nymphs conveyed her to Nereus, who

> gave her to his daughters to imbathe
> In nectar'd lavers strew'd with Asphodil,
> And through the porch and inlet of each sense
> Dropt in Ambrosial Oils till she reviv'd,
> And underwent a quick immortal change ...   (ll.837–41)

Here Milton is recollecting Alcaeus of Messene's epitaph on Homer,[6] which tells how the sea-nymphs anointed his body with

---

[1] xiv. 293 ff.   [2] x. 294 ff.
[3] II. xii. 49.   [4] II. xii. 57.
[5] *The Tempest*, III. ii. 99 f.   [6] The Greek Anthology, vii. i.

nectar, and Homer's descriptions in the *Iliad* of how Thetis
dropped ambrosia and nectar into the nostrils of Patroclus that
his flesh might be ever sound,[1] and of how Aphrodite anointed
the body of Hector with ambrosial oil, in order that Achilles
might not tear it as he dragged it round the walls of Troy.[2]
Even a phrase of Shakespeare's has been seamlessly incorporated
into this entirely classical description, for

> through the porch and inlet of each sense
> Dropt in

is not merely a paraphrase of Homer's στάζε κατὰ ῥινῶν
('instilled into his nostrils'), but a recollection of the Ghost's
words to Hamlet

> And in the porches of my ears did pour
> The leperous distilment.[3]

In the list of sea-deities appealed to by the Spirit in his invocation of Sabrina, beginning

> Listen and appear to us
> In name of great *Oceanus*   (ll. 867 f.)

every epithet and every attribute is drawn with the greatest care
and reveals how carefully Milton had read the classical poets.
Professor Mario Praz passingly refers to it with the words,
'Here is a neo-classical pageant of deities, each with his conventional attribute',[4] as though it were an example of something
common enough, but we shall find nothing like it in any English
poet before Milton, and certainly not in Spenser. The eighteenth-
century editor Newton showed more awareness when he remarked:

It will be curious to observe how the poet has distinguished the sea-
deities by the epithets and attributes, which are assigned to each of
them in the best classick authors.

---

[1] *Iliad*, xix. 38–9.   [2] *Iliad*, xxiii. 186–7.   [3] *Hamlet*, I. v. 63–4.
[4] 'Milton and Poussin' in *Seventeenth-Century Studies presented to Sir Herbert Grierson*,
1938, p. 202.

You may consult Newton's exhibition of Milton's sources for these epithets and attributes either in his own edition, or in those of Warton or Todd, where his comments are incorporated: I will limit myself to a comment on one of them,

> By *Thetis* tinsel-slipper'd feet.   (l.877)

Homer regularly calls Thetis ἀργυρόπεζα, silver-footed, and through Chapman's translation the epithet seems to have become quite common: Jonson, for example, in *Neptune's Triumph* has '*siluer-footed* Nymphs'[1] and in *Pan's Anniversarie* 'silver-footed Fayes'.[2] Verity is probably right in suggesting that Milton avoided 'silver-footed' because it had become hackneyed and, accordingly, coined the phrase 'tinsel-slipper'd'. To Milton and his contemporaries the word *tinsel* (derived from old French *estincelle*) still meant a kind of cloth or gauze scintillatingly interwoven with gold or silver thread, and had no suggestion of that tawdriness which later came to be associated with cheap imitations of the originally costly material. Nevertheless, beautiful as it is, the phrase has a certain curiousness and daintiness which is not strictly classical; Milton would not have used it at a later period, and probably even in *Comus* he would not have admitted it into a blank verse, as distinct from an octosyllabic passage. In the Spirit's Epilogue Milton's allusion to classical legend and classical mythology is especially exquisite, but it is all done with such apparent effortlessness and ease that probably few readers have suspected how much industrious and select reading lies behind it.

> To the Ocean now I fly,
> And those happy climes that ly
> Where day never shuts his eye,
> Up in the broad fields of the sky:
> There I suck the liquid ayr
> All amidst the Gardens fair
> Of *Hesperus*, and his daughters three
> That sing about the golden tree.

---

[1] *Ben Jonson*, ed. C. H. Herford and Percy and Evelyn Simpson, 1925–52, vii. 694 (l.397).
[2] ibid., vii. 536 (l.208).

I will not linger over the general resemblance, noticed by most commentators, between these opening lines and Ariel's farewell, for again and again in *Comus* Milton seems to be writing like an infinitely more learned Shakespeare. Professor Wright is probably correct in insisting[1] that Milton is still alluding to the 'true earth' of Plato's *Phaedo*, as he had done in the first lines of the Prologue, 'Before the starry threshold of *Joves* Court'. In that passage he originally had fourteen lines further identifying the 'true earth' with the Gardens of the Hesperides, lines which he later cancelled. Professor Wright also insists that Milton is revealing his awareness of the relation between the Platonic myth of the true earth and the earlier Greek conceptions of Elysian Fields and Islands of the Blest. Homer placed the Elysian Fields on the western edge of the Earth, beside the Ocean Stream; Hesiod and Pindar transferred this Elysium to the Islands of the Blest, and it became identified with the Gardens of the Hesperides. In the Trinity Manuscript Milton at first wrote

> Of Atlas & his daughters three,

which he corrected, first to 'Atlas & his neeces' and then to 'Hesperus & his daughters'. It seems almost certain that Milton had been led into making this mistake by Spenser, who, in his description of the Garden of Proserpina, had incorrectly made the Hesperides the daughters of Atlas, whereas, as their name implies, they were the daughters of Atlas's brother Hesperus. Spenser says of the golden apples in the garden that none like them were ever seen unless they had been brought from that place:

> For those, which *Hercules* with conquest bold
> Got from great *Atlas* daughters, hence began,
> And planted there, did bring forth fruit of gold.[2]

In the details of classical mythology Spenser was a very unsafe guide: for example, in three lines of *Daphnaïda* he manages to confuse three legends, those of Orpheus and Eurydice, Cybele and Attis, Demeter and Persephone:

---

[1] Milton, *Shorter Poems*, pp. 148–9.   [2] *The Faerie Queene*, II. vii. 54.

> But as the mother of the Gods, that sought
> For faire *Eurydice* her daughter deere
> Throughout the world.   (ll.463–5)

(Nevertheless, I think that 'Throughout the world' lingered in Milton's memory.) Milton probably soon detected the error into which his recollection of Spenser had betrayed him.

Even behind the apparently simple line, 'That sing about the golden tree', there is industrious and select reading. Ovid, according to Warton, is the only ancient author who says that the trees as well as the apples in the Garden of the Hesperides were of gold:

> arboreae frondes auro radiante nitentes
> ex auro ramos, ex auro poma tegebant[1]

('Arborial leaves, shining with radiant gold, apples of gold they covered'); and Warton further observes that Apollonius Rhodius in his *Argonautica* (a poem which Milton later read with his pupils) is the only ancient author who celebrates the *singing* of the Hesperides:

Where even until yesterday the earth-serpent Ladon guarded golden apples in the dwelling-place of Atlas; and round about minister the Hesperian nymphs, sweetly singing.[2]

It may well be that Milton was remembering this passage, but it is not true, as Warton asserts, that it is the only one in ancient literature where the singing of the Hesperides is celebrated: their singing is celebrated (or, more strictly speaking, they are invoked as singers) by an earlier poet, Milton's favourite Euripides, in one of the choruses of the *Hippolytus*—in a passage, moreover, which I think it very likely that Milton was remembering as a whole when he wrote the first lines of the Spirit's epilogue:

Let me take my way to the apple-planted court of the Hesperides, the singers,[3] where the sea-ruler of the purple flood assigns to sailors no further course and fixes the sacred boundary of the sky that Atlas

---

[1] *Metamorphoses*, iv. 637–8.   [2] iv. 1396 ff.
[3] Ἑσπερίδων δ'ἐπὶ μηλόσπορον ἀκτὰν ἀνύσαιμι τᾶν ἀοιδῶν.

bears—there where ambrosial fountains flow before the nuptial chamber of Zeus, there where the life-giving hallowed earth augments felicity for the Gods.   (ll.742–51)

In the rest of the Spirit's description of the abode to which he is returning Milton deals very freely with classical legend, and has both Plato and Spenser in his mind. His association of the Garden of Adonis with the Garden of the Hesperides and his making it an abode of celestial lovers was almost certainly suggested by Spenser's description of the Garden of Adonis in the third book of the *Faerie Queene* (vi. 29–49): Spenser also places Cupid and Psyche, together with Venus and Adonis, in this garden, although not, as Milton characteristically does, 'farr above' them. It is also probable that he had in mind that paradise of faithful lovers described by Spenser in his *Hymn of Love* (ll.280–7); but Milton was a much stricter, a much less popular kind of Platonist than Spenser; he does not, like Spenser, attempt to combine Platonism with chivalry and courtly love, and about his Cupid and Psyche, whom he places 'farr above' Venus and Adonis, there is a strong suggestion of the Platonic φιλοσοφία or love of wisdom:

> Where young *Adonis* oft reposes,
> Waxing well of his deep wound
> In slumber soft, and on the ground
> Sadly sits th' *Assyrian* Queen;
> But farr above in spangled sheen
> Celestial *Cupid* her fam'd Son advanc't,
> Holds his dear *Psyche* sweet intranc't
> After her wandring labours long,
> Till free consent the gods among
> Make her his eternal Bride.

(2) *Personifications*

Perhaps the best way to begin a study of the diction of *Comus* will be to collect various passages where personification appears, for nowhere else can one so profitably compare Milton's style, on the one hand, with his own later practice, and, on the other hand, with that of Shakespeare, to whom he is so deeply indebted. Consider this passage:

They left me then, when the gray-hooded Eev'n
Like a sad Votarist in Palmers weed
Rose from the hindmost wheels of *Phœbus* wain.   (ll.188–90)

This is perhaps as close as any of the personifications in *Comus*
to the style of Milton's later poetry; it is also, as it so happens, a
passage with which several in his later poetry immediately present
themselves for comparison:

Lycidas (ll.186f):

Thus sang the uncouth Swain to th'Okes and rills,
While the still morn went out with Sandals gray;

P.L., IV. 598–9:

Now came still Eevning on, and Twilight gray
Had in her sober Liverie all things clad;

Paradise Regained, IV. 426–7

Thus passd the night so foul, till morning fair
Came forth with Pilgrim steps in amice gray;

P.L., VII. 373–4:

                                        the gray
Dawn, and the *Pleiades* before him danc'd.

I think you will agree with me that the personification in *Comus*
is a shade less classical than the four later examples I have quoted;
and the reason why it seems so is, oddly enough, the rather
conventional classical allusion in the last line,

Rose from the hindmost wheels of *Phœbus* wain.

The later Milton would have felt that that prolongation was
unnecessary—it is, in comparison with his later style, a piece of
Shakespearean or Spenserian exuberance. Professor Mario Praz
has said of Milton and Poussin that 'they eliminate whatever is
curious, picturesque, particular, not universal. A bareness of pure
and austere lines becomes their ideal'.[1] This, perhaps, requires
some qualification: even in what Professor Praz calls 'the austere

---

[1] 'Milton and Poussin' in *Seventeenth-Century Studies presented to Sir Herbert Grierson*,
1938, p. 209.

nakedness' of *Paradise Regained* there is some gorgeously picturesque description. What, though, one can safely affirm is that Milton's later style is less Shakespeareanly exuberant than that of *Comus*.

> Ere the blabbing Eastern scout,
> The nice Morn on th' *Indian* steep
> From her cabin'd loop hole peep,
> And to the tel-tale Sun discry
> Our conceal'd Solemnity.   (ll.138–42)

This might be described as characteristically late Elizabethan, with a strong touch of Shakespeare and with a possible reminiscence of Dante. Shakespeare, in the second part of *Henry VI* wrote of

> The gaudy, blabbing and remorseful day,[1]

and Phineas Fletcher (possibly remembering this line and improving upon it) wrote in *Britain's Ida* (published in 1628, and attributed by the publisher to Spenser)

> The thicke-lockt bowes shut out the tell-tale sunne,
> (For *Venus* hated his all blabbing light).[2]

Of 'morn peeping' (though not indeed of that queer Shakespearean conception, a 'cabin'd loop hole') there are numerous examples in numerous sixteenth- and seventeenth-century poets, while 'on th' *Indian* steep' is a possible reminiscence of Dante's 'al balco d'oriente'.[3]

Here is a third personification:

> And envious darknes, ere they could return,
> Had stole them from me, els O theevish Night
> Why shouldst thou, but for som fellonious end,
> In thy dark lantern thus close up the Stars,
> That nature hung in Heav'n, and fill'd their Lamps
> With everlasting oil, to give due light
> To the misled and lonely Travailer?   (ll.194–200)

---

[1] IV. i. 1.
[2] Canto II, stanza 3. *Works*, ed. F. S. Boas, 1908–9, ii. 350.
[3] *Purgatorio*, ix. 2.

This ingenious, elaborate, and yet, in its way, beautiful and vivid personification might almost have been spoken in one of their soliloquies by Romeo or Juliet. Certainly it was Shakespeare who taught many other poets to write, or to try to write, like this, although none of his pupils proved so apt as Milton. This 'envious darkness' may possibly have been suggested by the 'envious' streaks in Romeo's

> look, love, what envious streaks
> Do lace the severing clouds in yonder east[1],

just as his 'theevish night' may have been suggested by a passage in one of Phineas Fletcher's *Piscatory Eclogues*, published in 1633,

> the theevish night
> Steals on the world, and robs our eyes of sight;[2]

but the most Shakespearean passages in *Comus* are not always those where Milton has actually imitated or adopted Shakespeare's phrases or even Shakespeare's images. Sometimes, though, Milton distils Shakespeare as he distils the classics:

> How sweetly did they float upon the wings
> Of silence, through the empty-vaulted night
> At every fall smoothing the Raven doune
> Of darknes till it smil'd.   (ll. 249–52)

Here, as Miss Seaton has observed,

from many lines and images in *Romeo and Juliet* Milton has woven a fresh pattern of meaning and melody: from Romeo's answer to Juliet, 'How silver-sweet sound lovers' tongues by night, Like softest music to attending ears' (II. ii. 165–6); from Juliet's summons to Romeo (III. ii. 18–9),

> For thou wilt lie upon the wings of night
> Whiter than new snow on a raven's back;

and finally from Friar Laurence's salute of the dawn, 'The grey-eyed morn smiles on the frowning night' (II. iii. 1).[3]

---

[1] *Romeo and Juliet*, III. v. 7 f.
[2] Eclogue V, stanza 20. *Works*, ed. Boas, ii. 204.
[3] '*Comus* and Shakespeare' in *Essays and Studies by Members of the English Association*, 1945, pp. 70 f.

The spirit disguised as Thyrsis declares that when the roar of
Comus's rout began he

> listen'd[1] them a while,
> Till an unusuall stop of sudden silence
> Gave respit to the drowsie frighted steeds
> That draw the litter of close-curtain'd sleep   (ll. 551–4)

This personification of sleep was almost certainly suggested by
Shakespeare's personification of Night in that same speech at
the beginning of the fourth act of the second part of *Henry VI*
which, as we have already noticed, probably suggested Milton's
'blabbing Eastern scout'—that speech which begins

> The gaudy, blabbing and remorseful day,

and which continues:

> And now loud-howling wolves arouse the jades
> That drag the tragic melancholy night;
> Who, with their drowsy, slow and flagging wings,
> Clip dead men's graves. . . .

This personification poses a very interesting textual and stylistic
problem. Although the Bridgewater manuscript and all three
printed texts (1637, 1645, 1673) read 'drowsie frighted', the
Trinity manuscript reads 'drowsie flighted', a reading which
several editors have preferred. The strongest argument in its
favour is that, like 'flowry-kirtl'd', 'rushy-fringed' and many
others, it is a characteristically Miltonic compound epithet; that
it is *in pari materia* with Shakespeare's jades of night, with their
drowsy slow and flagging wings, in the passage which probably
suggested the whole personification; and that about the phrase

---

[1] For this use of 'listen' as a transitive verb, cp. the following passage from a religious
eclogue entitled *Hermes & Lycaon* by Edward Fairfax, the translator of Tasso,
transcribed by his grand-nephew the Lord General Fairfax in the autograph collection of his own poems and verse-translations now in the Bodleian Library (MS
Fairfax 40, p. 648):

> Yee sedgie lakes & peble-paued wells
> And thou great Pales in these feilds that dwells
> How oft have you hid in the shadie spraies
> Listned Lycaon's songes, his loues and laies.

'drowsie frighted' there is something recalcitrant, whether we attempt to read it as a (probably impossible) compound epithet, 'frighted while drowsy', or (as Milton, although he has no comma, seems more likely to have intended) as two separate words, '(normally) drowsy, (but now) frighted'. Nevertheless, in a most interesting and penetrating study, Lascelles Abercrombie has to my mind convincingly defended the reading 'drowsie frighted', on both bibliographical and aesthetic grounds.[1]

As Thyris continues his speech another magnificent personification arises:

> At last a soft and solemn breathing sound
> Rose like a steam of rich distill'd Perfumes,
> And stole upon the Air, that even Silence
> Was took ere she was ware, and wish't she might
> Deny her nature, and be never more
> Still to be so displac't. I was all eare,
> And took in strains that might create a soul
> Under the ribs of Death.
>
> (ll.555–62)

This is not an imitation of any particular passage or passages in Shakespeare, but the whole movement of it, together with what I may call the 'dynamic abstractions', is inevitably Shakespearean.[2] Milton, in fact, the Milton of *Comus*, has done what no other English poet has done, he has written passages that Shakespeare might have written. It seems to me very likely that Warton was right in supposing that the comparison of sound to scent in this passage may have been suggested by Bacon's essay *Of Gardens*: 'And because the breath of flowers is farre sweeter in the aire,

---

[1] 'Drowsie Frighted Steeds' in *Proceedings of the Leeds Philosophical Society*, vol. II, pt. i, pp. 1–5; reprinted by Chorley and Pickersgill, Leeds, in November 1928. My own view is this: that Abercrombie is right in preferring Milton's original reading and that Milton was right in adhering to it, but that there is nonetheless something not wholly satisfactory about 'drowsie frighted', as Milton himself seems to have perceived. The two epithets do not like one another, or, rather, they are alternatively attracted and repelled.

[2] Compare, for example, in respect of their rhythm and their compressed syntax, the lines on Silence with the following passage from *Cymbeline* (I. vi. 44–6):

> Sluttery to such neat excellence opposed
> Should make desire vomit emptiness,
> Not so allured to feed.

where it comes and goes like the warbling of music.' Nevertheless, we may remember that Shakespeare's Orsino had compared a strain of music to a breeze which had stolen fragrance from a bank of violets.

Even in brief, fleeting, and sometimes only half-suggested personifications these Shakespearean dynamic abstractions appear. What I call dynamic abstractions are one of the most striking characteristics of Shakespeare's natural style, both in the sonnets and in the plays. A single sonnet (the 66th) will sufficiently illustrate what I have in mind:

> Tired with all these, for restful death I cry,
> As, to behold desert a beggar born,
> And needy nothing trimm'd in jollity,
> And purest faith unhappily forsworn,
> And gilded honour shamefully misplaced,
> And maiden virtue rudely strumpeted,
> And right perfection wrongfully disgraced,
> And strength by limping sway disabled,
> And art made tongue-tied by authority,
> And folly doctor-like controlling skill,
> And simple truth musicall'd simplicity,
> And captive good attending captain ill:
>> Tired with all these, from these would I be gone,
>> Save that, to die, I leave my love alone.

As examples of such brief but dynamic personifications in *Comus* I will mention 'visor'd falshood' in the Lady's exclamation,

> Hast thou betrai'd my credulous innocence
> With visor'd falshood, and base forgery?   (ll.697–8);

'the lean and sallow Abstinence' (l.709); and, more elaborate but equally Shakespearean,

> swinish gluttony
> Ne're looks to Heav'n amidst his gorgeous feast,
> But with besotted base ingratitude
> Cramms, and blasphemes his feeder.   (ll.776–9)

How Shakespearean is that last line! But the whole passage is Shakespearean, and the diction, with its native and homely vigour, conveying the moral and emotional attitude, is, just as in similar passages in Shakespeare, inseparable from the image. It is, too, the sort of diction of which Milton reveals such an inexhaustible command in the more bitter and contemptuous passages in his prose pamphlets. According to the Oxford Dictionary, Milton was the first to use the word *besotted* in the sense of 'intellectually or morally stupefied or blinded', as distinct from the earlier sense of 'having the affections foolishly or dotingly engaged', as when North says that Antony was 'besotted by Cleopatra'.

The younger Brother tells the Elder that he may as well try to persuade him that treasure is safe beside an outlaw's den

> As bid me hope
> Danger will wink on Opportunity,
> And let a single helpless maiden pass.   (ll.400–2)

Here 'wink on' means 'close the eye to, fail to notice'. This is very near to Shakespeare's gnomic or didactic style; indeed, one of many Shakespearean passages with which it might be compared is one where there is also a personification of Opportunity: Ulysses exclaims of Cressida:

> O, these encounterers, so glib of tongue,
> That give accosting welcome ere it comes,
> And wide unclasp the tables of their thoughts
> To every ticklish reader! set them down
> For sluttish spoils of opportunity
> And daughters of the game.[1]

Equally Shakespearean is the combination of personification and dynamic abstraction in the Elder Brother's reply:

> I do not, brother,
> Inferr, as if I thought my sisters state
> Secure without all doubt, or controversie:
> Yet where an equal poise of hope and fear
> Does arbitrate th'event, my nature is
> That I incline to hope, rather then fear,
> And gladly banish squint suspicion.   (ll.407–13)

---

[1] *Troilus and Cressida*, IV. v. 58–63.

Not only is 'squint suspicion' a thoroughly Shakespearean personification: 'arbitrate th'event' is a thoroughly Shakespearean phrase, and the subject of that phrase, 'an equal poise of hope and fear' is, in combination with that phrase, an excellent example of those 'dynamic abstractions', as I have called them, which are so frequent in Shakespeare.

Here, finally, in the Spirit's description of Comus's liquor, is what seems to me a most interesting combination of late Milton and mature Shakespeare:

> whose pleasing poison
> The visage quite transforms of him that drinks,
> And the inglorious likenes of a beast
> Fixes instead, unmoulding reasons mintage
> Character'd in the face.　　　　　　　　　　(ll. 526–30)

The second line, with its inversion, 'The visage quite transforms of him that drinks', might almost have appeared in *Paradise Lost*, but about the rest of the passage there is something essentially Shakespearean. Todd quotes from *The Rape of Lucrece* (ll. 807–8):

> The light will show, character'd in my brow,
> The story of sweet chastity's decay,

but this might have appeared in numerous Elizabethan poets, and seems to me different not merely in degree but in kind from

> unmoulding reasons mintage
> Character'd in the face.

In this and in several of the other passages we have been considering it is a question, not of the imitation of particular Shakespearean phrases, but of the achievement, whether consciously or unconsciously, of a manner of expression essentially similar to that of the mature Shakespeare—an achievement which, I repeat, has been beyond the reach of any other English poet.

❯❯ 9 ❮❮

Lycidas

THE OTHER COMMEMORATIONS OF EDWARD KING

Edward King entered Christ's College, Cambridge, in 1626, a year later than Milton. He came of a good family which was presumably able to exercise some political influence, for in 1630, when he had only taken his B.A. degree, he was elected by royal mandate to a vacant fellowship. This, however, does not seem to have affected his popularity in the college, to which he left his whole fortune; and when, in August 1637, he was drowned off the Welsh coast while crossing to visit his family in Ireland, his Cambridge friends soon set about preparing a volume of commemorative poems—perhaps shortly after the beginning of Michaelmas Term, for in the Trinity College manuscript Milton has dated the poem for which he himself was requested 'Novemb: 1637'. It has indeed been suggested that some inter-university rivalry may have been at work, and that, since Oxford was at this time preparing to commemorate Ben Jonson, who had also died during the summer of 1637, in the collection of poems entitled *Jonsonus Virbius*, Cambridge poets resolved to show what they could do by commemorating Edward King. Their book, which was published early in 1638, consists of two parts, which in the few surviving copies are sometimes found separately and sometimes together. The first part, entitled *Justa Edovardo King*, contains nineteen Latin and three Greek poems, preceded by an anonymous prose panegyric; the second part, entitled *Obsequies to the memorie of Mr Edward King*, contains thirteen English poems, of which the last is Milton's *Lycidas*.[1]

---

[1] For another study of this subject see G. Williamson, 'The Obsequies for Edward King', *Seventeenth-Century Contexts*, London, 1960. A.L.

It is worth while to spend a little time considering these
poems, because they reveal most strikingly how remote Milton's
conception and practice of poetry had now become from that of
many of his academic contemporaries, and how old-fashioned he
must have seemed to them. A modern reader, unfamiliar with the
by-ways of seventeenth-century poetry, would probably be
astonished and even shocked by what seemed to him the extreme
impropriety of most of the English elegies. It would seem to him,
not merely that the writers had been no more afflicted by King's
death than Milton and others had been by that of Hobson the
carrier, but that they took it no more seriously: King, his death,
and the manner of his death would seem to him to have become
mere topics for wit, mere opportunities for saying something
ingenious. That the charge of callous indifference and want of
feeling cannot justly be applied to the writers themselves, whatever we may think of their poems, is proved by the fact that even
King's brother Henry writes in the same strain.

In the Latin elegies this kind of wit with its excesses is not
so apparent as in the English ones, partly, no doubt, because the
writers were there more restrained by tradition. In fact, most of
the Latin elegies are just dull. However, one Coke (initial and
college unknown) may be seen straining, as it were, at the Latin
leash, and in his Alcaics, of which I will translate a portion,
there is a most curious combination of something like Cleveland's
wit and something like Milton's neo-classicism:

To think that shameless waves can overwhelm so many studious
acquirements; that a single night can sweep away the labours of so
many nights and so many days!

That dumb fishes can swallow into their entrails a tongue filled
with dripping sweetness of Latin and Attic honey, tongue worthy,
alas, of a better grave!

No dolphin, I think, traverses the Hibernian main. . . .

Faithless pine, inhospitable ship, why does it split? Why did its
impious side admit the wave? Its voyager deserved safer planks.

(p. 19)

In the last of the Latin elegies, by Ralph Widdrington, Fellow of
Christ's, Christ's College complains to the sea-nymphs. It begins
quite in the pastoral tradition:

Nymphs, that owe your illustrious origin to the cerulean waves, natives of the white shore, nymphs, if any traces of your ancient fame remain and you have not become all frozen among your waters, weep a little. Amphitrite shall proffer mournful elegies, and the waves shall now learn to lament their crime.

Then Christ's College reflects that perhaps they have made King the genius of their waves:

Treat gently, I beg you, that dearness, and let not that inoffensive head fall a prey to fishes. Maybe even that flock grows milder in its savage channel, and claims among its waters a wandering divinity. This indeed was what the swelling waves portended and the sky all threatening with pregnant clouds: the lord of the sea wished to resign his empire and savage trident to a god to come. Alas that with you, as you reign throughout your glassy world, your mother cannot be a portion of your soul! Yet I myself am not less whelmed with waves: behold waves coming and going over my unkempt cheeks. (p. 35)

Milton, whose poem concludes the volume and may well have been the last received, perhaps saw copies of some at least of the poems already written: were his wafting dolphins, his 'fatall and perfidious Bark', his sea-nymphs and his 'Genius of the shore' in any way suggested by some of the detail in these two elegies, which, despite some intrusions of contemporary wit, are less remote than the majority from the tradition he himself elected to follow? We can only guess.

When, though, we turn to the English elegies, Milton and the pastoral tradition seem far away indeed. Of these thirteen poems, all but *Lycidas* are in couplets: eight entirely and one mainly in the heroic couplet, and three in the octosyllabic. The heroic couplet had long been established as the standard metre for funeral elegy, as also for satirical, complimentary and epigrammatic verse; and, although I have no statistics, I think it probable that more seventeenth-century poetry was written in that metre than in all the rest put together. Certainly, it is the grand repository of that kind of wit which so many of Milton's academic contemporaries admired and practised, and it was probably better suited to their purposes than any other.

The first of these elegies is by King's brother Henry, also of

Christ's. Although I said that even he wrote in the same strain as the rest, his poem is by no means continuously Clevelandish; it contains passages in that strain of serious hyperbole which we find in some of Donne's verse-letters, and in one or two places it is not unworthy of Donne. The loss of his brother, he declares, is more grevious than all the famines, earthquakes and other afflictions that were brought in by original sin:

> His, whose perfections had that Atheist seen,
> That held souls mortall, he would straight have been
> In t'other extreme, and thought his body had
> Been as immortall, as his soul was made.
> Whose active spirit so swift and clearly wrought
> Free from all dregs of earth, that you'd have thought
> His body were assum'd, and did disguise
> Some one of the celestiall Hierarchies.
> Whose reason quite outstript our faith, and knew
> What we are bound but to beleeve is true.

Then, after some estimable but rather prosaic reflections that he may now praise without immodesty the brother who shed lustre on their whole family, he curses the water, and achieves conceits of the kind which Cleveland elaborated:

> Thou sav'dst but little more in the whole ark,
> Then thou hast swallow'd now in this small bark . . .
> (Though drowning but a second baptisme was,
> T' admit him to the other Churches place).

Henceforth he will not own one drop of water in his composition, but throw it all away in tears. If the sun should drink up the whole sea and rain it down in tears, they would not expiate this crime. Those who cross those seas henceforth shall say:

> Here lyes one buried in a heap of sand,
> Whom this sea drown'd, whose death hath drown'd the land.

Then, after a long and undistinguished poem in octosyllabics by Joseph Beaumont, Fellow and later Master of Peterhouse and author of *Psyche*, a vast allegorical and Spenserian poem about the soul's pilgrimage, the redoubtable John Cleveland, Fellow of St John's, appears. I say 'then', because although the next poem is unsigned, it is undoubtedly by the author of the one that follows it, and that is signed (though it scarcely needed signing) 'J. Cleveland'. The best part of this first poem (best, I mean, in its own kind) is the beginning, where he develops the ingenious conceit that, just as stars only become visible after the sun has set, so poets only dare to appear after King's death.

> Whiles Phebus shines within our Hemisphere,
> There are no starres, or at least none appear;
> Did not the sunne go hence, we should not know
> Whether there were a night and starres, or no.
> Till thou ly'dst down upon thy western bed,
> Not one Poetick starre durst shew his head;
> Athenian owls fear'd to come forth in verse,
> Untill thy fall darkned the Universe:
> Thy death makes Poets: Mine eyes flow for thee,
> And every tear speaks a dumbe elegie.

Cleveland's second poem consists entirely of the development of ingenious conceits suggested by tears, the sea, and drowning, on each of which topics his wish, as Dr Johnson would express it, was only to say what he hoped had never been said before. It seems very unlikely that it ever had. The poem is a brilliant thing of its kind, and the very *ne plus ultra* of that out-of-one's-own-head kind of originality at which so many of these poets were aiming. I will offer a brief prose analysis, not as a substitute for your own reading of the poems, but in order to reveal, so to speak, the skeleton of Cleveland's dialectical and hyperbolical wit. There are roughly five stages. (1) He will not attempt to *scan* his tears; his pen is merely a spout for the rain-water of his eyes. The Muses are no mermaids, although the ocean may well have turned into Helicon at King's death. (2) But can King really be buried in the sea, which, in comparison with the depth of his learning, is so shallow? (3) Aristotle bequeathed his widow Philosophy to King as his wife. It has been affirmed that every terrestial thing has its counterpart in the sea. Hitherto books and arts were wanting there, but now Neptune has got a whole university. (4) The seaman will now welcome storms in the hope that they will bring him to a tomb more precious than his merchandise. (5) In order to understand our loss we must study whole libraries;

then our sorrow will vent itself in such elegies

> As that our tears shall seem the Irish seas,
> We floating Islands, living Hebrides.

William More, of Christ's, does not attempt to scale these heights, and writes an elegy that is decorous and flat, but one W. Hill, about whom nothing seems to be known, after doing what he can with tears and the sea, proceeds to consider the bark as an appropriate coffin:

> Heav'n would (it seems) no common grave intrust,
> Nor bury such a Jewel in the dust.
> The fatall barks dark cabbin must inshrine
> That precious dust, which fate would not confine
> To vulgar coffins. Marble is not fit
> T'inclose rich jewels, but a cabinet.
> Corruption there shall slowly seise its prize,
> Which thus embalm'd in brinie casket lies.

Or perhaps, he suggests, Heaven was anxious to prevent idolatry, and therefore quenched King's celestial fire in water lest we should adore his ashes in an urn. If King's grave were known, it would become a shrine for idolatrous pilgrims, or they might voluntarily melt into tears there, and save death the trouble of taking them. Having considered so many examples of the way in which Milton was ready to borrow even from the most minor poet any phrase he felt able to use or improve, we may perhaps think it not unlikely that Hill's 'fatall bark', together with the 'infida pinus, navis inhospita' in Coke's Alcaics, suggested to him his own 'fatall and perfidious Bark'. Hill concludes his poem with an idea which Milton also used, although he expressed it rather differently:

> Thus doth the setting sunne his evening light
> Hide in the Ocean, when he makes it night;
> The world benighted knows not where he lies,
> Till with new beams from seas he seems to rise:
> So did thy light, fair soul, it self withdraw
> To no dark tombe by natures common law,
> But set in waves, when yet we thought it noon,
> And thence shall rise more glorious then the sunne.

Was it, I wonder, these not very memorable lines that suggested the unforgettable

> Sunk though he be beneath the watry floar,
> So sinks the day-star in the Ocean bed,
> And yet anon repairs his drooping head,
> And tricks his beams, and with new spangled Ore,
> Flames in the forehead of the morning sky:
> So *Lycidas* sunk low, but mounted high,
> Through the dear might of him that walk'd the waves?

Sampson Briggs, Fellow of King's, begins with comparative sobriety: when common souls depart nature does not seem disturbed, but at the departure of the nobler sort she travails with some strange prodigy. Then he becomes really possessed by his muse: King,

>   rigg'd and fraught
> With Arts and Tongues too fully, when he sought
> To crosse the seas, was overwhelm'd; each wave
> Swell'd up, as coveting to be his grave;
> The winds in sighs did languish; Phebus stood
> Like a close-mourner, in a sable hood
> Compos'd of darkest clouds; the pitying skies
> Melted and dropt in funerall elegies.
> Such generall disturbance did proclaim,
> 'Twas no slight hurt to Nature, but a maym:
> Nor did it seem one private man to die,
> But a well order'd Universitie.

As we have seen, this last brilliant idea also occurred to Cleveland, though he made more of it, and connected it with that of sub-marine counterparts of the terrestrial world. Briggs concludes with a bold rhetorical question, for which, however, he hastens to apologise, telling his muse that it is not her business to question providence: could God have forgotten his covenant when he allowed another flood to drown this little world?

Isaac Olivier, Fellow of King's, has no hesitations. He makes a quick start, and throughout his short poem keeps his eye steadily fixed upon his object, which is water:

> What water now shall vertue have again
> (As once) to purge? The Ocean't self's a stain.

Were Pindar now alive he would regret the praises he had bestowed on water. Then comes the dolphin which Coke, in his Latin Alcaics, had also desiderated:

> Why did not some officious dolphine hie
> To be his ship and pilot through the frie
> Of wondring Nymphs?

The excuse must be that the waters which had baptised him loved him so that they hoped to regain some virtue from a touch:

> They clung too fast; great Amphitrite so
> Embraces th'earth, and will not let it go.

King ought to have swum unscathed through the Irish Seas just as Achelous runs untainted through salt Doris to meet his Arethusa,

> Or else (like Peter) trode the waves: but he
> Then stood most upright, when he bent his knee.

(This is an allusion to the report that King knelt in prayer while the vessel was sinking.)

John Hayward, Chancellor and Canon Residentiary of Lichfield Cathedral, a little o'erparted in this brilliant company, writes a poem 'To the deceased's vertuous sister the Ladie Margaret Loder', declaring that he is sure that her religion and good churchwomanship, as he remembers them, will enable her to support her loss. 'C.B.', probably Christopher Brembridge, Fellow of Christ's, who contributed a Latin elegy, also consoles the 'vertuous sister', in octosyllabics, but much more ingeniously and academically than the old-fashioned Chancellor of Lichfield: he begs her not to add waters to the sea, declares that her brother lives on in her, transformed into a different sex, and implores her to stay with them yet awhile before they be compelled to mourn her brother a second time.

R. Brown, otherwise unknown, arranges his decasyllabic couplets in three stanzas with final triplets, each stanza forming a stage in a three-fold argument. (1) Is King really drowned? Will he not return like gold from the refiner's fire or streams to the ocean? (2) Yes, but what have we gained if he lives ensphered

where only stars can applaud him? (3) Weep for him, then.
Tears retained might spread into a Lethe that would drown his
memory. Weep them away:

All waters are pernicious since *King* dy'd.

This is nearer to Donne in his more seriously hyperbolical manner
than to the sheer intellectual fireworks of Cleveland. Indeed, I
am inclined to wonder whether it may not have been Donne's
Valediction: of weeping that suggested to these poets the many
ingenious things that might be said about tears and seas, true
though it be that conceits of a less intellectual kind about sea-
like tears and gale-like sighs were common enough in European
poetry long before Donne began to write. Perhaps, though, they
required no suggestion, but perceived at once the enormous
possibilities of their subject.

The last poem before Milton's is by Thomas Norton, Fellow
of Christ's, a short poem in octosyllabics, of which the beginning
is slightly reminiscent of Wootton's 'You meaner Beauties of the
Night': let the Moor haste north, for there is a jewel in the Irish
seas more precious than all those he possesses. Let poets no
longer feign that Apollo retires to rest on the western billows:

I'th' Irish sea, there set our Sun;
And since he's set, the day's undone.

This, then, was how Milton's Cambridge contemporaries
thought fit to commemorate Edward King, and no doubt many
fully believed that this blaze of wit would continue to coruscate
over the Irish Sea for ever and for ever. If, as I have suggested,
Milton saw copies of some, or even perhaps all, of the other
contributions, their effect upon him was like that of masterpieces
upon Gerard Manley Hopkins, who said that they inspired him
to go and do otherwise. This parallel, as perhaps I need scarcely
insist, is not intended to be exact. Masterpieces inspired Hopkins
to do something out of his own head: the own-headedness, the
untraditionality, of most of the other elegies on King, seems
merely to have confirmed Milton in his convictions about what
he (unlike many of his modern critics) regarded as the true
tradition both of English and of European poetry.

'LYCIDAS' AND PASTORAL ELEGY

Although Milton seems to have taken a few hints and even a few phrases from these examples of the new style in funeral elegy, he returned to a far older tradition. The ingenious conceits and the colloquial diction of his contemporaries must have seemed strangely remote, for an other and statelier music was vibrating in his memory—something, perhaps, like this:

> Groan welaway for me now you glades and Dorian waters,
> Make a lament, you streams, for loved and lovable Bion.
> Mourn with me now, you orchards, and moan you whispering
>   woodlands,
> Breathe your fragrance, flowers, from grief-dispirited clusters;
> Now be for sorrow alone your redness, roses and windflowers,
> Utter now, Hyacinthus, the word inscribed, and for ever
> Babble it forth with your petals: the lovely singer has
>   perished . . .
> Satyrs mourned you as well and sable-vestured Priapi,
> Pans deplored the loss of your song and in every woodland
> Naiads burst into weeping and waters turned into tears.
> Echo too in the rocks laments that now she is silent,
> No more able to mimic your lips. And, loth to have lost you,
> Trees have cast their fruit to the ground and the flowers have
>   faded.
> No good milk has flowed from the flocks, from the hives no honey,
> Perished with grief it lies in the comb; for, alas no longer,
> Now that honey of yours has gone, shall the other be garnered.

That is from the Ἐπιτάφιος Βίωνος, the *Lament for Bion*, the third of the Greek bucolic or pastoral poets, after Theocritus and Moschus, as he was reckoned in antiquity, although very little of his surviving poetry is really pastoral at all. The lament was for long attributed to Moschus, but it seems rather to have been by an unknown pupil of Bion's. It is, I believe I am correct in saying, the only classical poem, whether in Greek or Latin, that can be correctly described as a pastoral elegy. The matter is important, for many of Milton's editors seem to suggest that in classical antiquity the pastoral elegy, as a literary form, was almost as recognised and established as the pastoral itself. Milton, you will find them saying, has taken over certain fixed con-

ventions: the fiction that all nature is mourning the dead shepherd; the reproach addressed to the Guardian nymphs for their
heedlessness; the procession of appropriate mourners; the list of
flowers scattered on the dead shepherd's grave; the consolation,
or change of tone, from sadness to joy at the thought of his
immortality.

Let us consider, first, which of these supposedly fixed conventions are to be found in the Lament for Bion, which, as I have
said, is the only true example of a pastoral elegy that has survived
from classical antiquity; next, which of them are to be found in
one poem of Theocritus, one of Bion and one of Virgil which,
though not strictly pastoral elegies, seem to have been regarded
as such by various Renaissance poets and by Milton's modern
editors; and finally, which of them are to be found in various
examples of the English pastoral elegy before Milton.

In the passages I have translated from the beginning of the
Lament for Bion nature is both exhorted to lament and described
as lamenting. There is no formal procession of mourners, but
merely a mention of those who mourned: Apollo, the Satyrs,
Pans, Priapi and nymphs; Galatæa; many cities and towns.
There is no mention of flowers to be scattered on Bion's grave,
although at the beginning of the poem roses and windflowers
are exhorted to let their redness henceforth be a sign of mourning and Hyacinthus is exhorted to utter the letters (αἰ, αἰ, alas,
alas!) inscribed on his petals. And so far from there being a
transition to consolation, there is this memorable passage:

> Ah, for alas! when mallows about the garden have perished,
> They and the parsley green and the curly-clustering anise
> Live yet again and flourish another year in their season:
> We, though, who grow so greatly in height, in strength and
>   wisdom,
> We, so soon as we die, in hollowed earth without hearing
> Sleep on soundly for ever a wakeless, infinite slumber.

> ἄμμες δ'οἱ μεγάλοι καὶ καρτεροί, οἱ σοφοὶ ἄνδρες

Wordsworth remembered that line from the Lament for Bion,
and indeed it may well have been his recollection of the whole
passage where it occurs that largely inspired one of his most

I

memorable sonnets.[1] And more than a hundred years later Professor Arnold Toynbee, at the conclusion of an eloquent letter to *The Times* (22 April 1936), introduced the same line into a Greek epitaph on the Abyssinians and the Europeans:

They, naked and barbarous though they were, did not fear the weapons of terrifying Ares, but fighting bravely hand to hand, still free, went down unshrinking into Hades. We, though, the great and powerful, we the wise (ἡμεῖς δ' οἱ μεγάλοι καὶ κάρτεροι, οἱ σόφοι), our fate is to die after tasting the sore pains, but not by a martial death: that gift God has never given to those who have broken their oaths.

I have digressed, perhaps, but it seemed worthwhile to insist that this so living and life-begetting line occurs in a pastoral, a form which Dr Johnson described as 'easy, vulgar, and therefore disgusting'. Many pastorals, like many sonnets, tragedies and epics, have been whelmed in everlasting darkness, but only *carent quia vate sacro*. A poetic form, like a game at chess, is what you make of it.

There is, then, no transition from mourning to consolation in the *Lament for Bion*, although it is true that at the very end of his poem the poet indulges a half-tender, half-playful fancy, and begs Bion in Hades to sing some song of Sicily to Persephone the Maid, whom Pluto ravished from the Vale of Enna, in the hope that, remembering Sicily, she may restore Bion to his native hills, just as she once restored Eurydice to Orpheus.

Among the surviving poems of Bion himself is a Lament for Adonis, which cannot be regarded as a pastoral elegy, but rather as a literary version of the kind of song that was sung at the Adonis festivals. Here, though, there is some suggestion of a procession of mourners: the poet describes how the Erotes, or Loves, come to tend Adonis, how Hymen has put out every torch before the door, how the Graces bewail him, and even the Fates.

---

[1] Valedictory Sonnet to the River Duddon ('I thought of Thee, my partner and my guide'). This contains the lines:

While we, the brave, the mighty, and the wise,
We men, who in our morn of youth defied
The elements, must vanish.

Very important in the history of pastoral elegy, although it is not really an elegy at all, is the song on the Afflictions of Daphnis which Theocritus introduced into his First Idyll. In that Idyll a shepherd and a goatherd meet and compliment one another on their piping, and in return for a cup which he describes the goatherd persuades Thyrsis the shepherd to sing him the song or ballad of the Afflictions of Daphnis. This poem, which begins as narrative and then passes into a long lament by the dying Daphnis himself, describes the results of a situation which is not explicitly stated but which seems to have been this: that Daphnis had vowed himself to Chastity, had then fallen desperately in love, but had preferred to die of unconfessed and unrequited love rather than break his vow.[1] There is no flower-strewing and there is no transition to consolation, but the other three conventions, as they have been called, are very clearly present. First, the lamentation of Nature: the narrative portion describes how foxes, wolves, lions and cattle mourned for Daphnis, and Daphnis himself exclaims that now, for all he cares, briars and thistles may bear violets, narcissi grow on junipers, pines bear figs, and the nightingale be outsung by the owl. Then, although there is not, strictly speaking, a procession of mourners, there is quite an elaborate procession of those who come either to console or to expostulate: his fellow shepherds, together with the neat-herds and goat-herds, gather round him; Priapus, the flouted god of fertility, taunts him, but gets no reply; the slighted Aphrodite mildly rebukes him, whereupon he threatens her with vengeance after his death. As for the reproach to the tutelary nymphs for their negligence, it is there at the very beginning of the poem (I quote from Calverley's translation):

The voice of Thyrsis. Aetna's Thyrsis I.
Where were ye, Nymphs, oh where, while Daphnis pined?
In fair Penëus' or in Pindus' glens?
For great Anapus' stream was not your haunt,
Nor Ætna's cliff, nor Acis' sacred rill.

---

[1] See A. S. Gow's commentary in his edition of Theocritus, 1950. Gow rightly insists that what we are told of Daphnis in the poem is not reconcilable with any other known version of the Daphnis legend.

Virgil, who so often imitated Theocritus, has partly imitated this First Idyll in his Fifth Eclogue, where two shepherds engage in a song contest, Mopsus relating the death of Daphnis and Menalcas his deification. Mopsus' song is a very abbreviated and purely narrative version of the *Afflictions of Daphnis*, and concentrates almost exclusively upon the mourning of nature: the nymphs wept for Daphnis, the neat-herds did not water their kine; beasts ate no food, even African lions mourned. Pales and Apollo have now forsaken the fields, weeds choke the corn, thistles and thorns have replaced violets and narcissi. There is no procession of mourners and, although the nymphs are said to have wept for him, there is not, as in Theocritus, any apostrophe of the tutelary nymphs of his region and reproach to them for having failed to protect him. Virgil, however, has imitated this passage, together with several other details in Theocritus's poem, including the procession of comforters, in another Eclogue, the tenth,[1] where he places his friend Gallus in Arcadia and celebrates his unrequited love:

> Quae nemora aut qui vos saltus habuere, puellae
> Naides, indigno cum Gallus amore peribat?

('What groves or what glades held you, virgin naiads, while Gallus was pining with an unrequited love?') At the end of his song on the death of Daphnis in the Fifth Eclogue Mopsus makes mention, very briefly it is true, of funeral honours and of the strewing, if not of flowers, at any rate of leaves, a detail which, as I have said, we do not find in Theocritus or in the Lament for Bion: 'Strew the turf with leaves, shepherds, curtain the springs

---

[1] J. H. Hanford ('The Pastoral Elegy and Milton's *Lycidas*', *P.M.L.A.*, xxv (1910), 420–1) has remarked that 'In general outline this poem resembles *Lycidas* much more closely than any other of the poems of Virgil or Theocritus. In both we have an invocation at the beginning but no mention of the shepherd singer until the end; in both the motive of a procession of mourners is employed; both poems close with eight lines, very similar in spirit, referring to the end of the day and the departure of the shepherd.' In neither the First Idyll nor the Tenth Eclogue is the procession, strictly speaking, one of 'mourners', but rather of those who come either to sympathise or to expostulate. Virgil's procession consists of a shepherd, some swineherds and Menelcas, followed by Apollo, Silvanus, and Pan, and it occupies only twelve lines (19–30). Apollo rebukes Gallus for pining for one who has forsaken him and Pan exclaims against the cruelty of love.

with shade—such honours Daphnis requires of you.' Then—a
piece of Virgilian originality without, so far as we know, any
Greek precedent—Menalcas sings of the deification of Daphnis,
and in this modern scholars are probably right in seeing an
allegorical allusion to the apotheosis of Julius Caesar, belief in
which, for imperial and dynastic reasons, Augustus and his
admirers were doing their best to encourage. Menelcas's song
begins (I quote from the Loeb translation):

Daphnis, in radiant beauty, marvels at Heaven's unfamiliar threshold,
and beneath his feet beholds the clouds and the stars. Therefore frolic
glee seizes the woods and all the countryside, and Pan, and the
shepherds, and the Dryad maids. The wolf plans no ambush for the
flock, and sets no snare for the stag; kindly Daphnis loves peace. The
very mountaine, with woods unshorn, joyously fling their voices
starward; the very rocks, the very groves ring out the song: 'A god is
he, a god, Menelcas!'

This, it seems almost certain, was the precedent for the transition
from lamentation to consolation which is a feature of almost all
Renaissance pastoral elegies. These poets derived their conception of the pastoral elegy mainly from this Fifth Eclogue of
Virgil's, and, appreciating neither the uniqueness of Menalcas's
song nor Virgil's allusion to the apotheosis of Julius Caesar, they
believed that they had classical precedent for concluding a pastoral elegy with the Christian hope of immortality. Indeed, apart
from such pastoralisms as the allusion to shepherds and their
flocks, which are common to all forms of pastoral, the great
majority of English pastoral elegies before Milton use only two
of the five conventions, or characteristics, we have been discussing: they begin with a description of the lamentation of
nature and they conclude with a description of the dead shepherd's immortality. But before proceeding to examine some of
these English elegies I will remark that there are at least two
passages in ancient poetry which, although they do not occur in
pastoral elegies or semi-elegies, are of a pastoral kind and may
well have strengthened and, as it were, amplified the precedent
provided by Virgil's Fifth Eclogue for descriptions of the
lamentations of Nature in pastoral elegies. Both occur in that

most widely read of all Latin poems, Ovid's *Metamorphoses*, and the first of them,[1] describing the laments for the satyr Marsyas after he had been flayed by Apollo, whom he had presumptuously challenged to a contest in flute-playing, may also have provided hints for some of those fancies about tears and the sea in the Cambridge elegies on Edward King.

The rustic Fauns, divinities of the woodlands, wept for him, and his brother satyrs, and Olympus,[2] who even then was still dear to him, and the Nymphs, and all who on those mountains pastured fleecy flocks and horny herds. Fertile Earth grew moist and, moistened, gathered the tears they had let fall and imbibed them into her inmost veins, and, when she had made them into water, emitted them into the empty airs. Thence, hastening through steep banks to the devouring main, the Marsyas, Phrygia's most limpid river, takes its name.

The second of these passages[3] describes the lamentations for Orpheus after the Maenads had torn him to pieces:

You the mournful birds, Orpheus, you the multitude of beasts, you the rigid rocks, you the woods that had often followed your songs bewept; shedding their leaves and cutting their hair, the trees grieved for you; even rivers, they say, were augmented by their own tears and naiads and dryads wore their veils black-edged and hair unbound.

The first pre-Miltonic English pastoral elegy I will mention is the Lament for Basilius in Sidney's *Arcadia*,[4] a not very distinguished poem in fifteen-line stanzas. There seem to be some echoes of the Lament for Bion, which Sidney may or may not have known directly, and also of Virgil's Fifth Eclogue, but the classics are seen through a very medieval glass. The poem begins with a series of invitations to mourn, addressed to a long list of what Wordsworth called natural objects. Then, instead of the usual transition to consolation, comes a complaint against Nature and a rather medieval meditation on the vanity of life:

---

[1] vi. 392–400.
[2] Not the mountain, but the pupil and friend of Marsyas, whom he had instructed in flute-playing.
[3] xi. 44–9.
[4] 1590 edn, Bk. iii, ch. 25; *Works*, ed. A. Feuillerat, 1922–6, i. 498 ff.

the snake renews her skin, the trees their leaves, but man perishes. Justice, bounty, goodness, have died with Basilius. We see that death is our home and life but a delusion.

A far finer poem—indeed, despite those inequalities of style which its author so seldom avoids, by far the finest English pastoral elegy before *Lycidas*—is Spenser's Lament for Dido in the November Eclogue of *The Shepherd's Calendar*. Dido, it has been plausibly suggested, was the daughter of his patron, Young, Bishop of Rochester. 'E.K.' says, in the brief argument prefaced to it:

This Æglogue is made in imitation of Marot his song, which he made vpon the death of Loys the frenche Queene. But farre passing his reache, and in myne opinion all other the Eglogues of this booke.

It is, as Professor Renwick has demonstrated, an eclectic version of Marot's *Complainct de Madame Loyse de Savoye*, which, with various additions of his own, may be described as a series of variations on the two main themes of Virgil's fifth Eclogue, the description of Nature lamenting the death of Daphnis and the description of his apotheosis. Spenser, as I have said, in comparison with Milton, nearly always tends to view the classics through a kind of medieval glass but, making due allowance for this, one may roughly indicate the relation between classical and medieval tradition in his elegy by means of a short analysis. The poem is made up as follows. An unclassical invocation of Melpomene—unclassical at least as far as pastoral went. A classical exhortation to the shepherds to mourn. An unclassical interrogation whether, now that its fairest flower has faded, life is still worth living? A possibly classical, but equally possibly Old Testament, reflection that Man, unlike the flowers, does not revive. An exaggerated treatment, such as Renaissance poets favoured, of the classical theme of the lamentations of Nature, the nymphs and the Muses. A medieval reflection on the world's brittleness. A transition to Christian consolation, followed by a description of the apotheosis and sanctification of Dido.

Whence is it, that the flouret of the field doth fade,
And lyeth buryed long in Winters bale:

Yet soone as spring his mantle doth displaye,[1]
It floureth fresh, as it should neuer fayle?
But thing on earth that is of most availe,
  As vertues braunch and beauties budde,
  Reliuen not for any good.
    O heauie herse,
The braunch once dead, the budde eke needes must quaile,
  O carefull verse.   (ll. 83-92)

The corresponding passage in Marot is as follows:

D'où vient cela, qu'on voit l'herbe sechante
Retourner viue, alors que l'Este vient?
Et la personne au Tombeau trebuchante
Tout grande soit, iamais plus ne reuient?

This may possibly have been suggested by that beautiful passage in the Lament for Bion about the willows, the parsley and the anise, but equally possibly by *Job*, xiv. 7-10:

For there is hope of a tree, if it be cut down, that it will sprout again, and that the tender branch thereof will not cease. Though the root thereof wax old in the earth, and the stock thereof die in the ground; yet through the scent of water it will bud, and bring forth boughs like a plant. But man dieth, and wasteth away: yea, man giveth up the ghost, and where is he?

Marot has greatly expanded passages in Virgil's description of nature lamenting for Daphnis, and Spenser in his turn has expanded Marot: faded locks fall from the lofty oak, rivers are dried up and replaced by floods of tears, flocks refuse their food, beasts wail, wolves chase the sheep that now lack their shepherdess, the turtle-dove and the nightingale lament, the nymphs carry cypress instead of olive and the Muses wear elder instead of bay. Indeed, this theme of the lamentation of nature gave only too much encouragement to the natural extravagance of Elizabethan rhetoric, and in the hands of lesser poets than Spenser easily passed into the ludicrous.

---

[1] 'doth displaye': the true reading is almost certainly 'hath displayde'. In every other stanza in this poem the first line rhymes with the third: why should Spenser have here used the infinitive rather than the past participle, thus depriving himself of the obvious rhyme with 'fade'?

I have mentioned Sidney's Lament for Basilius. On Sidney's own death numerous collections of elegies were published, including one by each of the two universities. A collection of eight elegies, opened by Spenser's *Astrophel*, was appended to the 1595 edition of Spenser's *Colin Clouts come Home Again*, and with a brief review of these and of Spenser's *Daphnaïda* we may conclude our examination of English pastoral elegies before *Lycidas*.

Astrophel is one of Spenser's least successful poems. It lacks all distinction of phrase, and, as in *Daphnaïda*, there is a curious attempt to blend classical tradition with something like medieval allegory. The allegorical framework is provided by the legend of Adonis as told by Ovid in the tenth book of the *Metamorph-oses*—and the poem is mainly concerned with Astrophel's love for Stella, who is regarded as the spur to all his noble deeds, and who is represented as bewailing his destruction by the Spanish boar. Professor Renwick seems to suggest that Spenser also has in mind Bion's *Lament for Adonis* and the anonymous *Lament for Bion*, together with Theocritus's First Idyll and Virgil's Fifth Eclogue: if so, he is viewing these poems from a great distance and through a very dark glass. For example, instead of apostrophising the tutelary nymphs, as Theocritus and Milton do, he apostrophises Astrophel's companions:

> Ah where were ye this while his shepheard peares,
> To whom aliue was noght so deare as hee. (ll.127 f.)

He pretends that Stella immediately followed him in death and (after Ovid's version of the Adonis story) that the Gods transformed both of them into a single flower.

Spenser's poem is followed by *The Dolefull Lay of Clorinda*, by Sidney's sister, the Countess of Pembroke, a poem in which the rhetorical pattern is rather wordily filled out and where the classical connections seems to be discerned mainly through the medium of Spenser's lament for Dido in the *Shepherd's Calendar*. Nature, we are told, is disconsolate:

> Woods, hills and riuers, now are desolate,
> Sith he is gone the which them all did grace:
> And all the fields do waile their widow state,
> Sith death their fairest flowre did late deface. (ll.25–8)

The exhortation to mourn is unclassically addressed to the Shepherd lasses instead of to the guardian nymphs:

> Breake now your gyrlonds, O ye shepheards lasses,
> Sith the faire flowre, which them adornd, is gon.

Then comes the transition to consolation: Astrophel lives in eternal bliss, where a thousand celestial birds carol to him day and night.

The Countess of Pembroke's poem is followed by *The Mourning Muse of Thestylis*, by Spenser's friend Lodowick Bryskett. It is in Alexandrine quatrains, and its style, as might be expected of such a metre, seldom rises above that of the Masque of the Nine Worthies in *Love's Labours Lost*. After exhorting the nymphs to lament, he describes the lamentations of nature with conscientious thoroughness. Thames, Seine, Mosel, Scheldt and Danube all roared with grief; the sylvan gods lamented him and the beasts forsook their food. Father Ocean, roused by their cries, rebuked the mourners, declaring that destiny was unalterable. Then, after Astrophel has uttered his dying prayer, there is further mourning by Nature and natural objects: the sun shrouded his beams, the mountains shook, the rivers reversed their streams, ghosts and portents appeared, dogs howled. Then comes a description of Stella's weeping and of her lament and of the Countess of Pembroke's weeping, so ingeniously exploited by Cupid:

> The blinded archer-boy, like larke in showre of raine
> Sat bathing of his wings, and glad the time did spend
> Vnder those cristall drops, which fell from her faire eies,
> And at their brightest beames him proynd in louely wise.

Nature wept so much that there was danger of a second flood. The poem concludes with a description of Astrophel in Elysium.

There follows *A Pastorall Aeglogue upon the Death of Sir Philip Sidney*, also by Bryskett, which is metrically, at least, more satisfying, or less rebarbative! It is mainly a dialogue on Sidney's virtues and exploits, but it contains further description of the lamentations of nature.

That process of medievalisation which, together with more or less of Elizabethan extravagance, we have noticed in all these examples of the pastoral elegy, is still more strikingly apparent in Spenser's *Daphnaïda*, which he wrote in 1590 to commemorate Douglas Howard, the first wife of Arthur Gorges. The title, as Professor Renwick has suggested, seems to have been made out of the name Daphne (adapted, perhaps, from the *Daphnis* of Theocritus and Virgil), on the analogy of *Odysseis* and *Aeneidos*. Except for a stanza or two describing the lamentations of nature, the only Theocritean or Virgilian element in Spenser's poem is the pastoral convention itself, into which, in the guise of a shepherd, he has introduced the Man in Black from Chaucer's *Book of the Duchess*. This mourning shepherd tells the poet how he caught and tamed a young white lioness (the Howard coat of arms was a white lion) and kept her on a silver chain until she was killed by a cruel satyr. Having heard all this described at length, the puzzled poet asks him to 'aread this doubtfull case', whereupon the mourner replies that Daphne is dead, and proceeds with a more formal lament. Except for one or two passages (e.g. lines 308–29) it is a dreary and undistinguished poem.

It should now be clear, not only that Milton could have learnt little from his English predecessors about the writing of pastoral elegy, but that *Lycidas* is a much more original, a much more unprecedented, kind of poem than has commonly been supposed. Even if we regard only the five so-called conventions which I mentioned at the beginning of this discussion, it is a fact that in not one of the four possible classical models (only one of which, the *Lament for Bion*, is in the strict sense a pastoral elegy) do they all occur; that the only classical precedent we shall find for Milton's procession of mourners is the procession (or rather, for it has not the formality of a procession, the successive appearances) of sympathisers and expostulators in Theocritus's song on the Afflictions of Daphnis, together with (partly imitated from Theocritus) Virgil's procession of those who come to question and comfort Gallus in the Tenth Eclogue; and that the only classical precedent we shall find for his catalogue of flowers (an afterthought, by the way, as we shall see later) are two lines at the end of Mopsus's Song on the Death of Daphnis in Virgil's

Fifth Eclogue. Indeed, whether in a pastoral context or elsewhere, it is difficult to recall anything like an elaborate list of
flowers in classical poetry, and I strongly suspect that it was
suggested to Milton by the flower passages in Spenser's March
eclogue, in *The Winter's Tale*, and in *Cymbeline*. 'Ay', as Hamlet
exclaims in the Bad Quarto, 'Ay, there's the point': we can always
find other poets suggesting details to Milton, but we cannot find
them suggesting his designs. From *L'Allegro* and *Il Penseroso*
onwards it is above all in structure and design, in architectonic
power, that his genius is apparent. In *Comus* we can point to
numerous details of phrasing, of thought, and of incident that
were suggested to Milton by earlier writers, both classical and
English, but we cannot point to any particular play, or masque,
or pastoral drama and declare that this was his main source.
He has absorbed and largely transmuted a vast amount of
industrious and select reading and has combined his acquisitions
into a design that is essentially his own. Here, subject though it is
to various distinctions and qualifications which I cannot now
develop, I will suggest that there is an interesting and characteristic difference between Milton and Shakespeare: in Shakespeare's maturer work the phrasing and the details are essentially
original, but he generally takes his plots and designs from
wherever he can find them, and the success of his play is often
largely dependent on the luckiness of his choice; Milton's
originality, on the other hand, consists rather in his adaptation,
transmutation, and combination of detail suggested to him by his
vast and various reading. One could spend a lifetime tracing this
detail back to its literary sources, but for the plot, design, and
structure of *Comus* and *Lycidas*, of *Paradise Lost*, *Paradise Regained*
and *Samson Agonistes*, the only source was Milton himself.

Lycidas, in fact, is an even more original poem than *Comus*.
Not only has Milton, from his reading of the classic pastoral
elegies, or pastoral semi-elegies, and also, no doubt, of various
Renaissance imitations, accepted five conventions and developed
each of them with an emphasis and a formal clarity such as it
had never received before; he has also accepted and developed
many other details from classic pastoral poetry in general, and,
above all, he has enlarged the scope of the pastoral elegy in

a manner analogous to that in which various Renaissance poets, and chiefly Spenser in *The Shepherd's Calendar*, had enlarged the scope of the ordinary pastoral. Just as Spenser introduced into *The Shepherd's Calendar* his views on poetry and on religion, Milton has introduced into *Lycidas* two most impressive digressions, one on the self-dedication required of those who would achieve the highest poetry and on the nature of true fame, and the other on the difference between true shepherds such as King and the many false ones. It has been objected (a point to which I shall return later) that the poem is as much about Milton as about King; nevertheless, King is never allowed to drop out of the poem. Every part of the poem, which, if not a continuous argument, is at any rate a continuous reflection, follows naturally and inevitably from what has gone before and leads naturally and inevitably to what comes next, and in everything that is said King and his death are more or less immediately present. Milton insists no less than the other Cambridge elegists on King's learning and poetic gift, on his piety, and on the circumstances and manner of his death, although he does so in a far more classical and traditional, a far less ingenious and fashionable way. This poem has been accused of impersonality, but his pastoral and allegorical description of King and himself as fellow-students is more personal than anything in the other elegies. And although he does not say ingenious things about tears and the sea, he finds in the circumstances of King's death an opportunity (partly suggested, perhaps, by certain details in the other Cambridge elegies) for an apostrophe to the tutelary nymphs of that region, for some magnificent and original evocation of local scenery and legend, and for a beautifully managed transition to consolation in the reflection that

> *Lycidas* sunk low, but mounted high,
> Through the dear might of him that walk'd the waves.

Milton, in fact, has transformed the pastoral elegy almost as completely as in *Comus* he has transformed the masque. The only other example of the form that, in sheer power of style, may justly be compared with *Lycidas* is the earliest of all, the *Lament for Bion*, and even that is inferior to it in variety and design. Shelley's

Adonaïs also, perhaps, presents itself for comparison, for although it is not, strictly speaking, a *pastoral* elegy, it is certain that but for *Lycidas*, and the hints that *Lycidas* suggested, it could not have been what it is.

The power of *Lycidas* is so inseparably connected with its wonderful architecture and continuity that, before proceeding, I shall offer a short analysis of the poem, following, with a few modifications, the excellent one given by Oliver Elton in his edition.[1] In the Trinity manuscript Milton has divided it into eleven clearly marked sections or paragraphs, beginning the first line of each new paragraph in the left-hand margin. This paragraphing is followed exactly in the 1645 edition, except that there, as was customary, the first line of each new paragraph is indented. 1645 even follows the Trinity manuscript in one curious error: Milton, through some oversight, begins his third paragraph at line 25, in the middle of a sentence,

> Together both ere the high Launs appear'd,

instead of at line 23

> For wee were nur'st upon the selfe same hill.

Elton introduces two further paragraph divisions, at line 108 and line 152: these I shall refer to as 8a and 9a.

(1) ll.1–14. Lycidas the singer must himself be sung.

(2) ll.15–22. May someone perform the like office for me!

(3) ll.23–36. For we were nurst upon the self-same hill.

(4) ll.37–49. All nature speaks of his loss.

(5) ll.50–63. Apostrophe to the guardian nymphs, followed by the reflection that it is idle to blame them, since even the Muse herself could not save Orpheus.

(6) ll.64–84. (First digression). Why labour at verse? Why not dally or write songs of dalliance? Atropos prevents what Fame spurs us on to. Not so, replies Phoebus, true Fame is rewarded in Heaven, not on earth.

(7) ll.85–102. Invocation of the Theocritean Arethusa, a fountain at Syracuse, and of Virgil's native river the Mincius, as

---

[1] *Milton's Minor Poems*, ed. Oilver Elton, 1910.

symbolising, respectively, the muses of Sicilian and of Latin pastoral: partly, it may be, in order to suggest that the foregoing reflections had a higher source of inspiration than the pastoral muses, partly to signify that he is now returning to the pastoral mood, and partly, perhaps, to apologise for the apparent breach of *decorum* he has committed by writing, during the digression, in a strain higher than is appropriate to pastoral poetry. Beginning of the procession: Neptune's herald announces that it was not the waves or winds but 'that fatall and perfidious Bark' that destroyed Lycidas.

(8) ll.103–7. Continuation of the procession: Camus laments his dearest pledge.

(8a) ll.108–31. Continuation of the procession and second digression: St Peter could well have spared for Lycidas the many false shepherds whose fall is foretold.

(9) ll.132–51. Invocation, for the same reasons as after the first digression, of the river Alpheus, lover of Sicilian Arethusa, and of the pastoral Muse. Let the Sicilian vales send all their flowers to strew Lycid's hearse.

(9a) ll.152–64. But the hearse is empty, and his bones are buried—where? To the Hebrides, or to the mount where Michael gazes? Michael, restore him!

(10) ll.165–85. Weep no more, for Lycidas has sunk only to rise through the dear might of him that walked the waves.

(11) ll.186–93. Day and dirge are over, but tomorrow brings new labour and shepherding.

Such is the plan and structure of what I venture to regard as the most perfect poem of its length in the English language. It may be regarded either as the greatest of English elegies or (with Wordsworth's Immortality Ode as its only rival) as the greatest of English odes.[1] For metrically, with its long paragraphs, its irregularly placed rhymes, and its occasional admixture of short lines, it may be regarded as an ode, having affinities both with the Italian canzone and with Spenser's *Epithalamion* and

---

[1] Perhaps Leishman might have taken Gray's Odes and Hopkins' 'The Wreck of the Deutschland' into consideration. Ed.

Prothalamion.[1] Milton has here achieved, in a poem of nearly two hundred lines, and in an entirely different tradition, that consecutiveness and untransposability which is the distinguishing characteristic of Donne's *Songs and Sonnets* and of many of George Herbert's poems. He has so completely absorbed and transmuted the various conventions and traditions he has accepted and the vast amount of industrious and select reading he displays that they never for a moment impede or hinder the long majestic march and energy divine.

Dr Johnson's objections to the poem are well known: that 'its form is that of a pastoral, easy, vulgar, and therefore disgusting'; that it is 'not to be considered as the effusion of real passion'; and that with trifling fictions Milton has mingled 'the most awful and sacred truths'.[2] At this stage in our argument it scarcely seems necessary to embark upon any elaborate defence of the pastoral form: I will merely remark that Milton could adapt any form to his purposes and use it greatly; I will point to the Lament for Bion; and I will quote Thomas Warton: 'Lycidas,' he declares, replying to Dr Johnson,

has but little of the bucolick cant, now so fashionable. The Satyrs and Fauns are but just mentioned. If any trite rural topics occur, how are they heightened!... We cannot blame pastoral imagery, and pastoral allegory, which carry with them so much natural painting.... Subordinate poets exercise no invention, when they tell how a shepherd has lost his companion, and must feed his flocks alone without any judge of his skill in piping: but Milton dignifies and adorns these common artificial incidents with unexpected touches of picturesque beauty, with the graces of sentiment, and with the novelties of original genius.[3]

In reply to Dr Johnson's objection to the mingling of pagan and Christian images and ideas, I will merely point to the general

---

[1] For his occasional unrhymed lines (10 out of 193) Milton if he required it, had ample precedent in Tasso's *Aminta* and Guarini's *Pastor Fido*: in both, but especially in the latter, there are numerous passages where sometimes unrhymed lines predominate and where hepta-syllabics are mingled in varying proportions with hendecasyllabics. Indeed, in the *Pastor Fido*, where pastoral drama seems so often to be aspiring towards pastoral opera, such passages greatly predominate over those in pure blank verse.

[2] *Lives of the Poets*, ed. G. B. Hill, 1905, i. 163, 165.

[3] *Poems upon several Occasions by John Milton*, ed. Thomas Warton, 1785, p. 34.

practice of Renaissance poets, which I have already made some attempt to explain and justify in my remarks on the Doctrine of *Comus*, and I will add that in the invocations of Arethusa and Mincius and of Alpheus, which follow the two digressions, Milton almost seems to be insisting on the distinction between his beliefs and his fancies, as also in the lines (152–3) which immediately follow the flower passage:

> For so to interpose a little ease,
> Let our frail thoughts dally with false surmise.

On the other hand, Dr Johnson's objection that the poem is 'not to be considered as the effusion of real passion' and that 'where there is leisure for fiction there is little grief', requires a more careful reply, because there are still many readers who believe, mistakenly, that the function of an elegy is to express grief. I have already more than once insisted that the purpose of an elegy is to make the person commemorated remembered, and that the authors of the so un-Miltonic other elegies on King were aware of this, although their conception of poetic memorability was at fault. The point has been splendidly put by Professor Wright, in a passage I will quote:

The elegy is not, as often thought, merely a lament for an individual, but an elaborate literary memorial intended to perpetuate his memory. The duty or practical job of the elegist, as of the sculptor in similar circumstances, is to commemorate the dead by creating a worthy and enduring work of art; only if the work endures as literature has the intention of the elegy been fulfilled. Consequently the predominant motive of the elegist, however sincere his personal grief, must be an artistic one, implying a literary detachment such as is evident in the opening and closing lines of 'Lycidas'. Milton chose to work in a form of the elegy sanctioned by long tradition and by the oustanding names of Theocritus, Vergil, and Spenser; and the poem is partly inspired, as all Milton's greatest work is, by a literary ambition—the ambition to produce in English a consummate example of the pastoral elegy. His success in this literary ambition measures his success as an elegist; but for 'Lycidas' the name of Edward King would long ago have been forgotten.[1]

---

[1] John Milton, *Shorter Poems*, p. 173.

THE TWO DIGRESSIONS

When Milton included *Lycidas* in the 1645 edition of his poems he appended to it the following sub-title:

In this Monody the Author bewails a learned Friend, unfortunatly drown'd in his Passage from *Chester* on the *Irish* Seas, 1637. And by occasion foretels the ruine of our corrupted Clergy then in their height.

Partly because of this last sentence (written, it should be remembered, in the middle of the Civil War), and partly because of inadequate literary and historical knowledge, many readers seem almost to have supposed that Milton seized the occasion in order to attack the clergy, that this was the subject uppermost in his mind, and accordingly, for them, what I have called the second digression has come to assume a quite exaggerated importance, to throw the whole poem rather out of focus, and thereby to impair that structural unity on which I have been insisting. It will therefore perhaps be as well to begin a more detailed consideration of the poem with some remarks on this passage. First, I will remark that this solemn, stately, and tremendously impressive passage is far removed both from the almost playful description of those who came to console or to rebuke the dying Daphnis in Theocritus's ballad-like poem and from Virgil's very brief description of the coming of Menalcas, Apollo, Silvanus and Pan to question the pining Gallus in the tenth Eclogue, the only possible precedents for it in classic pastoral elegy or pastoral semi-elegy. It is reminiscent rather of Homer's description of the shades of the great Achaeans, Agamemnon and Achilles, who approach and speak to Odysseus when he visits Hades to consult Teiresias, or of Virgil's imitation thereof in the sixth book of the *Aeneid*. Nevertheless, the impressiveness and memorability of the passage must not blind us to the fact that, in sheer vehemence of denunciation, it by no means surpasses many things which Spenser, both in *The Shepherd's Calendar* and in *Mother Hubbard's Tale*, had written about corrupt clergy and the Popish peril, and many things that many of Milton's quite orthodox contemporaries were writing and saying on the same subject. It was also, we should remember, included without question in what was almost an official University publication. For a most interesting and important examination of the whole passage I will refer you to an article by Mr E. S. de Beer, entitled 'St Peter in "Lycidas" ', in the *Review of English Studies* for 1947. Mr de Beer is almost certainly correct in assuming that the reason why Milton has introduced St Peter is because of his denunciation of false teachers at the beginning of the second chapter of his Second Epistle:

But there were false prophets also among the people, even as there shall be false teachers among you, who privily shall bring in damnable heresies, even denying the Lord that bought them, and bring upon themselves swift destruction.

In the 'grim Woolf' Milton's readers, like Spenser's, would have immediately recognised an allusion to the Roman Church. To quote Mr de Beer,

George Con(n) had come as papal agent to the Queen's court in the summer of 1636 and his proselytising had met with such success, chiefly among the court ladies, that in October 1637 Laud was compelled to protest; as a result a proclamation was issued against the Roman Catholics on 20 December.

Mr de Beer suggests that Milton's readers would perhaps see an allusion to this proclamation in the words 'and little sed' at line 129. They may have done, although Milton, who began to write his poem in November, must surely have finished it before the proclamation was issued. Perhaps, however, it was the proclamation that caused him to make an interesting correction in his already completed poem. In the Trinity manuscript he originally wrote 'and nothing sed', but corrected it to 'and little sed', and this is the reading in the King memorial volume. In 1645 Milton withdrew his qualification and returned to his original 'and nothing sed': a little had indeed been said, but it had amounted to nothing.

Generations of scholars and readers have made a tremendous and, as it seems to me, quite unnecessary puzzle out of the lines

But that two-handed engine at the door,
Stands ready to smite once, and smite no more.

partly as the result of failing to perceive the Biblical allusions, and partly as the result of misinterpreting the word 'engine' and the phrase 'at the door'. At this time and for long afterwards the word 'engine' could be applied to almost any contrivance devised by human ingenuity to extend human power. Aubrey, for example, describes a 'little engine' which one of the subjects of his characterisations had invented to remove phlegm from his throat. Milton's 'two-handed engine' is simply an impressive way of saying 'that two-handed sword', that sword that required two hands to wield it. Further, 'at the door' or 'at the doors' was then a quite common metaphorical phrase for 'at hand', a fact of which Mr de Beer is aware, although he does not seem to perceive that Milton could not possibly be using it here in any other sense. Robert Baillie wrote in 1637 that 'the whole people thinks Poperie at the doores', and in his translation of *Clavis Apocalyptica*, 1651, p. 36, Samuel Hartlib wrote:

It is very likelie that for certain, som great things are at the door, and that wee may look for fearful and terrible revolutions.

Milton's use of the phrase is partly pleonastic and for the sake of rhyme: all he means is 'that two-handed sword stands ready to strike.' With regard to the Biblical allusions, I cannot do better than quote Mr de Beer:

The most important passage in the Bible concerned with the smiting of shepherds is that in which Christ repeats Zechariah's prophecy: 'For it is written, I will smite the shepherd, and the sheep of the flock shall be scattered abroad' (St Matthew, XXVI. 31; also St Mark, XIV. 27). Here the weapon is not stated, but Zechariah is explicit: 'Awake, O sword, against my shepherd ... smite the shepherd, and the sheep shall be scattered' (XIII.7). Here it is the Lord's shepherd who is to be smitten, but Zechariah also gives the sword as the weapon which is to punish the bad shepherd: 'Woe to the idol shepherd that leaveth the flock! the sword shall be upon his arm and upon his right eye: his arm shall be clean dried up, and his right eye shall be utterly darkened (XI.17 ...).[1]

---

[1] Although Mr de Beer has not suggested it, it seems possible that Milton may also have had in mind a passage from *Revelation*, that book where Protestants were continually discovering prophecies of the pride and iniquity of the Roman Church and of its destruction: xix. 11–21, 'And I saw heaven opened, and behold a white

Although I began with this passage primarily in order to restore it, as it were, to its place and to its context, and to show that the Milton of 1637, who could still regard St Peter's 'Miter'd locks' without suspicion, is not to be regarded as a crusading anti-episcopalian, I will not leave it without two comments on the verbal detail.

First consider this passage:

> And when they list, their lean and flashy songs
> Grate on their scrannel Pipes of wretched straw:

that, if anything, one might suppose, was the original invention of the man who in his prose pamphlets was to reveal himself such a master of rich and racy invective. Nothing, surely, could be more natively English; and it is indeed true that the *Oxford Dictionary* quotes no earlier example of that brilliantly chosen word *scrannel*, meaning thin or meagre. Nevertheless, that most spontaneously invective line is actually a paraphrase of one in Virgil's Third Eclogue, where Menalcas replies to Damaetas's boast that he had beaten Damon in a singing-match:

---

horse; and he that sat upon him was called Faithful and True, and in righteousness he doth judge and make war. . . . And the armies which were in heaven followed him upon white horses. . . . And out of his mouth goeth a sharp sword, that with it he should smite the nations. . . . And I saw the beast, and the kings of the earth, and their armies, gathered together to make war against him that sat on the horse, and against his army. And the beast was taken, and with him the false prophet that wrought miracles before him, with which he deceived them that had received the mark of the beast, and them that worshipped his image. . . . And the remnant were slain with the sword of him that sat upon the horse, which sword proceeded out of his mouth.' In the autograph manuscript volume of his own poems in the Bodleian Library (MS Fairfax 40) the Lord General Fairfax has transcribed (pp. 647 ff.) a religious eclogue entitled *Hermes and Lycaon*, by his great-uncle Edward Fairfax, the translator of Tasso. At the conclusion of this eclogue, with an obvious allusion to the above-quoted passage from *Revelation*, Hermes described how Flora (the Roman Church) and her servants were finally destroyed by a crowned monarch on a white horse:

> Sitting on Isis flowrie banke I spied
> On a white horse a crowned Monarch ride
> Vpon his thigh was write his wondrous name
> Out of his mouth a sword two-edged came
> Flora her beast & all her goats he slew
> And in a lake of fire ther bodys threw
>   This king is Phyches [*sic*] spouse wth him she went
>   And rul'd the world for Floras lease was spent.

Cantando tu illum? aut umquam tibi fistula cera
iuncta fuit? non tu in triviis, indocte, solebas
stridenti miserum stipula disperdere carmen?

(ll. 25–7)

('You beat him in singing? When did you ever own a wax-jointed
pipe? Was it not you, you dunce, who at the cross-roads used to
murder a wretched tune on a strident straw?') My second comment concerns the lines:

The hungry Sheep look up, and are not fed,
But swoln with wind, and the rank mist they draw,
Rot inwardly, and foul contagion spread.

Not only is this not specifically Puritan, it is not even a specifically
Protestant denunciation of corrupt clergy: in fact, as the
eighteenth-century commentator Peck pointed out, Milton very
probably had a passage of Dante in his mind—one in the
Paradiso[1], where Beatrice, like Milton's St Peter, is denouncing
false and vain teaching:

Florence hath not so many Lapos and Bindos as the fables of such
fashion that yearly are proclaimed from the pulpit on this side and on
that; so that the sheep, who know no aught, return from their pasture
fed with wind, and not to see their loss doth not excuse them[2]—

sì che le pecorelle, che non sanno,
tornan del pasco pasciute di vento.

As masters of invective and denunciation Milton and Dante may
be profitably compared.

Since we have begun our more detailed examination of the
poem with a consideration of the second digression, it seems
natural, before proceeding, to devote some attention to the first,
where Milton meditates on the self-dedication required of those
who would achieve the highest poetry, and then on the distinction
between terrestrial and celestial fame. These two digressions compose the doctrinal or didactic element of the poem, as distinct
from the descriptive, a fact which is indicated by Milton himself
when, in the two invocations, or re-invocations, of the pastoral

---

[1] xxix. 103–8.
[2] *The Paradiso of Dante*, tr. P. H. Wicksteed and ed. P. H. Wicksteed and H. Oelsner,
1899, p. 357.

muses, by which each is followed, he exclaims, after the first,

> That strain I heard was of a higher mood,

and, after the second,

> Return *Alpheus*, the dread voice is past,
> That shrunk thy streams; Return *Sicilian* Muse.

The first part of the first digression contains both a distinction between two kinds of muse and also a definite allusion:

> Alas! What boots it with uncessant care
> To tend the homely slighted Shepherds trade,
> And strictly meditate the thankles Muse,
> Were it not better don as others use,
> To sport with *Amaryllis* in the shade,
> Or with the tangles of *Neæra's* hair?[1]

Milton is here distinguishing between the 'thankles Muse', the muse of epic and tragedy, and the elegiac Muse, the Muse of love-poetry such as that of Ovid and Propertius, which had been written in the elegiac couplet. He had made the same distinction in the sixth of his Latin elegies, written just after the completion of the Nativity Ode, and addressed to his friend Diodati, who had excused himself for the badness of his verses on the ground that he was in the midst of Christmas festivities. Milton rejected the excuse: wine and festivity, mirth and dancing and dalliance, were, he had then replied, precisely the things most likely to inspire an elgiac, or love-poet, to excel; whereas one who (like himself, he meant) aspired to be an epic poet and to celebrate gods and

---

[1] Milton's original version of this line, the version which appeared in the King Memorial Volume was

> Hid in the tangles of Neera's hair.

He later substituted, both in the Trinity Manuscript and in the 1645 edition, 'Or with' for 'Hid in'. Since it is scarcely possible to suppose that he imagined the person sporting with Amaryllis in the shade as being at the same time hidden in the tangles of Neæra's hair (a difficult position from which to sport with Neæra's companion), I assume that, if he really meant what he said, he meant 'To sport in the shade with an Amaryllis hidden in the tangles of a Neæra's hair', Amaryllis being the more bashful of the two with whom this bad character, this 'vulgar amorist', was simultaneously sporting. It seems possible, however, that Milton (with unusual carelessness) neither meant what he said nor said what he meant, and only discovered the fact after the 1638 version had been printed.

heroes must live with Pythagorean simplicity:

> Additur huic scelerisque vacans, & casta juventus,
> Et rigidi mores, & sine labe manus.
> Qualis veste nitens sacrâ, & lustralibus undis
> Surgis ad infensos augur iture Deos. (ll.63–6)

('More than this, his youth must be chaste and free from sin, his manners strict, and his hand without stain, even like you, O priest, when in sacred vestment and gleaming with the waters of cleansing you rise as augur to face the angry gods.')[1] Milton, then, had already declared that the life of the would-be heroic poet must be as strict as that of a true priest, and, although the fact was not then generally noticed, he is doing the same in *Lycidas*; for 'the homely slighted Shepherds trade' means the office of priest or pastor, and Milton associates it with, speaks of it in the same breath with, the life of the strict meditator of the thankless muse. King was preparing himself to be a true priest, just as Milton, who might also be cut off by an untimely fate, is preparing himself to be a true heroic poet. And thereupon Milton finds himself tempted (or pretends to find himself tempted) to ask whether it would not be better to follow the example of at least one famous modern Latin poet; for as Thomas Warton, in a passage I will quote, pointed out in a concluding note on the palinode to Milton's seventh Latin elegy, the phrase 'as others use', and the mention of Neæra and her hair almost certainly contain an allusion to George Buchanan, who addressed several poems to a certain Neæra, whose golden hair makes what Warton calls 'a very splendid figure' in one of his elegies and in one of his epigrams. Warton, it is true, rather weakened his case by a piece of careless scholarship, for he assumed that Buchanan had another mistress whom he called Amaryllis, and that Milton's 'to sport with *Amaryllis* in the shade' was an allusion to the poem which Buchanan addressed to her. The poem in question is entitled *Desiderium Lutetiae*, which, as Warton ought to have known, means 'Longing for Paris', *Lutetia Parisiorum*, as the Romans called it, and it is not a woman but his beloved city that

---

[1] *The Latin Poems of John Milton*, ed. and tr. W. MacKellar, New Haven, 1930, pp. 99, 101.

Buchanan there celebrates under the pastoral name of Amaryllis. It is, I suppose, just possible that Milton, in his reading of Buchanan's poem, made the same mistake as Warton. Since, however, Milton does not particularise Amaryllis, and since the pastoral name was very common, we may be content to leave her in the shade, and to base the argument that Milton was probably alluding to Buchanan entirely on the fact that Buchanan actually did celebrate 'the tangles of *Neæra's* hair'. In his last elegy, declares Warton,

he raises the following extravagant fiction on the luxuriant *tangles* of this lady's hair. Cupid is puzzled how to subdue the icy poet. His arrows can do nothing. At length, he hits upon the stratagem of cutting a golden lock from Neæra's head, while she is asleep, with which the poet is bound; and thus *entangled* he is delivered a prisoner to Neæra: EL. ix. p. 46. ut supr.

> Fervida, tot telis, non proficientibus, ira
>   Fugit ad auxilium, dia Neæra, tuum;
> Et capiti assistens, te dormitante, CAPILLUM
>   AUREOLUM FLAVÆ tollit ab ORBE COMÆ:
> Et mihi ridenti (quis enim non talia *vincla*
>   Rideat?) arridens brachia vinxit Amor;
> Luctantemque diu, sed frustra, evadere, traxit
>   Captivum, dominæ restituitque meæ.

[His hot anger at so many darts' being unavailing betakes itself, divine Neaera, to your aid; and sitting by your head while you sleep he takes a golden lock from your orb of yellow hair: and as I laughed (for who would not laugh at such bonds?) Love laughingly bound my arms; and led me captive, struggling long but vainly to escape, and restored me to my mistress.]

This fiction is again pursued in his Epigrams. Lib. i. xlv. p. 77. ibid.

> Liber eram, vacuo mini cum sub corde Neæra
>   Ex oculis fixit spicula missa suis:
> Deinde unam evellens ex AURICOMANTE CAPILLUM
>   Vertice, captivis *vincla* dedit manibus:
> Risi equidem, fateor, vani ludibria *nescus*,
>   *Hoc laqueo* facilem dum mihi spero fugam:
> Ast ubi tentani spes irrita cessit, *ahenis*
>   Non secus ac *manicis* implicitus genui.
> Et modo membra *pilo vinctus* miser abstraher *uno*.

[I was free, when Neæra fixed beneath my vacant heart the darts sent from her eyes: then, uprooting a single lock from her golden-haired crown, she put fetters upon my captive hands. I laughed, I confess, at this vain mockery of a binding, and promised myself an easy escape from such a snare; but when I made the attempt and my hope was disappointed, I groaned to find myself enfettered as with manacles of brass. And now I am wretchedly dragged off, my limbs bound by a single hair.]

And to this Neæra many copies are addressed both in Buchanan's *Epigrams*, and in his *Hendecasyllabics*. Milton's insinuation, *as others use*, cannot therefore be doubted. 'Why should I *strictly meditate* the *thankless* muse, and write *sublime* poetry which is not regarded? [Rather, Warton should have said, 'prepare myself for a kind of poetry which I may never live to write.'] I had better, like some other poets, who might be more properly employed, write idle compliments to Amaryllis and Neæra.'[1]

I may add that Buchanan's golden-haired Neæra may well have been suggested to him by the Neæra of a still more famous Renaissance Latin poet, his predecessor Johannes Secundus (Jan Everaerts, 1511–1536). Of the mistresses whom Secundus celebrated, the one who occupies the most prominent place in his verse is Neæra, a blonde Spaniard of great beauty and easy morals, whom he met while acting as secretary to the Archbishop of Toledo. It is true that he only twice refers to the 'tangles of her hair' briefly and incidentally in his *Basia*: once in the phrase *tortiles capillos*,[2] and once in *Basium* XV where he describes how Cupid was drawing his bow to wound her, when, seeing her brow and the hair overspeading it ('Cum frontem sparsosque videns in fronte capillos') together with the rest of her charms, he dropped his arrow and became himself her captive. It is also possible that the name Neæra may have been suggested both to Secundus and to Buchanan by that chestnut-haired Neæra whom Horace, at the end of the fourteenth ode of his third book, sends his boy to fetch, together with perfumes, garlands, and a jar of wine, to help him celebrate Augustus's return from Spain:

dic et argutae propertet Neærae
murreum nodo cohibere crinem

---

[1] *Poems upon Several Occasions by John Milton*, 2nd edn 1791, pp. 474–5.
[2] viii. 20.

('And bid clear-voiced Neæra hasten to bind in a knot her chestnut hair'). At the same time, I think Warton is right in supposing that the 'tangles' of Neæra's hair were suggested to Milton by Buchanan, and that in his general allusion to elegiac or love-poetry Milton has Buchanan more particularly in mind.

But it is the second part of this first digression, where Milton distinguishes between terrestrial and celestial fame, that is especially interesting, because it enables us, looking backwards and looking forwards, to answer that question which has often presented itself: where, exactly, and how, into this deep devotion to his art and to ancient literature, did Milton's Christianity enter? We have seen how Christianity modified his Platonism: how did it modify his humanism in general, his tremendous literary ambition, his almost fanatical dedication, as some might consider it, to the art of poetry? The argument of the passage, perhaps because of the metaphors and the classical allusions, has not always been clearly recognised. It is as follows: Why should one lead an ascetic and almost priestly life in order to obtain at last the reputation of a great heroic or tragic poet, when perhaps one may die before one has been able to begin? Because, although one may not live to obtain the praise of men, one will certainly, if one has deserved it, obtain the praise of God, which in the end is all that matters:

> *Fame* is the spur that the clear spirit doth raise
> (That last infirmity of Noble mind)
> To scorn delights, and live laborious dayes;
> But the fair Guerdon when we hope to find,
> And think to burst out into sudden blaze,
> Comes the blind *Fury* with th'abhorred shears,
> And slits the thin-spun life. But not the praise,
> *Phœbus* repli'd, and touch'd my trembling ears;
> *Fame* is no plant that grows on mortal soil,
> Nor in the glistering foil
> Set off to th' world, nor in broad rumour lies,
> But lives and spreds aloft by those pure eyes,
> And perfet witnes of all-judging *Jove*;
> As he pronounces lastly on each deed,
> Of so much fame in Heav'n expect thy meed.

Consider the first two lines of that passage. 'Spur' may well have
been suggested to Milton by a notable passage in Spenser's
Teares of the Muses, where Calliope, the Muse of Heroic Poetry,
declares that it is hope of the immortal fame she can confer that
spurs noble minds to great deeds:

> Or who would euer care to doo braue deed,
> Or striue in vertue others to excell;
> If none should yeeld him his deserued meed,
> Due praise, that is the spur of dooing well?   (ll.451–4)

—a passage in illustration of which Professor Renwick quotes
in his commentary from North's translation of Amyot's Preface
to Plutarch's *Lives*:

> The immortal praise and glorie wherwith History rewardeth wel-doers,
> is a verie lively and sharpe spurre for men of noble courage and
> gentleman-like nature, to cause them to adventure upon all manner
> of noble and great things.

In connection with 'the clear spirit' we may note that the Oxford
Dictionary distinguishes no less than twenty-five uses of the
adjective *clear*. I think it is probably correct in placing this
passage under sense 14, 'pure, guileless, unsophisticated', which
it regards as a figurative use of sense 3, 'allowing light to pass
through, transparent'; for this meaning accords well with
Milton's conception of the scale of being and of the sublimation
of matter into spirit. The 'clear' spirit is the spirit that has purged
itself (to borrow a Shakespearean phrase that Milton seems to
have remembered) of such mortal grossness, that has moved
farther than most from the brute, nearer than most to the divine.
It is the 'erected spirit', unlike Mammon,

> the least erected Spirit that fell
From Heav'n.

Indeed, in the *Remonstrant's Defence against Smectymnuus* Milton
was again to use the phrase 'clear spirit' and to contrast it with
the spirit of Mammon, when he asked whether learning was to be
sought in the den of Plutus or the cave of Mammon, and replied;

Certainly never any cleare spirit nurst up from brighter influences
with a soule inlarg'd to the dimensions of spacious art and high
knowledge ever enter'd there but with scorn.[1]

And it was with glory as the spur of 'most erected spirits' that
he was to make Satan tempt Christ in the third book of *Paradise
Regained*:

> glory the reward
> That sole excites to high attempts the flame
> Of most erected Spirits, most temperd pure
> Ætherial, who all pleasures else despise,
> All treasures and all gain esteem as dross,
> And dignities and powers all but the highest. (ll.26–30)

In the phrase 'That last infirmity of Noble mind' the word 'that'
has the force of Latin *ille*, and means that well-known infirmity,
that infirmity which even the noblest minds of antiquity, whom
Milton so greatly admired, were never, except perhaps with some
few rare exceptions, really able to transcend. One might quote
innumerable passages. Here is Cicero in the *De Officiis*:

in maximis animis splendidissimisque ingeniis plerumque exsistunt
honoris, imperii, potentiae, gloriae cupiditates;[2]

('in the greatest souls and the most brilliant geniuses there
usually spring up ambitions for civil and military authority, for
power and for glory'). And here is a passage from Sillus Italicus

---

[1] Columbia edn, iii. 162. Later still Clarendon memorably applied the phrase to
Montrose: 'And then there was the marquis of Mountrose, with more of the
nobility, as the earls of Seaforte and Kynoole and others, who adhered to
Mountrose, and believed his clear spirit to be most like to advance the King's
service'. (*History of the Rebellion*, ed. W. D. Macray, 1888, v. 16.) Fulke Greville,
in *Caelica*, Sonnet lxxx, had contrasted

> Cleare spirits, which in Images set forth
> The wayes of Nature by fine imitation

with the 'Dull Spirits'

> which loue all constant grounds,
> As comely veyles for their vnactiuenesse.

> (*Poems and Dramas*, ed. G. Bullough, i. 130)

[2] i. 8.

which Milton almost certainly had in mind when he wrote that
speech of Satan's I have just quoted:

> fax mentis honestae
> gloria,[1]

('glory, the enkindling torch of the erected mind'). The Stoics, in
a sense, transcended it, and there is Stoicism behind a famous
phrase of Tacitus which may well have suggested to Milton the
line in *Lycidas* which we are now considering, *etiam sapientibus
cupido gloriae novissima exuitur*[2] ('even with wise men the desire of
glory is the last to be discarded'), but Stoicism, as Milton was to
make Christ declare in *Paradise Regained*, was really a kind of
self-glorification, and the Stoics made their virtuous man the
equal of God:

> Ignorant of themselves, of God much more,
> And how the World began, and how man fell
> Degraded by himself, on Grace depending.[3]

For Satan in *Paradise Regained*, both in the third book when he
tempts Christ with glory, and in the fourth book, when he
tempts him with the promise of wisdom, with the achievements
of Greek philosophy and Greek literature (a passage where
Milton's intention has been so often misunderstood and where he
has sometimes been represented as narrowly, and in the spirit of
a fundamentalist, denying his own cultural inheritance)—Satan
is to be regarded as the spokesman of merely human virtue, merely
human motives, merely human ideals, of the highest reaches of a
merely human wit, of the aspirings of merely human minds.
These things are in some ways noble, but they do not go far
enough, they lack what for a Christian is the one thing needful, the
love of God and the recognition of man's insignificance apart
from God: without that they may easily turn to corruption, and in
comparison with that they are nothing. To Satan's temptation
with glory, Christ replies that glory merely means the praise of
the people, a miscellaneous rabble.

> Of whom to be disprais'd were no small praise,

---

[1] vi. 332–3.   [2] *Histories*, iv. 6.   [3] iv. 310–12.

and that true glory consists in earning the approval of God, as Job did:

> This is true glory and renown, when God
> Looking on th' Earth, with approbation marks
> The just man, and divulges him through Heaven
> To all his Angels, who with true applause
> Recount his praises.[1]

If we ask, what was the relation between Milton's humanism and his Christianity, and where exactly did his Christianity, so to speak, come in, the fullest reply is to be found in *Paradise Regained*. I do not say that the Milton of *Lycidas* had either experienced his Christianity so profoundly or integrated it to the same extent with his humanism as had the Milton of *Paradise Regained*: nevertheless, here already in *Lycidas*, even though through the mouth of Phoebus, even though partly in the phraseology of Virgil, and even though in naming only the ruler of the classical Olympus, Milton is declaring that the only fame, the only praise, that ultimately matters is that conferred by God. I say 'partly in the phraseology of Virgil', because the lines

> But not the praise,
> *Phœbus* repli'd, and touch'd my trembling ears

were undoubtedly suggested by the opening lines of Virgil's Sixth Eclogue, where he says that he began as a pastoral poet, and that when he felt inclined to sing of kings and battles

> Cynthius aurem
> vellit et admonuit: 'pastorem, Tityre, pinguis
> pascere oportet ovis, deductum dicere carmen'

('the Cynthian (i.e. Apollo) twitched my ear and warned me: "A shepherd, Tityrus, should feed fat sheep, but sing a slender song" '). This passage, incidentally, may have also suggested Milton's subsequent apology to Arethusa and Mincius for having, in this digression, overstepped the limits of pastoral poetry. It was not merely in descriptive and decorative passages that Milton adapted phrases and images from his beloved classics;

---

[1] *Paradise Regained*, iii. 56 and 60–4.

he often used them to express convictions that were characteristically his own, or even characteristically Christian, as in the deeply felt conclusion of the sonnet on his twenty-third birthday,

> Yet be it less or more, or soon or slow,
>> It shall be still in strictest measure eev'n,
>> To that same lot, however mean, or high
> Toward which Time leads me, and the will of Heav'n—

a passage which, as we have already noticed, was almost certainly suggested by one in Pindar's Fourth Nemean Ode. It is also worth remembering that in the letter accompanying a transcription of the sonnet Milton had mentioned, as further proof that his apparent inactivity was not the result of a mere love of studious retirement, but of the presence in himself of that 'desire of honour & repute & immortall fame seated in the brest of every true scholar', a motive which he described as 'if not of pure yet of refined nature'.

There were indeed deep conflicts and tensions in Milton, but they cannot be explained, as has too often been attempted in recent times, in terms of the psychology of repression. Milton himself was well aware of them, or rather, perhaps I should say, he grew increasingly aware of them. He had great literary ambition, and he was aware of the temptation to set the praise of men above the praise of God, the temptation to worship the talent, that one talent which was death to hide, rather than the giver of the talent, in whose service it was to be used. He had also, no doubt, felt a temptation to set an almost excessive store upon that 'old and elegant humanity of Greece' and upon what, in *Areopagitica*, he called 'those ages, to whose polite wisdom and letters we ow that we are not yet *Gothes*, and *Jutlanders*',[1] and, in contemplating these splendours of human achievement, to trust too much in man and to forget, or, at any rate, to underemphasise, what, in his Tractate *Of Education*, he defined as the end of learning, namely, 'to repair the ruines of our first Parents by regaining to know God aright.'[2] His own 'honest haughtinesse, and self-esteem',[3] as he called it, no doubt tempted him to admire

---

[1] Columbia edn, iv. 295–6. [2] Columbia edn, iv. 277.
[3] Columbia edn, iii. 304.

overmuch certain specifically classical virtues and to nourish an un-Christian contempt for misguided multitudes, miscellaneous rabbles, and lesser breeds. That immense fund of creative energy which, in addition to the specific gift of language, is required to make a great poet, has often been generated by great tensions and polarities, and in Milton, I am inclined to think, the chief tension was the unceasing attempt to impose Christianity upon a mind and temper in many ways not naturally Christian, to reconcile his humanism with his Christianity. No doubt the reconciliation was never quite complete, and Milton's habitual attitude to antiquity, his habitual manner of thinking and feeling about it, was perhaps never quite that of Christ in *Paradise Regained*. That, though, is bringing in the infinite, as Gerard Manley Hopkins would have said. In a letter to Robert Bridges, written in 1886, Hopkins reminded him and Canon Dixon and all true poets that fame, though one of the most dangerous things, was nevertheless the true and appointed end of genius and its works, which ought to aim at being known. True, in comparison with virtue, genius and its works were nothing, but that was only by bringing in the infinite. Looked at from the ordinary point of view, he would apply to them Christ's words about virtue: 'Let your light so shine before men, that they may see your good works [say, of art], and glorify your Father which is in heaven.'[1] Milton, however, just because of the very dedicatedness and exclusiveness with which he cultivated his talent, may well have been peculiarly aware of the dangerousness of fame and of the love of fame, and may well have felt a continual need to remind himself that, in comparison with virtue, with Christian virtue, genius and its works were nothing. I may, perhaps, have exaggerated the tension and the conflict: the fact remains that when his Christian faith was tested by what, for him, must surely have been the severest of all possible trials, it was not found wanting. By 1652 he had become totally blind, and now that the exhilarating task of replying to Salmasius, the task which finally cost him his sight, was over, it must have been with a heart-chilling shock that he recognised that his one talent was now

---

[1] St Matthew, v. 16.

K

lodged with him useless. For in verse he was a most careful and fastidious writer, and it must have seemed to him that, without a pen in his hand and paper before him and the ability to make endless rough drafts and revisions and continually to review what he had written, he would never be able henceforth to write more than very short poems, and that his hope of composing the great poem to which he had dedicated so much of his life must now be abandoned. A possibility had occurred which he had not contemplated when he wrote *Lycidas*: he had not, like King, been cut off by an early death, but his ability to use his talent had been destroyed. The manner in which he accepted the situation as it then appeared to him is the measure of his Christian faith:

> When I consider how my light is spent,
>   Ere half my days, in this dark world and wide,
>   And that one Talent which is death to hide,
>   Lodg'd with me useless, though my Soul more bent
> To serve therewith my Maker, and present
>   My true account, least he returning chide,
>   Doth God exact day-labour, light deny'd,
>   I fondly ask; But patience to prevent
> That murmur, soon replies, God doth not need
>   Either man's work or his own gifts, who best
>   Bear his milde yoak, they serve him best, his State
> Is Kingly. Thousands at his bidding speed
>   And post o're Land and Ocean without rest:
>   They also serve who only stand and waite.

The task of the poet and humanist (so it seemed) had been ended; the task of the Christian, to stand and wait, in cheerfulness and without repining, had now really begun.

> Teach us to care and not to care
> Teach us to sit still
> Even among these rocks,
> Our peace in His will—[1]

So wrote a modern poet who has often spoken disparagingly of Milton. Milton had indeed been there and sat still, and if need

---

[1] T. S. Eliot, 'Ash Wednesday'.

were would have remained there, in what Wordsworth called 'cheerful godlines', until the end. Gradually, though, he found that he could dispense with pen and paper, and that he could compose long passages in his mind and retain them in his memory: his muse returned,

> not parted from him, as was feard,
> But favouring and assisting to the end.[1]

In this discussion of the first digression I have perhaps myself shown some tendency to digress, but it seemed a fit occasion to glance, as I said, backwards and forwards, and to collect our thoughts on the subject of Milton the Christian Humanist.

REVISIONS AND AFTERTHOUGHTS

We may begin our more detailed examination of the style and diction of the poem by considering, first, Milton's three revisions of what may be called the Orpheus passage (ll.56–63), and then his addition, followed by a revision, of what may be called the flower passage (ll.136–51)—two extended pieces of re-writing from which we may learn almost as much about his art as from the successive drafts of *At a Solemn Musick*. He made several other revisions, but, interesting and important as many of them are, they do not extend beyond the alteration of single words or phrases, and it will not be necessary to consider them all in detail.

The text of *Lycidas* in the Trinity manuscript may be regarded as Milton's first fair copy, made from a draft which is not preserved. He made certain alterations in this fair copy, and he re-worked the Orpheus passage and extended and re-worked the flower passage on the blank verso facing the page on which he had begun the fair copy. He also seems to have begun by transcribing on this scribble-page a revised version of the opening lines of the poem, in which, before starting his fair copy, he made certain alterations.

Before examining the revisions of the Orpheus passage, I will insist that, considered so to speak, as a rhetorical figure, it is a profoundly original extension of the traditional apostrophe to the

---

[1] *Samson Agonistes*, ll. 1719 f.

guardian nymphs, and, so far as I know, without classical precedent, although it is just what Theocritus or Virgil *might* have done.

> Where were ye Nymphs when the remorseless deep
> Clos'd o're the head of your lov'd *Lycidas*?
> For neither were ye playing on the steep,
> Where your old *Bards*, the famous *Druids* ly,
> Nor on the shaggy top of *Mona* high,
> Nor yet where *Deva* spreads her wisard stream.   (ll. 50-5)

The first example in ancient literature of such an apostrophe to the guardian nymphs occurs, as I have already remarked, at the beginning of Theocritus's ballad-like poem on the Afflictions of Daphnis. Where were you, nymphs, exclaims Thyrsis, when Daphnis was pining with love? Were you in Thessaly, in the vale of the river Peneius or in the glens of Mount Pindus? For certainly you were not in Sicily, by the rivers Anapus or Acis, or on Mount Etna. Mount Pindus in Thessaly was one of the traditional seats of the Muses, but I doubt whether Theocritus is considering it as such: his Thyrsis regards the nymphs he invokes, not as Muses, but simply as the guardian spirits of the regions where Daphnis lived and loved, and he asks them whether, since they were not where they might have been expected to be, they were somewhere else—for example, in Thessaly. Virgil has imitated this apostrophe, together with much else in Theocritus's poem, in his Tenth Eclogue, where he places his friend Cornelius Gallus in Arcadia and celebrates his unrequited love. Virgil, though, no doubt as a compliment to the poetical pretensions of his friend, invokes the nymphs, not as the guardian spirits of various named regions in Arcadia, but as Muses: at any rate, the only three localities he names, Mount Parnassus in Phocis, Mount Pindus in Thessaly, and the spring Aganippe in Bœotia, were all traditional haunts of the Muses:

What groves or what glades held you, maiden Naiads, while Gallus was pining with unrequited love? For it was not the heights of Parnassus or of Pindus that detained you, nor Aonian Aganippe.

Milton, in his own apostrophe to the nymphs, combines in a most original way the element of locality in Theocritus's apos-

trophe and the element of compliment in Virgil's. His nymphs
are guardian spirits of places near the spot where Lycidas was
drowned—of the 'steep' where the Druids lie, that is to say, of
the mountains of Denbighshire, of the Isle of Anglesey (Mona),
and of the river Dee; and yet at the same time the emphatic
'your' in the line

> Where your old *Bards*, the famous *Druids* ly

suggests that he also regards the nymphs, Virgilianly, as Muses,
British Muses, who should have devoted special care to the
preservation of Lycidas the singer. I say 'suggests', because I
do not feel absolutely certain that this is what Milton intends;
although Warton seems to have no doubts whatever that Milton
is apostrophising the nymphs as Muses. 'It is', he declares:

. . . with great force and felicity of fancy, that Milton, in transferring
the classical seats of the Muses to Britain, has substituted places of
the most romantic kind, inhabited by Druids, and consecrated by the
visions of British bards. And it has been justly remarked, how coldly
and unpoetically Pope, in his very correct pastorals, has on the same
occasion selected only the *fair fields* of Isis, and the *winding vales* of
Cam.[1]

This, incidentally, is another example of that 'romanticism' which
Warton and some of his contemporaries discovered and admired
in Milton, and further confirmation of my remark, in considering
L'Allegro and *Il Penseroso*, that the classical Milton has some title
to be regarded as the most romantic of seventeenth-century
poets. For the moment, though, we are more particularly concerned with his classicism. Whether or no my suggestion and
Warton's conviction be correct, there can be no doubt that the
rhetorical form of Milton's apostrophe is Virgilian, and that
his 'Where were ye . . . For neither were ye' was suggested by
Virgil's 'quae nemora . . . nam neque'. Milton, however, without
any classical precedent, but entirely in the classical tradition, at
once proceeds to extend the apostrophe, declaring (I quote his
final version):

---

[1] *Poems upon Several Occasions by John Milton*, ed. Thomas Warton, 1785, p. 13.

> Ay me, I fondly dream!
> Had ye bin there . . . for what could that have don?
> What could the Muse her self that *Orpheus* bore,
> The Muse her self, for her inchanting son . . .

To the Virgilian formula 'Where were ye . . . For neither were ye' he adds 'Yet even had ye been there', and cites, as an *exemplum*, the inability of the Muse herself to save Orpheus.

This very original addition to the Virgilian apostrophe may perhaps have been suggested to Milton by his recollection of a passage in Ovid's elegy on Tibullus. This, the Ninth Elegy in the Third Book of Ovid's *Amores*, is the only funeral, or memorial elegy in that collection of love-poems, and its place there is justified by the fact that Tibullus was himself a love-poet, 'a smooth elegiac poet', as Milton would have said, and that the elegiac couplet, a metre first used in short epitaphs or memorial inscriptions, is here being restored to its original use. I may add that, after the pastoral *Lament for Bion*, this is the only other notable ancient poem in which a poet laments the death of a fellow-poet—a fact which might well have recalled it to Milton's attention and reminded him of the passage in question, in which, reflecting on the inescapability of all-profaning death, Ovid exclaims (ll. 21–2):

> Quid pater Ismario, quid mater profuit Orpheo?
> carmine quid victas obstipuisse feras?

('What did his father, what did his mother avail for Ismarian Orpheus? What his having held wild beasts spell-bound with his song?')

Just as *Comus* contains numerous personifications and phrases such as Shakespeare might have written, *Lycidas* is full of descriptions and turns and rhetorical devices and formulae which we might expect to find in Theocritus or Virgil but which, as a matter of fact, we do not. Milton does not merely imitate or adopt passages or phrases in the classical poets, any more than he merely imitates or adapts passages in Shakespeare: he combines adaptation and insertion, and he is so penetrated by the style and spirit of the classical poets that we are aware of no artistic gap, no change of texture, between his adaptations and his inventions.

Indeed, readers with only a slight knowledge of the classics may often have assumed that he is imitating or adapting when he is really inventing. Except for the doctrinal and didactic substance in the two digressions and the proffer of Christian consolation at the end, there is scarcely anything in *Lycidas* which some classical poet—Theocritus or Virgil or Ovid, or one of the Greek tragedians, or even Homer—might not have said. It is not merely the accuracy and often (to borrow a seventeenth-century word) the 'curiosity' of his classical allusions that distinguishes Milton's classicism from Spenser's, it is this wonderful unity of texture, this ability, not merely to imitate, but to continue, the classical tradition. There is nothing naive or medieval and there is nothing indiscriminately imitative about Milton's classicism: he sees the classics, not through a glass darkly, but face to face.

Let us now consider Milton's successive revisions in this very original extension of the traditional apostrophe to the guardian nymphs. After asking where the nymphs were when the remorseless deep closed upon Lycidas, he originally continued:

> ay mee I fondly dreame
> had yee bin there, for what could that have don?
> what could the golden hayrd Calliope
> for her inchaunting son
> when she beheld (the gods farre sighted bee)
> his goarie scalpe rowle downe the Thracian lee.

Very soon (one may suppose) Milton perceived that the last two lines would not do. He erased them, and replaced them in the margin by four new ones, so that the passage now read:

> what could the golden hayrd Calliope
> for her inchaunting son
> whome universal nature might lament
> and heaven and hel deplore
> when his divine head downe the streame was sent
> downe the swift Hebrus to the Lesbian shore.

The passage had now been completely transformed, but Milton was still dissatisfied, and he worked out a new version on his scribble-page. First, perhaps, he perceived that Calliope's golden hair was a mere piece of prettiness, quite irrelevant either to her

power or to her grief. Keats was to commit the same sentimentalism, as one may call it, in a youthful sonnet,[1] where he
wrote

> Of fair-hair'd Milton's eloquent distress,
> And all his love for gentle Lycid drown'd.

The suggested connection between the eloquence of Milton's
distress and the colour of his hair is the kind of sentimentalism
that might occur to a sub-editor and lead him to compose the
head-line 'Platinum blonde weeps in court'. Milton ejected
both Calliope's golden hair and her name, and made of her a much
more impressive being and a much stronger antithesis to the
guardian nymphs[2] by referring to her in one of those descriptive
phrases or periphrases, which could become tiresome and
mechanical in the hands of lesser poets, but of which he himself,
like Dante, was a master:

> What could the Muse her self that *Orpheus* bore?

There are other examples of such periphrases in *Lycidas*: 'the
Pilot of the *Galilean* lake' (l.109), 'the great vision of the guarded
Mount' (l.161), 'the dear might of him that walk'd the waves'
(l.173). It may well be that this kind of expression was suggested
both to Dante and to Milton by Virgil, as when he says that among
the monsters Aeneas found at the entrance to Avernus was, not
the giant Geryon, but *forma tricorporis umbrae*,[3] 'the form of the
three-bodied shade'. In the hands of lesser artists than Virgil,
even among the poets of antiquity, especially those of the later
Roman empire, this device can be quite as frigid and pedantic as
among the lesser moderns. It makes, for example, a damping and
dispiriting appearance in the one really memorable poem of
Ausonius, in that earliest (so far as I am aware) and, on the whole
most charming example of what Dr Johnson called 'local poetry',

---

[1] 'Keen, fitful gusts are whisp'ring here and there.'

[2] It is this strong antithesis between the guardian nymphs and the Muse herself that
makes me a little uncertain as to whether Milton is really apostrophising the nymphs
both as guardian spirits and, Virgilianly, as Muses. Or is his meaning something
like: 'What could mere British muses have availed, when even the Muse that bore
Orpheus could not save her son?'

[3] *Aeneid*, vi. 289.

the *Mosella*: the architecture of the castles along the banks would not, declares Ausonius, have been disdained by x or y or z, and he gives a long list of famous architects, beginning with 'the Gortynian winger, builder of the Euboic temple', which is his way of referring to Daedalus, and including him 'who, praised even by the enemy, protracted the renowned contests of the Syracusan war', which is his way of referring to Archimedes (ll. 300 ff.).

The line 'What could the Muse her self that *Orpheus* bore' was originally followed by a short line:

> for her inchaunting son;

but in 'the Muse her self' Milton had hit upon a phrase capable of effective repetition: he accordingly used it to lengthen, with expressive effect, the line that followed:

> the muse her selfe for her inchanting son.

Then he perceived that after the line

> whom universal nature might (later 'did') lament

the following line

> and heaven and hel deplore

was merely space-filling and rhyme-supplying. He accordingly replaced it by a new line in which the presence of the Bacchanals, hitherto merely implied, was thrillingly evoked—evoked, not by naming them, but, as with Calliope, by means of a periphrasis:

> when by the rout that made the hideous roare.

Having now used 'when' at the beginning of this line, he had to remove it from the next which originally read

> when his divine head downe the streame was sent.

At first he wrote, substituting 'visage' for 'head' to supply the missing syllable:

> his divine visage downe the streame was sent;

then, perceiving that the collision between the last syllable of

K*

'divine' and the first syllable of 'visage' made an awkward and unnecessary pull-up, he substituted 'goarie', the adjective he had used in his original and not very happy version of the last two lines:

> When shee behelde (the gods farre sighted bee)
> his goarie scalpe rowle downe the Thracian lee.

He had now achieved his final version, that of the 1645 edition:

> What could the Muse her self that *Orpheus* bore,
> The Muse her self, for her inchanting son
> Whom Universal nature did lament,
> When by the rout that made the hideous roar,
> His goary visage down the stream was sent,
> Down the swift *Hebrus* to the *Lesbian* shore.

It is a pity that Milton did not find some way of dispensing with the expletive 'did' in 'did lament'. He had previously used 'might', no doubt an attempt, later rejected as unsatisfactory, to escape from 'did'. The use of 'did', 'do', 'doth', or 'does', sometimes merely in order to supply a syllable, but most often in order to be able to use the infinitive form of the verb as a rhyme with some word one had already thought of, was an all too common practice with sixteenth- and seventeenth-century poets, and does not seem to have been generally recognised as a blemish until the time of Dryden. Milton himself did not escape the contagion, although he used these enfeebling rhyme-suppliers more sparingly than most of his contemporaries, and less frequently in his later rhymed verse than in his earlier. There are three of them in *Lycidas*: 'did lament' here, 'doth raise' at l.70, and 'did go' at l.108.[1] Since these successive revisions of a single passage were

---

[1] Leishman dealt more fully with this matter in *The Art of Marvell's Poetry*, pp. 147 ff. Perhaps he accepted too readily Pope's principle of rejecting these expletives. No poet would now think of using them; but Wordsworth at least did so, perhaps in an attempt to achieve a less loaded line than Pope desiderated. Surely there was something to be said for these expletives when as late as the early nineteenth century Wordsworth could write:

> The moon doth with delight
> Look round her when the heavens are bare.

Perhaps Wordsworth is the last great poet to use them. They were in his day

made in a poem which had already reached the stage of a fair copy, we can only guess how much labour it had cost Milton to raise the rest of his poem to its present level.

Let us now consider the flower passage (ll.136–51). In his fair copy Milton originally wrote:

> yee vallies low where the mild whispers use[1]
> of shades, and wanton winds, and gushing brooks
> on whose fresh lap the swart starre sparely looks
> throw hither all yor quaint enamel'd eyes
> that on the greene terfe suck the honied showrs
> and purple all the ground wth vernal flowrs
> to strew the laureat where Lycid' lies.

That is to say, the catalogue of flowers (ll.142–50) was an afterthought, which Milton worked out on his scribble-page after he had transcribed his fair copy of the poem. When he was satisfied with it he drew a line between the last two lines of the passage I have quoted and wrote in the margin 'Bring the rathe &c.', thus indicating the place where his addition was to be inserted.

Before examining his two versions of this catalogue of flowers and the various hints he seems to have taken from earlier poets, I will repeat that the only precedent for it in classical pastoral elegy or pastoral semi-elegy is so inconspicuous that it can itself scarcely be considered as more than a hint: Mopsus exclaims, towards the end of his song on the death of Daphnis in Virgil's Fifth Eclogue:

> spargite humum foliis, inducite fontibus umbras,
> pastores (mandat fieri sibi talia Daphnis).

('Strew the turf with leaves, shepherds, curtain the springs with shade—such honours Daphnis commands you to pay him'). Virgil does not even mention flowers—only leaves. Indeed, so

---

entirely obsolete in spoken English, except for purposes of emphasis. ('I did do it.') In her review of Leishman's book on Marvell (*Review of English Studies*, Nov. 1967) Dame Helen Gardner suggested that Leishman should perhaps have thought a little longer on this subject. Ed.

[1] frequent, resort, inhabit. In this sense (O.E.D. 16) the verb use, both transitively (e.g. 'use a tavern') and (as here) intransitively, seems to have lingered on until almost the end of the nineteenth century.

far as I can remember, the only precedent in classical pastoral
for a list of flowers occurs, not in pastoral elegy or semi-elegy,
but in Virgil's Second Eclogue (ll.45–55), where the shepherd
Corydon promises gifts of flowers and fruit to the disdainful
Alexis:

Come hither, lovely boy! See, for you the Nymphs bring lilies in
heaped-up baskets; for you the fair Naiad, plucking pale violets and
poppy-heads, blends narcissus and sweet-scented fennel flower; then,
twining them with cassia and other sweet herbs, sets off the delicate
hyacinth with the golden marigold. My own hands will gather
quinces, pale with tender down, and chestnuts, which my Amaryllis
loved. Waxen plums I will add—this fruit, too, shall have its honour.
You too, O laurels, I will pluck, and you, their neighbour myrtle,
for so placed you blend sweet fragrance.

It may well be that better scholars than I could produce from
elsewhere in Greek and Latin poetry other lists of flowers offered
as gifts; nevertheless, I think I am right in saying that in the
whole of classical poetry there is only one memorable passage
about the scattering of flowers as a tribute to the dead—that passage in the Sixth Book of the *Aeneid* (ll.883–6), where Virgil,
availing himself of the Pythagorean and Platonic doctrine of re-
incarnation, makes the Spirit of Anchises in the Elysian Fields
show his son Aeneas, who has been conducted thither by the
Sibyl, the spirits of future Roman heroes, among them that of
Marcellus, Augustus's nephew and adopted son, who was to
perish in his twentieth year. 'Let me strew by handfuls lilies',
exclaims Anchises,

> manibus date lilia plenis
> purpureos spargam flores, animamque nepotis
> his saltem accumulem donis, et fungar inani
> munere.

('Let me strew by handfuls lilies, those purple flowers, and with
such gifts at least endow my offspring's shade and perform an
unavailing rite.')[1] It would probably be possible to discover many
lists of flowers in English poetry before Milton, but I think there

are only five really memorable ones: Spenser's in the Song in praise of Eliza in the April eclogue of *The Shepherd's Calendar*; and four in Shakespeare—the flowers that the mad Ophelia distributes[2], the flowers Perdita distributes and the spring flowers she wishes for at the Shepherds festival,[3] the flowers that Marina is gathering to strew upon the grave of her nurse Lychorida,[4] and the flowers with which Arviragus promises to sweeten Fidele's grave.[5] Of these, only the flowers promised Fidele and Lychorida are funeral flowers,[6] although it is true that when Perdita concludes her desiderated list of spring flowers with the words

> O, these I lack,
> To make you garlands of, and my sweet friend,
> To strew him o'er and o'er!

Florizel exclaims 'What, like a corse?' to which she replies:

> No, like a bank for love to lie and play on;
> Not like a corse; or if, not to be buried,
> But quick and in mine arms.

Milton, as we shall see, certainly remembered Perdita's description of the primrose, and it seems just possible that he also remembered her delightful exchange with Florizel, and that it was this which suggested to him the idea of an elaborate list of flowers to be strewn for Lycidas, an addition for which he doubtless found sufficient classical precedent in those two inconspicuous lines in Virgil's Fifth Eclogue. One might be inclined to say that the elaborate list of flowers is an English, not a classical thing, that it was Spenser who began it, and that even Shakespeare probably

---

[1] In this famous passage I have adopted the construction proposed by Kennedy and Page, who insist that *spargam* (as well as the two following subjunctives) is dependent on *date*: 'grant me to scatter lilies, those purple flowers', not 'give me lilies . . . let me scatter purple flowers', which assigns to the subjunctive *spargam* a meaning it will not bear.

[2] *Hamlet, IV.* v. 175–86.   [3] *The Winter's Tale,* IV. iv. 73–132.
[4] *Pericles,* IV. i. 14–8.   [5] *Cymbeline,* IV. ii. 218–29.
[6] The Queen (*Hamlet,* v. i. 266–9) scatters flowers upon Ophelia's coffin, but they are not particularised.

got the idea of it from Spenser. Nevertheless, it seems to be very likely that Spenser himself got the idea of it from Virgil, not from any of Virgil's better known poems, but from his mock-heroic *Culex*, which Spenser translated with the title of *Virgil's Gnat*. The gnat, at the cost of its own life, saves a shepherd's by stinging him in the eye and wakening him just as he is about to be attacked by a serpent, and the poem concludes with a description of the tomb which the grateful shepherd built for the gnat and of the flowers he planted around it. Here is Spenser's translation of the flower-passage:

> And round about he taught sweete flowres to growe,
> The Rose engrained in pure scarlet die,
> The Lilly fresh, and Violet belowe,
> The Marigolde, and cherefull Rosemarie,
> The *Spartan* Mirtle, whence sweet gumb does flowe,
> The purple Hyacinthe, and fresh Costmarie,
> And Saffron sought for in *Cilician* soyle,
> And Lawrell th'ornament of *Phœbus* toyle.
>
> Fresh *Rhododaphne*, and the *Sabine* flowre
> Matching the wealth of th'auncient Frankincence,
> And pallid Yuie building his owne bowre,
> And Box yet mindfull of his olde offence,
> Red *Amaranthus*, lucklesse Paramour,
> Oxeye still greene, and bitter Patience;
> Ne wants there pale *Narcisse*, that in a well
> Seeing his beautie, in loue with it fell.   (ll.665–80)

Spenser's translation is rather loose and inaccurate, but that does not here concern us; what does concern us is the fact that it may well have been this list of flowers which suggested to him, and served as a kind of precedent for, two further lists. One of these (the earlier, perhaps, since it is closer to its Virgilian precedent) is the list, in *Muiopotmos* (ll.185–200) of the flowers rifled by the butterfly:

> And then againe he turneth to his play,
> To spoyle the pleasures of that Paradise:
> The wholsome Saulge, and Lauender still gray,
> Ranke smelling Rue, and Cummin good for eyes,

The Roses raigning in the pride of May,
Sharpe Isope, good for greene wounds remedies,
Faire Marigoldes, and Bees alluring Thime,
Sweete Marioram, and Daysies decking prime.

Coole Violets, and Orpine growing still,
Embathed Balme, and chearfull Galingale,
Fresh Costmarie, and breathfull Camomill,
Dull Poppie, and drink-quickning Setuale,
Veyne-healing Veruen, and hed-purging Dill,
Sound Sauorie, and Bazill hartie-hale,
Fat Colworts, and comforting Perseline,
Colde Lettuce, and refreshing Rosmarine.

This, perhaps, with its herbalistic emphasis on the virtues rather
than on the appearances of the flowers, is more medieval than
Virgilian. Far more beautiful and memorable is the list of flowers
in the April Eclogue of *The Shepheards Calendar*, ancestor, as I
think, of the flower-passages in Shakespeare and in Milton:

Bring hether the Pincke and purple Cullambine,
  With Gelliflowres:
Bring Coronations, and Sops in wine,
  worne of Paramoures.
Strowe me the ground with Daffadowndillies,
And Cowslips, and Kingcups, and loued Lillies:
  The pretie Pawnce,
  And the Cheuisaunce,
Shall match with the fayre flowre Delice.   (ll. 136–44)

Before leaving this question of analogues, I will add that
between *Cymbeline* and *Lycidas* there is at least one other memorable passage about the *strewing* of flowers, a passage which
Milton, with his unerring eye for anything he felt able to use or
improve upon, almost certainly remembered and perhaps transcribed into that notebook, that English *Gradus*, whose existence
I have found it almost necessary to postulate. The passage occurs
in an otherwise unmemorable sonnet-epitaph on Prince Henry,
which Drummond of Hawthornden inserted in the third edition
(1614) of his not very memorable elegy on Prince Henry, *Teares
on the Death of Moeliades*:

Th' immortall *Amaranthus*, princely *Rose*,
Sad *Violet*, and that *sweet Flowre* that beares,
In Sangvine Spots the Tenor of our Woes,
Spred on this *Stone*, & wash it with thy Teares.[1]

My reason for saying that Milton remembered his passage is that
it seems to me almost certain that he has adapted the phraseology
of Drummond's mythological description of the hyacinth in his
own allusion to the same flower in his description of Camus's
bonnet,

> Inwrought with figures dim, and on the edge
> Like to that sanguine flower inscrib'd with woe.

Let us now examine Milton's two versions of the inserted
flower-passage. His first attempt was as follows:

> Bring the rathe primrose that unwedded dies
> colouring the pale cheeke of uninjoyd love
> and that sad floure that strove
> to write his owne woes on the vermeil graine
> next adde Narcissus y^t still weeps in vaine
> the woodbine and ye pancie freak't wth jet
> the glowing violet
> the cowslip wan that hangs his pensive head
> and every bud that sorrows liverie weares
> let Daffadillies fill thire cups with teares
> bid Amaranthus all his beautie shed
> to strew the laureat herse &c.

Before proceeding to the alterations which Milton made in this
passage, let us first consider the very varied sources of some of its
imagery and diction. This first and unabbreviated version of
Milton's allusion to the primrose was obviously suggested by
Perdita's

>   pale primroses,
> That die unmarried, ere they can behold
> Bright Phœbus in his strength—a malady
> Most incident to maids.

---

[1] *Poetical Works*, ed. L. E. Kastner, 1913, i. 83.

Rathe ('the rathe primrose') is from Anglo-Saxon hræð, quick, soon, from which our comparative *rather* (which means literally 'sooner') is derived. The notion that it was an obsolete word which had been revived by Spenser (e.g. *Shepheard's Calendar*, December, l.98) is quite wrong: especially as a description of flowers and fruit it is very common during the sixteenth and seventeenth centuries, not only in poets, but in writers on husbandry, where we read of 'rath or timely Peares' and 'Raith, (or early ripe) Pease'. Nevertheless, it seems probable, as Warton suggested, that the phrase 'rathe primrose' came to Milton from a poem by Edmund Bolton entitled *A Palinode* and printed in *Englands Helicon*[1]:

> And made the rathe and timely Primrose grow.

The metamorphoses of Hyacinthus and of Narcissus into flowers had been told by Milton's favourite Ovid, and the author of the Lament for Bion had exhorted Hyacinthus to utter the letters of woe inscribed on his petals. The 'pensive head' of the cowslip may have been suggested by the same phrase in another context in Giles Fletcher's *Christs Triumph over Death*, St. 39,

> The headlong Jew hung downe his pensive head:

if so, it would be a superb example of Milton's power of perceiving, in a context which did not release them, the possibilities inherent in a phrase which he himself might one day hope to use more effectively.[2] An almost equally good example, perhaps, is the phrase 'sorrows liverie' in the line

> and every bud that sorrows liverie weares,

---

[1] *Muses' Library* edn, pp. 8–9.

[2] Curiously enough, the phrase was twice used by Davenant in a volume published in the same year as *Lycidas, Madagascar, with other Poems*, 1638 (entered March 13); in the ode 'In remembrance of Master *William Shakespeare*':

> each Flowre
> (As it nere knew a Sunne or Showre)
> Hangs there, the pensive head (p. 37);

and in 'The Queen returning to London after a long absence':

> Each Violet lifts up, the pensive Head (p. 74).

This suggests that the phrase had already become part of the general stock of poetic diction and that a search might reveal earlier examples than the one I have quoted from Giles Fletcher.

for, as Todd pointed out, the phrase had been used, in a quite unmemorable context, by Wither:

> my *Muse*, as yet vnknowne,
> Should first in *Sorrowes* liuery be showne.[1]

It is also likely that Milton remembered the phrase 'sad livery' in William Habington's poem *Upon the death of a Lady* (Venetia Digby) in *Castara*, 1634:

> shee perfum'd all
> The banks she past, so that each neighbour field
> Did sweete flowers cherisht by her watring, yeeld.
> Which now adorne her Hearse. The violet there
> On her pale cheeke doth the sad livery weare,
> Which heavens compassion gave her.[2]

Had Milton remained satisfied with his first version, I suppose we should have remained so too; however, he crossed it out and began again, and we, wise after the event, can agree that every alteration he made was an improvement. The general result of his revision was the achievement of a greater unity of texture and a better balance. In the first five lines of the first version only three flowers are mentioned, and the elaborately metaphorical or mythological description of them tends to make these lines top-heavy in comparison with the rest of the passage. Milton reduced the total number of lines from eleven to nine, and yet, although he rejected one flower (the narcissus), he found room for three more (the jasmine, the white pink, and the musk rose). With no loss, and with immeasurable gain, he compressed into a single line the description of the rathe primrose; he discarded entirely the periphrastic and mythological description of the hyacinth and simply mentioned the flower by its ordinary Elizabethan name of crow-toe; and he discarded both the legend of Narcissus and his flower:

> Bring the rathe primrose that forsaken dies
> the tufted crowtoe and pale Gessamin.

---

[1] *Juvenilia*, 1622, p. 351.
[2] *Poems*, ed. Kenneth Allott, 1948, p. 64, ll.8–13.

Since the woodbine (or, as Milton at first inclined to prefer, the columbine) was now required to rhyme, not very perfectly, with the narcissus-extruding 'Gessamin', some other flower had to be brought in to keep the pansy company, so Milton continued:

> the white pinke, and yᵉ pansie freakt wᵗʰ jet
> the glowing violet.

Now the columbine (later to give way to the original woodbine) must supply its rhyme, and there must be another flower to keep it company and fill the line:

> the muske rose and the garish columbine.

This is later revised to 'the well-attir'd woodbine'. The next line becomes

> wᵗʰ cowslips wan that hang the pensive head

which is neater and smoother than the original:

> the cowslip wan that hangs his pensive head.

Then follows

> and every flower that sad escutcheon beares.

The last phrase is later changed to 'that sad imbroidrie weaves', which is equally, if not more, beautiful in itself than 'sad escutcheon beares', and more subdued to the texture of the passage, less outstanding, less 'conceited' than either that phrase or the original 'sorrows liverie weares'. In his first version of this line Milton wrote 'and every bud', in order to avoid repetition of the word 'flower', which he had used in the third line of that version: 'And that sad floure that strove'. The reason for 'bud' had now disappeared. The passage ends:

> let daffadillies fill thire cups wᵗʰ teares
> bid Amaranthus all his beauties shed
> to strew &c.

Later these lines are rearranged:

> bid Amaranthus all his beauties shed
> & daffadillies fill thire cups wᵗʰ teares
> to strew &c.

Here not only are an unnecessary pause and an unnecessary verb ('let') avoided, but the conceit, 'fill thire cups wth teares', is made more justifiable by being made the climax.

The great improvement in mere neatness, continuity, and flow may be revealed by exhibiting, as it were diagramatically, the syntax of the two versions: (1) Bring the primrose that does this and that flower that does that; next add Narcissus that does this, the woodbine and the pansy, the violet, the cowslip that does this and every flower that does that: let daffadillies do this, bid Amaranthus do that, to strew ... (2) Bring the primrose that does this, the crow-toe and jasmin, the pink and the pansy, the violet, the musk-rose, and the woodbine, with cowslips that do this and every flower that does that; bid Amaranthus do this and daffadillies do that, to strew ... By discarding the mythological and (as one might be tempted to say, wise after the event) the conventionally classical descriptions of the hyacinth and the narcissus, Milton has not only made the passage more natively English, more Shakespearean, but more truly classical, in the sense of more harmonious, more uniform in texture, more of a piece. Shakespeare himself, it is true, has introduced a good deal of classical allusion into Perdita's list of spring flowers: Proserpina and Dis's waggon, Juno's eyes, Cytherea's breath, bright Phoebus in his strength; but these allusions are glancing and fleeting, scattered and distributed, not coagulated and—one is almost tempted to say—laboured like those in the three lines which Milton discarded. For he was careful to preserve *decorum*, not merely in his poem as a whole, but in its particular sections and passages. He perceived that while such a solemn periphrasis as

Like to that sanguine flower inscrib'd with woe

was entirely appropriate in the description of Camus, his later periphrastic description of the hyacinth was out of place in the list of flowers. Here, as in *Comus*, we see him ruthlessly sacrificing in the interests of *decorum* and unity of texture, lines and phrases which most poets could not have borne to part with.

Before leaving the flower-passage, I will pause to remark on the manner in which it is both led up to and continued. I have already noticed the exquisitely original, the half-apologetic, invocations, or re-invocations, of the pastoral muse after each of the two digressions. In the second of these invocations the Sicilian Muse is exhorted to

> call the Vales, and bid them hither cast
> Their Bels, and Flourets of a thousand hues.

Then, at the end of this passage, which, as we have seen, Milton extended, he has a transition and a turn no less original than that which he added to his Virgilian apostrophe of the guardian nymphs, or nymph-muses, when he reflected that even had they been there, it could have availed nothing, since not Calliope herself was able to save Orpheus.

> ... To strew the Laureat Herse where *Lycid* lies.
> For so to interpose a little ease,
> Let our frail thoughts dally with false surmise.

Was Milton, I wonder, remembering the words with which Guiderius interrupts Arviragus in his description of the flowers he will bring to sweeten Fidele's grave?—

> Prithee, have done;
> And do not play in wench-like words with that
> Which is so serious.[1]

The surmise, the notion, that these flowers can ever reach Lycidas is no more than a sentimentally consoling fiction, for his body is not reposing on a laureat hearse but being carried by the tides northwards, for all we know, to the Hebrides, or southwards to the Land's End. This gives opportunity for a characteristically Miltonic adaptation (subsequently made less Shakespearean, and, as so often, less outstanding) of Pericles's phrase about his queen's corpse being o'erwhelmed by humming water, and for a superbly evocative and impressingly periphrastic description of St Michael's Mount—a passage which, it is true, concludes with what seems to me the one really unsatisfactory line in the poem:

> And, O ye *Dolphins*, waft the haples youth.[2]

---

[1] *Cymbeline*, IV. ii. 229–31.
[2] 'Waft' here means 'convey safely by water', (*N.E.D.* 'Waft' v.[1], 2). Ed.

If for no other reason than that consoling fictions have now professedly been dismissed, this conventional allusion to the legend of Arion is here singularly out of place, and was perhaps suggested by the two allusions to dolphins in the other elegies on King. Nevertheless, in spite of his irrelevancy, the contemplation of Lycidas's ocean grave leads naturally to the fine transition, the reflection that he has sunk low only to mount high 'Through the dear might of him that walk'd the waves'.

Of Milton's other revisions in *Lycidas* I will limit myself to the consideration of six. In three of these his intention seems to have been to replace a more outstanding or curious phrase by one that attracted less attention to itself and blended more completely with its context. In two of these subduings, as I may call them, his original phrase seems to have been suggested to him by Shakespeare. There are some examples in *Comus* of this alteration of originally Shakespearean phrases (e.g. at line 63 Circe's originally 'potent' art becomes 'mightie'; at line 117 the originally 'yellow' sands become 'tawnie'; and at line 208 the 'ayrie toungs' that originally 'lure night wanderers' eventually 'syllable mens names'), and even there I cannot agree with Miss Seaton that Milton's intention was merely to avoid a too obvious echo of Shakespeare and to provide, as it were, something more 'out of his own head'. Here, though, his intention seems to be clearer. At ll.45–9 he originally wrote:

> as killing as the canker to the rose
> or taint-worme to the weanling heards that graze
> or frost to flowrs that thire gay buttons weare
> when first the white thorne blows
> such Lycidas thy losse to shepheards eare.[1]

---

[1] The rhetorical pattern or rhetorical formula exemplified in this passage, and which may perhaps be described as the comprehensive comparison, was, I think, first memorably practised by Theocritus, from whom it was occasionally imitated by Virgil in his Eclogues and very extensively by Ronsard and other Renaissance poets. It is one of those classical formulas which may be indefinitely expanded—the list, that is to say, of things which the good or evil, pleasant or unpleasant subject is *like* may be indefinitely prolonged—and it permits of endless variation. Thus, in his Eighth Idyll (ll.57–9; imitated by Virgil, Third Eclogue, ll.80–1) Theocritus declares that winter is as bane to trees, drought to waters, snares to birds, nets to beasts, and love to men; in his Ninth (? spurious) Idyll, ll.31–5,

It is almost certain, as Warton remarked, that this simile of the canker in the rose was suggested to Milton by Shakespeare, for it occurs very often in his plays and records a fact which that 'universal and accurate observer of real nature' had observed for himself, namely, that the wild or 'dog' rose is especially subject to this disease:

> . . . the most forward bud
> Is eaten by the canker ere it blow;[1]

> But now will canker sorrow eat my bud;[2]

I had rather be a canker in a hedge than a rose in his grace;[3]

> But let concealment, like a worm i' the bud,
> Feed on her damask cheek.[4]

But although Milton retained this Shakespearean simile he rejected the Shakespearean 'buttons': I say 'Shakespearean', because although the word had been applied both to buds and to other button-like parts of flowers long before Shakespeare, Shakespeare had used it in two notable passages, one of them containing yet another example of that canker in the bud simile which Milton had already borrowed from him:

> The canker galls the infants of the spring,
> Too oft before their buttons be disclosed,

---

cricket is dear to cricket, ant to ant, hawk to hawk, and to the poet his Muse. Not sleep, or swift-coming Spring are sweeter, or flowers to bees, than the Muses are dear to him. In his Tenth Idyll (ll.30–1) Bucaeus the reaper says of Bombyca the flute-girl: 'The goat pursues the clover, the wolf the goat, the crane the plough, and I am made for you.' Virgil, in his Second Eclogue (ll.63–6) had imitated this with variations: 'The grim lioness pursues the wolf, the wolf the goat, the wanton kid pursues the flowery clover, and Corydon, O Alexis, pursues you.' In his Twelfth Idyll, 'The Beloved' (ll.3–9), Theocritus employs the formula in a very original way: instead of saying 'As sweet as Spring after Winter is your coming', he says: 'As Spring is sweeter than Winter and an apple than a damson, as a ewe is fleecier than its lamb, as a maiden excels a thrice-married wife, as a fawn is fleeter than a calf, as the clear-voiced nightingale is more minstrel-like than all winged things, even so much do you gladden me with your coming, and I run to you as a traveller, when the sun is scorching, runs under a shady oak.'

[1] *Two Gentlemen*, I. i. 45–6.   [2] *King John*, III. iv. 82.
[3] *Much Ado*, I. iii. 28–9.   [4] *Twelfth Night*, II. iv. 114–15.

And in the morn and liquid dew of youth
Contagious blastments are most imminent.[1]

The other passage where the word occurs is perhaps the most
memorable one in the whole of Shakespeare's contribution to
The Two Noble Kinsmen:

O Queene *Emilia*,
Fresher then May, sweeter
Then hir gold Buttons on the bowes, or all
Th'enamelld knackes o'th Meade or garden.[2]

Milton felt, I think, that 'gay buttons' was not quite in key with
the rest of the passage: it was a too definite and particularised
piece of visual detail, unlike 'white thorne', which gave, as it
were, a mere outline for the imagination to work upon; it was
also a shade too familiar and jaunty. He therefore substituted the
more general, more dignified, and, so far as we know, original,
'gay wardrope'. It is possible, however, that it was an earlier
and minor revision that gradually led him to make this much
more important one. Having first written 'buttons weare' he
altered it to 'buttons beare', which sounds much better, not
merely because of the alliteration, but because the combination of
final and initial consonants '-s b-' is much smoother than the
combination '-s w-'. Nevertheless, it may well have been the
alliterative 'buttons beare' that partly suggested the alliterative
'wardrope weare'—an interesting example of the way in which, as
Aristotle remarked, art and chance can co-operate.

Although I am here primarily concerned with the question of
Milton's revisions, and only incidentally with his indebtedness to
Shakespeare, I will not leave this passage without remarking that,
even after the extrusion of 'buttons', it still remains one of the
most Shakespearean in the poem. For not merely are the rose and
canker simile and the original 'buttons' Shakespearean: consciously or unconsciously, Milton was also remembering a
passage where both the white thorn (or hawthorn) and the phrase
'shepherd's ear' occur—a passage in *A Midsummer Night's*

---

[1] *Hamlet*, I. iii. 39–42.   [2] III. i. 4–7.

Dream where Helena exclaims to Hermia, for whom she has been forsaken by Demetrius,

> Your eyes are lode-stars; and your tongue's sweet air
> More tuneable than lark to shepherd's ear,
> When wheat is green, when hawthorn buds appear.[1]

The staple diction of *Lycidas*, as also of *Comus*, is that of the more figurative and descriptive passages in Shakespeare a little sobered and that of Spenser and his sixteenth- and seventeenth-century disciples considerably sifted and choicened.

In the second of the three 'subduings' I shall consider, Milton's original phrase seems also to have been suggested to him by Shakespeare:

> Ay mee whilst thee yᵉ shoars[2] and sounding seas
> wash farre away, where ere thy bones are hurl'd
> whether beyond the stormie Hebrides
> where thou perhapps under the humming tide
> visit'st the bottome of the monstrous world.   (ll. 154–8)

It is almost certain, I think, that the phrase 'humming tide' was suggested to Milton by a phrase in Pericles' speech over his dead queen's body, which the sisters had insisted should be committed to the sea:

> A terrible childbed hast thou had, my dear;
> No light, no fire: the unfriendly elements
> Forgot thee utterly: nor have I time
> To give thee hallow'd to thy grave, but straight
> Must cast thee, scarcely coffin'd, in the ooze;
> Where, for a monument upon thy bones,
> And e'er-remaining lamps, the belching whale
> And humming water must o'erwhelm thy corpse,
> Lying with simple shells.[3]

'Humming tide' remained unaltered in the Trinity manuscript and duly appeared in the King Memorial Volume, but in his own copy of that volume Milton corrected 'humming' to 'whelming', and 'whelming' is the reading of the 1645 edition. Why did

---

[1] I. i. 183–5.   [2] originally 'floods'.   [3] III. i. 57–65.

Milton make the alteration? Not, I think, in order to get rid of a
too obvious indebtedness to Shakespeare, for 'whelming' might
just as easily have been suggested by Shakespeare's 'O'erwhelm',
which occurs in the same line as 'humming'. And not merely
because, on second thoughts, it occurred to him that an already
drowned man could no longer, like a drowning man or a diver,
hear the water 'humming' in his ears (cf., in Clarence's description of his dream: 'What dreadful noise of waters in mine ears!')[1].
But chiefly, I think, because the word 'humming' was not sufficiently subdued to its context and conjured up associations not
strictly relevant. Lycidas being hurled hither and thither by the
tide which had overwhelmed him—with that image, and with
that image alone, Milton wished his reader's imagination to be
filled. Shakespeare, with his tremendous exuberance, continually
introduces into his descriptions details and associations such as
Milton, as his art matured, came more and more to regard as
irrelevant. He would perhaps have agreed with Dr Johnson's
criticism of the famous description of Dover cliff in *King Lear*,
that the 'one great and dreadful image of irresistible destruction'
was dissipated and counteracted by the 'enumeration of the
choughs and crows, the samphire-man and the fishers'.

My third example of what I have called a 'subduing' is from
the description of Camus. Milton first wrote:

> Next Camus reverend sire went footing slow
> his mantle hairie, and his bonnet sedge
> scraul'd ore wth figures dim, and on the edge
> like to that sanguine flowre inscrib'd wth woe.   (ll. 103–6)

Warburton was probably right in taking the 'figures dim' as an
allusion to 'the fabulous traditions of the high antiquity of
Cambridge'. Milton's original phrase, 'scraul'd ore' did indeed
very vividly suggest parchments, manuscripts, charters and the
like, but, on the other hand, it was one of those too literally
worked-out conceits in the so-called metaphysical manner which
he had used in the *Passion*. The image of a 'scraul'd ore' or
'inscribed' bonnet no doubt struck him as incongruous, so he

---

[1] *King Richard III*, I. iv. 22.

substituted the more indeterminate 'inwraught'. Many a seventeenth-century poet, especially of the more argumentative or dialectical kind, would not have troubled about the incongruity: to him the important thing would have been the vivid suggestion of written scrolls. So long as he had made his main point clearly and vividly he would have been inclined to regard any incongruity among the parts of his metaphor or simile as a mere means to an end, a means to make a point. When the point had been made, the image could be forgotten. Milton's images are, in comparison, much more autonomous and, in this sense, much more pictorial: they can be contemplated as a whole, like pictures; we can linger over them. Everything in Milton's poetry is a means to an end, but nothing is a *mere* means: he proposes to himself, in Coleridges' phrase, such pleasure from each of the parts as is compatible with the maximum pleasure from the whole.

I will conclude this examination of the minor revisions with three examples of the substitution of a more for a less significant epithet. At lines 25-31 Milton first wrote:

> Together both ere the high Launs appear'd
> under the glimmering eyelids of the morne
> wee drove afeild, and both together heard
> what tyme the gray fly winds her sultrie horne
> batning our flocks wth the fresh dews of night
> oft till the ev'n starre bright
> toward heavens descent had sloapt his burnisht weele.

This passage appeared unchanged in the King memorial volume, but between then and the 1645 edition Milton made several alterations:

> Oft till the Star that rose, at Ev'ning, bright
> Toward Heav'ns descent had slop'd his westering wheel.

In this revised version the imagination is much more filled with the impression of evening and of the lapse of time from the first appearance of the evening star until its disappearance at dawn. It is true that the evening star does not, strictly speaking, rise, but only appears, and that it is always 'westering': nevertheless, Milton achieves his intention, which is to fill the reader's imagination with the sky and with the passage of time from sunset till

dawn. And for this purpose 'westering' is a much more appropriate epithet than 'burnisht', which not only insists too much on
the fleetingly suggested image of the evening star as a burnished
chariot driven by Hesperus (an image which might have occurred
to any Elizabethan poet), but insists on the brightness of the star
at the very moment when it has paled before the dawn and is about
to disappear.

In the second line of this passage the substitution of the
more natural or, if you will, the more conventional 'opening
eye-lids of the morn' for the more arresting 'glimmering eyelids'
may be regarded as yet another example of what I have called a
'subduing'. As he was to reveal in *Paradise Lost*, Milton was quite
willing to speak of a 'glimmering dawn':

> But now at last the sacred influence
> Of light appears, and from the walls of Heav'n
> Shoots farr into the bosom of dim Night
> A glimmering dawn;[1]

but he seems to have decided that his first version of the line in
Lycidas was an attempt to combine personification and natural
description in a manner that was really incongruous—in other
words, that if he was to retain 'glimmering' he must sacrifice
'eyelids' and that if he was to retain 'eyelids' he must sacrifice
'glimmering'. He decided to sacrifice 'glimmering', and to retain
the Biblical personification 'eye-lids of the morn'—Biblical,
because although, with or without variations, it had been used
by earlier English poets, its ultimate sources, as Todd pointed
out, were two passages in the *Book of Job*: iii. 9, where 'the dawn-
ing of the day' is marginally glossed as 'the eyelids of the morn',
and xli. 18 (of Leviathan), 'By his neesings (i.e., "sneezings")
a light doth shine, and his eyes are like the eyelids of the morning'. Warton had already noticed that Milton's whole phrase had
actually been used by the dramatist Thomas Middleton in *A
Game at Chesse* (published 1625):

> . . . like pearl
> Dropt from the opening eyelids of the morn
> Upon the bashful rose.[2]

---

[1] ii. 1034-7.   [2] I. i. 78-80.

Since this is just the sort of passage that might well have found its way into Milton's notebook, it may have been Middleton who suggested 'opening' as an alternative to 'glimmering': although the more one thinks about it, the more certain it appears that, if the Biblical personification was to be retained, 'opening' was the only possible epithet. If it was neither original nor particularly striking, it had the more important virtue of being exactly right, and it was in getting the right word or phrase in the right place that Milton's originality very largely consisted. Nevertheless, although he greatly improved his first version—or rather, perhaps I should say, his first known version—of these seven lines, he might, I think, have improved them still further. Writing, in November 1831, to his young friend William (later Sir William) Hamilton, whose flirtations with verse seemed to be deflecting him from the path of science, Wordsworth warned him that absolute success in poetry depended upon innumerable *minutiae*, 'which it grieves me you should stoop to acquire a knowledge of'. In spite of Milton's words about 'pouring easy his unpremeditated verse', Wordsworth could, he declared, point to five hundred passages in Milton's poetry upon which labour had been bestowed, 'and twice five hundred more to which additional labour would have been serviceable'. Perhaps we can find some too:

> . . . and both together heard
> What time the Gray-fly winds her sultry horn,
> Batt'ning our flocks with the fresh dews of night,
> Oft till the Star . . .

Here, I think, additional labour would have been serviceable, for the construction is harsh, obscure, and even a little clumsy, and the four periods of dawn, noon (when the gray-fly is active), night and second dawn do not follow one another as clearly and consecutively as they should do. The phrase 'what time', or 'at what time', meaning 'at such time as', 'at the time when', 'whenever' was probably already a little old-fashioned in prose and conversation, but Milton's use of it here is scarcely idiomatic and it compels him to use 'heard' (necessary as a rhyme to 'appear'd'), again rather unidiomatically, as an intransitive verb. *Either* 'we *heard* the gray-fly wind her horn', or 'we *listened* what time the gray-fly winds her horn', but *not* 'we heard what time the gray-fly winds her horn'. A modern reader (I am not sure how it would have been with a seventeenth-century one) even has to suppress some tendency to construe 'we heard at what time (at what hour) the gray-fly winds her horn'. Then, too, the present participle 'Batt'ning', which Milton probably used in order to avoid the interruption of another 'and', remains for a moment suspended in mid-air, until the reader has succeeded in relating it either to 'drove' or 'heard'. Greatly daring, I will venture to suggest how the passage might have been improved:

> We drove a field, and both together heard
> The busy Gray-fly wind her sultry horn,
> And fed our flocks with the fresh dews of night
> Oft till the Star that rose, at Ev'ning, bright
> Toward Heav'ns descent had slop'd his westering wheel.

The last two revisions I shall consider can be described with less qualification as examples of the substitution of a more for a less significant epithet. At lines 85–6 Milton at first wrote:

> Oh Fountaine Arethuse and thou smooth flood
> soft sliding Mincius crown'd wth vocall reeds.

He soon perceived that this was pleonastic, and that a smooth flood would obviously slide softly, so he substituted 'fam'd' for 'smooth' and 'smooth' for 'soft':

> and thou fam'd flood
> smooth sliding Mincius.

'Fam'd' was not merely a conventional epithet, for it contained an allusion to Virgil, by whom the Mincius, his native river, had been celebrated. Later, though, Milton made the allusion to Virgil still more explicit by substituting the less conservative 'honour'd' for 'fam'd': the Minicus had been honoured by Virgil's birth as well as celebrated in his poetry. Keats, in a phrase partly borrowed from Spenser, once urged Shelley to load every rift of his subject with ore[1]; the remark has often been quoted out of its context,

---

[1] In a letter of 16 August 1820. cf. *Faerie Queene*, II. vii. 28 (the House of Mammon): 'And with rich metall loaded euery rift.'

and has sometimes been understood as a demand for consistent 'poeticalness'. It is probable that Keats wanted Shelley to do more of what we can see Milton doing here: trying to ensure that each word carries the maximum amount of meaning, works its passage, and does not travel as a mere line-filler or rhyme-supplier.

I will not leave this invocation of Arethusa and the Mincius without remarking that it alone is sufficient to reveal how close was Milton's study of the classics. Arethusa was a spring or foun-tain, at Syracuse, and at the end of his Sixteenth Idyll, in praise of Hiero King of Syracuse and of the Muses, Theocritus declares that he himself is one of those many poets, dear to the daughters of Zeus, who are concerned to celebrate Sicilian Arethusa, together with her people and Hiero her warrior-king. Hence Arethusa came to be regarded as the Muse of Sicilian pastoral poetry, and as such is invoked by Virgil at the beginning of his Tenth Eclogue:

> Extremum hunc, Arethusa, mihi concede laborem:
> pauca meo Gallo, sed quae legat ipsa Lycoris,
> carmina sunt dicenda: neget quis carmina Gallo?

('Arethusa, permit me this final task: for my Gallus I must utter a song, slight but such as Lycoris herself may read. Who would deny a song to Gallus.') And he proceeds to celebrate, with many reminiscences of Theocritus's First Idyll and its song on the Afflictions of Daphnis, the love of his friend Cornelius Gallus for a mistress who had deserted him. But just as the successors of Theocritus, including Virgil, had exalted the Sicilian and Theo-critean Arethusa into a kind of pastoral Muse, so Milton (originally, I think) exalts Virgil's native river the Mincius into the Muse of *Latin* pastoral. Milton's description of the Mincius, 'crown'd with vocall reeds', echoes Virgil's own description of it in the *Georgics* (iii. 10–15), in a passage where he mentions his ambition of writing an epic poem that shall glorify Caesar and Italy: if life remains, he will return to his country bringing the Muses with him in triumph from the Aonian mount; he will bring back to Mantua the palms of Idumaea, and on the green plain will raise a marble temple beside the water where great

Mincius wanders in slow windings and fringes his banks with
slender reeds:

> propter aquam, tardis ingens ubi flexibus errat
> Mincius et tenera praetexit harundine ripas.

Since Milton's exaltation of the Mincius into a Muse, or kind of
Muse, was original, he evidently wanted to make the allusion
unmistakable: to readers who had forgotten that the Mincius
was Virgil's river 'smooth flood' would convey no hint; 'fam'd
flood' came nearer, but was still too general: 'honour'd flood'
(honoured by Virgil's birth, honoured in Virgil's verse, honoured
for Virgil's sake) came as near as Milton could get without
actually naming Virgil. That epithet, together with the allusion
to the Third Georgic, should be sufficient for any reader whom
Milton cared to reach.

The last revision I shall consider may be particularly recom-
mended to the notice of those who are inclined to suggest that
Milton was a poet more concerned with sound than with sense.
At the end of the description of those flowers with which the
valleys, at the command of the Sicilian Muse, are to strew
Lycid's hearse (ll.133–51) he at first wrote:

> for so to interpose a little ease
> let our sad thoughts dally wth false surmise.

Then he replaced 'sad' by 'fraile'. The new word is more beautiful,
more moving, than the old one, but is not its greater beauty
indistinguishable, in this context, from its greater truth? That the
body of Lycidas, instead of being tossed hither and thither by
the tides, is lying on a hearse where it can be strewn with flowers
—permission to indulge this fancy is craved as a concession, not
to human sadness, but to human frailty. Milton is, at it were,
saying more clearly what he means.

'INDUSTRIOUS AND SELECT READING'

In the preceding sections I have often had occasion to notice
Milton's indebtedness to his predecessors and his attention,
albeit with characteristic eclecticism, to 'best example'. I have,

though, been chiefly concerned with the larger aspects of the poem and with that careful subordination of the parts to the whole in which, as I have so continuously insisted, Milton's originality is most apparent. I will conclude with a fairly rapid survey of some of those particular indebtednesses to his predecessors, classical and English, which I have not hitherto had occasion to mention—a survey which will reveal that his poetic originality and poetic greatness were compatible with a degree of literary dependence upon his predecessors which to many modern readers must seem almost incredible, and certainly incompatible with poetic 'originality' as they have been taught to understand it. Perhaps one of the chief functions of the criticism of poetry should be to make us sceptical of any general definition of that art, to make us aware that almost unbridgeably *different* kinds of excellence are possible, and to persuade us that, in the most valuable sense, Milton's poetry is no less 'original' than that of Hopkins or of Rilke.

In surveying Milton's indebtedness to the classics, I will begin by remarking that his use of five proper names (one in periphrasis) and of one adjective is alone sufficient to indicate how much more exact was his scholarship than that of previous English poets, and how much more continuous his awareness of 'best example'.

First, the very name of 'Lycidas': of all the names in classical pastoral—Damon, Thyrsis, Daphnis, Menalcas, Damoetas and the rest—it was the most suitable for Milton's purpose. It was musical and dignified, it was free from any irrelevant or incongruous associations, and, being dactylic (in English, though not, of course, in Greek and Latin, where it was always used, in one of the oblique cases, as an anapaest), it could be used with equal effectiveness in at least four different places in a decasyllabic line—though Milton uses it in three only:

> For *Lycidas* is dead, dead ere his prime . . .
> Who would not sing for *Lycidas* ? he knew . . .
> Clos'd o're the head of your lov'd *Lycidas*.

It could also, if necessary, be abbreviated without too much loss of dignity:

L

To strew the Laureat Herse where *Lycid* lies.

The two other dactylic names that most readily occur, those of Corydon and Thestylis, had been used too often in lighter contexts. Todd noticed that the name had been used at least once in English poetry before Milton, by William Lisle in 1625, dedicating a portion of his translation of Du Bartas to the King:

> My former Shepheards song deuised was
> To please great *Scotus*, and his *Lycidas*.[1]

Nevertheless, I think it probable that Milton obtained it directly either from Theocritus's Seventh Idyll or from Virgil's Ninth Eclogue: more probably, perhaps, from Theocritus, where the narrator recites Lycidas's Song, and mentions that he said on meeting him 'dear Lycidas, all declare you to be a piper great excelling, whether among hersdmen or among harvesters'. It would be appropriate that the name of a Doric singer should be given to the subject of what Milton called a 'Dorick lay':

> With eager thought warbling his *Dorick* lay.   (l.189)

'Dorick', because Theocritus, the master of all succeeding pastoral poets, had written in the Doric dialect; because, more specifically, he had written that pastoral semi-elegy 'The Afflictions of Daphnis'; and because an unknown author (whom Milton probably supposed to be Moschus) had written in the Doric dialect a pastoral elegy on Bion. In these matters Milton knew and perceived far more clearly than his predecessors who was who and what was what.

Next consider the personage referred to periphrastically:

> But now my Oate proceeds,
> And listens to the Herald of the Sea
> That came in *Neptune's* plea: (ll.88–90)

the allusion is to Triton, Neptune's herald. Almost any other English poet would have been content to say that Neptune came. Similarly (and perhaps not altogether without some touch of pedantry) the answer of the questioned winds is brought by

---

[1] *Part of Du Bartas, English and French*, 1625, sig. g.2.

'sage *Hippotades*', that is to say, by Aeolus, son of Hippotes. The epithet occurs frequently in Homer, but always, I think, as an addition to the proper name of Aeolus, and although it occurs a few times in Ovid it would probably have mystified readers who did not know their Homer.

The fourth proper name is Panope:

> The Ayr was calm, and on the level brine,
> Sleek *Panope* with all her sisters play'd.   (ll.98–9)

Panope was one of the fifty Nereids, or daughters of Nereus. Homer, in a passage in the *Iliad*[1] where he names no less than thirty-three of the sisterhood, mentions Panope without even a distinguishing epithet. Virgil, however, refers to her in two passages in the fifth book of the *Aeneid*: in the second (ll.825–6) along with several of her sisters, but in the first (l.240) alone, as though she were the leader of the band:

> Nereidum Phorcique chorus Panopeaque virgo.

And there can, I think, be no doubt that Milton is here following Virgil's example. 'Sleek', I may remark, is one of Milton's happiest epithets; it means, as Elton rightly observed, 'smooth and shining with the water, like a seal'.

It also seems likely that a single passage in Virgil was Milton's authority for the allusion to the legend of Alpheus and Arethusa in the invocation that follows the second digression:

> Return *Alpheus*, the dread voice is past,
> That shrunk thy streams; Return *Sicilian* Muse.   (ll.132–3)

The legend was that the nymph Arethusa was bathing in the Arcadian Alpheus when the river-god fell in love with her; she fled to Ortygia, an island in the bay of Syracuse in Sicily, where Diana changed her to a fountain, but Alpheus flowed on under the sea to reach her there. Homer and Hesiod several times mention the river Alpheus, but neither has any allusion to this legend; nor indeed has the Sicilian Theocritus, who only mentions Alpheus twice. So far as I know, the first allusion to the

---

[1] xviii. 39–49.

legend by an ancient poet is by Virgil, when he says of Ortygia:

Alpheum fama est huc Elidis amnem
occultas egisse vias subter mare, qui nunc
ore, Arethusa, tuo Siculis confunditur undis.[1]

('Hither, it is said, Alpheus, river of Elis, forced a secret passage
beneath the sea, he who now at your fountain, Arethusa, is
mingled with the Sicilian waves.') Milton's meaning in this
rather recondite allusion (too recondite for the common reader)
is as follows: 'Alpheus, the voice that caused your stream to
shrink back in terror has now passed: you may continue on your
way to Arethusa, and the Sicilian (i.e. pastoral) Muse may return
to me.'

It is possible that Milton intends a Biblical as well as a Virgilian
allusion, and that the phrase 'dread voice' is meant to recall it:

Thou coveredst it [the earth] with the deep as with a garment: the
waters stood above the mountains. At thy rebuke they fled; at the
voice of thy thunder they hasted away.[2]

The invocation, though entirely in the classical tradition, is
even more original than the Virgilian invocation of Arethusa
and Mincius at the end of the first digression, which we have
already considered in detail.

More in the nature of an inherited formula is the invocation of
the Muses at line 15,

Begin then, Sisters of the sacred well.

The line:

Ἄρχετε βουκολικᾶς Μοῖσαι φίλαι ἄρχετ ἀοιδᾶς,

('Begin, dear Muses, begin a pastoral strain') is the refrain of
'The Afflictions of Daphnis' in Theocritus's First Idyll; and

Ἄρχετε Σικελικαὶ τῶ ἄενθεστ ἄρχετε Μοῖσαι,

('Begin, Sicilian Muses, begin the dirge') is the refrain of the
Lament for Bion.

Each of these Greek refrains is an example of those 'beautiful

---

[1] *Aeneid*, iii. 694–6.   [2] Psalm civ, 6–7.

turns of words and thoughts', that Dryden declared he had been unable to find examples of in Milton.[1] Had he studied Milton more carefully, he would have found plenty of them, both in the earlier and in the later poems. Of classic, and more especially Virgilian, repetition, the more subtle and elaborate forms of which Dryden would have called 'turns', there are at least three examples in *Lycidas*.

> For *Lycidas* is dead, dead ere his prime
> Young *Lycidas*, and hath not left his peer:
> Who would not sing for *Lycidas*? he knew
> Himself to sing, and build the lofty rhyme.   (ll.8–11)

Here it seems almost certain that Milton had the opening lines of Virgil's Tenth Eclogue in mind:

> Extremum hunc, Arethusa, mihi concede laborem:
> pauca meo Gallo, sed quae legat ipsa Lycoris,
> carmina sunt dicenda: neget quis carmina Gallo?

Spenser, whom Dryden was probably right in supposing to have learnt the device from Virgil, is usually content with a much simpler kind of repetition:

> Young *Astrophel* the pride of shepheards praise,
> Young *Astrophel* the rusticke lasses loue.

Indeed, in Spenser one comes to regard repetition less as a rhetorical device than as a mere manifestation of his tendency to diffuseness. Milton, on the other hand, reproduces classical formulae, idioms, and phrases in a manner with which there is no parallel except in the verse-translators, or in original poets when they happen to be translating. Spenser, for example, when translating Lucretius's address to Venus at the beginning of the *De Rerum Natura*,

> te, dea, te fugiunt venti, te nubila caeli,[2]

preserves the formula 'te . . . te' in

> Thee goddesse, thee the winds, the clouds doe feare.[3]

---

[1] See above, pp. 118–19.   [2] i. 6.   [3] *The Faerie Queene*, IV. x. 44.

Milton employs the same formula in his description of nature lamenting for Lycidas[1]:

> Thee Shepherd, thee the Woods, and desert Caves,
> With wilde Thyme and the gadding Vine o'regrown,
> And all their echoes mourn.   (ll.39–41)

This strongly suggests that he had in mind two passages in classical poets which also describe lamentation: Ovid's description of nature lamenting for Orpheus:

> Te maestae volucres, Orpheu, te turba ferarum,
> te rigidi silicces, te carmina saepe secutae
> fleverunt silvae.[2]

('For you, Orpheus, the mourning birds, for you the throng of beasts and the hard rocks wept; for you wept the wood which had often followed your songs'), and Virgil's description of Orpheus lamenting for Eurydice:

> te, dulcis coniunx, te solo in litore secum,
> te veniente die, te decedente canebat.[3]

('Of you, sweet bride, he sang, by himself on the lonely shore; of you he sang at the coming of day, and of you as day was departing.') On the other hand, with simpler repetition

> Weep no more, woful Shepherds weep no more   (l.165)

a close Spenserian parallel can be produced:

> Sing now ye shepheards daughters, sing no more.[4]

Of Milton's appropriation or adaptation of classical phrases there are several notable examples in *Lycidas*. It is commonly said that the memorable 'build the lofty rhyme' (l.11) is an imitation of *condere carmen*, a phrase twice used by Horace;[5] but this phrase means no more than 'compose' or 'construct' a

---

[1] Milton was perhaps remembering a passage in the Lament for Bion (ll.30–1): 'Echo too laments among the rocks that she is silent and no longer imitates your lips.'

[2] *Metamorphoses*, xi. 43–5.   [3] *Georgics*, iv. 465–6.

[4] *The Shepheardes Calender*, November Eclogue, l.78.

[5] *Epistles*, I. iii. 24; *Ars Poetica*, l.436.

poem (the literal meaning of *condere* is 'put together'). It is much more likely that, as Hurd was the first to suggest, Milton had in mind the figurative use of Greek πυργᾶν (from πύργος, a tower), 'raise to a towering height', as when Aristophanes (*Frogs*, 1004) speaks of Aeschylus as having been the first to uptower lofty (or majestic) phrases, πυργώσας ῥήματα σεμνά. 'Meditate the muse' in

> And strictly meditate the thankles Muse (1.66)

is a Virgilianism:

> Tityre, tu patulae recubans sub tegmine fagi
> silvestrem tenui musam meditaris avena.[1]

('You, Tityrus, reclining beneath the canopy of a spreading beech-tree, are meditating the woodland Muse with your slender pipe.')

The epithet 'gadding' in

> Thee Shepherd, thee the Woods, and desert Caves,
> With wild Thyme and the gadding Vine o'regrown (ll.39-40)

was probably suggested, as Warton supposed, by Cicero's description of the vine as spreading itself *multiplici lapsu et erratico*[2]. The phrase has often been exhibited as an example of Milton's literariness and of his tending to read nature through the spectacles of books; nevertheless, I should not feel able to declare confidently that he had never seen wild vines near Cambridge unless I knew more of that neglected subject, the history of English viticulture. Phineas Fletcher at least twice introduces vines into the landscape of 'Chame': in the sixth of his *Piscatorie Eclogues* he says of Thirsil and Thomalin

> Under a sprouting vine they carelesse lie (st. 2)

and in a poem 'To Master *W.C.*' he writes from Cambridge:

> Return now, *Willy*; now at length return thee:
> Here thou and I, under the sprouting vine,
> By yellow *Chame*, where no hot ray shall burn thee,
> Will sit, and sing among the Muses nine.[3]

---

[1] *Eclogues*, i. 1-2. [2] *De Senectute*, xv.
[3] St 3; *Poetical Works of Giles and Phineas Fletcher*, ed. F. S. Boas, 1908-9, ii. 227.

The line 'And now the Sun had stretch'd out all the hills', meaning the setting sun had lengthened the shadows cast by the hills (l.190), is imitated from the concluding lines of Virgil's First Eclogue,

> et iam summa procul villarum culmina fumant,
> maioresque cadunt altis de montibus umbrae.

('and now smoke rises from the roofs of the cottages far off, and larger shadows fall from the high mountains.')

In his imitations of the classical poets Milton has often provided examples of 'poetic diction': 'meditate the Muse', 'build the lofty rhyme'. 'Your sorrow', meaning 'the cause of your sorrow', in

> For *Lycidas* your sorrow is not dead   (l.166)

is a deliberate Latinism: in Ovid, for example, the river-god Inachus, having at last found his daughter Io transformed into a heifer, exclaims

> tu non inventa reperta
> luctus eras levior.[1]

('unfound you were a lighter grief to me than now discovered'). As examples of this use of the word 'sorrow' the Oxford Dictionary (*Sorrow*, sb. 2c) quotes only this passage and Shelley's imitation of it in *Adonais* (st. x),

> Our love, our hope, our sorrow, is not dead.

In 'watry bear',

> He must not flote upon his watry bear   (l.12)

and 'watry floar',

> Sunk though he be beneath the watry floar   (l.167)

We have examples, first of a traditional, and then of an original Latinism; and these two phrases may provide a convenient

---

[1] *Metamorphoses*, i. 654–5.

transition from this brief survey of Milton's indebtedness to the diction of classical poets to a survey of his indebtedness to that of his English predecessors. The actual phrase 'watery bier' had not, so far as I know, been used by any earlier poet, but Ben Jonson has 'watrie hearse',[1] a phrase which Phineas Fletcher has probably borrowed in *The Purple Island*, where the swan

> ... chaunting her own dirge tides on her watry herse;[2]

and Shakespeare has both 'watery tomb',

> Such a Sebastian was my brother too,
> So went he suited to his watery tomb,[3]

and 'watery grave';

> Let it suffice the greatness of your powers
> To have bereft a prince of all his fortunes;
> And having thrown him from your watery grave,
> Here to have death in peace is all he'll crave.[4]

What Elizabethan poet first used the adjective 'watery' in such phrases I do not know,[5] but I think it may be regarded as a Latinism. Ovid has the interesting combination 'watery mother', in a passage where Briseïs recalls how Achilles swore by his mother Thetis:

> ... iuratus per numina matris aquosae;[6]

and Virgil, in a notable passage in the Sixth Book of the *Aeneid*, where Anchises, in the underworld, in replying to the questions

---

[1] *Cynthia's Revels*, I. ii. 59; *Ben Jonson*, ed. C. H. Herford and Percy and Evelyn Simpson, 1925-52, iv. 50.

[2] i. 30; *Poetical Works of Giles and Phineas Fletcher*, ed. F. S. Boas, 1908-9, ii. 18.

[3] *Twelfth Night*, V. i. 240-1.

[4] *Pericles*, II. i. 8-11.

[5] In Sylvester's translation of Du Bartas, one of the great sources of this kind of diction, I have noticed only two phrases with 'watery': '*Neptunes* Watry Front' (First Week, Third Day, edn 1621, p. 64) and 'watry Citizens' (First Week, Fifth Day, edn 1621, p. 95). There may well be other examples which I have failed to notice.

[6] *Heroides*, iii. 53.

M

of Aeneas, has the phrase *campi liquentes*, 'liquid' or 'watery' plains:

> Principio caelum ac terram camposque liquentis
> lucentemque globum lunae Titaniaque astra
> spiritus intus alit, totamque infusa per artus
> mens agitat molem et magno se corpore miscet.   (ll.724–7)

('First, the heaven and the earth and the watery plains and the
morn's shining orb and Titan's star a spirit within sustains, and
mind, diffused through all its members, sways the whole mass and
mingles with the mighty frame.') Joseph Hall's 'the watery playne'
in *The Kings Prophecie*[1] (1603), should probably be regarded as a
deliberate imitation of the phrase *camposque liquentes* in this passage from Virgil. 'Watery' in phrases such as 'watery bier' (where
it means 'composed of water', as distinct from merely 'like
water') may, I repeat, be regarded both as a Latinism and as a
piece of specifically poetic diction. It was a great favourite with
William Browne: in the First Book of *Britannia's Pastorals* we
have: 'wat'ry nymph' (Song ii, l.179), 'wat'ry rulers' (l.239),
'wat'ry regiment' (Song iii, l.88), Britain's 'wat'ry zone' (Song v,
l.251), 'Neptune's wat'ry thieves' (l.338). But it is not merely in
the Spenserian and pastoral poets and in the translators that we
find such phrases: they are no less frequent in Shakespeare, whose
diction certain modern critics are pleased to regard as the very
polar opposite of Milton's and of which they write as though it
were habitually as un-Spenserian and un-Miltonic as Donne's.
In addition to the two examples I have mentioned ('watery
tomb' and 'watery grave'), Shakespeare has: 'watery glass'
(*M.N.D.*, I. i. 210), 'watery Neptune' (*Rich. II*, II. i. 63),
'watery kingdom' (*M. of V.*, II. vii. 44), 'watery empire' (*Pericles*,
II. i. 54), 'watery arch' (*Tempest*, IV. i. 71), 'watery main' (Sonnet
64, l.7).[2]

While, though, Milton's use of 'watery' in these two phrases
is thoroughly traditional, his use of 'floor' in 'the watry floar'

---

[1] Stanza 46; *Poems*, ed. A. Davenport, 1949, p. 118.

[2] Phrases with the adjective πηγᾶιος, 'welly', from πηγή, 'spring', 'well', are very
frequent in the Greek tragedians: for example, in the *Electra* of Euripides the returned Orestes, seeing—without, of course, recognising her—his peasant-married
sister carrying a pitcher of water, says to Pylades: 'I see some servant carrying a
welly burden (πηγαῖον ἄχθος) on her shaven head' (ll.107–9).

should perhaps be regarded as an original attempt to recover the original meaning of *aequor*, so frequent in Latin poetry, but which we tend to forget is really a metaphor. It is derived from *aequus*, and originally meant an even, level surface. Hence it came to be applied to the even, level surface of a calm sea.

Before leaving this survey of Milton's indebtedness to the classical poets, I will add a word or two, in addition to what has been said in the preceding sections, on his use of what may be called classical 'properties'. Only, I think, in one extended passage (as distinct from two pieces of detail which I shall mention later) is he at all liable to that charge of pedantry, artificiality, and incongruity which Dr Johnson brought against the whole poem. When he declares that he and King were nursed upon the self-same hill (Cambridge) and that they drove afield before dawn and often did not return until after the paling of the evening star (i.e. that they began their studies early and quitted them late), his pastoral allegory is exquisitely beautiful, but in what follows his imitation of various details in Virgil's *Eclogues* produces, at any rate upon a modern reader, a slightly incongruous, or even ludicrous, effect:

> Mean while the Rural ditties were not mute,
> Temper'd to th'Oaten Flute,
> Rough *Satyrs* danc'd, and *Fauns* with clov'n heel,
> From the glad sound would not be absent long,
> And old *Damœtas* lov'd to hear our song.   (ll.32–6)

This is not *in pari materia* with what has preceded: the dancing of satyrs and fauns cannot be interpreted allegorically in the same immediate and spontaneous fashion as can the driving afield. It is a mere piece of decoration. If we try to interpret it allegorically, we conjure up a ludicrous image of yokels or horny-handed townsmen or philistine undergraduates being moved to ecstatic admiration by the poetry-readings of Milton and King. I fear that the Fauns (bringing with them the Satyrs) are here for no better reason than that they appear in Virgil's description of the effect of Silenus's singing in the Sixth Eclogue:

> tum vero in numerum Faunosque ferasque videres
> ludere, tum rigidas motare cacumina quercus   (ll.27–8)

('then indeed you might see Fauns and wild beasts sporting in measured time, then rigid oaks nodding their tops'). And 'old *Damœtas*' listens partly, at least, because Meliboeus listens to the songs of Corydon and Thyrsis in Virgil's Seventh Eclogue. But for the intrusion of the Fauns and Satyrs, he would have been *in pari materia* with what has preceded, and could be immediately and effortlessly interpreted as an approving and encouraging tutor in whom grammar had not stifled the humanities. Such merely *mechanical* introduction of classical properties is precisely what Milton (unlike so many of the lesser neo-classicists) generally avoids. In contrast to it, I may remark on the beauty, economy and restraint of the immediately following description of the mourning of nature: a passage which may be contrasted, not merely with the exaggerations of Elizabethan pastoral elegists on the same theme, but with the tearful lions, wolves and foxes who in Theocritus and Virgil mourn for Daphnis.

I have already referred to the incongruous and rather trivial introduction of dolphins at the conclusion of the superbly evocative description of St Michael's Mount:

> Or whether thou to our moist vows deny'd,
> Sleep'st by the fable of *Bellerus* old,
> Where the great vision of the guarded Mount
> Looks toward *Namancos* and *Bayona's* hold;
> Look homeward Angel now, and melt with ruth,
> And, O ye *Dolphins*, waft the haples youth.   (ll.159–64)

Milton needed a couplet to conclude this soaring apostrophe, which otherwise would have remained suspended in mid-air, but the device he hit upon to turn its flight and bring it back to earth was trivial and artificial. The allusion to the myth of Arion (who, to save himself from some sailors who had plotted to rob and murder him, flung himself overboard and was saved by a dolphin he had charmed with his lyre) is not only out of place now that frail dallyings with false surmise have been professedly dismissed, but is one of those merely conventional, decorative, and unsynthetised classicisms which Milton generally avoids. For Milton's sake one may like to suppose (as I have already suggested) that these intruding dolphins were put into his head by

two passages in the other elegies on King: one in the Alcaics of
the shadowy 'Coke', and the other in the elegy by Isaac Olivier,
Fellow of King's.[1]

Slightly incongruous, perhaps, and slightly trivial, though
much less seriously so than the dolphins, is the declaration that
the already enshrined and sainted Lycidas has become the classic
'Genius of the shore'—a declaration that occurs immediately
after the beautiful adaptation of the language of *Revelation* (vii.
17 and xxi. 4: 'And God shall wipe away all tears from their eyes'):

> There entertain him all the Saints above,
> In solemn troops, and sweet Societies
> That sing, and singing in their glory move,
> And wipe the tears for ever from his eyes.
> Now *Lycidas* the Shepherds weep no more;
> Henceforth thou art the Genius of the shore,
> In thy large recompense, and shalt be good
> To all that wonder in that perilous flood.   (ll.178–85)

Was it the phrase and the rhyme 'weep no more' that combined
with a reminiscence of Virgil and a more recent reminiscence of a
passage in Ralph Widdrington's elegy on King to suggest the
phrase and the rhyme 'Genius of the shore'?

> Sis bonus o felixque tuis!

exclaims Menalcas in his song on the deification of Daphnis in
Virgil's Fifth Eclogue (l.65); and Ralph Widdrington makes
Christ's College exclaim:

> Scilicet hoc fuerat tumidæ monuere quod undæ,
>   Et cœlum gravidis nubibus omne minax:
> Imperium pelagi Dominus sævúmque tridentem
>   Venturo voluit deposuisse Deo.[2]

('This indeed was what the swelling waves portended and the
sky all threatening with pregnant clouds: the lord of the sea
wished to resign his empire and savage trident to a god to come.')

>   ... and shalt be good
> To all that wander in that perilous flood:

---

[1] See above ,p. 249.   [2] *Justa Edovardo King*, p. 35.

Milton's rather unusual use of 'good' in the sense of 'propitious' was probably suggested to him by Virgil's *bonus* in 'Sis bonus o felixque tuis'. It is also possible that Milton was recalling a passage in the first of Sannazaro's Piscatory Eclogues, a lament by a shepherd for a drowned shepherdess. Hailing the departed spirit in whatever celestial or Elysian region it inhabits, the shepherd exclaims:

> Aspice nos, mitisque veni. Tu numen aquarum
> Semper eris; semper laetum piscantibus omen. (ll.97-8)

('Look upon us and come with mercy. You shall be for evermore the divinity of these waters; for evermore a joyful omen for the fishermen'). There is, I think, some distinction between this passage and the characteristically Spenserian and Renaissance mingling of Christian and pagan imagery in, for example, the passage in *Comus* in which the Attendant Spirit describes his abode as

> Amongst the enthron'd gods on Sainted seats; (l.11)

in the description of Lycidas, in the Christian heaven, Homerically laving his oozy locks with pure nectar (l.175), a much more fleetingly suggested classicism than the more elaborate description in *Comus* of the revival of Sabrina with its various reminiscences;[1] and, most astonishingly of all, at the conclusion of the *Epitaphium Damonis*:

> Ipse caput nitidum cinctus rutilante corona,
> Letáque frondentis gestans umbracula palmæ,
> Aeternùm perages immortales hymenæos;
> Cantus ubi, choreisque furit lyra mista beatis,
> Festa Sionæo bacchantur & Orgia Thyrso.

('Then, even thou, thy lustrous head circled with ruddy-glowing crown and bearing joyous branches of leafy palm, shalt perform for ever the eternal nuptials, where song and lyre wildly mingle with the dances of the blest and sacred orgies riot to the beat of the Thyrsus of Sion.') The invocation of Lycidas as 'the Genius of the shore' is not just a piece of allegorical, or semi-allegorical

---

[1] See above, pp. 233-4.

description; it brings in, not merely a pagan image, but a distinctively pagan and non-Christian *idea*, and may perhaps be regarded as the insufficiently considered introduction of a classical 'property'.

Dolphins, satyrs and fauns, genius of the shore; these, in descending order of flagrancy, are, I think, the only classical properties that may justly be regarded as excrescent and open to the charge of pedantry, artificiality and incongruity. At the same time, they may help us to appreciate more deeply the wonderful art which Milton has displayed in the rest of his poem—that judicious combination of imitation, adaptation and invention with which he has transmuted his industrious and select reading into a beautiful and satisfying artistic whole. Perhaps no other poet except Virgil could have displayed such learning and such literariness without becoming cold and pedantic. Milton, unlike so many of his neo-classic contemporaries, especially in Italy, had not been educated beyond either his intelligence or his poetic capacities. I also think I can perceive how his moral and spiritual ardour, that quality so conspicuously lacking in his Italian contemporaries, provided, in ways which I cannot precisely define, much of the fuel and fire which enabled him to transmute this vast load of literariness into great poetry. His art, his unique art, depended as much upon his character as upon his learning: without his character his learning would have degenerated into pedantry.

I remarked that Milton's use of the traditional Latinism 'watery' would provide a convenient transition from this review of what may be called his 'classicisms' to a brief survey of his indebtedness to the diction of his English predecessors. Since I have already noticed many examples of this indebtedness in previous sections, I will here content myself with a few characteristic ones which I have not yet had occasion to mention. Here, as in *L'Allegro* and *Il Penseroso* and in *Comus*, we can observe Milton drawing upon that stock of poetic diction which English poets had been accumulating since the time of Spenser, and sometimes, like Spenser himself, upon the language of the English Bible, especially that of the *The Revelation*.

Since I have already described Shakespeare as a great creator of specifically poetic diction, I will begin by citing a phrase which Milton has been supposed to have derived from Horace, but which I think he is more likely to have derived from Shakespeare: 'wanton winds' in the lines (136-7)

> Ye valleys low where the milde whispers use,
> Of shades and wanton winds, and gushing brooks.

Sir John Sandys[1] (I do not know whether he was the first to do so) suggested that this was a rendering of *protervis ventis* in the twenty-sixth Ode of Horace's First Book:

> Musis amicus tristitiam et metus
> tradam protervis in mare Creticum
>   portare ventis.

('Dear to the Muses, I will give gloom and fear to the wanton winds to carry away to the Cretan sea.') Nevertheless, Shakespeare (whether or no he himself derived it from Horace) has the identical phrase in *A Midsummer Night's Dream*, where Titania refuses to yield up to Oberon the 'little changeling boy' with whose mortal and departed mother she had sat on the sea-shore,

> When we have laugh'd to see the sails conceive
> And grow big-bellied with the wanton wind.[2]

Elsewhere Shakespeare, with whom (as with other sixteenth- and seventeenth-century poets) the word 'wanton' seems to have been a great favourite, has 'wanton air':

> On a day—alack the day!—
> Love, whose month is ever May,
> Spied a blossom passing fair
> Playing in the wanton air;[3]

and 'wanton summer air':

> A lover may bestride the gossamer
> That idles in the wanton summer air.[4]

---

[1] 'The Literary Sources of Milton's "Lycidas" ', *Transactions of the Royal Society of Literature*, Second Series, xxxii (1914), 233-64.
[2] *A Midsummer Night's Dream*, II. i. 128-9.
[3] *Love's Labours Lost*, IV. iii. 101-4.   [4] *Romeo and Juliet*, II. vi. 18-19.

and, since there is something memorable about all these contexts, it seems to me much more likely that Milton derived the phrase from Shakespeare than that he derived it from Horace. He had already in *Arcades* (l.47) used the words 'quaint' and 'wanton',

> To nurse the Saplings tall, and curl the grove
> With Ringlets quaint, and wanton windings wove,

in a line which, as Warton noticed, had almost certainly been suggested to him by a line in *A Midsummer Night's Dream*:

> And the quaint mazes in the wanton green
> For lack of tread are undistinguishable.[1]

In the lines (157-8),

> Where thou perhaps under the whelming tide
> Visit'st the bottom of the monstrous world,

commentators from Warton onwards seem to have assumed that the phrase 'monstrous world' must have been suggested by a passage in Horace's Ode to Virgil Sailing for Greece, where Horace expatiates on the well-worn topic of that over-weeningness which led men to tempt the sea (and Providence) with ships:

> quem mortis timuit gradum,
>   qui siccis oculis monstra natantia,
> qui vidit mare turbidum et
>   infamis scopulos, Acroceraunia?[2]

('What form of death's approach did that man fear who gazed with dry eyes on the swimming monsters, the stormy sea, and the ill-famed cliffs of Acroceraunia?') and by a line in Anchises's philosophical discourse to Aeneas in the Sixth Book of the *Aeneid*, where, after speaking of men and beasts and birds, he refers to 'quae marmoreo fert monstra sub aequore pontus' (l.729)—('those monsters which the ocean bears beneath its glassy floor'). The fact is, though, that Horace's entirely unremarkable mention of 'swimming monsters' and Virgil's entirely unremarkable mention of 'monsters' *tout court* are no more likely to have suggested Milton's very remarkable phrase than any

---

[1] II. i. 99. [2] *Odes*, I. iii. 17-20.

number of allusions to sea-monsters in Shakespeare, Spenser and other English poets. I call the phrase 'remarkable', because the only other example of the word *monstrous* cited by the *O.E.D.* in this sense (3b), which it defines as 'abounding in monsters', occurs in an obvious imitation of Milton's line in Pope's version of the *Odyssey*,

> Whelm'd in the bottom of the monstrous deep.[1]

The *O.E.D.*'s definition, 'abounding in monsters', is not strictly accurate—'inhabited by monsters' would be better,[2] although it is, I admit, more difficult to define Milton's use of the word than to define the phrase in which he uses it. By the 'monstrous world' he means the world of monsters as distinct from the world of animals and of men, as distinct from the 'animal world' or the 'human world'. The phrase (or rather, perhaps I should say, the same combination of words) does actually occur once in Shakespeare, in that speech where Iago professes to be horrified that Othello should seem to doubt his honesty:

> O wretched fool,
> That livest to make thine honesty a vice!
> O monstrous world! Take note, take note, O world,
> To be direct and honest is not safe.[3]

Here, though, Shakespeare is using the word *monstrous* in a sense substantially the same as that which it could bear in a similar context today: Iago is not professing to believe that the earth, like the sea, is now entirely inhabited by, in the literal sense, monsters, but that it is inhabited by men who behave with monstrous, or monster-like, unnaturalness and ingratitude. This, together with the fact that Milton, who in the Tractate *Of Education* and in the Preface to *Samson Agonistes* was to dismiss all English tragedy with contempt, reveals no clear indebtedness to the language of Shakespeare's later tragedies, although he was steeped in that of *Romeo and Juliet*, of the comedies, and of the romances, makes it seem very improbable that his own use of the

---

[1] iv. 658.
[2] 'Consisting of monsters' would perhaps be best of all.
[3] *Othello*, III. iii. 375–8.

phrase 'monstrous world' was suggested to him by Shakespeare's very different use of it in *Othello*. Much nearer to Milton's use of the word 'monstrous' here is its use by Drummond of Hawthornden in a line which Todd added, without comment, to Warton's two unparallel 'parallels' from Horace and Virgil. In his first volume of *Poems*, 1616 (as also in its undated predecessor, which perhaps appeared in 1614), Drummond has a sonnet[1] (the eighth in the First Part) which is an expanded paraphrase of the first eight lines of Petrarch's famous sonnet beginning

> Or che 'l ciel e la terra e 'l vento tace

and in which occur the lines

> And Birds and Beastes a Silence sweet doe keepe,
> And PROTEVS monstrous People in the Deepe.

Indeed, Drummond's use of the word *monstrous* is here almost identical with Milton's, for his meaning is, not that Proteus rules over a monster-like people, but that Proteus rules over a people consisting of monsters, rules the world of monsters, 'the monstrous world'. If Milton is indebted to anyone for this phrase he is indebted to Drummond. It may well be, though, that here Milton was indebted only to himself; for in *Comus* (l.533) he had made the Attendant Spirit speak of Comus's 'monstrous rout', meaning thereby his company consisting of monsters:

> ... this bottom glade, whence night by night
> He and his monstrous rout are heard to howl
> Like stabl'd wolves, or tigers at their prey.

In the passage from *Lycidas* which we have been discussing, while two traditionally cited classical 'parallels' may be frankly dismissed, Milton's indebtedness to an English predecessor cannot be clearly established. The case is different with the phrase 'occasion dear' in the lines

> Bitter constraint, and sad occasion dear,
> Compels me to disturb your season due.   (ll.6–7)

---

[1] *Poetical Works*, ed. L. E. Kastner, 1913, i. 7.

Dear in this passage is a now obsolete word, etymologically quite distinct from the one which has the sense of Latin *carus* and French *cher* and which is related to modern German *teuer*. It is descended from *deor*, a word very common in Anglo-Saxon poetry, which sometimes means 'brave', 'hardy', but more often 'hard, severe, heavy, grievous'. It occurs frequently in Middle English poetry and also in Spenser and Shakespeare. 'I, made lame by fortune's dearest spite', Shakespeare exclaims in his thirty-seventh sonnet. The phrase 'occasion dear', as Todd observed, had actually been used by Sidney in Philoclea's Sonnet on Time in the Third Book of the *Arcadia* (1593 edn),

> Thou art the father of occasion deare;[1]

and Richardson noticed that 'constraint', the other substantive in Milton's line, had been used with 'dear' by Spenser:

> Loue of your selfe, she said, and deare constraint
> Lets me not sleepe.[2]

The phrase 'sable shroud', in

> And bid fair peace be to my sable shrowd   (l.22)

had already been used, though in a different context and with a different meaning, by Sylvester in his translation of Du Bartas:

> Still therefore, cover'd with a sable Shrowd
> Hath She kept home; as all to Sorrow vow'd.[3]

'Footing slow', in

> Next *Camus*, reverend Sire, went footing slow   (l.103)

is a Spenserian phrase:

> A damzell spyde slow footing her before;[4]

---

[1] *Complete Works of Sir Philip Sidney*, ed. A. Feuillerat, 1922–6, ii. 33.
[2] *The Faerie Queene*, I. i. 53.
[3] 'Bethulian's Rescue', Bk. iv; edn 1621, p. 991.
[4] *The Faerie Queene*, I. iii. 10.

and it had been used in a context very similar to Milton's by that admirer of Spenser, Giles Fletcher:

> At length an aged Syre farre off he sawe
> Come slowely footing.[1]

Line 171 of *Lycidas*,

> Flames in the forehead of the morning sky,

(a line which, if we may credit James Joyce, Dowden loved to quote) is an excellent example of what we have seen Milton doing several times in *L'Allegro* and *Il Penseroso*: releasing, by means of context and emphasis, the magic latent in a phrase which until then had remained, as it were, neutral. The 'humorous' senator Menenius in *Coriolanus* describes himself as one that 'converses more with the buttock of the night than with the forehead of the morning',[2] and Sylvester, in a passage in his Du Bartas which Milton is more likely to have remembered, exclaims

> Shall I omit a hundred Prodigies
> Oft seen in forehead of the frowning Skies?[3]

It is partly by his use of the word 'flames' and partly by the weight that falls on the whole line, as the climax of his simile, that Milton makes the phrase memorable and (I will repeat, in the most valuable sense) original:

> Sunk though he be beneath the watry floar,
> So sinks the day-star in the Ocean bed,
> And yet anon repairs his drooping head,
> And tricks his beams, and with new spangled Ore,
> Flames in the forehead of the morning sky:
> So *Lycidas* sunk low, but mounted high,
> Through the dear might of him that walk'd the waves
> (ll. 167–73)

I might, perhaps, have included the use of 'repairs' in this passage,

---

[1] *Christ's Victorie on Earth*, st. xv; *Poetical Works of Giles and Phineas Fletcher*, ed. F. S. Boas, 1980–9, i. 43.
[2] II. i. 56–8.
[3] First Week, Second Day; edn 1621, p. 35.

And yet anon repairs his drooping head,

in my survey of Miltons' 'classicisms'. Todd referred to a passage in Phineas Fletcher's *Purple Island* on the corruption and redemption of the human understanding:

> Can one eclipse so dark his shining brow,
> And steal away his beautie glittering fair?
> One onely blot so great a light empair,
> That never could he hope his waning to repair?
>
> Ah! never could he hope once to repair
> So great a wane, should not that new-born Sun
> Adopt him both his brother and his heir.[1]

It is indeed possible that Milton had this passage in mind, but it is also possible that he (and perhaps Fletcher too) was remembering a phrase in that Ode of Horace which A. E. Housman considered to be the most beautiful poem in the Latin language:

> damna tamen celeres reparant caelestia lunae;
> nos ubi decidimus,
> quo pius Aeneas, quo Tullus dives et Ancus,
> pulvis et umbra sumus.[2]

('The losses of the heavens the swift moons make up again. But we, when we have gone down where pious Aeneas has gone, and wealthy Tullus and Ancus—we are dust and shadow.')

'Pastures new', in the last line of the poem (a line so often quoted incorrectly) is another example of a phrase which its context alone has made memorable—one might almost say, proverbial. This phrase too Milton may well have borrowed from Phineas Fletcher's *Purple Island*, from the conclusion of the same canto in which occurs the phrase that may have suggested 'the forehead of the morning sky':

> Home then my lambes; the falling drops eschew:
> To morrow shall ye feast in pastures new,
> And with the rising Sunne banquet on pearled dew.[3]

---

[1] Canto vi, st. 70–1; *The Poetical Works of Giles and Phineas Fletcher*, ed. F. S. Boas, 1908–9, ii. 84.
[2] *Odes*, IV. vii. 13–16.
[3] Canto vi, st. 77; *The Poetical Works of Giles and Phineas Fletcher*, ii 86.

The line

And hears the unexpressive nuptiall Song   (l.176)

is an interesting combination of Shakespearean diction and
Biblical allusion:

And I heard as it were the voice of a great multitude, and as the voice
of many waters, and as the voice of mighty thunderings, saying,
Alleluia: for the Lord God omnipotent reigneth. Let us be glad and
rejoice, and give honour to him: for the marriage of the Lamb is come,
and his wife hath made herself ready.[1]

Mr C. S. Lewis has recently suggested that the supposed influence
of the English Bible upon English prose has been considerably
exaggerated. Its influence, however, upon English poetry, from
Spenser onwards, has not, I think, been sufficiently noticed. I
have already remarked that the word 'unexpressive' seems to
have been used only three times in the whole course of English
literature: first, by Shakespeare in *As You Like It*, then by Milton
in the Nativity Ode, and finally by Milton in the present passage.[2]

It is fitting that we should conclude this long study both of
Lycidas and of Milton's shorter poems with the mention of
Shakespeare, to whom, among his predecessors, Milton owed
little less than he did to Spenser and Virgil. The differences
between the least and the most scholarly of great English poets are
indeed great, but their affinities, both with one another and with
a common tradition, are greater than is generally recognised.

---

[1] *Revelation*, xix, 6–7.
[2] See above, pp. 62–3.

APPENDIX

James Blair Leishman

1902–1963

James Blair Leishman, the eldest son of a tea merchant, was born at Thursby, Cumberland, on 8 May 1902. He was educated at Earnseat School, Arnside, Westmorland, from which he removed to Rydal Mount, Colwyn Bay, in 1916.

At Arnside he is still remembered for his remarkably retentive memory and indomitable will power, but also for his preference for long walks in country lanes to the football field, where it was said that he would not move except to get out of the way of the ball. He himself recalled with special pleasure a trip to Ambleside and a walk with a few boys through Clappersgate to Rydal. As they gazed along the drive of a house called Fox How, an elderly lady invited them into the garden and showed them round, drawing their attention particularly to a tree planted by her father Dr Arnold, and to another planted by her brother Matt.

At Oxford, where he matriculated from St John's College in 1922, he was debarred from reading Classical Moderations by ignorance of Greek, but he set himself to learn the language so as to qualify himself for Literae Humaniores in which he obtained Second Class Honours in 1925. Two years later he was rewarded with a First in English Language and Literature. The prospect of an academic career was opened to him and he decided to read for the higher degree of Bachelor of Letters, submitting as his dissertation a study of the three Parnassus plays written for performance at Cambridge at the end of the sixteenth century. He was without doubt the most able student of his year, and it was not surprising that he was appointed to the only post which fell vacant in the summer of 1928, an assistant lecturership at University College, Southampton. He was to stay there for eighteen years. In 1946 he left to take up a university lecturership at Oxford, and was promoted to a senior lecturership the following year. He was elected to a research fellowship at St John's College in 1959, and to a Fellowship of the British Academy in 1963.

During his last year at Oxford he had begun to teach himself German and to take an interest in recent German poetry. His enthusiasm for the work of Rilke led a friend to express the wish to be able to read the poet in translation, and this induced him to attempt an English version. He translated a selection of thirty-five poems and offered them to the Hogarth Press, who had already published versions of Rilke's *Duino Elegies* and his *Notebook of Malte Laurids Brigge*. The reception of this volume (1934) encouraged him to attempt the whole corpus of Rilke's poetry in English: *Requiem and Other Poems* appeared in 1935 (2nd edn, 1949), *Sonnets to Orpheus* in 1936 (2nd edn, 1948), *Later Poems* in 1938, the *Duino Elegies* (translated in collaboration with Stephen Spender) in 1939 (2nd edn, 1948), *Selected Poems* in 1941, *From the Remains of Count C. W.* in 1952, *Poems 1906–1926* in 1957, and *Selected Works. Vol. II, Poetry* in 1960. With this volume he supposed his work as a translator of Rilke to be complete. But there was still needed a complete translation of *Neue Gedichte*, only half of which was included in the last published volume. He therefore set himself to the task. The work was complete at the time of his death, and he had finished correcting the proofs.

In the meanwhile he had also translated selections from Hölderlin (1944 and 1947), and thirty odes of Horace (1956). The latter, prefaced by a long and valuable introduction on the differences between Latin and English versification and on the poetical character of Horace, was undertaken, like the first selection from Rilke, to help a friend to some understanding and appreciation of the original. Throughout these works Leishman invites comparison with his author: a scholarly translation was his first consideration, and he taxed the rhythmic and syntactic resources of English to the utmost in his effort to obtain closeness of rendering; but he never allowed himself to forget that he was translating poetry, and he might have claimed, though he never did, that his versions were themselves poetry of a high order.

[Professor Eudo C. Mason has kindly contributed the following assessment of Leishman's work in German studies: 'His reading in German literature never ranged more than desultorily beyond Rilke and the two writers in whom he became interested as a direct result of his Rilke studies, Hölderlin and Rudolf Kassner. He felt no urge to grapple with the interesting but intrinsically not very rewarding German poetry of the sixteenth and seventeenth centuries, with which he was chiefly concerned in his work on English literature, nor was he more than moderately attracted by Goethe and his age. He would have deprecated the suggestion that he was a Germanistic scholar in the stricter sense of the word. But within the field to which he confined himself— a very exacting field—he was deeply read and earned recognition particularly as one of the soundest and profoundest authorities on Rilke. The uncertainty regarding linguistic niceties observable in his earlier translations soon disappeared, and even such scholars as Ernst Zinn, who to begin with had helped him, were later glad to consult him on knotty problems of interpretation. In his modesty he failed to recognise how, in the correspondence which he maintained for years with various fellow Rilke specialists in Germany and this country, they learnt certainly quite as much from him as he did from them, if not more. The final summing-up of his views on Rilke in the long introduction to *New Poems* is an excellent synthesis of erudition and intuitive perception, of critical detachment and enthusiastic admiration.']

Although the introductions and commentaries accompanying several of his volumes of translations, no less than the translations themselves, had brought him a reputation as a German scholar, he regarded himself primarily as an Anglist. His postgraduate work upon the Parnassus plays was completed in an edition published in 1949; but by that time his principal field of interest had become the literature of the seventeenth century. A letter written to him by George Gordon in 1931 shows what he then had in mind to do: a selection from the Cambridge Platonists to replace Campagnac's, or a book on Donne, Herbert, Vaughan, and Traherne, or, with a prophetic leap into the future thirty years ahead, a book on 'Shakespeare's characteristic ideas'. Gordon was inclined to favour the book on the seventeenth-century poets, especially 'since you have tested it so successfully with classes'. It appeared in 1934 with the title *The Metaphysical Poets*. At that time there were few studies of these poets available, and the book is still in many respects a valuable exposition of the work of the four poets chosen. Leishman long nursed a hope of revising it, but in this he was impeded by the outstanding success of his study of Donne, entitled *The Monarch of Wit* (1951; 6th edn, 1962). This was the first book of his maturity, the first to display his characteristic excellences in ample form. The kind of poet Donne is he establishes by some initial comparisons with Ben Jonson and, incidentally, Horace, and then by a painstaking discussion of what might be regarded as minor groups, the elegies (with their counterparts in Ovid), epigrams, satires, and verse epistles. The Songs and Sonnets are reached only half-way through the book; but by that time the reader has been taught to recognise the use of language, the handling of ideas, and the appeal to a contemporary coterie that mark the poet's work, and he has his sights properly adjusted for Donne's most famous poems. The most learned and perhaps the most stimulating of his books is *Themes and Variations in Shakespeare's Sonnets* (1961), in which he places the *Sonnets* in their European setting, compares and contrasts the handling of topics by Shakespeare, Horace, Ovid, and Propertius, Petrarch and Tasso, Du Bellay, Ronsard, and many others, notes which familiar topics were not touched by Shakespeare, and which are peculiar to him, and succeeds in showing that 'Shakespeare transfigured and Shakespeareanised his reading to a far greater extent than any other Renaissance poet'. In fact, he once expressed the hope that his book might prove a corrective to those studies of Renaissance thought which, by habitually quoting Shakespeare in illustration, lead us to assume that Shakespeare was typical of his times.

An illuminating examination of *L'Allegro* and *Il Penseroso*

(1951) was designed as the first instalment of an expository study of Milton's minor poems.[1] This, like so many of his books, was based upon courses of undergraduate lectures undertaken with a major interest of his own in mind; it was carefully revised and kept up to date, and it may well be published. A similar work upon the poetry of Marvell had been on his hands for ten years or more. A small portion of it was delivered as a Warton Lecture before the British Academy on 4 October 1961. This had since been much expanded and revised, and the whole was within sight of completion at the time of his death. The character of the book is essentially similar to that of his *Themes and Variations in Shakespeare's Sonnets*, in that it explores the individuality of a poet, his resemblance and his difference from contemporaries and predecessors, by showing how he and they handled certain favourite topics. It is not surprising therefore that in writing to a friend he mentioned the subject for a future book on the History of Topics in Seventeenth-century Literature. For work of this kind he needed to keep the great classics in repair; but this was his pleasure, too, as well as the support for his conviction that only a knowledge of the classics prevents a man becoming too provincial in his judgement. When the present writer published, a few years ago, a selection from Pope's letters, he received a long ten-page letter in Leishman's small, crabbed, and highly idiosyncratic hand commenting on detail and generalising most fruitfully on Pope's literary character; but when another friend tried to persuade him to look again at *The Cloister and the Hearth*, Leishman told him that he had read it as a boy and did not feel he had time for such books now. The nature of a typical six-weeks holiday reading in the long vacation indicates the scope at which he was accustomed to aim; the trunks that were returned from Switzerland after his death contained the following books: the *Æneid* in a German translation, the Loeb editions of Martial's *Epigrams* and of the Greek Anthology, Rousseau's *Confessions*, Dryden's *Poems*, with Van Doren's study, *The Oxford Book of Italian Verse*, and all the appropriate dictionaries.

---

[1] The present book is the result. Ed.

Leishman was a striking figure in any gathering. He was large-framed, though a little bowed in the shoulders of recent years. His features were sharply pointed and were set off by hair brushed wispily back from a central parting, with straggling side-whiskers which looked as though their owner were not altogether aware of their existence. To some he gave the appearance of a genial and benevolent witch; but no witch even on a benevolent expedition ever wore such clothes. They seemed to alter very little in point of style over the years. A plus-four suit of heavy brown tweed with a brown bow-tie was normal day-time wear in most seasons, with a pair of long trousers for greater evening comfort. A subfusc suit lurked in a wardrobe. Many years ago some friends, anxious that his normal appearance should not too greatly startle an appointment committee, mistakenly advised him to model himself for the occasion upon a bank clerk. As they sped him to his train, they noticed that the dark blue suit and a belted mackintosh of the same colour had been pressed into service, but that the hairiness of the tweeds had been transferred to a black hat of vast proportions. He was not a bank clerk but, as nearly as could be matched, a very distinguished savant from Ruritania.

His manner of life was shaped at an early date into a fixed routine, and being a bachelor he never found occasion to alter it. He spent his mornings at work; but a serious illness as a schoolboy had weakened his chest and determined him in a habit of spending every afternoon on foot or on a bicycle in the countryside, and he resented and resisted any interference with this routine, such as the expectation that he should attend academic business meetings. It was his custom on these expeditions to meditate and polish his translations. When asked why he had limited his translations of Horace to thirty odes, he replied that that was all that he found he could hold in his memory at one time. He especially appreciated the permission granted him to walk in Wytham Woods, and he exercised the permission with weekly regularity. Perhaps he did not know that he was overprivileged, that the keepers (who respected him) kept an eye over him and their charge when, his powerful pipe failing to disperse the flies in summer, he lit a fire of sticks and leaves and sat with his head, hands, and a copy of Homer all suffused in smoke.

Week-ends permitted him expeditions to friends living a little further afield. These were undertaken on a heavy-framed bicycle (replaced by a lighter machine in summer), which he loaded like the White Knight's horse. The Christmas and Easter vacations were spent in more distant parts of the country. Since his step-sister lived in Glasgow, he was always to be seen in the north at Easter. He would arrive with a brief-case full of books, his other belongings slung in a huge grey pack on his shoulders. If his visit was to a country farmhouse, his arrival was preceded by a case of wine—sometimes the panniers of his bicycle contained a bottle or two—and he gave every encouragement to the farmer's wife to search for a few sprigs of chervil for his salad, and to pay particular attention to the date-stamp in a packet of St Ivel cheese. But the summer vacations were invariably spent abroad when the country was not at war, in Germany and Switzerland, and for some years in the Sudeten parts of Czechoslovakia. He had many friends, among them Rudolf Kassner, men and women who had known Rilke or who could share Leishman's scholarly interest in the poet's work. He was warmly welcome in the houses of all his friends, for he was by nature, simple, affectionate, and gentle; children and women liked him instinctively.

At his solitary meals in Oxford he indulged his passion for music from a huge collection of gramophone records, some of which were specially chosen as a suitable background for his post-prandial studies. By Oxford standards he was a recluse; but those friends who sought him out were rewarded by a warmly affectionate welcome and by conversation, at once learned and playfully allusive, which ranged over a wide field of European history and literature both ancient and modern, and irrupted with explosive force whenever it turned to local or national politics. He did not read daily newspapers, claiming that his eyesight was not good enough; but he read the *New Statesman and Nation* regularly, and growled alike at Tory and at Labour perversities.

Though a shy man, he was warm-hearted and took great delight in entertaining his pupils at his open Thursday-evening

At Homes. On these occasions there was talk, and music, and reading and sometimes the opportunity of meeting some of his continental friends. The pupils who made a practice of returning to these parties must have come in the first place drawn by their respect, and even reverence, for a tutor whose work was more than usually inspiring: 'you realised', said one of them, 'that a Leishman tutorial was something very special, absolutely genuine, of its own kind'; and another remarked that 'the intellectual discipline to which he subjected us and the spiritual exhilaration which he engendered in us were the most valuable things in our whole university career'.

He projected his learning better on these semi-formal occasions than at a lecture, where his enunciation was poor. He did not practise any of the little histrionic arts of persuasion, and relied too much on the sheer merit of his material. The audience was apt to feel frustrated at catching so little of what had been said. Yet it was these lectures, revised, expanded, repointed, and annotated, that became the books of his maturity.

While returning from a walk near Zeneggen in Switzerland, he missed his footing on a mule-track, stumbled, and fell to his death on 14 August 1963.

JOHN BUTT

Index